ESSAYS

On Economic Topics

of

J. A. Schumpeter

Professor Joseph A. Schumpeter

ESSAYS

On Economic Topics

of

J. A. Schumpeter

Edited by

RICHARD V. CLEMENCE
Wellesley College

1951

KENNIKAT PRESS/PORT WASHINGTON, N. Y.

ESSAYS OF J. A. SCHUMPETER

First published 1951
Reissued in 1969 by Kennikat Press
Library of Congress Catalog Card No: 79-86567
SBN 8046-0585-8

Manufactured by Taylor Publishing Company Dallas, Texas

ESSAY AND GENERAL LITERATURE INDEX REPRINT SERIES

TABLE OF CONTENTS

PREFACE

For some time prior to Professor Schumpeter's death I had been trying to persuade him to make a collection of his more important essays as an aid to the instruction of students of economics. He had, however, little interest in his own earlier work, and he was already fully occupied with his history of economic analysis. I finally suggested, therefore, that I undertake to make a collection of papers for him, and to this proposal he immediately agreed.

I am not sure exactly what the resulting volume would have contained. My intention was merely to act as his assistant, making the publication arrangements, and attending to such details as would not require his personal attention. Professor Schumpeter, I hoped, would himself choose the contents, and write at least a brief introduction to the book. No more than a beginning had been made, however, at the time of his death, and without the aid of Mrs. Schumpeter this volume would never have appeared.

As it stands, I believe that the volume includes all the important articles published by Professor Schumpeter in English before 1950, with the exception of the biographical essays that are being collected separately. I have attempted no translations from foreign languages, but have simply arranged these papers in chronological order, doing my best to see that they were accurately reproduced. Photography has been used wherever possible, and papers that have had to be reset have been carefully checked against the originals. I have not thought it appropriate to compose an introduction to the book, or to comment on any of the individual essays in it. These papers are the work of one of the great figures in the history of economics, and the object of the book is to make them available to students of the subject.

R. V. C.

ACKNOWLEDGEMENTS

In addition to the invaluable assistance given me by Mrs. Schumpeter, I wish to acknowledge various courtesies extended by the following: Professors Edward H. Chamberlin, Gottfried Haberler, Wassily Leontief, and Arthur Smithies of Harvard University; Mr. Paul M. Sweezy of Wilton, New Hampshire; Professor Francis S. Doody of the College of Business Administration, Boston University; and Roberta Grower Carey of Wellesley College.

The time and place of original publication of each paper are identified in the table of contents.

R. V. C.

ON THE CONCEPT OF SOCIAL VALUE

Reprinted from *Quarterly Journal of Economics*, Feb. 1909, 213-232.

SUMMARY.

I. Methods of pure theory are individualistic, 214.— II. Meaning of the concept of social value, 217.— III. Concept of social value opens up an optimistic view of society and its activities, 222.— IV. Relation of the theory of prices to the concept of social value, 225.— V. Summary, 231.

It is but recently that, in pure theory, the concept of social value came into prominence. The founders of what is usually called the "modern" system of theory, as distinguished from the "classical," never spoke of social, but only of individual value.[1] Recently, however, the former concept has been introduced by some leaders[2] of economic thought, and has quickly met with general approval. To-day it is to be found in nearly every text-book. Since it is generally used without careful definition, some interest attaches to a discussion of its meaning and its rôle; and it is the purpose of this paper to contribute to such a discussion. The reader is asked to bear in mind, first, that our question is a purely *methodological* one and has nothing whatever to do with the great problems of individualism and collectivism; further, that we shall consider the question for the purposes of pure theory only; and, finally, that we confine our inquiry to the concept of social value without including several other concepts which also have social aspects.[3]

[1] Jevons, Walras, and others.

[2] Especially Professor J. B. Clark, whom the writer desires especially to thank for his kindness in revising this manuscript. It is interesting to note that Professor v. Wieser's "natural value" is a kind of "social value," too. Much less importance than to either of these attaches to Stolzmann (Die soziale Kategorie, 1896).

[3] For instance, social capital, national dividend, national income, *Volksvermögen, richesse sociale.* They were mostly used by Adam Smith and have been carefully discussed often since. Marshall, Held, A. Wagner, among others, have paid special attention to them. *Cf.* also R. Meyer, Wesen des Einkommens.

I. At the outset it is useful to emphasize the individualistic character of the methods of pure theory. Almost every modern writer starts with wants and their satisfaction, and takes utility more or less exclusively as the basis of his analysis.[1] Without expressing any opinion about this *modus procedendi*, I wish to point out that, as far as it is used, it unavoidably implies considering individuals as independent units or agencies. For only individuals can feel wants. Certain assumptions concerning those wants and the effects of satisfaction on their intensity give us our utility curves,[2] which, therefore, have a clear meaning only for individuals. These utility curves, on the one hand, and the quantities of procurable goods corresponding to them, on the other, determine marginal utilities for each good and each individual. These marginal utilities are the basis and the chief instruments of theoretical reasoning; and they seem, so far, to relate to individuals only. It is important to note that, for the purposes of a theory of utility and value, it is not sufficient to know merely the quantities of goods existing in our theoretical country taken as a whole. Not only must the sum of individual wealth be given, but also its distribution among individuals. Marginal utilities do not depend on what society as such has, but on what individual members have. Nobody values bread according to the quantity of it which is to be found in his country or in the world, but everybody measures the utility of it according to the amount that he has himself, and this in turn depends on his general means. The distribution of wealth is important for determining values and shaping production, and it can even be maintained that a country with one and the same amount of general wealth may be rich or poor according to the manner

[1] In case there should be any doubt about this point of our argument, *cf.* Marshall's Principles, which can be taken as typical.

[2] *Cf.* W. S. Jevons's theory. These curves are what Professor v. Wieser calls *Nützlichkeitsskalen*.

in which that wealth is distributed. For two reasons we have to start from the individual: first, because we must know individual wants; and, secondly, because we must know individual wealth.

Marginal utilities determine prices and the demand and the supply of each commodity; and prices, finally, tell us much else, and, above all, how the social process of distribution will turn out.[1] We gather from the theory of prices certain laws concerning the interaction of the several kinds of income and the general interdependence between the prices and the quantities of all commodities. This, *in nuce*, is the whole of pure theory in its narrowest sense; and it seems to be derived from individualistic assumptions by means of an individualistic reasoning. We could easily show that this holds true not only for modern theories, but also for the classical system. It is submitted that this treatment of economic problems is free from inherent faults, and, as far as it goes, fairly represents facts.

It now becomes clear that the same reasoning cannot be directly applied to society as a whole. Society as such, having no brain or nerves in a physical sense, cannot feel wants and has not, therefore, utility curves like those of individuals. Again, the stock of commodities existing in a country is at the disposal, not of society, but of individuals; and individuals do not meet to find out what the wants of the community are. They severally apply their means to the satisfaction of their own wants. Theory does not suggest that these wants are necessarily of an exclusively egotistical character. We want many things not for ourselves, but for others; and some of them, like battleships, we want for the interests of the community only. Even such altruistic or social wants, however, are felt and taken account of by individuals or their agents, and not by so-

[1] The reader will observe that here and elsewhere Dr. Schumpeter uses the word "price" in the manner of the German *Preis*,—substantially in the sense of value-in-exchange. *Editors.*

ciety as such. For theory it is irrelevant *why* people demand certain goods: the only important point is that all things are demanded, produced, and paid for because individuals want them. Every demand on the market is therefore an individualistic one, altho, from another point of view, it often is an altruistic or a social one.

The only wants which for the purpose of economic theory should be called strictly social are *those which are consciously asserted by the whole community*. The means of satisfying such wants are valued not by individuals who merely interact, but by all individuals acting as a community consciously and jointly.

This case is realized in a communistic society. There, indeed, want and utility are not as simple as they are in the case of individuals. Altho it would have to be determined somewhat artificially what the wants of such a society were, it is clear that we could speak of social utility curves. Furthermore, society would have direct control of all means of production, and could dispose of them much as could an isolated man. Production and distribution would, in fact, be ruled by social value and social marginal utilities; and in this part of economic theory such concepts have a place.

But outside of the domain of communism we see, so far, only individual wants, values, and demands and their interaction. It is true that in some connections, and, in particular, in applying pure theory to practical problems, it is desirable to combine all the individual demand and supply curves into general demand and supply curves. In similar connections we speak of general utility curves. But these are by no means the same as the utility curves of a communistic society. They resemble them and have about the same shape; but they refer to individual wants and to a given distribution of wealth. Being only combinations of individual curves, they cannot be understood without these, and they are not what they would be in a communistic society. In the two types of society different commodities would be produced, and the same commodities would have different values. They would be produced in different quantities and would be differently apportioned among the members.[1]

II. It follows from what we have said that no obvious or natural meaning attaches to the concept of social value in a non-communistic society. We shall proceed, therefore, to examine the uses made of it, in order to get a well-defined idea of the character and the importance of this instrument of economic thought.

Many writers call production, distribution, and exchange social processes, meaning thereby that nobody can perform them—at least the two last named—by himself. In this sense, prices are obviously social phenomena.[2] Others explain certain fundamental truths by means of a "representative firm"; that is to say, by considering society, for the moment, as one great establishment,[3]—a method which is very useful for certain purposes. It is very usual, finally, to speak of society as such consuming and producing, directing the agents of production, and so on. This is meant to emphasize the mutual interaction of individuals and the manifold social influences under which all of them live and work. Altho not quite precise, this way of expressing one's self is often a convenient *βραχυλογία*. The concept of social value is frequently used in connection with such sayings, but here its rôle

[1] The principle upon which our general demand curves are constructed is this: their abscissas represent quantities demanded in a market, and the ordinates equilibrium prices corresponding to those quantities. These equilibrium prices are given by the individualistic theory of prices, and the curves which describe them are different from what we should call social demand curves or curves of a communistic society. The expressions "general curves" and "social curves" ought to be kept distinct.

[2] *Cf.* Professor J. B. Clark's Essentials of Economic Theory.

[3] This metaphor is very often used, especially by Marshall.

is not very important and its use does not involve any opposition to the individualistic methods and concepts of theory. It is a summary expression for certain phenomena, and its meaning is pretty clear. It expresses the fact of mutual interaction and interdependence between individuals and the results thereof.

So far we have not, I think, travelled over very controversial ground. But we now approach two more important applications of our concept, which fairly cover the whole range of applications of it within the field of pure theory. In the first of these it is said that "it is society—and not the individual—which sets a value on things";[1] and in the second that "exchange-value is social value-in-use."[2]

That it is society as a whole which sets values on things can be true in different senses, which are admirably stated by Professor Seligman. This dictum may be nothing more than the short expression already referred to. It is evidently true, moreover, that, if value means "exchange-value," it is, of course, not fixed by any single individual, but only by the action of all. Even then, however, it would not simply be the aggregate of wants that fixes values, but only this aggregate acting according to the self-interest of individuals and to the distribution of wealth among them. But our question is whether social value can be considered as an independent agency, which can be substituted, partly at least, for the idea of individual values; and we need to examine this wider claim. There are two important facts to support it. First, it is only so long as an individual is isolated that the total as well as the marginal utilities of all commodities he may pos-

[1] *Cf.* Professor Seligman's Principles, p. 179 *seq.* The present writer agrees entirely with most of his statements. This paper analyzes our concept more with a view to what can be expected from it in future than to a criticism of its present uses.

[2] "Tauschwert ist gesellschaftlicher gebrauchswert." *Cf.* Rodbertus, "Zur Erkenntnis unserer staatswirtschaftlicher Zustande," *passim.*

sess depend exclusively on him. All utilities are changed when he lives within society, because of the possibility of barter which then arises. This possibility alters at once the individual's appreciation of his goods. It has an effect on their values similar to the discovery of new ways of using them. Our individual will now put a new value on his goods because of what he can get for them in the market; and this new value depends on how much *other* people want them. This fact may be said to show a direct social influence on each individual's utility curves.

Secondly, there are other influences of a similar kind. Every one living in a community will more or less look for guidance[1] to what other people do. There will be a tendency to give to his utility curves shapes similar to those of other members of the community. Every one's valuations will be influenced by the fact "that he compares them consciously or unconsciously with those of his neighbors." The phenomenon of fashion affords us an obvious verification of this. Moreover, the same holds true of the "cost side" of economic phenomena. Every one's costs depend, in an easily perceptible way, on every one else's costs, so that the individual cost curves, for each community, are interdependent and govern each other.

This is important. Social influences like these are the keys to a deeper understanding of the whole life of the functions of the body politic, and the analysis of them may lead to new and valuable results. To-day we know very little about our utility curves, and are forced to make assumptions[2] about their shape.[3]

We must look at individual demand curves and marginal

[1] *Cf.* Seligman, *loc. cit.*

[2] A most interesting assumption would be that, at a given time and in a given place, individual utility curves for each commodity do not differ very much from each other. To-day we do not assume anything of this sort, but fashion, imitation, etc., might support such an hypothesis, the importance of which it is needless to emphasize.

[3] This has been tried, without however meeting approval, by W. Launhardt.

utilities as the data of purely economic problems outside a communistic society. Social influences *form* them, but *for us* they are data, at once necessary and sufficient, from which to deduce our theorems. We cannot substitute for them "the community of wants" or the idea of society as such fixing values. That this is so we shall try presently to prove; but, *if* so, it would follow that this way of expressing things has, except for the case of a communistic society, no other than a metaphorical meaning; that it may not be wrong, but that it is superfluous and only synonymous with what the concept of "interaction of individuals" expressed; and that we had better avoid it, since it lends itself to doubts and to misinterpretation.

If it be really society that fixes values, then the exchange values of things could be called social values-in-use. This theory we may proceed to discuss now. Rodbertus held this view, and it amounts to saying that exchange-values, as represented by prices in a market, are identical with the values which the same commodities should have in a communistic society. Perhaps it is implied that, if society as such should value things, it would put the same values on them as are expressed by their prices under present circumstances, or that market prices express relative values of things which correspond to what they are worth from the standpoint of society as a whole. It may, in explicit terms, be held that what appears *prima facie* as the result of individual actions turns out, in the end, to be the very thing that would be brought about by the conscious action of society itself. This would, at any rate, be the proper and the most interesting meaning of the formula. This interpretation is confirmed by sayings like these: "The group finds, after comparing individual preferences, that the desire unsatisfied, for instance, by the lack of an apple is three times as great as that unsatisfied by the lack of a nut." "Value is the expression of social marginal utility."[1]

Is this true, and under what conditions? It is obviously true for a communistic society. But for a non-communistic one it would be a fair representation of facts on these conditions only,—

(1) if its members were in the habit of meeting to express their wants and if equal account were taken of all of them, regardless of their wealth;

(2) if the same kinds and amounts of commodities were produced in both cases;

(3) if the principle of distribution were the same in both cases.

These conditions are not fulfilled. We have already touched upon the first. As to the second, it seems to be beyond doubt that production, under the influence of demand from individuals possessing different amounts of wealth, will take a different course from that which it would take in a communistic society, and that different kinds and amounts of commodities will be produced. This fact will alter the values of the products. The principle of distribution might, indeed, conceivably be the same in either case. But the principle now in operation is that of marginal efficiency; and it is probable that, in many cases, another principle—that of want, for example—would more commend itself to a socialistic community. Such a community might apportion goods among its members according to their several needs. But, disregarding this, we easily see that, even if the principle of efficiency were applied in both cases, it would mean, in the one case, distribution according to *personal* efficiency, in the other distribution according to the efficiency of the *productive agency* one may possess. Land and capital are factors in the second case, and this makes a decisive difference.

[1] Seligman, pp. 180, 182.

Hence it follows that to substitute for the many individual values the idea of a social value cannot lead to more than an analogy. This analogy is separated from reality by a great gulf,—by the fact that values, prices, and shares in the social product all depend on, and are dominated by, the original distribution of wealth. Rodbertus's saying, taken verbally, is altogether wrong. This we shall prove more fully by discussing its application to the problem of distribution.

III. We now approach the most important aspect of the theory of social value, and that which makes the subject worth discussing. The concept of social value is chiefly instrumental in opening up a thoroughly optimistic view of society and its activities. It affects an important theory and great practical conclusions, and in these the chief interest of the subject centres. Vastly more than terminology is at stake. As the reader knows, the theory is that even in a non-communistic society each factor of production ultimately gets what its services are worth to the community.

The practical importance of this theory is obvious. It tends to show that economic forces are not only of the same nature, at all times and everywhere, but also that they lead, under a régime of free competition, to the same results as in a communistic society. Competition and private ownership of productive agents are held to bring about a distributive process quite similar to one regulated by a benevolent and intelligent ruler. This theory attributes, indeed, to the law of social value the functions of such a ruler. Society itself is called upon to sanction what is actually happening, and it is assumed that, apart from minor grievances, there is little to complain of.

It would be possible to trace this view to a period far back in the past. Some of the classical economists and their immediate followers inclined toward it. With McCulloch political economy was not always a dismal science; and others went much farther in this direction,—Bastiat and such later writers as M. Block, P. Leroy-Beaulieu, and G. de Molinari. But it is essential to distinguish this group of economists, whose importance, never very great, is now rapidly declining, from those modern writers with whom we are here concerned. While the former confine themselves to general philosophies about the excellence of free competition and *laisser faire*, the latter have developed a scientific theory, the originality and merits of which have rightly led to its present vogue. The former are individualists in every sense, the latter emphasize the social aspect of economic things. This new theory was first expounded by J. B. Clark and v. Wieser.[1] The work most typical in this respect is, as far as I know, Carver's *Distribution of Wealth.*[2]

For the system of economic science the main importance of this theory lies in the fact that, if distribution can be described by means of the social marginal utilities of the factors of production, it is not necessary, for that purpose, to enter into a theory of prices. The theory of distribution follows, in this case, directly from the law of social value. This theory, indeed, seems to be the starting-point of the concept of social value and the main theoretical reason for its introduction; and it helps to set forth all economic phenomena, and especially those of wages and interest, in a very simple manner,—one that is much more lucid and attractive than that derived from an intricate and cumbersome theory of prices. The first step is to describe things in a communistic society. Then it has to be shown or assumed that what happens in a non-communistic society is not essentially different, and that the same

[1] I know not of any followers of v. Wieser in the respect under discussion.

[2] The reader who is interested in Professor Carver's views should compare with this statement his own interpretation of the social bearing of the theory under discussion. See this Journal, vol. xv. p. 579. *Editor*.

theorems apply in both cases. From this follows, on the one hand, the theory of social value as the guiding principle of economic activity, and, on the other hand, that brighter view of everything happening in competitive society.

This last step follows as a consequence of the two others. There is no doubt about the first step; for, certainly, the concept of social value is the only available instrument for explaining the economic life of a communistic society. It enables us to show satisfactorily how such a society carries on its daily existence, how the values of all its commodities will be adjusted, how its means of production will be employed, how they will be arranged on fixed scales of social utility, and how their marginal utilities will be determined. These marginal utilities, in their turn, are the barometer of the social importance of the means of production and fix the share of the value of the product which each productive agent may claim. There is no doubt that v. Wieser's work gives a thoroughly sound theory of a communistic and static society. But it is the second step—the extension of the domain of social value to competitive society—that requires discussion. If tenable, it would much simplify matters and constitute a great step in advance. The concept of social value would, in this case, acquire in economics an importance similar to that of the fiction of a "central sun" in astronomy.

This is what has been tried; and, surely, success has been attained to a certain extent. The fundamental theorems concerning value can be applied, whatever may be the organization of society. Therefore, some of the results obtained by the study of communistic society can serve usefully as a foundation of, and introduction to, the study of economic phenomena in general,—a rôle which formerly Crusoe was called upon to fulfil. But what we have to decide is whether this study can do more, and whether it gives a perfectly sufficient and correct view of all the features of competitive distribution. The writers referred to have used an interesting device to obtain this end. Whilst retaining the idea of values governed by society as such, they have introduced into their picture of a communistic economy some characteristics of a non-communistic one. They speak of land-owners and capitalists, and even of competition. The society they deal with is one which admits private ownership of factors of production, but retains a control of production and distributes the national product according to the principle of efficiency. Land-owners and capitalists have to submit to this social control, and really *are* land-owners and capitalists only in so far as they receive rent and interest. Every one, so to speak, keeps his factor of production, but gets his orders from society as to what to do with it; or, to put it differently, every one is regarded according to the social appreciation of what he produces. It is held, not that this is a description of an existing organization, but that, given a régime of free competition, everything happens in the way that it would if society were so organized. This, at least, would be the last consequence of the theory of social value.

We seem to be faced by this alternative: either we are to assume social utility curves,—in which case society must be the sole owner of capital and land, the society is communistic, and no rent or interest will be paid to individuals; or rent and interest are paid, in which case there are no social values, but only individual ones, and society as such does not control production. It may still be held that the final results are the same as they would be if society were in control; and this theory we shall further discuss.

IV. We have laid stress on the theory of prices as necessary for dealing with distribution, since its explanation rests on individual marginal utilities; but we have also seen that we can represent the phenomena of the market, and therefore of distribution, by what we called general demand and supply curves. This does not, however, enable us to leave out of account the theory of prices. For, as has been explained, these "general curves" cannot be constructed without the help of the concept of prices; they, in fact, embody the whole theory of prices and represent its results.

Now, to make it quite clear that the theory of distribution cannot be based on value *sans phrase*, but can only be indirectly so based with the help of the theory of prices, let us discuss the following example. Let us, for the moment, consider land-owners, capitalists, and workmen as three distinct groups, each organized so as to exclude competition between its members and enable the group to act as a unit. Then rent, interest, and wages appear to be the result of a barter between these groups. The outcome, as we are taught by the theory of prices, is indeterminate; we cannot give an exact formula fixing it, but only limits between which it must fall. An equilibrium will be attained in each concrete case, but other equilibria would be, from the standpoint of pure theory, just as possible as the one which happens to result,—and just as unstable.

What our case teaches us is this: the *utilities* of the services of land, capital, and labor are perfectly determined,—since each group values its agent according to a definite scale,—and so are their marginal utilities. Nevertheless, their prices and consequently their share in the social product lack determination. Hence we see, at least in one special case, that *values* of productive factors do not necessarily determine their shares of products, and that we cannot find the shares if we do not know their prices. We may conclude that distribution has directly more to do with prices than with values, in spite of prices being, in their turn, dependent on values. Nor is this all. If society, consisting of our three groups, would form utility curves of its own and enforce them upon the groups, even then, if they were allowed to fight for their shares, the results of distribution could not be foretold. Determination of values and determination of prices, therefore, are vastly different things.

There is, however, one possibility of making our problem determinate. If our three groups aim at the greatest satisfaction, not of their own wants, but of those of all of the three,—that is, those of "society,"—then their shares become determinate. But, in this case our society realizes all the characteristics of a communistic one, and is so for all intents and purposes. Here social value would become a reality and play its true rôle. But this shows more clearly than anything that, at least in the case supposed, a theory based on the concept of social value leads to results that differ from those reached under the assumption of individual values,—to results which are true for certain cases, but cannot be extended to others.

It could be replied that competition alters all that. Indeed, only for a régime of perfect competition is it held that every one gets what his contribution is worth to the community. Free competition only is said to bring about results such as can be represented by social utility curves and social marginal utilities,—results which are identical with what they would be if brought about by the conscious action of society as a whole. Competition is supposed to fix marginal utilities determining the shares of productive agents and having every right to be called social ones. Distribution, so regulated, works out for all members of the community and for the community as a whole in such manner that they reap a maximum of benefit, and hence competition overcomes all the difficulties we found in the case just discussed. It indicates and justifies the representation of distribution in a non-communistic society by social curves and the theory that distribution can be directly explained by the phenomenon of value.

To this we offer the following remarks:—

(1) What is determined now (competition having been introduced), and has not been determined before, is not values, but prices. Values—utility curves as well as marginal utilities—were fully determined before. It is, therefore, due only to the phenomena described by the theory of prices that the concept of social value can be applied at all in a non-communistic society, and that we are able to speak of social marginal utilities regulating distribution. To understand thoroughly how it is that in a non-communistic society things work out in some such way, it is not sufficient to say that "social valuation decides," but it is necessary to study the theory of prices. Some knowledge of it is indispensable, and, even if the theory of social value were otherwise quite satisfactory, it would not enable us to explain distribution without the theory of prices.

(2) Nobody gets, or can get, all that his productive contribution is worth to the community, which is its *total-value*. For total-value is an integral of the function representing marginal utility. Nobody gets as much as that, but everybody is, by the theory under discussion, supposed to get what Professor Irving Fisher has called *utility-value;* that is, the product of the social utility of the productive agent he has to offer with the quantity of it he sells. This product, depending on marginal value only, is very independent of total-value. Every one, therefore, necessarily gets *less* than his contribution is worth to the community. Even if the total-utility of what he contributes were very great, he might get very little if the marginal utility of it happened to be small.

(3) It is true that equilibrium in a non-communistic society corresponds to a maximum of satisfaction, just as does equilibrium in a communistic one; but the two maxima are different, for they are subject to the conditions of given circumstances. Both are maxima of that satisfaction which can be attained *under those circumstances.* Among the circumstances, in a non-communistic society, is a given distribution of wealth, where only that maximum will be attained which is compatible with the existing distribution. In the case of a communistic society there is no such condition. If we represent the phenomena of distribution under a competitive régime by "general curves," then it must be borne in mind that they relate not to given quantities of productive agents simply, but to given quantities in a given distribution among the members of the community; and the consequences of this, as contrasted with what would happen in a communistic society, can be explained only by the study of the phenomenon of prices.

Only one point remains to be mentioned. The smallest or marginal utilities of commodities within the community can be said to decide what each commodity will fetch in the market; and so the smallest or marginal utilities of land, capital, and labor may, in the same sense, be said to determine the distribution of the social product. There is, for this reason, some ground for calling them *social* marginal utilities as distinguished from those of the individuals. In fact, if there is any phenomenon in the market which has a claim to that name, it is such marginal utility, and we are far from denying the value of this terminology. But there are social reservations to be made. It is clear, to begin with, that they cannot be called marginal utilities of society in the same sense as individual marginal utilities are the marginal utilities of some individual. For they are not derived from social utility curves, but are merely marginal utilities of those individuals who, in each case, happen to be "marginal sellers" or "marginal buyers." They do not enable us to do without the theory of prices, since we need it to tell us why these marginal utilities play their rôle and by what influences they are put in the position to play it. Not being derived from social wants and social utility curves, but representing the outcome of a struggle between individuals, they do not tell us all that might naturally be expected from them. They do not reflect the state of satisfaction of the community as a whole,—do not indicate up to what degree society is able to satisfy its wants. There may be wants, much more important from the social standpoint, which remain unsatisfied for lack of means of those who feel them, so that it would be wrong to represent the social marginal utility as the lowest ordinate of a steadily declining social curve. We cannot say whether the weakest buyer, whose marginal utility is the social one, is the weakest because he is the poorest, or because he cares least for the good,—a fact which deprives this marginal utility of much of its interest. It is also not sure whether what in this sense is the social marginal utility of labor—that which has been said to determine wages—is equal to social marginal disutility. For the workman who is the weakest in one sense is not necessarily the one who feels the pain of labor most heavily, but perhaps the one who, having some other means of subsistence, does not compete keenly for work. This case may be of little practical importance, but it helps to clear up the question of principle.

Finally, we must not overrate the importance of these marginal utilities. It is true that, in a certain sense, they determine prices; but they cannot be called the cause of them. It would, in some cases, be just as true that prices determine the marginal utilities of productive agents, because they decide how much of them will be offered for the production of a certain commodity. There are several ways of expressing these facts, and none of them has an exclusive claim to use. The whole truth is not contained in any of them; but the key to it under any form of expression is the clear recognition of mutual interdependence of all individual quantities, values, marginal values, and prices of all commodities within society. All these things govern each other, as is shown by the theory of prices. It is possible, for many purposes, to call some of them the causes of the others; but the reverse is also true. Besides, four social marginal utilities are said to determine prices. This does not mean that all the other marginal utilities of those individuals who are not marginal sellers or buyers are indifferent. Every one has his marginal utility for each commodity; and for every one, if equilibrium is to be attained, it must be true that for the commodities to which they relate prices must express ratios between his marginal utilities, and that prices must have the same proportions to each other as every one's marginal utilities for the same commodities.

But this is brought about only by the joint action of marginal and intra-marginal sellers and buyers; and the result would be different if the marginal utilities of any of them were not what they are. All of them contribute towards fixing prices. It appears, therefore, that the theory of prices is not to be dispensed with in a full explanation of social distribution; and this theory of prices is based on individual values.

V. To summarize: First of all, it is here claimed that the term "methodological individualism" describes a mode of scientific procedure which naturally leads to no misconception of economic phenomena.[1] It is further claimed that in a non-communistic state no reality corre-

[1] This point is more fully elaborated in the present writer's recently published book, Wesen und Hauptinhalt der theoretischen Nationalökonomie (1908).

sponds to the concept of social values and social wants properly so called. It has been shown, on the other hand, that this concept has its great merits. By its help the great fact has been pointed out that society forms individuals and directly influences their economic value, so as to give them a remote approach to similarity. Further, it has been shown that the concept of social value is indispensable in the study of a communistic society. But its importance does not stop here. For some purposes it is most useful to introduce it, by way of a scientific fiction, in the study of non-communistic society. In this case, however, the theory of social value cannot be accepted as a fully satisfactory statement of facts. It is never true, moreover, that in this case social industry yields the same results as if society itself were directing it. No conclusions as to the justification of the competitive régime can be drawn from this theory, and, on the other hand, it does not enable us fully to explain distribution without the theory of prices. The present way of testing economic phenomena emerges justified out of our discussion. It is —in the respect investigated here—a fair picture of facts, and does not, so far, need reform. Whatever may be said against it, there seems to be far more in its favor.

JOSEPH SCHUMPETER.

VIENNA.

THE EXPLANATION OF THE BUSINESS CYCLE

Reprinted from *Economica,* Dec. 1927, 286-311.

§ I. The childhood of every science is characterised by the prevalence of " schools," of bodies of men, that is, who swear by bodies of doctrine, which differ *toto cælo* from each other as to philosophic background and fundamentals of methods, and aim at preaching different " systems " and, if possible, different results in every particular—each claiming to be in exclusive possession of Truth and to fight for absolute light against absolute darkness. But when a science has " gained man's estate," these things, whilst never ceasing to exist, tend to lose importance : the common ground expands, merits and ranges of " standpoints " and " methods " become matter of *communis opinio doctorum,* fundamental differences shade off into each other; and what differences remain are confined within clear-cut questions of fact and of analytic machinery, and capable of being settled by exact proof.

Our science is past its childhood, but has not reached its manhood yet. On the one hand, our patience is still being tried by the phraseology of " schools " and " -isms," and there is still plenty of scope and shelter for the products of bad workmanship passing themselves off as new departures ; but, on the other hand, the really living part of our science shows hopeful signs of, if I may say so, that *convergence of effort,* which is the necessary and sufficient condition of serious achievement. Those economists who really count do not differ so much as most people believe ; they start from much the same premises ; problems present themselves to them in much the same light ; they attack them with much the same tools ; and, although some of them have a way of laying more stress on points of difference than of points of agreement, their results mostly point towards common goals. This is not only true of fundamentals of fact and machinery, but also of what is going on within the precincts of every one of our time-honoured problems.

The problem of the business cycle is a case in point. It presented itself to the economists of the classic period and their immediate successors in the aspect of the striking fact of recurring "crises." Two first results were speedily established. The one, negative only but of the greatest "diagnostic" importance, was that there can be no such thing as a general glut. The other, that crises are—I really ought to say that it is *extremely probable* that crises are—an essential element of the capitalistic process and not merely occasional breakdowns to be individually explained by accidents different in each case—just breakdowns which happen if anything of sufficient importance goes wrong.[1] But barring these two points, discussion went to pieces on fundamental differences in the views about the capitalistic process, each author drawing different conclusions from different fundamentals; and finally languished in an atmosphere of theoretic hopelessness. Then came the great impulse due to the genius of Clément Juglar. He, first, by showing that crises are only elements of a much wider and deeper cyclical movement, unearthed the real problem; he, second, succeeded in *describing* empirically this cyclical movement; and, third, he contributed substantially towards its *explanation*. Few only were his immediate successors, such as Des Essars. But later on set in the great torrent of descriptive studies of the cycle which is one of the characteristic features of modern economics and which—not perhaps consciously inspired by Juglar, but still flowing from his source, by virtue of the logic of the scientific situation—permits us to *see*, where our predecessors had to *guess*. This torrent does not, by itself, supply us with a solution of the problem. Part of its waters are, besides, more useful in helping us to understand the peculiar features of individual cycles than in answering the great question: *Why there are such things as cycles at all.* But it gives endless opportunities to the analyst—whose own tools have been much improved meantime—for finding explanations and verifying them. And so we have reached a stage, perhaps for the first time, where facts and problems are before all of us in a *clear* and in the *same* light, and where analysis and description can co-operate in something like the spirit of physical science.

[1] It is part of the nature of the problem, that it is not very easy to prove this in strict logic. For there are *always* things happening to which an individual crisis can be attributed without any glaring absurdity. All we can say is: (1) That from our knowledge of the phenomenon we gather a strong *impression* that its causes are more than casual and that they operate from within the system and not from without *on* the system. (2) That if we find, by analysis, a cause *adequate* to produce the phenomenon without extraneous influences—though such influences may be operating in each case—we are justified in accepting this cause as an explanation of what we may call the "essence" or "nature" of the phenomenon.

§ 2. As a matter of fact, this is the line along which we are now moving. It stands out clearly in all the best work done, for instance, in the important theory of Spiethoff. But, hopeful as the situation is, it calls for aptitudes not often found together. And as few men unite, as Professor Pigou does, consummate mastery of statistical facts and of the art of handling them to unrivalled command of the analytic engine, it is but natural for us to approach his recent work on the subject[1] with the very highest expectations. These expectations have been amply fulfilled. The book is an admirable achievement. It is impossible to give, within the limits of an article, an adequate impression of all its fruitful and original contributions. We shall, in the main, confine ourselves to Part I—" Causation "— and refrain from entering, except incidentally, upon a discussion of the vast and complex issues dealt with in Part II—" Remedies ".

There are really—subject to a qualification to be introduced later—four groups of problems which come under the head of " Industrial Fluctuations " : the seasonal fluctuations, the " cycle," the " long waves," and the secular trend. Professor Pigou's analysis is limited to the second, and we shall follow his example, although we confess to a feeling that it is the two last-named which will before long absorb the attention of the workers in this field, and that the problems of the cycle cannot be dealt with quite satisfactorily without reference to them.

Now a distinction occurs at the outset, the triviality of which does not deduct anything from its importance. By " theory of the business cycle " we may mean, first, an analysis of any single one of the cycles which history records, or, arising out of such analysis of many or all recorded cycles, a reasoned history of the phenomenon. The most eminent instance of this type is Professor Mitchell's book. Second, we may mean by that expression a general theory, as exhaustive as may be, of all the elements contributing, or likely to contribute, to the phenomena we observe and of their interaction. Third, we may mean something different again, viz., a theory of what we conceive to be the fundamental cause. Neglect of this distinction has repeatedly led to misunderstanding. So, for instance, Pareto held that there is no sense in asking the question, what " *the* " cause of interest is—interest being evidently the result of *all* elements of the economic system But although it is, of course, true that the rate of interest, at any given moment, is a function of all other economic quantities existing at that moment, it does not follow that that question is

[1] *Industrial Fluctuations*, London, 1927 (Macmillan). 25s.

futile, and saying so only serves to confuse issues. Nowhere is the fallacy alluded to more specious and dangerous than in the particular case of the theory of cycles. For nowhere is it more difficult to disentangle the fundamental from the accidental, or more easy to cover the shortcomings of an explanation by a wealth of secon dary considerations, and insufficiency of analysis by an appeal either to the complex mass of detail, always so convincing to the "practical-minded," or to the great principle of economic interdependence, which occasionally covers a multitude of analytic sins.

Professor Pigou's theory is of the second type. I do not mean to imply that he fails to offer a "fundamental explanation" of the phenomenon. But he aims at more than that, and it is precisely this comprehensiveness of survey which makes the book so valuable—not only to the student but also to the business man, whose needs are but little served by a mere "pure" theory of the cause or causes of the cycle—and assures it of a high place in the first rank of the contributions to its subjects. To discuss only the fundamental explanation of the cycle which it offers, and to neglect that it clears up many problems of industrial movement in general as its argument unfolds itself, is to do much less than justice to it. This is, however, what limits of space in some measure compel us to do. We can only mention in passing that the author deals with important subjects, relevant to industrial movement of any sort besides the cyclical one, with a mastery all his own, for instance, with the "autonomous monetary causes of industrial fluctuations" (Ch. VIII)—which he quite rightly distinguishes from those monetary causes which belong in a special sense to the mechanism of the cycle and will come in for discussion in the second part of this paper—or with the part played by rigidity in wage-rates or by the imperfect mobility of labour (Chaps. XIX and XX), subjects, to be sure, without which there is no understanding of all that happens in the cycle and which, therefore, form part of its "causation" in Professor Pigou's sense, but subjects too, I submit, which do not form part of its "causation" in the sense which we mean here and which will be made clearer presently. The writer begs leave to avail himself of the Editor's invitation to start, in discussing Professor Pigou's theory, from his own views, arrived at in 1909, first published in 1912 and capable of being compressed into a very few propositions:

§ 3. (1) The first of these is that there would be no cycles under "static" conditions. This seems self-evident, because we are still in the habit of mixing up "static" and "stationary" conditions, a habit, by the way, responsible for much that is unsatisfactory in our apparatus of analysis. What I want to say is : Those elements of the economic process, *the description of the interaction of which makes up the theory of economic equilibrium, do not contain anything out of which a tendency towards cyclical movement could automatically arise.* This is not self-evident, but still need not be proved to readers familiar with Marshallian analysis.

(2) " Static " conditions are compatible with continuous " growth " (or decline) such as would be the consequence of *the mere fact* of an increase (or decrease) of population and capital. For it is no part of the system of assumptions of " static " theory that there should be no shifting of the centre of gravitation of the economic cosmos. All that is required is that the economic process should adapt itself to such shifting simply by trying to find the new equilibrium by small alterations of quantities. We may, then, speak either of an equilibrium of growth or—as we prefer—of an equilibrium which, though continually disturbed by growth, continually tends to be re-established. There is nothing in this which, by itself, could produce the business cycle. Professor Pigou lends the weight of his authority to this proposition, by word as well as *tacendo.* And indeed theories looking for an explanation of the cycle in the increase either of population or of capital seem to me hardly worth discussing.

(3) I always thought, and still think, that in order to find out whether or not cycles are a phenomenon *sui generis,* clearly standing out as such from the rest of industrial fluctuations and arising from *within* the economic system, we ought, in the first instance, to assume the absence of outside disturbances—non-economic ones, or economic ones which cannot be produced or avoided by economic action, both of which we are going to call " casual "—acting on the system. We shall, then, see either that the economic system *never* (and not only not under " static " conditions) evolves that particular kind of fluctuations of itself, in which case outside disturbances *must* be looked upon as responsible for them; or else that the economic system would of itself display " cyclical " movement, in which case we should have to recognise the presence of a problem of a " normal cycle " ; we should, moreover, have to conclude that the whole of purely economic phenomena cannot be exhausted by means of the " static " apparatus ; and we should, finally, have to look upon the influence of outside disturbances as a fifth set of problems within the genus of industrial fluctuations, which would, indeed, also form part of any comprehensive survey

of all that happens *in* cycles (because outside disturbances of some kind never fail to arise and always must react upon the cyclical movement), but which would have to be kept aloof in a theory of causation, in a sense which I hope is now quite clear.

Professor Pigou, after having rather severely reproved those who uncritically look for " causes " of industrial fluctuations,[1] proceeds to draw a distinction similar to and still fundamentally different from ours. He distinguishes the problem of " initiating impulses " from what I may term the mechanism of the cycle. His " initiating impulses " being substantially what I mean by outside disturbances, such as exceptional harvests, wars, social unrest and so on, he merges what are our second and fifth sets of problems into one ; and his views seem to us to come to holding that there are *no* causes within the system sufficient to produce the cycle and that its theory can only consist in describing the mechanism through which initiating impulses act[2] as they arise, some of them sporadically, others periodically. This does not, indeed, diminish the value of Professor Pigou's contributions to our knowledge of that mechanism—which proves to be applicable to even a much wider range of facts beyond the cycle—but it does interfere with his doing justice to the fundamental problem, and puts a gulf between him and what seems to us the line of advance chalked out by the best work done so far : and in fact, we grieve to say, he does not so much as mention Juglar, and even the name of Spiethoff is absent from his pages.

We only need, however, look at the way in which any disturbing element acts in order to be confronted with a distinction, both natural and important, which points in our direction. If, say, a war breaks out and upsets existing equilibrium, people can try to adapt themselves to altered conditions by infinitesimal steps, reducing, for instance, their consumption or, in their business, accepting the higher takings they get and paying their higher expenses, adjusting the quantity of their product accordingly. They may not be able to so adapt themselves and perish. They will, in so adapting themselves, be of course subject to all sorts of error. Still, we have here a well-defined type of behaviour admirably fitting in with " static " theory ; and a type of behaviour, too,

[1] I do not know that anyone ever did look for *the* cause of industrial fluctuations *in general*. But I submit, that no looseness of thinking need be implied in looking for *the* cause of the cycle in the sense I have been at pains to define.

[2] He also includes invention, of which more presently. He is careful, moreover, not to rely merely on these disturbing elements themselves, but on the expectations they give rise to. But this makes no difference just here.

which we have before our eyes in real life, *for this is the only way in which the majority of people do act and are capable of acting.* But however high we may put the explanatory value of error and friction, this is emphatically *not* the way in which booms arise, and *not* the kind of events of which booms *fundamentally* consist, as will be seen as we go on.

There evidently is another way of reacting, clearly distinguishable from this, although shading off into this on the border. People can also drop their attitude of passive adaptation, they can react by doing new things or things in a new way, incompatible with the fundamental arrangements that exist. The clerk, instead of reducing consumption, can go into business for himself; the manufacturer can change his cotton-mill into an ammunition factory. Some people—never all nor ever more than a minority—do that. This is a different kind of behaviour and not within reach of marginal variations; and it is productive of different consequences.

Now, on the one hand, although, if distinguishable, these two kinds of reaction are both of them invariably set into motion by any "initiating impulse," it is only the first of them which can be said to follow automatically from the outside impulse by virtue of a causal connection exhaustively described—and determined—by theory. The second kind of reactions is not gripped by our analytic machine—although of course their consequences are—unless we "put a new arm" to it, which is precisely what I have been trying to do since 1912; and they cannot, with any certainty, be relied on to happen, or be predicted to happen, in any definite way in practice: they *could* fail to show up, in which case there would be no boom; whilst *if* they show up, it is never the *mere* occurrence of the disturbance which produces them, but *a certain attitude of certain people.*

Again this attitude, on the other hand, exists and shows itself quite independently of the presence of any disturbance. To avoid misunderstanding—of course, the type of behaviour we are glancing at now always has to do with a given environment, and environment always includes some sort of disturbance. But if there were not the one disturbance there would be another. And if there be none, the "impulse" would be *created* by our type. There is always scope for this. Industrial and commercial methods are never perfect in any sense except relatively to the average light and energy of the business community. Knowledge—scientific and other—is always far in advance of actual practice, not only in things which it could not, or not yet, pay to carry out, but also in things which it would. Results of invention—not only, again, impracticable ones—are always offering themselves, but may lie unused indefinitely. Why? Because doing what has not yet stood the test of experience is no mere act of ordinary business practice, such as we primarily think of when applying our theoretic apparatus, and such as the average man of business can be relied on to do promptly, but something else which wants an *attitude* and an *aptitude*, different indeed from what is required for the act of invention, but equally rare—an attitude and aptitude more of character—" power," " leadership "—than of intellect. Hence there are always great prizes to be won by those who have them,[1] the business community does not, and cannot, proceed to new methods, as it were, *in line*: some rush ahead, others lag behind; and the latter are forced onwards or ruined by competition setting in from those who lead. Nor are these things mere frictions such as theory can afford to neglect; fundamental phenomena of modern industrial life depend on them for explanation—the business cycle among them, for the explanation of the nature of which this set of facts—which lies outside the domain of static theory but still within the economic system itself—is both necessary and sufficient, as I hope to show. Meanwhile, we only want to point out that willingness and capacity to do new things will always and necessarily find, or be able to create, the opportunity on which to act, being, in fact, itself the one fundamental " initial impulse " of industrial and commercial change.

In this sense, therefore, I claim " independence " of the cycle and of those booms and depressions *which form the normal cycle* of impulses from without: in the face of the facts, first, that such events do also lead to booms and depressions displaying a very similar mechanism and very similar features; second, that every one of the " normal cycles " is, as a matter of fact, powerfully influenced and coloured by some disturbances from without—*any* given situation being subject to such disturbances, which may help on, or rein in, any given upward or downward movement, and offer, as it were, part of the material of which the fabric of every boom consists, but which, if absent, would be supplemented by other material always at hand.

I also submit that this distinction of phenomena, which in

[1] The attitude and aptitude making up willingness and capacity of carrying out new things—which may be very trivial of course—is probably distributed among people according to the normal law of error. We must not be understood to hold that some people have it all in a high degree whilst the rest are entirely without it. But this does not affect the gist of our argument, and we cannot go into details.

reality always go on together and react upon one another, is no matter of theoretic nicety. For to the distinction in theory corresponds a distinction in reality. If we are furnished with sufficient details of a case, we are always able to tell whether it belongs to the static or non-static sphere—a movement of the rate of interest, for instance. Nor is this all. It is of very considerable practical importance to distinguish between booms of different nature, and it makes a great difference both to diagnosis and to remedial policy, whether we have to do, say, with a crisis of deflation or with the depression of a normal cycle. Neglect of this distinction vitiates, I think, part of what I otherwise consider most valuable results of recent research.

(4) Our fourth proposition is the one due to Juglar: " La cause unique de la dépression c'est la prospérité." That is to say, that the phenomena which we have got in the habit of calling " depression " are no irregular heap of disturbances, but can be understood as the reaction of business life to the situation created by the boom or, more precisely, as the movement of business life towards a new state of equilibrium conforming to the data created by the boom—such being what I may term " normal " depression as distinguished from " abnormal " havoc, incidentally wrought by panic, and productive of consequences of its own. It is important to note that by reaction I do not mean a psychological one, although this, too, must always play an important, though secondary, part, a part, that is, which is secondary not only in importance but also as to its position in the chain of causation. The new data, created by the boom and upsetting all the bases of industrial and commercial calculation, are an " objective " fact. As such they enforce " objective " adjustments. And these and the losses they entail would account for what happens in the period of depression, even if nobody lost his head or turned, by zoological miracle, into a " bear."

It may not be superfluous to ask the reader to bear in mind two more points: we should not, of course, be justified in applying the same sort of reasoning to the boom. There are authorities who barely escape this sort of *perpetuum mobile* reasoning, according to which there would be booms because there are depressions, and depressions because there are booms. This reasoning derives some support from the fact that depression, by lowering prices of materials, machines, labour and " going concerns," affords the opportunity of buying cheaply. I need not stay to show why this support is insufficient. But I want to emphasise that we are doing nothing of the sort.

As will be readily seen, moreover, *all* theories of the cycle—including those of, say, Marx, Hawtrey, Pigou—are at liberty to accept this proposition. Whatever their explanations may be, they all consider what happens in depression to be the consequence of something which happened in the boom, or, anyhow, before the crisis or depression itself.

(5) We shall, therefore, have explained the cycle when we have explained those booms which are so clearly before our eyes ever since (at least) the Napoleonic wars, which we can so well distinguish from other fluctuations, and in which we can, I think, equally well distinguish what they owe to their own and to extraneous impulses. Those booms consist in the carrying out of innovations in the industrial and commercial organism. By innovations I understand such changes of the combinations of the factors of production as cannot be effected by infinitesimal steps or variations on the margin. They consist primarily in changes in methods of production and transportation, or in changes in industrial organisation, or in the production of a new article, or in the opening up of new markets or of new sources of material. *The recurring periods of prosperity of the cyclical movement are the form progress takes in capitalistic society.*

By saying this we mean to state a fact requiring both proof and explanation. Whilst we hope to be able to contribute, by our two last propositions, something towards the latter, it is impossible here to satisfy the reader as to the former. But the fact is becoming recognised more and more, and it is, for instance, clearly hinted at by Mr. Robertson—with that amiable diffidence of his—on p. ii of his important little book, to which we shall return in the second part of this paper. The reader needs only to make the experiment. If he cares to survey industrial history from, say, 1760 onwards, he will discover two things; he will find, first, that very many booms are unmistakably characterised by revolutionary changes in some branch of industry which, in consequence, *leads* the boom—railways for instance in the 'forties, or steel in the 'eighties, or electricity in the 'nineties—and that, if he will take a bird's-eye view of our industrial organism, he will be able to follow up every one of its leading features to a source originating in a boom. And he will find, secondly, that *all* the booms which he may find himself unable so to characterise can be shown, by other and independent reasons, to be casual phenomena outside the cyclical movement and distinguishable from it, such as the booms ending in the collapses of 1793, 1799, 1810 and 1922, which, to my mind, lead to the most palpable mistakes both of analysis and policy if mixed up with the cyclical ones. It is equally important—and possible—to distinguish cyclical depressions from mere " breaks " such as the crises of 1866 and 1901—even as a doctor must distinguish between the going down of the temperature of his patient owing to his progress towards health, and the breaks the curve of temperature may occasionally display for all sorts of reasons.

Further corroboration is afforded our proposition by the fact, brought out beyond doubt by statistical investigation and quite universally admitted, of the prominence of the constructional trades, both as to priority in time and as to amplitude of fluctuation, within the events of the cycle. I do not know one modern writer who would deny it. But if the fact be undeniable, it evidently fits in admirably with our thesis: it could not indeed prove it, for there is no such thing as statistical proof. But it is eminently apt to serve as verification; for it derives a very natural explanation by our thesis, which alone, in fact, gives it its proper significance and sheds on it its true light.

It is instructive to look at Professor Pigou's treatment of these points from this angle. He overlooks none of them. The question of instrumental industries he deals with in § 9 of his second, and again in his ninth chapter, and " inventions " come up for discussion in §§ 11-13 of Chapter IV. But he arrives at results substantially negative in much less space than he devotes to what seem to me secondary points. I submit, with due deference, that this would have been impossible, if he had:

First, used the Spiethoff index, which brings out the salient features much more clearly than Professor Pigou's figures do, or those of the authorities he quotes on page 20; then he would hardly have called the evidence " less clear " than that which establishes other characteristics of the cycle.

Secondly, taken hold of the link obviously existing between what he calls " invention " or, rather, the putting into practice of it and the constructional industries or, to use Spiethoff's[1] term, goods of reproductive consumption; for although it would still have been logically possible to dismiss, as he does in Chapter IX, the significance of the fluctuations of these industries on the ground that these fluctuations being larger does not prove that the cycle originates there, that significance, by being connected with new improvements, would have more strongly impressed itself. Whatever the nature of the innovation actually being carried out, there will

[1] In emphasising the importance of the work of my eminent friend and colleague, I must be careful not to attribute to him any views of mine. His theory is different from mine in several points, and what we both consider the fundamental " cause " is among them.

be always the necessity of providing new buildings, machines and so on, which means that innovation or reorganisation must always, in the first instance, show itself in an increase in the consumption of iron and steel.

Thirdly, not focussed his attention so strongly on the element of "invention," which it is, indeed, easy to dismiss by pointing out that it is not invention that matters, but its adoption and actual working (p. 44). This very fact points in *our* direction. And so does his saying that we are not justified in inferring from the fact that without Stephenson's invention there could have been no railway mania, that there would have been no boom in 1845-7; for railway development may have been merely a channel into which industrial activity, caused in some quite different way and due to come into play, found it convenient to flow. Quite so. But does not this apply to any initiating impulse? If no, why then to this one? If yes, is it not imperative to develop for the purposes of fundamental explanation an analysis independent of the occurrence of impulses from without—an analysis of the way in which new things come to be done in industrial life, and old methods come to be eliminated, together with those firms who cannot rise above them?

(6) But innovations would be powerless to produce booms, if they went on continuously in time. By this we mean, that if it were possible to choose units of time such that to each of them would correspond one new thing done—it need of course be no "invention" carried out—then the disturbances which would still be caused would be small as compared with the whole of the industrial life of a nation, so that they would be capable of being continuously absorbed—just as simple "growth" is—without producing consequences important enough to show. There would be no cycles, though still, of course, irregular disturbances owing to wars, earthquakes, and the like.

Therefore, the problem of causation of the cycles reduces itself to the question (the answer to which contains what we shall call in a sense not now admitting any more of ambiguity, the only " cause " of cycles):

Why is it that industrial and commercial change is not continuously distributed in time, but proceeds by leaps which, it is easy to understand, must fundamentally alter the bases of calculation and upset the existing equilibrium beyond the possibility of all people adapting themselves successfully by marginal variations?

(7) It is simply because as soon as any step in a new direction has been successfully made, it at once and thereby becomes easy to follow. Business life, like any other, consists mainly of routine work based on well-tried experience, partly ancestral; only within the

boundaries of routine do people function both promptly and similarly; it is only to routine work that received theory applies; outside routine most people find it difficult—and are often unable to act; those who can are rare and therefore not subject to competitive conditions, whence the phenomenon of profit; but whenever in a given situation (which theory has the right and the duty to assume to be in the first instance "static") new things have been successfully done by some, others can, on the one hand, copy their behaviour in the same line—whence prominence of one industry at the time—and on the other hand, get the courage to do similar things in other lines, the spell being broken and many details of the behaviour of the first leaders being applicable outside their own field of action. And therefore the first success draws other people in its wake and finally crowds of them,[1] which is what the boom consists in.

§ 4. I beg leave to ask the reader not to be deterred by what must necessarily look like a highly abstract if not one-sided view of the thing. Of course this is *no* theory of the cycle, if we understand by this a complete explanation of all that happens. This can only be found in a reasoned history of industrial life. It is only the backbone of it. But I submit that Professor Pigou's analysis of detail, or Professor Mitchell's, or, indeed, Professor Clapham's facts, do fit in exactly with the view explained—in some points much better than with the fundamental views of those eminent authors themselves. I also submit that our propositions, whilst strikingly verified by experience, are hardly open to objections on theoretical grounds. Propositions (1), (2), (4), (6) I do not even see a possibility of denying. Proposition (3) does no more than introduce a distinction, which might be useless, but could not possibly be false. For Proposition (5) I can point both to statistical evidence and to what we have before our eyes in real life. It is true, as has often been pointed out, and as Professor Pigou points out again, that there seems to be more "brain" in business during depression. But this does not prove anything against our theory, for it is but natural that competition setting in from the side of innovators should force the "crowd" to try their best to save themselves by improving their methods. Proposition (7) seems to me to be a very natural way of explaining what remains to be explained when once we accept the six others. I may also say that, as far as I can claim having had any practical insight at all, it seems to me but to formulate what I think I have

[1] Let me ask the reader to bear in mind that these "crowds" need not necessarily be making any mistakes in following a lead. They are, of course, very likely to. But depression, though milder, would still come about even without any errors.

seen. A sort of verification is finally afforded by two facts, which I am sorry not to be able to go into more thoroughly.

There is, first, the fact of booms as well as depressions becoming milder—the last real "crash" in Europe having taken place in 1873. Now there are many ways of accounting for this, all of them compatible with our theory. But there is one which we can, I think, directly derive from it, viz., the steadying influence of great units, especially of trusts. As the industrial units tend to grow, the management tends more and more to be divorced from ownership. Therefore, whereas the rising men had, in the times of our fathers, typically to found new businesses and to get their things done by under-selling the old ones, the rising men of a later period are not confined to this method, but can and do conquer leading positions in the new big units now existing, and impose on them their plans. It is evident that, as far as this is being done and as far as, consequently, the new things tend more and more to grow out of the units already existing, the simple change of the managers does what formerly had to be done by a struggle in the markets, conducive to bankruptcies and other well-known features of depressions; and this of course tends to mitigate them and to prevent many losses.

There is, second, the rhythm. Evidently if our explanation be true, we should be justified in seeing more in periodicity than Professor Pigou naturally sees in it in Chapter XXII. Similarly, the period of gestation of instruments, already adverted to by Marx and Mr. Robertson and discussed by Professor Pigou,[1] would then acquire an additional and deeper significance. And inasmuch as there are probably only few people to agree with Mr Hull's saying, that there is literally nothing in periodicity, we may perhaps point to the fact that the phenomenon of periodicity would be without difficulty explained by our theory, as not irrelevant.

The features of depression explain themselves not wholly by equilibrium being upset by new enterprise pouring forth new products at prices with which all firms cannot complete, and driving up prices of means of production beyond what they can afford to pay, nor even by the secondary waves, which it would be easy to insert in our picture. We ought to take account of all

[1] I am afraid, however, I have not quite caught his meaning. For as far as I can make out, his argument (p. 207-8) would suppose one boom to have happened, after which secondary booms would have a tendency to recur periodically. But this cannot be his meaning, as the quotation from Fisher shows, which would amply refute it. I also have to confess that I cannot get over a similar difficulty in Mr. Robertson's argument.

sorts of frictional elements in order to put the necessary flesh on the bare bones of our argument—in fact, we ought to superimpose on it the whole of Professor Pigou's mighty structure. This we cannot do and, indeed, we need not, feeling that the best we can do for the reader is to ask him to follow into all the complications of the subject an analyst so much our superior. We want to draw his attention especially to Chapters VI and VII, where Professor Pigou deals with the element of error—which acquires from our standpoint added importance by the fact that action outside of routine, and action in a situation disturbed by action outside of routine, evidently is exposed to error in a way amounting, as compared to error within routine, to a difference in kind. This particular importance of error can hardly stand out as it ought to without account being taken of the facts covered by our argument; for without them the explanatory value of error is much reduced by observing that, what looks like error *after depression has set in*, need not have been error at all before—so that of all the errors we think we see, a large part does not range with causes but with consequences.

But although we must discard whatever we possibly can, we yet must enter into some discussion of the part played by the machinery of credit, for what we consider the fundamental cause acts through it, and is in acting so much bound up with it, that quite essential things would be either missing altogether or going on differently if that machinery did not function as it does; and that without going into it, we could not claim completeness for our argument even in the limited sense we wish to.

§ 5. If the members of a community which has so far known no methods of payments other than the physical handing over of gold coins suddenly elect to deposit their holdings in a "bank," and to effect henceforth payments to one another by means of cheques, the managers of the bank will find that a great part of the coins in the tills will show a habit of staying with them for good—all in fact, except what may be required for shipment to other communities and, perhaps, for small payments which may still be effected by the old method. If managers feel sure of the confidence of depositors they will, therefore, be able to lend out a considerable part of the deposits and if borrowers, again, leave the sums borrowed with them and behave, as they probably would under the circumstances, exactly like the other depositors, a similar proportion of the loans granted will again be available for further lending and so on, as S. Newcombe pointed out long ago. The same thing could be shown by means of any other form of bank money, uncovered bank notes for instance, or bills accepted by banks and so on.

Now everyone knows that what I have said is but a way of describing what actually happens. The point to get hold of is not, of course, the mere fact of what has been called the "manufacture" by banks of means of payment, but the fact that they can and do, not by way of mistake or aberration from sound principles, but systematically and "significantly" create "credits" exceeding on the one hand the sum of savings existing and entrusted to them and, on the other, the value of commodities existing at the moment. A short footnote is all we can contribute here towards sheltering this statement from the misunderstandings to which it is exposed.[1] In fighting the fact and the important inferences flowing from it, economists seem to have felt themselves to be under a well-nigh moral obligation since the time of A. Smith. They were right in many respects. But they went much too far and now they block the very road they themselves have opened up.

There are, of course, limits to this creation of additional purchasing power: to this purchasing power, that is, which is additional to the sum of legal tender, to the sum of saving *and* to the sum of purchasing power represented by the value of existing commodities. They are obvious in our case of a perfect

[1] Even if banks, to begin with, only lent out what customers entrusted to them, there would be "manufacture of credit" as far as current accounts are concerned. For current accounts are as good as cash, they *are* cash, for the depositor. And if part of the sums paid in on current accounts be loaned to other customers, that part would be cash for these too. So there would be duplication of existing, or creation of new purchasing power, even if banks did only lend what they receive.

But this is not the case. No doubt, savings in the hand of savers or banks are, normally, the backbone of the supply of "money" in the sense of the money-market article: of mobile resources. But over and above this supply at their command, banks can and do extend their credits; and that part of the savings entrusted to them, which they can count upon for lending, is not so much the fund they have to lend, but the reserve against the sum they actually lend. I may also refer to the fact that "Bankakzepte" were in Germany, 1900-14, about five times the banknotes outstanding, or even to the methods of financing American crops before the War.

Since Fullarton's days, or longer, it is commonly held that creations of credit only correspond to the volume of commodity transactions, the classic instance being the three-months commercial paper, and that, therefore, the sphere of money and credit cannot harbour anything which could escape us, if we deal with the economic process in terms of goods only, except indeed, technical disturbances. There is truth in this, but not the whole truth. Even if strict parallelism of the volumes of "regular" banking credit and of the social product were assured —which it is not—there would still be a "non-regular" credit not displaying this parallelism, and covered neither by savings nor by goods; and without this credit, of which the old Scotch "cash-credit" is a well-known instance, business could not be carried on as it is. The question of collateral does not, of course, enter into this argument: if a loan be secured on something which is not normally meant to change hands, such as an industrial plant, the effect of the purchasing power created is the same as if there were no cover at all.

gold standard and equally present, if less obvious, in the case of any other standard. But within these limits, credit or money can be and is being " manufactured," to use Mr. Hartley Withers' or Sir J. Stamp's expression. The reason why this is possible in the sphere of money whilst it is impossible in the sphere of goods does not concern us here. I always explain it to my students by saying that whilst you cannot ride on the claim to a horse you can pay with a claim to money.[1] It is for this reason too that I do not think it advisable to speak of money as a commodity or to apply the ordinary apparatus of supply and demand to it.[2]

Now whenever purchasing power is created in such a way, there being no additional commodities and no reductions of money-expenditure by savers to correspond to it, prices must rise, first the prices of the commodities on which that new purchasing power is expended, later on all or nearly all of them. Parallelism between the flow of money and the flow of goods being destroyed, we have inflation, the features of which can be in the first instance best explained by the example of inflation by Government paper money. But it is a peculiar sort of inflation. Whilst Government paper inflation produces a state of things which lasts indefinitely unless remedied by a distinct and painful operation, inflation by banking credit normally rectifies itself automatically—ending normally in a process of " *self-deflation*." Business men apply for credit to banks, they spend it on the markets of the " factors of production " ; as far as the sums so spent have been newly created *ad hoc*, the existing money demand increases, therefore the prices of labour and so on rise, and incomes of workmen, owners of natural agents or of " capital-goods " will increase in consequence ;[3] and prices on the markets of articles of consumption will rise too, the process going on *until enough means of production have been*, by the rise of prices, *wrung from those firms* which had

[1] It may be replied that you could occasionally discharge a debt with your claim to a horse. This is true but off the point. It is no part of the function of horses to serve as means of payment, but to do so is the only function of money.

[2] The question of limits of " created " purchasing power is of great interest. But here I can do no more than disclaim any sympathy with the exaggerated statements sometimes met with. Although not *quite* agreeing with everything in Mr. Crick's paper in the June number of this journal, I yet need not ask the reader to grant more than what he finds there.

[3] There is, therefore, nothing in the general theory of this process which would warrant any general assumption of wages lagging behind if we mean by " wages " the sum total of real wages. Cases of such lags in wages must be dealt with as they arise on their individual merits.

This is, although in a lesser degree, true even in case of the quantity of money being increased by an increase in the production of gold as pointed out by Professor Pigou in his masterly paper on Prices and Wages from 1896 to 1914. It is still less true, and even not true at all, in the case of the issue of Government paper money.

been in the habit of buying them *to satisfy the additional demand of the newcomers at the new prices.* Now there would be no sense for newcomers (including people already in the market but desirous of extending their business) to borrow in order to buy means of production in markets rising against them, if they only intended to produce what is already being produced by the same methods. For if we start, as for clearness sake we must, from a state of perfect equilibrium, it will be readily seen that they could, by doing so, *never earn the interest they have to pay*: they could indeed earn the capital sums borrowed, if prices of products rose in proportion, but under competitive conditions, in the absence of friction, and production having already been everywhere carried up to the margin, never more than that. But if they happen to be those innovators we met with in the first part of this paper, then things are different. By means of " new combinations," the same flow of quantities of factors of production which had been regularly bought and used before by other people may now be used to greater advantage and may produce what will not only fetch a sum equal to capital and interest but normally also—as long as competition has not caught them up—profits. Sooner or later, therefore, if things go right, they will be able to pay back what they borrowed with interest, which is synonymous with saying that the " created " purchasing power will automatically eliminate itself.[1] This we mean by " self-deflation," which then comes about, first, by the new products appearing after a time on the markets of articles of consumption—the nature of the thing is best seen if we imagine the improvements to consist of new methods by which *more* of a product already produced before can be got out of the same quantity of labour and natural agents—and, secondly, by the repayment of loans, thereby re-establishing the parallelism previously destroyed by the " creation of credit." There will be, in fact, *more* than compensation of the previous inflation, as I perhaps need not stay to show. *And this is indeed the true explanation of the secular downward trend of prices during the period of Capitalism, only partially and occasionally offset by the vagaries of the production of gold.*

§ 6. I have now to submit two theorems which have been

[1] Perhaps I ought not, even when writing for English readers, to be so short as this. Of course cases must be very rare in which the whole *capital* could be repaid out of earnings within one boom; but the argument is not altered if we extend the period of amortisation, nor by the fact that repayment to the bankers or financiers takes the form in the first instance of *saved up* capital stepping in to relieve the banks in the form of the taking up of shares for instance, nor finally, by what I should have to say, if I had space, to fit the theory to some of the peculiarities of the English financial system.

since 1912 and are still the objects of many attacks in my country :

First, in a perfectly static state, there would not be this scope, barring Government inflation, for the creation by banks or other agencies of such purchasing power. There would not be even the possibility of it for, as shown above, there would be no demand.[1] The process of production could and would be financed by previous takings and only small and relatively unimportant discrepancies, properly included among " frictions," would occasionally have to be smoothed over by banks. It is only the fact that society is not " static," that the industrial and commercial process is always being reorganised and revolutionised, that accounts for the phenomenon of a sort of money which is indeed still a " ticket "— in J. Stuart Mill's sense—admitting holders to the " national heap " of goods, but not or not yet also a " certificate " representing productive service rendered. Although the device once evolved will then serve many purposes, it would never have been evolved without the innovators', the entrepreneurs' demand for mobile resources, which always remains its *raison d'être*.

Second, just as in strict theory there is no other demand for the creation *ad hoc* of purchasing power but that of the entrepreneur, there would in strict theory be no other sources from which to satisfy it but such creation. It is not so in practice because that constant revolution of industrial and commercial methods is constantly yielding profits, the first, most natural and most important source of " mobile resources " or of " savings," which however would not exist in a static state, from which we have to start in order to avoid explaining things by what are their consequences; nor would there be in a static state nearly as much motive to save out of other resources besides profits as there actually is. The analytic value of this proposition does not depend on what important or unimportant rôle " creation of credit " may play in a given country at a given time. Situations are possible of great wealth and little activity in which this rôle would be nil. To point to such, or nearly such, situations would be easy but irrelevant.

But as the innovators' or entrepreneurs' demand for credit could not, in the highly abstract case we are considering, be met by *other* resources, so it always *could* be met by this. That is to

[1] It might be objected that there would be always something to be gained by inflation. This is true of inflation of the Government paper pattern but not of banking credit under competitive conditions, under which no producer and no banker could, by his own single act, raise the level of prices, and if they cannot do it the producer would *ex hypothesi* be producing what he could only sell at a loss and the banker would risk insolvency.

say, saving, though still of primary importance, turns out to be a shade less important than one would think. "Mobile resources" are not necessarily the result of previous saving, just as economic progress is not *primarily* the result of an increase in factors of production, but the result of applying the quantities of them already existing to ever new ends and by ever changing methods. As we have seen, this is done by withdrawing them from the uses they are serving and the persons who manage them, in order to hand them over to those who will use them better, by means of purchasing power created in favour of the latter and of a consequent rise in prices which cuts down the demand of the former. It remains true, as Ricardo knew, and as we do not deny, that no wealth can be created by "banking operations." It even remains true, although in a sense not quite natural, that productive forces must be saved before there can be new production. But those "banking operations" are an important device for bringing about a better arrangement of productive forces; and if saving there be it is not the usual sort of saving, but what we may term "forced saving" (*erzwungenes Sparen*).

§ 7. It is not possible here to unfold all the applications by which this analysis lights up many points of the theory of money, credit, interest and other matters, which cannot, I submit, be dealt with satisfactorily without it. I only wish to show or rather hint at how it links up with the theory of the cycle.

The periods of prosperity or booms being the periods in which "innovations" in, or reorganisations of, the productive process are mainly taken in hand, they consequently are the periods of creation of new purchasing power as, in fact, is shown by statistics.[1] This, and not simply fluctuation of the "K" in the Marshall-Pigou-Keynes[2] formula, accounts for the rise of prices in every boom, which could hardly be explained otherwise. There may be a lag because of the presence of accumulated stock, and a rise in articles of consumption before a rise in the *rate* of wages, because of the presence, at the beginning, of unemployment. This is why

[1] It is true that statistics are more likely to show more secondary phenomena such as the issue of shares and so on; but as everyone knows who has seen these things being done, no big issue is ever made without the help of purchasing power created *ad hoc*.

[2] Mr. Keynes is, however, quite right in emphasising the importance of the movements of "K" in dealing with the post-War situation, with which we are not here concerned. Much must, moreover, remain unsaid in a sketch like this, but I want to mention (1) that movements of "K" can, and often do, accentuate or mitigate the effects of credit-creation; (2) that movements of "K" may, and often do, effect what otherwise would have to be effected by credit-creation; (3) that movements of "K" may sometimes technically enforce and so *cause* credit-creation, whence a very complex tissue of mutual interaction.

the Spiethoff index is so much better than some others, but this does not alter any fundamentals.

The periods of depression, being typically the periods in which the changes in the productive organism, especially those embodied in new industrial plants which now have got into working order—the theoretical turning-point—begin to make themselves felt and to exert their pressure on the rest of the community, are consequently periods of deflation. This explains the downward movement of prices we observe. It is, first, deflation of the sort we have been describing as self-deflation. But it is, naturally, aggravated by what I may term autonomous deflation by frightened banks, who not only see and expect difficulties arising with their debtors but also anticipate difficulties with depositors and sources of rediscount. Here, too, there may be lags through producers trying to keep prices up and through frozen credits defying the endeavours to contract them, but here, too, this does not affect the basic argument, although it very much does affect the situation.

No more need be said about the function which this movement of general prices—the upward one as well as the downward one—actually fulfils. It is clear enough. Nor need we stay to explain how far and why we are unable to accept Mr. Hawtrey's dictum by which he so gallantly exposed himself to attack, viz., that the cycle is a "purely monetary phenomenon," which most undoubtedly it is not. We rather think it our duty to explain how far we do agree with him.

We agree with him, first, in recognising that the fundamental cause, whilst in its nature independent of the machinery of money and credit, could not without it produce the particular kind of effects it does. Booms and consequently depressions are not the work of banks :[1] their " cause " is a non-monetary one and entrepreneurs' demand is the initiating cause even of so much of the cycle as can be said to be added by the act of banks. But booms

[1] Nor is it in their interest to favour them. There is much misunderstanding about this. Of course a boom affords the chance of unloading such investments as banks would rather be without or *any* investments at great profit ; there are many similar sources of gains, differing very much in importance in different countries. But the banking business itself would probably prosper more under stable conditions than it does in conditions in which the higher rate of interest and the lucrative deals of booms are constantly being offset by the slackness of business and by the losses in crises and depression. As a matter of fact I think I have observed that the banker of high standing does not relish booms particularly, and that he actually does something towards stopping them within his own sphere.

But whilst the banks, if acting in concert, *could* probably keep down any boom, they cannot be said to have the power of entirely preventing depression. The mere " injection " of credit is powerless to do so, even if it were possible ; but producers will simply refuse credits at ever so favourable conditions, in certain circumstances, as shown by post-War experience in many countries and as is rightly pointed out by Professor Gregory.

and depressions would not without banks be what they are, and it remains utterly misleading to say, as has been said ever since Fullarton, that banks are only following the lead of demand and unable "to force their money on people"; for it lies with them to satisfy *this* and to create *additional* demand in a sense quite different from the sense in which it would be true of sellers of a commodity: the latter acting under the pressure of cost which is absent, within limits, in the case of the former.[1] So there is for banks a range of freedom of action to which nothing corresponds in other branches of business: this range would exist even without national or international understandings which, however, powerfully extend it.

It follows—which is indeed a second point of agreement—that banks can and do, even without knowing it, exert influence on the pace of prosperity and depression, although, for the reason given in a footnote, more on the former than on the latter; and they do more than this. They not only finance innovators' or entrepreneurs' demand, but also the demand of other people, who simply want more credit because they see prices rise. They are even specially willing to give in to those people, for they are their old customers. Hence, they help the coming up of a secondary wave of the boom to which, although it also increases forced savings, it is impossible to attribute the function of the "primary wave." Other waves may and often do follow, and among them the great wave of mere speculative punting, all of which makes prices rise still more.[2] It is these things which make up the physiognomy of both boom and depression, and which we have looked to when warning the reader not to judge our theory merely from what we said in the first part of this paper. They are, in fact, the bridge which leads from what we consider the keystone to the complexities of the "real" phenomenon. Now I believe that it is these things, too, that Mr. Hawtrey—and Mr. Bellerby still more—has had primarily in mind. And as to them we, within wide limits, agree with him, just as we think that we could get him to agree in some measure with our view of the initiating impulse, if indeed he were so unfortunate as to fall into our hands.

Third, we also agree as to the practical possibility of stopping any normal boom by a proper management of credit. It may be

[1] There are, we repeat, limits other than cost, and there is also cost, but there are no additional prime costs incident to, say, the carrying out of a decision to be content with a smaller reserve-proportion and to extend loans and advances correspondingly.

[2] In this sense it is true that according to a saying of Marshall's, prices rise because they have risen and conversely in depression. It is also true that gains and losses consequent upon this have no, or nearly no function.

difficult, and discount policy may be insufficient to effect it[1] except in quiet times. Into this we cannot enter; but it is surely possible. This does not imply indeed that it is in any sense desirable. But inasmuch as I am strongly under the impression that these discussions and the theoretic views of the parties to them are influenced by views held as to policy, and that such views are suspected to be at the bottom of every theory propounded, I am most anxious to say that I do not wish to advocate or fight any policy whatever. And although I feel debarred from entering upon questions of desirability of measures by the purely scientific character of my argument—the mixing up of which with practical policy I should indeed look upon as a misdemeanour—I still wish, in order to appease suspicions, to say that if I think that the cycle cannot be successfully held to be merely an "evil," serving no social interests whatever, I do not mean thereby to imply that it is to be complimented on the way it fulfils what we have seen to be its "function." It may well be argued that it does its work at very great costs, that these costs might be saved or reduced by proper arrangements and that a policy of keeping the level of prices stable might do but little harm to improvement, while greatly reining-in secondary phenomena which are universally (or nearly so) felt to be evils and are the main source of error, losses, unemployment, and so on. Some slackening down of improvement might even be held to be no more than a reasonable price to pay for benefits such as these. Without receding from our protest against using post-war phenomena when discussing points of general theory, we may still point to the instance of recent American experience as a proof that booming *activity* is

[1] If the efficiency of discount policy has often been grossly exaggerated it has been also sometimes underrated. Thus by writers using the argument that so small an alteration of conditions of production as is implied in the rate going up by, say, 1 per cent., must be powerless to put an effective brake on activity in a boom. This is never quite true, not in quiet nor in disturbed times. In quiet times, when money markets function properly, there is a class of speculators who act on the basis of comparison between the *yield* of shares and the rate they have to pay for loans. This kind of operation is calculated to a nicety and a rise of even ½ per cent. may turn it the other way; and from this point of attack, insignificant as it seems, effects of restrictive credit policy may expand to reach much farther than one would think. It is this point, too, which well-nigh immediately acts on the interest of Mr. Robertson's "long lacking," for first, many long-time purposes are being directly financed by short-term money, and secondly, interest of long-term investment is being indirectly affected because long-term securities and shares usually financed in part by short credits will be offered and, therefore, the interest they bear raised, by the class of speculators mentioned. In disturbed times such as war booms small changes in the rate of interest do not act like this; discount policy is really an instrument only for fighting disturbances which are small and do not last too long. But still, the effect of raising the bank-rate is seldom quite lost, the business community knowing that if a small rise would prove ineffective, larger ones would follow, and, moreover, although no central bank could very well go up to, say, 50 per cent., other sources of credit can and do.

quite possible without booming *prices.* This is no problem for us, nor any *instantia contraria* against us. Having said this much, we can venture to say, without danger of being misunderstood, that Mr. Bellerby seems to us to have injured an admirable argument by over-statement and by failing to distinguish sufficiently "normal" and post-War phenomena. But in our argument there is nothing to get on the nerves of our money-reforming friends.

§ 8. Nor is there anything in it to get on other nerves, viz., on the sound-money nerves of those to whom the very word of "credit-creation" is abomination, savouring as it does to them of old popular fallacies on the one hand and of advocating inflation on the other. We respect all theoretical, political and moral views implied. We do not stand for John Law. We do not advocate anything, but least of all inflation, although we do draw a distinction between inflation which does, and inflation which does not, automatically "deflate" just as, without advocating the use of morphine, we draw a distinction between the use of morphine for mitigating pain and the use of morphine for the pleasure of it. We admit that the term "credit-creation" is open to objection.[1] Any term is. But we are doing nothing but analyse patent and undeniable facts. And as they seem to us important, we should now try to convince an authority so very highly respected by us as is Professor Cannan of the fact that what seems startling in an over-simplified and at the same time highly abstract argument like this may still be perfectly compatible with sound (theoretical) conservatism, which we value very much ourselves.

But we need not do it, for Professor Pigou has undertaken the task (Chaps XII, XIII, XIV). It is a very great pleasure to us to be able to state that we find ourselves in perfect accord with him on important points of this important subject. I have explained as best I could, and it was indeed but ill, part of what I wrote in 1912. But I should probably have served my purpose better if I had started from Professor Pigou's chapters or from Mr. Robertson's powerful argument in his book on *Banking Policy and the Price Level.*[2] And I think that by these chapters the new

[1] I usually say "creation of purchasing power" (Kaufkraftschaffung).

[2] Priority of publication of the essential points seems to be Mr. Robertson's, although there are hints at them in Professor Pigou's contribution to the volume, *Is Unemployment Inevitable*? which appeared in 1925. But in his article in the *Economic Journal* for June, 1926, Professor Pigou made himself the interpreter of Mr. Robertson's views in such a way as it is hardly given to Man receiving truth really new to him.

Now I think Mr. Robertson's book a most original, fruitful and suggestive performance, making a new departure which may lead very far. And it is a most amiable book, sincere to a degree, never slurring over perplexities, never trying

theory of credit has come to stay—not the *facts*, from which it starts, for they were always known and made use of in the limited sphere of money and banking, but the *theory* of them as a necessary part of the *general* theory of the economic process.

There is, first, the recognition of the importance of credit-creation and of the theoretic issues raised by it. It is seen to be a " levy " by Professor Pigou and as producing forced savings, or, as Mr. Robertson says, " imposed lacking." Many consequences, explaining much of what has been hitherto looked at as inexplicable deviations of real life from theory, are immediately drawn.

Both authors, but Professor Pigou especially, go on, secondly, to explain points of detail not only of technique but also of theory, and, in so doing, already leave the present writer far behind, who never so much as attempted to touch some of them,[1] such as the question of how large a real levy banks will achieve—the first of the three problems distinguished by Professor Pigou in his paper quoted in our footnote.

But there is more than that. In propounding the thesis, in §§ 4-6 of Chapter XIII, that any year's addition to bank deposit, is, subject to qualifications, a rough index of the quantity of bank credit for " industrialists," Professor Pigou comes near to one essential element of our argument. And Mr. Robertson in his book, and Professor Pigou in his article dealing with it (Sub-problem the third) hold that, " sudden additions to the supply of circulating capital can, in fact, only be obtained through the creation of new money by the banks." This is, to be sure, only meant as a result of analysis interesting in itself and practically important as it stands, and must not, of course, impute to those

to be original—although being it—strictly fair to its problems and to co-workers. I, for one, find it easy reading, although I do not quite like its terminology in every particular, especially where it implies approval or disapproval of facts analysed. I may as well say at once, that I also admire his thought for depth more than his technique for elegance. I should not indeed quite feel at ease if I had to answer Mr. Harrod's attack on him in the last number of ECONOMICA.

Finally, I hope Mr. Robertson will not take it unkindly from a sincere admirer of his most valuable gifts to science, if this admirer ventures to say that Mr. Robertson, whilst negotiating his hurdles most neatly, has a way of stopping dead after the jump: He does not, I thereby mean, really take hold of the points he makes. This explains, I think, that, although we find all elements needful for a complete theory in the pages of this book and of other publications of his, the constructional trades and the period of gestation and so on, on the one hand, and " imposed lacking " and so on, on the other, they do not somehow work up into a whole. Even the " secondary cases " are there and still there is no getting hold of the cause of the primary ones. But the book is nevertheless full of new truth and its argument emerges, I think, entirely unscathed from Mr. Hawtrey's criticisms levelled at it in the *Economic Journal* for September, 1926.

[1] He begs leave, however, to refer to his papers : " The Control of Credit " (Kreditkontrolle, Archiv. f. Sozialw., 1925) and " The Golden Brake of the Machine of Credit " (Die goldene Bremse an der Kreditmaschine, Kölner Vorträge, 1926).

eminent authors any tenets of mine. But the connection between statements such as these and my theory of the cycle is obvious—it is even obvious that creation of new money must have *something* to do with *new* transactions, and these with " innovation." And ἔσσεται ἦμαρ ὅταν, the positions so taken up will shade off into those I have been trying to sketch out.

If this should happen there will be, I think, reason to expect some repercussion on the theory of interest;[1] and other points may then be found to need readjustment, if we are to have, one day, a really satisfactory analysis of the capitalist process. But I do not now want to add to what, as it is, seems to me a stroke of temerity.

[1] I even think I see some signs already. Thus there is much more than occurs at first sight in Mr. Hawtrey's statements (*The Economic Problem*, p. 221), that " capital is accumulated mainly out of profits " and that " in so far as capital is used in business, the interest upon it is paid out of profits." If we link this up to a theory of profits different from Mr. Hawtrey's, and take account of the element of credit creation, we might be able to advance considerably beyond the positions held at present.

THE INSTABILITY OF CAPITALISM

Reprinted from *Economic Journal,* Sept. 1928, 361-386.

I. *Economic Stability under Static Conditions*

§ 1. The many "instabilities" created by the War and by post-war vicissitudes, whilst very properly engaging the attention of economists in all countries both as to diagnosis and as to remedial policy, do not, in themselves, present to science any new or startling problems. There is nothing strange in the fact that events such as the breakdown of Russia or, generally, disturbances arising from without the sphere of economic life, should affect its structure, its data and its working. In this paper I shall disregard them entirely, and deal merely with the question whether or not the capitalistic system is stable in itself—that is to say, whether or not it would, in the absence of such disturbances, show any tendency towards self-destruction from inherent economic causes, or towards out-growing its own frame. The interest of such an investigation is primarily scientific; still, an answer to that question is not without some diagnostic value, and, therefore, not without some, if remote, bearing upon policy; especially as there is, it seems to me, a marked tendency to reason upon post-war figures and about post-war problems, exactly as if they reflected something like the normal working of our economic system, and to proceed, on this basis, to conclusions about the system as such.

By way of clearing the ground, it may be well, first, to distinguish the kind of stability or instability we propose to discuss, from other phenomena covered by the same terms. Looking, for instance, at France, with her stationary population and enterprise and her vast colonial empire, and at the opposite state of things in Italy, the observer may well have an impression of instability—let us call it, "political" instability—which, however, has nothing to do with economic instability in our sense; for in the economic systems of these countries there might still be perfect stability. Or if we assume a state of things in which the whole of the industry of a country is monopolised by one single firm, we should probably agree in calling such a system unstable in a very obvious sense—let us label the case as one of "social instability"—whilst it could be highly stable economically. Instability in still another sense would obtain in a system, for which equilibrium wages were at a point below what workers will put up with—although there need not be any tendency in the economic conditions themselves to produce any change at all *by the mere working of the system.* Finally, special cases of instability may arise from particular influences from without, which cannot properly be charged to the economic system at all. England's return to the gold standard is a case in point. "Stabilising" the pound at what was, viewed from the standpoint of existing conditions, an artificial value, naturally meant dislocating business, putting a premium on imports and a tax on exports, intensifying losses and unemployment, thereby creating a situation eminently unstable. But this instability is evidently due to the act of politicians, and not to the working of the system which, on the contrary, would have evolved a value of the pound exactly fitting the circumstances. In short, the economic stability we mean, although it *contributes* to stability in other senses, is not *synonymous* with them, nor does it *imply* them. This view must, of course, seem highly superficial to anyone who assumes the existence of as close a relation between the economic and other spheres of social life as, for instance, Marx did. As, however, it would be waste of time to prove to English readers the necessity of separating these several spheres, I may confine myself to these remarks.

Secondly, we have to define what we mean by "our economic system": We mean an economic system characterised by private property (private initiative), by production for a market and by the phenomenon of credit, this phenomenon being the *differentia specifica* distinguishing the "capitalist" system from other species, historical or possible, of the larger genus defined by the two first characteristics. Although few things seem to me to be more firmly established by historical research than the fact that economic history cannot be divided into epochs corresponding to different systems, it is still permissible to date the *prevalence* of capitalistic methods from about the middle of the eighteenth century (for England), and to call the nineteenth century κατ' ἐξοχήν the time of *competitive,* and what has so far followed, the time of increasingly "*trustified,*" or otherwise "organised," "regulated," or "managed," capitalism.

Thirdly, capitalism may be stable or not, simply in the sense that it may be expected to last or not. Its history might be full of the most violent fluctuations or even catastrophes—as it undoubtedly has been so far—and these fluctuations or catastrophes might even be inherent in its working—which precisely is what we want to form an opinion about—and we might still, in a real sense, have to call it " stable " if we have reason to expect it to last. Whenever we mean no more than this—that is to say, when we merely mean to speak of the question of what may be termed the institutional survival of capitalism, we will henceforth speak of the capitalist *order* instead of the capitalist *system*. When speaking of the stability or instability of the capitalist *system*, we shall mean something akin to what business men call stability or instability of business conditions. Of course, mere instability of the " system " would, if severe enough, threaten the stability of the " order," or the " system " may have an inherent tendency to destroy the "order" by undermining the social positions on which the " order " rests.

§ 2. The business man's meaning of stability we have now to translate into the language of theory. It will shorten matters and facilitate exposition if I state at the outset that, barring differences on a number of particular points, the following remarks run entirely on Marshallian lines. But I could equally well call them Walrasian lines. For within serious economic theory there are no such things as " schools " or differences of principle, and the only fundamental cleavage in modern economics is between good work and bad. The basic lines are the same in all lands and in all hands : there are differences in exposition, in the manner—and mannerism—of putting things, for example, according to the relative importance different authors attach, respectively, to rigour and generality or to vicinity to " real life." Then there are differences in technique, the very greatness of Menger, Böhm-Bawerk and Wieser, for example, consisting in their having achieved so much with such shockingly clumsy and primitive tools, the use of which was an insurmountable bar to correctness. There are, furthermore, differences in individual pieces of the analytic machine—as, for example, between the Walrasian and the Marshallian demand curves, or between the rôle assigned to coefficients of production respectively by Marshall and Walras—Pareto—Barone. Finally, there are differences as to particular problems, the most important of which are the theories of interest and of the business cycle. But this is all. There is no difference in fundamentals—Clark's productivity or Walras' equilibrium or the Austrian imputation or Marshall's substitution or Wicksell's compound of Walras and Boehm-Bawerk being all of them in the last analysis the same thing, and all, in spite of appearances to the contrary, equally far removed from, and at the same time and in the same sense descendants of, Ricardo's patchwork.

The economic system in the sense of conditions and processes reduces itself for the purposes of Theory to a system in the scientific sense of the word—a system, that is, of interdependent quantities—variables and parameters—consisting of quantities of commodities, rates of commodities and prices, mutually determining each other. This system has been found to be stable, and its stability to be amenable to rational proof, under static conditions. Not as stable, it is true, as economists would have held sixty years ago, when most of them—nearly all, in fact, except the Marxists—would have most confidently asserted absolute stability both of the capitalist *order* and the capitalist *system*: stability has fared very much as the theory of maximum satisfaction did. Just as newer methods, whilst yielding correct proof of what they left of the competitive maximum, have considerably taken away from its importance, so similarly, whilst showing that we have, generally, as many equations as we have "unknown" quantities, and therefore a determined state of equilibrium corresponding to a given set of certain data which turns out to be stable under appropriate conditions, they have also shown that the exceptions to this general "determinateness" are considerable. Even apart from cases such as the possibility of the offer curve of labour [1] curling back or such as the case of the value of money in a system of bimetallism without legal ratio,[2] we have many instances where equilibrium cannot be said to be determinate. The case where both supply and demand are inelastic, is an example.[3] It may be said, for example, that the

[1] This, of course, does not make equilibrium entirely indeterminate, but only makes the system have several, mostly two, different solutions.

[2] It is worth while emphasising, however, that there is no indeterminateness when two or more commodities circulate as money and every transaction is concluded specifically in one of them. The instability only arises if contracts are in terms of "money" generally, so that payment can be made in any of those commodities.

[3] Another has been pointed out by Wicksell, *Geldwert und Güterpreise*: If coefficients of production be constant and if there be no alternative use for the factors of production—their quantity being, moreover, fixed—then there would be indeterminateness of their shares in the product. Still others have been discussed by Marshall, Edgeworth, Taussig ("Is Market Price Determinate?" *Quarterly Journal of Economics*, 1921, and Divisia (*Economique rationnelle*, 1928, p. 410: This case of indeterminateness arises only from the absence of any true marginal utility of money. It has been pointed out before by Prof. Cassel, and is, of course, easily remedied.)

home demand for wheat in the United States is highly inelastic within a considerable interval of price. Supply, again, though very variable, is equally inelastic—if it be permitted to apply this term to supply for shortness sake—within intervals of time too short to allow for extension or contraction of acreage; and this may, perhaps, partially explain the instability of American farming.

But although illustrations of this and other cases abound, the determinateness of static equilibrium under competitive conditions is yet a broad basic fact, and this equilibrium is stable, provided that supply price [1]—the price of "willingness to sell"—is an increasing function of quantity of product. This condition rests on the fundamental fact that the extending of production by any given industry means withdrawing quantities of factors of production from increasingly "important" other uses, which, of course, does not show within single firms—any more than the influence on demand price of increasing output shows within the field of action of single firms in a state of pure competition—but is yet the force the balancing of which against decreasing marginal utilities of product determines the distribution of resources between industries. There is, it is true, an interval for practically every industry in which this condition is not satisfied, owing to the tendency which it embodies being over-compensated by fixed costs distributing themselves over an increasing number of units of product. As long as this is the case, there cannot be a point of stable equilibrium.[2] But the

[1] The supply price schedule meant here is the series of supply prices at which, given the methods of production actually in use and embodied in given plants and under given general conditions and trade practices, the respective quantities of product would be forthcoming. The schedule, therefore, refers, in an obvious sense, to a point of time. It does not, however, take account of chance occurrences, such as momentary market situations on the one hand; and it does not, on the other hand, take account of any but marginal adjustments, *capable of being decomposed into infinitesimal steps:* so it might be called a short period, normal. But the objections to this would be the implication of the existence of some long-period normal and, besides, the emphasis which this manner of expression lays on the element of time, whilst the important thing is not the lapse of time as such, but what happens during it.

[2] Not even if, in the familiar illustration, the demand curve cut the supply curve negatively. For even then it must be to the interest of every single producer, who *ex hypothesi* neglects the influence of his own action on price, to go on producing in this case. Whilst this lasts, there is *movement* towards equilibrium (and this distinguishes *this* case of "increasing returns" fundamentally from others), but not equilibrium itself. Whilst other cases of the compound called "increasing returns" *vires acquirunt eundo,* and thereby may lead up to a monopoly, this one can hardly do so. It may offer, however, instances of increasing cost for an industry as a whole in the face of the presence of decreasing unit cost in every single firm.

effect of this spends itself necessarily and, therefore, stable equilibrium will nevertheless eventually emerge, although there may, and often will, be a prior instability—instability of the kind which is one of the sources of what is called "over-production."

Any other cause of "increasing cost" is excluded by the static hypothesis, the justification for accepting such an arrangement being that it separates clearly different sets of phenomena, which stand in need of different treatment. Innovations in productive and commercial methods, in the widest sense of the term—including specialisation and the introduction of production on a scale different from the one which ruled before—obviously alter the *data* of the static system and constitute, whether or not they have to do with "invention," another body of facts and problems. And so does that part of "external economies," which is represented by such instances as the trade journal, the bureau of standards, the "pooling" of reserve stocks of materials incident to the presence of a large market in them and so on. The reader is asked to stay judgment about the exclusion of these things until later. Here it is only necessary to point out that we should have to emphasize the heterogeneous nature of all these phenomena the very moment we included them. In any case we should have to recognise that there is no "law of decreasing cost" of the same kind as, and symmetrical to, the law of increasing cost.[1] The relation of the two can, perhaps, be best seen by means of the analogy with the "demand side"

[1] By law of increasing cost we may mean four things entirely independent of one another: first, we may, as above, mean what is of the very essence of the economic process and, indeed, only another way of stating the law of satiable wants, that the significance of successive doses of means of production must always increase as they are drawn into any one industry for the reason that they are actually or virtually taken away from others. Secondly, we may, as pointed out before, mean that successive doses of any one factor of production applied to a constant quantity of the others yield a decreasing physical increment of product, everything, especially method, remaining the same. The most "practical" way of making use of this proposition is to consider a given plant, embodying both a given method of production and an inelastic set of supplementary costs, and to vary elements of prime cost one at a time. This is perhaps the best tool we have to deal with the routine work of the management of a single firm. It has, however, nothing whatever to do, thirdly, with a community being driven in the process of expansion of production to exploit less and less fertile productive opportunities. This has been well stated in Prof. Sraffa's acute study, "Relazioni fra costo e quantita prodotta," *Annali di Economia*, 1925, epitomised in an article in this Journal, December 1926, and commented on by Prof. Pigou in the issue for June 1927. And, fourthly, there is the prophecy to which Ricardo owes the epithet of pessimist, that improvements (in agriculture) of productive methods will in the long run fail to counterbalance increasing costs in the second and third sense, in case population should keep on increasing.

of the problem. Empirically we evidently could arrive in very many cases at demand curves which would slope upwards instead of down (cp., for example, Prof. Moore's demand-curve for pig iron). And there are, of course, very many similar cases, the special point of interest about the pig-iron curve being the fact that its periodicity is indicative of the business cycle. Nobody, however, thinks less on that account of what is universally considered to be the "true" slope of the theoretic demand curve. Everybody, on the contrary, recognises that what happens in such cases is a shifting—by which term we mean to cover inexactly not only displacement but also distortion—of the theoretic curves, every one of which retains its fundamental characteristic in obedience to the "law" it has been constructed to represent, and that any curve displaying a positive slope is merely a statistical [1] or historical curve fitted through a family of successive theoretic ones. The same applies to—if I be permitted to waive for the sake of shortness the objections to speaking of so doubtful a thing—supply curves. There is only one theoretic supply curve; and it slopes upwards in all cases. Changes of data do not make it slope down, but shift it, or, more correctly, break it off [2] and start a new one. And through these changing positions—in all of which these curves retain their slope and meaning—we may, if we so choose, fit historical curves, which will certainly often slope down. They will, in fact, display

[1] The theoretic curve can, of course, be determined statistically without ceasing to be a theoretic curve, the above distinction not turning on the fact, or possibility, of statistical determination, but on whether or not the curve expresses or illustrates a *theorem*, thereby acquiring logical unity as distinguished from what could be termed "descriptional" unity. Now I am far from overrating the importance of this distinction: On the one hand, theory itself is only a way of describing facts; on the other hand, any descriptional unity may, by some progress of analysis, turn into a logical unity any moment—in fact, the frontier between the two continually shifts in the progress of science. But this is no reason for simply ignoring it and for co-ordinating things, which do not stand on the same plane.

[2] This links up with another distinction, the importance of which is best seen by means of an example: Von Böhm-Bawerk's theory of interest stresses the importance of the "roundabout" process of production. But it is not the *running* of production of a given degree of roundaboutness which matters, but *the act of introducing* greater "roundaboutness." There is a drop—in its nature discontinuous, irregular, "unpredictable" and "historically" unique—in costs the moment production starts on the new plan (on *any* successful new plan, no matter whether it involves roundaboutness or not), but there is no further and continuous saving of costs per unit of product in the running of it. Generalising: Changes of *data* may be represented by lines connecting the displaced and distorted theoretic curves. If they are small and frequent, these lines may themselves *look* like our curves. But they never *are* theoretic curves and have not, in this sense, any theoretic meaning.

no regularity at all. It may not even be quite easy, in some cases, to guard against the supreme misfortune of total cost being actually smaller for a greater output than for a lesser one, for changes of *data*, once admitted, would sometimes produce this result, which could not, in competitive circumstances, be handled by assuming that the larger quantity would be produced but partially destroyed.[1]

There is nothing new or startling in thus limiting the scope of this part of our analytic engine. In fact, we are doing no more than to sum up what has been an unmistakable doctrinal tendency ever since it came to be recognised, first, that increasing cost in the sense of decreasing physical response to productive effort applied to a constant quantity of one of the factors is no peculiarity of agriculture, but a general phenomenon—a phenomenon which, given the same conditions, applies to all kinds of production and, given other conditions, does not apply even to agriculture; secondly, that there is a more fundamental tendency at work to make the second derivative of total cost with respect to output positive, and one which has nothing to do with the physical "law of decreasing returns," whence the difficulty of filling certain empty boxes. We are merely clinching, on the one hand, what seems to us to be the true real-cost-phenomenon, and, on the other hand, what seems to us to be both the meaning of economic "statics" and the nature of static equilibrium. That this is perfectly in keeping with the fundamental drift of Marshallian analysis, I will try to show in a footnote.[2]

[1] Cf. H. Schultz, "'Theoretical Considerations Relating to Supply," *Journal of Political Economy* for August 29, p. 441. Therefore the assumption $\frac{dy}{dx} > 0$ remains arbitrary, unless reinforced by Cunynghame's criterion $\frac{dy}{dx} > \frac{y}{x}$.

[2] Marshall, indeed, repeatedly protests against the limitations of the static apparatus (cf. especially a letter of his to Prof. John B. Clark). Now if it were true that reasoning by means of it is "too far removed from life to be useful," then the greater part of the analysis of the *Principles* would be useless—as would be the greater part of any exact science: For Marshallian analysis rests just as much on static assumptions as Prof. Clark's structure. But it is not true. There is nothing unduly abstract in considering the phenomena incident to the running of economic life under given conditions taken by themselves. On the contrary, it means giving this class of problems the treatment they require. And Marshall himself has contributed substantially to the perfection of this treatment by forging such invaluable tools as his consumer's surplus and his quasi-rent. He has, furthermore, made use of static assumptions both in his theory of distribution and in the fundamentals of his catallactics; in fact, in one decisive point, when dealing with refinements calling for rigour of analysis, he has confined his argument to increasing cost. And he has, finally, himself insisted on the irreversibility of, and on the difficulties peculiar to, a declining supply curve, and come, in doing so, very near to saying much the same as what has been said above. Loyalty to

§ 3. There seem to be, however, two other sources of instability due to indeterminateness within the precincts of the "static" system. By universal consent, single monopoly yields determined and stable equilibrium, but dual and multiple monopoly, or, generally, the case in which firms can and do take account of their own influence on price, is held, by very high authorities, to fail to do so. Cournot's treatment and the objections raised against it, first by Bertrand and then by Edgeworth, are well known. As this case is not only more important practically than either of the cases of "free, pure or simple" competition on the one hand, and of single monopoly on the other, but also the more general one in a theoretic sense—for the competitive hypothesis is, after all, an additional condition and very much in the nature of a crutch—the breach in our wall seemed a rather serious one. To clear up the matter has been one of the last of the many services Knut Wicksell has rendered to science.[1]

---

tradition, aversion to appearing too "theoretical"—which carried so much weight with him—and that tendency of his, to which we owe so much in other respects, to take short cuts to the problems of practical life, may account for his not taking the final step and for what I cannot but agree with Mr. Keynes in considering the least satisfactory part of his analysis, successfully assailed by Prof. Sraffa. This entailed a string of consequences, but fundamentally what we have said is but a development of a trend overlaid indeed by other things, but yet present in the *Principles*.

We may add the weight of Prof. Pigou's authority. For in the article quoted in a previous note, he excludes, for the sake of "logical coherence" of the cost function, the bulk of those phenomena, which we ourselves propose to exclude for the same reason. He, indeed, even rules out what we have called the fundamental law of cost ($\phi''(x) > 0$). But this he does merely on the technical ground that it is "impossible to construct a cost function" in the event of changes in the relative values of factors of production being liable to occur in consequence of changes in the scale of production of an industry. On the other hand, he does not entirely rule out external economies. But what he retains of them are merely "variations in aggregate costs associated with, and due to, variations in the scale of output" (*l.c.* p. 189); and if we insert, as we must, the word "automatically" in this sentence, very few, if any, cases will be found to answer the criterion, as has been pointed out by Prof. Young (*Quarterly Journal of Economics*, August 1913, p. 678). Of course, expansion and improvement are closely allied in real life. But, as we shall try to explain in the text, the main causation is the one from improvement to expansion and cannot adequately be dealt with by static analysis at all. If this be correct, Prof. Pigou's position will be seen to approach closely the one taken up in the text, if the reader take hold of the fact, that economies, before becoming "external," must generally be internal ones in some firm or firms of the same *or some other* industry.

I do not mean, furthermore, to raise by what I have said objections to the attempts to determine cost functions statistically. On the contrary, I am a humble admirer of the pioneer work done by Prof. H. L. Moore and his followers, even though I beg leave to point out that to speak of "moving equilibria" may prove misleading, in the face of the fact that what really happens is *destruction* of equilibria in the received meaning of this term.

[1] It is with reluctance that I contradict the great shade of Edgeworth. But there seems to be no warrant to assume indeterminateness in the case of what

The simplest form of the second case of what I call "correspective prices" is presented by exchange between two monopolists. It is again Prof. Edgeworth's authority which accounts for well-nigh universal acceptance of the view—first expressed by him in his *Mathematical Psychics*—that there is indeterminateness of price within an interval (on the contract curve) which must in general be considerable. He even went so far as to describe the state of things in a trustified economic world as a "chaos." Here, therefore, is a rich source of instability opened up. Naturally, any theorist might well be tempted to link up what instabilities he sees with this possible explanation of them. Nor can we reply by pointing to the fact that prices fixed

---

Prof. Pigou calls Monopolistic Competition. Taking into consideration the limiting instance only, that of Duopoly, which can be easily generalised, and assuming both competitors to be in exactly the same position, we are, first, faced by the fact that they cannot very well fail to realise their situation. But then it follows that they will hit upon, and adhere to, the price which maximises monopoly revenue for both taken together (as, whatever the price is, they would, in the absence of any preference of consumers for either of them, have to share equally what monopoly revenue there is). The case will not differ from the case of conscious combination—in principle—and be just as determinate. The only other alternative which presents itself in the absence of any hope of driving the competitor out of the market, is best "visualised" by starting from one monopolist controlling the market and then introducing a second one (Cournot's procedure). It is perhaps more "realistic" to assume that the first monopolist will not, as would be to his ultimate advantage, readily surrender half of his market to the newcomer, but that the latter will have to force his way in. And this case is equally determinate, as has been shown by Wicksell in his review article on Prof. Bowley's "Groundwork" (*Ekonomisk Tidskrift*, 1925, and *Archiv für Sozialwissenschaft*, 1927). Taking, as the unit of the price p, that price at which the output would be zero, and, similarly, as the unit of the quantity sold x, that quantity which could be disposed of at the price zero (Edgeworth), we have $p = 1 - x$. A single monopolist would, if there are no costs, maximise px and charge a price of $\frac{1}{2}$, selling $\frac{1}{2}$. The second man, having to face this situation, will obviously maximise *his* output, x, multiplied by price—that is, $x_2 p = x_2 (\frac{1}{2} - x_2)$, and, therefore, sell $\frac{1}{4}$. Whereupon the first will have to readjust *his* output, x_1, and to offer $\frac{3}{8}$ and so on. This finally leads to a limit at the price of $\frac{1}{3}$, when each of the two sell $\frac{1}{3}$, the price being higher and the quantity sold smaller than under competition. There is nothing absurd in this. It cannot be objected that neither of the two competitors is justified to assume, in deciding on how to adjust his output, that the other will stick to *his*. For no such assumption is really involved, the above argument aiming only at describing the process of *tâtonnement*, out of which the equilibrium price is finally bound to emerge, and things would remain substantially the same if some of the steps were to drop out—just as the equilibrium of perfect competition does not necessarily come about by every one of the theoretical steps of bidding actually taking place in practice. Nor can it be said that the two monopolists would, on reaching what we have called the equilibrium price, try to retrace their steps. For neither of them could do so singly without losing his customers. They could do so only together—the case would become one of single monopoly. The same result has been independently arrived at by Dr. Chamberlin in his *Monopolistic Competition*, as yet unpublished.

by trusts display in many and important instances much less fluctuation than could be expected under competitive conditions; for non-economic forces, pressure of public opinion or fear of government action, for instance, might account for that. And the authority of Prof. Edgeworth has been reinforced by the not less weighty authority of Prof. Pigou.

Now it is perfectly true that there is, in this case, just as in the case of one-sided monopoly, much less *guarantee* of a tendency towards equilibrium prices actually asserting itself. We have much less reason to expect that monopolists will, in either case, charge an equilibrium price, than we have in the case of perfect competition; for competing producers *must* charge it as a rule under penalty of economic death, whilst monopolists, although having a *motive* to charge the monopolistic equilibrium price, are not forced to do so, but may be prevented from doing so by other motives. Furthermore, it is quite true also, that such things as bluffing, the use of non-economic force, a will to force the other party to their knees, have much more scope in the case of two-sided monopoly—just as cut-throat methods have in the case of limited competition—than in a state of perfect competition.

But there is yet more than academic interest in stating that our theory does not break down at this point. Equilibrium is determinate even in this case—even if we take so extreme an instance as a trade union comprising all the workmen of a country, quite sure of the allegiance of its members, capable of preventing immigration from abroad or from other strata of society, and an employers' union similarly constructed. If we assume that each party has a definite monopoly-demand-curve and knows the curve of the other; that each party wants to get the best terms it can—the workmen's union offering varying amounts of labour and providing for those of its members who may have to be kept unemployed—without attempting to attain victories or to inflict defeats; and that the contract is to cover the whole period of account (the "*uno actu*" condition), then the barter point between the parties is perfectly determined, and *not* only the range within which there will be barter. It could be indeterminate only for reasons which would make the case indeterminate also in competition. Nor can it be held that the assumptions alluded to are so very far from reality. They are, if anything, nearer to reality than the assumptions implied in the idea of theoretically perfect competition: It is, for instance, much more common than observers believe whose attention is naturally focussed on abnormal cases, for employers and workmen to meet in precisely the frame of mind assumed, and to view with misgivings all the economic, political and social risks of holding out or of a struggle, which may turn out bad business even in the case of success. By proceeding by way of Walras' *prix crié par hazard* or simply by inspecting the two schedules plotted against one another, our statement will too readily be found to hold good to make it necessary to give formal proof.[1]

§ 4. So there is rather more of stability [2] about the economic system than we should expect on most of the authoritative statements. But how much this amounts to, depends entirely on the nature of that other restriction, which we have introduced alongside of the competitive assumption just discarded: the "static state," which we define both by a distinguishable set of facts and by an analytic apparatus or theoretical point of view. The set of facts consists in the sum of operations which form the essence of the ever-recurring circular process of production and consumption and which make up a self-contained whole. It is no valid objection to say that this process cannot be thought of independently of growth or, generally, change. For it can.

[1] The well-known Edgeworthian apparatus commonly used to prove the contrary merely shows that the *elements described by it* do not suffice to determine more than a range. Prof. Bowley in his "Groundwork" reaches, in dealing with the case of one employer and one workman, the result of incompatibility of the respective maxima only by implying that the workman could produce the product by himself. The "Groundwork" contains, however, two most suggestive approaches to the problem of universal monopoly, the one embodied in a note carrying that title, the other leading to the theorem that there is determinateness in the case of *either* the products *or* the factors—but not both of them—being monopolised. Arguments analogous to those of our text seem to show that at least the same sort of determinateness obtains in these cases too.

[2] This stability is of the same nature, and its exact proof of the same value, as the stability of any other exact system. Of course, it is compatible with a large amount of instability in the actual phenomenon. Part of this instability is unimportant, both for theoretical and for practical purposes; another part, whilst practically important, is yet uninteresting in a discussion of principles; still another, however, has, as we shall see, both practical and theoretical importance. None of these groups of cases affects the fundamental importance of exact proof of stability in the sense meant, as would be obvious everywhere except in economics, where the sterility incident to the prevalence of interest in the "practical problem" has yet to be overcome and where scientific refinement is still an opprobrium. But it must be borne in mind that our arrangement excludes all important cases of determined but unstable equilibrium. For the above argument, therefore, and within our meaning of terms, determinateness spells economic stability under static conditions, although, of course, these two things do not coincide logically and always require separate proof. The shortest way to satisfy oneself on this point is by verifying the statement, that of all cases of equilibrium known to Marshallian analysis, only the stable ones remain—apart from chance equilibria which occur during the process of Walrasian *tâtonnement*—for a static theory as above defined. Correct proof of this stability has not been given so far, but does not seem to meet with any great difficulty.

Just as a child's blood circulation, although going on concurrently with its growth or, say, pathological change in its organs, is yet capable of being singled out and dealt with as a distinct real phenomenon, so that fundamental circular process can be singled out and dealt with as a distinct real phenomenon, and *every analyst* [1] *and every business man does so deal with it*—the latter realising that it is one thing to figure out the outlay on, and the income from, a building in given circumstances and another thing to form an idea about the future prospects of the neighbourhood, or that it is one thing to manage an existing building and another to pull it down and replace it by another of a different kind. Nor is our analogy with the circulation of the blood idle. For the first complete analysis of the static economic process, Quesnay's, was directly inspired by Harvey's discovery. The analytic apparatus or theoretic point of view of statics is presented by the concept of a determined equilibrium, the use of which, however, is not absolutely confined to the explanation of the circular process, as temporary equilibria occur outside of this process.

Because a set of facts, which form a coherent whole and are, in many cases, capable of statistical separation from the rest, corresponds to static theory, the static state is not merely a methodological device, still less a pedagogical one. And its range is much widened by the fact that it is not a state of rest. It is first, of course, no state of absence of motion, as it implies the ever-changing flow of productive services and consumers' goods, although this flow is looked upon as going on under substantially unchanging conditions. But, secondly, conditions need not be entirely constant. We can allow seasonal oscillations. We can also allow, without leaving the precincts of statics, chance variations, provided reaction to them is merely adaptive, in the sense of an adaptation *capable of being brought about by infinitesimal steps*. And we can, finally, deal with the phenomenon of mere growth of population, of capital and, consequent thereupon, of the National Dividend. For these changes occur continuously, and adaptation to them is essentially continuous. They may

[1] Of course, only a minority of economists are aware of the fact. And some of those who are, spoil the edge of the tool by speaking of a "stationary" state. Some of these, again, construct a state of harmonious progress to occupy the ground between "statics" and what too obviously lies outside of it. There is no objection to such a construction. But it is not always recognised that, owing to the fact that it implies consideration of long periods, the "normal," which pertains to it, is much bolder and much more dangerous an abstraction than the static one.

condition discontinuous changes; but they do not, directly and by their mere presence, bring them about. What they do bring about automatically are only variations at the margins.[1] Increase of population, for instance, will, by itself, merely tend to make labour cheaper, and diagnosis of the state of any particular nation in any particular point of time will have to recognise this as a real and distinct element of the situation, however much it may be compensated by other factors. From this it follows that mere growth is not in itself a source of instability of either the System or the Order of Capitalism, within the meaning given to " stability " in this paper. This disposes of some, if not most, theories of " disproportionality," past and present, and gives further help towards " localising " causes of instability.

II. *Stability and Progress*

§ 5. This might very well be all: Economic life, or the economic element in, or aspect of, social life might well be essentially passive and adaptive and *therefore, in itself, essentially stable.* The fact that Reality is full of discontinuous change would be no disproof of this. For such change could without absurdity be explained by influences from without, upsetting equilibria that would, in the absence of such influences, obtain or only shift by small and determined steps along with what we have called continuous growth. We could, of course, even then fit trend lines through the facts succeeding one another historically; but they would merely be expressions of whatever has happened, not of distinct forces or mechanisms; they would be statistical, not theoretical; they would have to be interpreted in terms of particular historic events, such as the opening up of new countries in the nineteenth century, acting on a given rate of growth—and not in terms of the working of an economic mechanism *sui generis.* And if analysis could not detect any purely economic forces within the system making for qualitative and discontinuous change, we

[1] Although, therefore, even these influences do not work within a given state of equilibrium and do not tend towards a given centre of gravitation, but displace this centre and propel the economic organism away from the old position, the static apparatus is admirably competent to deal with them. Treatment of such questions has been called " dynamics " by some authorities, foremost among whom was E. Barone. It would, perhaps, be best to drop the terms statics and dynamics altogether. Certainly they are misnomers, when used in the sense given to them in the text, and care should be taken not to think of them by way of analogy with their meanings in mechanics and not to confuse the different meanings attached to them by different writers. All the different meanings, I suppose, lead back to John Stuart Mill, who owes the suggestion to Comte, who, in his turn, expressed indebtedness to the zoologist de Blainville.

should evidently be driven to this conclusion,[1] which can never lack verification, as there are always outside influences to point to, and as a great part of the facts of non-equilibrium must in any case be explained largely on such lines, whether there be a definite piece of non-static mechanism in them or not.

Now it is always unsafe, and it may often be unfair, to attribute to any given author or group of authors clear-cut views of comprehensive social processes, the diagnosis of which must always rest largely on social vision as distinguished from provable argument. For no author or group of authors can help recognising many heterogeneous elements, and it is always easy to quote passages in proof of this. The treatment of the history of the analysis of value, cost and interest affords examples in point,[2] and it must be left to the reader to form his own opinion about the correctness or otherwise of our thus formulating what seems to us to be received doctrine: Industrial expansion, automatically incident to, and moulded by, general social growth—of which the most important purely economic forces are growth of population and of savings—is the basic fact about economic change or evolution or "progress"; wants and possibilities develop, industry expands in response, and this expansion, carrying automatically in its wake increasing specialisation and environmental facilities,

[1] As a matter of fact, this is what the position of our highest authorities comes to. It is certainly the position of Ricardo and John Stuart Mill, whose discussion of "progress" mainly turns on the question of relative growth of population and capital, occasionally affected by improvement of methods of production, which they glance at in passing as a disturber of the normal course of things. Such is the position, too, of Walras or, for that matter, of Böhm-Bawerk, who both of them seem convinced that everything of a purely economic nature must needs fit into one homogeneous body of doctrine, which is frankly "static" with Walras, whilst Böhm-Bawerk always rejected the static conception precisely because it excludes some things which yet are undoubtedly "purely economic." John B. Clark is the one outstanding exception, but Marshall, although embracing within his wide horizons every one of the elements essential to a distinct theory of "dynamics," still forced all of them into a frame substantially "static." The present writer believes that some of the difficulties and consequent controversies about Prof. Pigou's argument in his *Economics of Welfare* are traceable to the same source, and his work on *Industrial Fluctuations* is a monument to the view that economic life, in itself essentially passive, is being continually disturbed and propelled by "initial impulses" coming from outside.

[2] Even within the narrower precincts of problems such as these, it has become a fashion—a justified reaction, perhaps, from the opposite vice—to interpret older authors so very broadly as to make them "*see*" everything and *definitely say* nothing, and to frown on another way of stating their views as ungenerous. I submit, however, first that whilst this attitude is the correct one in evaluating individual theorists—provided that the same generous broadness be vouchsafed to all—it is not useful in bringing out characteristics; secondly, that mere "recognition" of a fact means nothing unless the fact be welded into the rest of the argument and made to do theoretic work.

accounts for the rest, changing continuously and organically its own *data*.

Grounds for dissent from this view present themselves on several points, but I am anxious to waive objections in order to make stand out *the* objection. Without being untrue, when taken as a proposition summing up economic history over, say, a thousand years,[1] it is inadequate, or even misleading, when meant to be a description of that mechanism of economic life which it is the task of economic theory to explain, and it is no help towards, but a bar to, the understanding of the problems and phenomena incident to that mechanism. For expansion is *no* basic fact, capable of serving in the rôle of a cause, but is itself the result of a more fundamental " economic force," which accounts both for expansion and the string of consequences emanating from it. This is best seen by splitting up the comprehensive phenomenon of general industrial growth into the expansion of the single industries it consists of. If we do this for the period of predominantly competitive capitalism, we meet indeed at any given time with a class of cases in which both entire industries and single firms are drawn on by demand coming to them from outside and so expanding them automatically; but this additional demand practically always proceeds, as a secondary phenomenon,[2]

[1] Different sets of problems require different distances from the objects of our interest; and different propositions are true from different distances and on different planes of argument. So, *e.g.*, for a certain way of describing historic processes, the presence of a military commander of Napoleonic ability may truly be said to be of causal importance, whilst, for a survey farther removed from details, it may have hardly any importance at all. Our analytic apparatus consists of heterogeneous pieces, every one of which works well on some of the possible " planes " of argument and not at all on others, the overlooking of which is an important, and sometimes the only, source of our controversies.

[2] We may conveniently enumerate, partly anticipating and partly repeating, the more important types of those secondary phenomena, which we hold received opinion, neglecting the primary phenomenon, exclusively deals with, and which would not entirely, but almost entirely, be absent without the primary one.

(1) Expansion of some industries called forth by primary expansion in others, as stated above: If a new concern establishes itself, grocers' businesses will expand in the neighbourhood and so will producers of subsidiary articles. *The expansion of all industries, which do not themselves display any break in their practice during the time under consideration* is to be accounted for thus.

(2) If the primary change results in turning out better tools of production, naturally this will expand the industries which use them. This must be taken account of in judging the comparative success of some State-managed railways surrounded by private industries, which force on them improved engines, fittings, and so on.

(3) Every given change starts from a given environment, and would be impossible without its facilities. But every given environment embodies the results of previous primary change, and, therefore, cannot be taken, except within static theory, as an ultimate datum, acting autonomously, but is itself, in great part, a secondary phenomenon.

from a primary change in some other industry—from textiles first, from iron and steam later, from electricity and chemical industry still later—which does not *follow*, but *creates* expansion. It *first*—and by its initiative—expands its own production, thereby creates an expansion of demand for its own and, contingent thereon, other products, and the general expansion of the environment we observe—increase of population included—is the *result* of it, as may be visualised by taking any one of the outstanding instances of the process, such as the rise of railway transportation. The way by which every one of these changes is brought about lends itself easily to general statement: it is by means of new combinations of existing factors of production, embodied in new plants and, typically, new firms producing either new commodities, or by a new, *i.e.* as yet untried, method, or for a new

(4) So is, in great part, what we have called growth. This is specially clear in the case of saving, the amount of which would be very much smaller in the absence of its most important source, the entrepreneurs' profits. It is also true as to increase of population. And expansion, incident to what would be left of growth in the absence of primary change, would soon be quenched by a (physical) law of decreasing returns acting sharply. *This, then, is the main reason why we think so little of the autonomous—as distinguished from secondary—importance of external economies incident to mere expansion and of what is left of increasing returns*, if we exclude all that is either primarily or secondarily due to the cause we are about to consider.

(5) Industrial evolution inspires collective action in order to force improvement on lethargic strata. Of this kind was, and is, Government action on the Continent for improving agricultural methods of peasants. This is not "secondary" in the sense we mean it, but if it comes to creating external economies by non-economic influence, it has nevertheless been due so far mainly to some previous achievement in some private industry.

(6) Successful primary change is followed by general reorganisation within the same industry, more and more other firms following the lead of some, both because of the profits to be gained and the losses to be feared. During this process, what have at first been the internal economies of the leaders soon become external economies for the rest of the firms, whose behaviour need be no other than one of passive adaptation (and expansion) to what *for them* is environmental advantage. But for us, the observers, to look upon the process as one of adaptation to expanding environment is to miss the salient point.

(7) Incident to all the phenomena glanced at, are, among other things, secondary gains going to all kinds of agents, who do not display any initiative. There is, however, another, a secondary, initiative, stimulated by the possibility of such gains becoming possible—extensions of businesses, speculative transactions and so on, calculated to secure them. The periodic rise and fall of the level of prices—an essential piece, as we shall see, of the mechanism of change in competitive capitalism—carries in its wake extensions and, to finance them, applications for credit merely due to the fact of prices rising, which greatly intensify the phenomenon. And this secondary phenomenon is being as a rule realised much more clearly by observers than the primary phenomenon which gives rise to it.

Our analysis neither overlooks nor denies the importance of these things. On the contrary, it aims at showing their cause and nature. But in a statement of fundamental principles within so short a compass they cannot loom large in the picture.

market, or by buying means of production in a new market. What we, unscientifically, call economic progress means essentially putting productive resources to uses *hitherto untried in practice*, and withdrawing them from the uses they have served so far. This is what we call " innovation."

What matters for the subject of this study is merely the essentially discontinuous character of this process, which does not lend itself to description in terms of a theory of equilibrium. But we may conveniently lead up to this by insisting for the moment on the importance of the difference between this view and what I have called the received one. Innovation, unless it consists in producing, and forcing upon the public, a new commodity, means producing at smaller cost per unit, breaking off the old " supply schedule " and starting on a new one. It is quite immaterial whether this is done by making use of a new invention or not; for, on the one hand, there never has been any time when the store of scientific knowledge had yielded all it could in the way of industrial improvement, and, on the other hand, it is not the knowledge that matters, but the successful solution of the task *sui generis* of putting an untried method into practice—there may be, and often is, no scientific novelty involved at all, and even if it be involved, this does not make any difference to the nature of the process. And we should not only, by insisting on invention, emphasise an irrelevant point—irrelevant to our set of problems, although otherwise, of course, just as relevant as, say, climate—and be thereby led away from the relevant one, but we should also be forced to consider inventions as a case of external economies.[1]

[1] There is another point which arises out of the usual treatment of these things: Nobody can possibly deny the occurrence or relevance of those great breaks in industrial practice which change the data of economic life from time to time. Marshall, therefore, distinguishes these, which he calls " substantive " inventions and which he deals with as chance events acting from outside on the analogy, say, of earthquakes, from inventions which, being of the nature of more obvious applications of known principles, may be expected to arise in consequence of expansion itself. This distinction is insisted upon by Prof. Pigou in the paper quoted above. This view, however, cuts up a homogeneous phenomenon, the elements of which do not differ from one another except by degree, and is readily seen to create a difficulty similar to that of filling the empty boxes. Exactly as the failure to distinguish different processes leads, in the case of the boxes, to a difficulty in distinguishing between groups of facts—and leads, also, to that state of discussion in which some authors hold that most industries display *increasing*, others that most industries display *decreasing*, still others, that normally any industry shows *constant*, returns—so it is obviously impossible to draw any line between these classes of innovations, or, for that matter, inventions; and the difficulty is not one of judging particular cases, but one of principle. For *no* invention is independent of existing data; and *no* invention is so dependent on them as to be automatically produced by them. In the case of important invention, change in data is great; in the case of unimportant invention it is small. But this is all, and the *nature* of the process and of the special mechanism set in motion is always the same.

Now this hides part of the very essence of the capitalist process. This kind of external economies—and, in fact, nearly every kind, even the trade journal must, unless the product of collective action, be somebody's business—characteristically comes about by first being taken up by one firm or a few—by acting, that is, as an internal economy. This firm begins to undersell the others, part of which are thereby definitely pushed into the background to linger there on accumulated reserves and quasi-rents, whilst another part copies the methods of the disturber of the peace. *That* this is so, we can see every day by looking at industrial life; it is precisely what goes on, what is missing in the static apparatus and what accounts both for dissatisfaction with it and for the attempts to force such phenomena into its cracking frame—instead of, as we think it natural to do, recognising and explaining this as a distinct process going on along with the one handled by the static theory. *Why* this is so, is a question which it would lead very far to answer satisfactorily. Successful innovation is, as said before, a task *sui generis*. It is a feat not of intellect, but of will. It is a special case of the social phenomenon of leadership.[1] Its difficulty consisting in the resistances and un-

[1] This does not imply any glorification. Leadership itself does not mean only such aptitudes as would generally command admiration, implying, as it does, narrowness of outlook in any but one direction and a kind of force which sometimes it may be hardly possible to distinguish from callousness. But economic leadership has, besides, nothing of the glamour some other kinds of leadership have. Its intellectual implications may be trivial; wide sympathies, personal appeal, rhetorical sublimation of motives and acts count for little in it; and although not without its romance, it is in the main highly unromantic, so that any craving for personal hero-worship can hardly hope for satisfaction where, among, to be sure, other types, we meet with slave-trading and brandy-producing puritans at the historic threshold of the subject.

Apart from this source of possible objections, there is a much more serious one in the mind of every well-trained economist, whom experience has taught to think little of such intrusions into theory of views savouring of sociology, and who is prone to associate any such things with a certain class of objections to received doctrine, which continually turn up however often they may have been refuted—sublimely ignorant of the fact—such as objections to the economic man, to marginal analysis, to the use of the barter hypothesis and so on. The reader may, I think, satisfy himself that no want of theoretic training is responsible for statements which I believe to tally fundamentally with Marshallian analysis.

No difficulty whatever arises as to verification. That new commodities or new qualities *or new quantities* of commodities are forced upon the public by the initiative of entrepreneurs—which, of course, does not affect the rôle of demand within the static process—is a fact of common experience; that one firm or a small group of firms leads in the sense meant above, in the process of innovation, thereby creating its own market and giving impulse to the environment generally, is equally patent (and we do not deny facts of other complexion—the secondary or "consequential" ones); and all we are trying to do is to fit the analytic apparatus to take account of such facts without putting its other parts out of gear.

certainties incident to doing what has not been done before, it is accessible for, and appeals to, only a distinct type which is rare. Whilst differences in aptitude for the routine work of "static" management only result in differences of success in doing what every one does, differences in this particular aptitude result in only some being able to do this particular thing at all. To overcome these difficulties incident to change of practice is the function characteristic of the entrepreneur.

Now if this process meant no more than one of many classes of "friction," it certainly would not be worth our while to dissent from the usual exposition on that account, however many facts might come under this heading. But it means more than this: Its analysis yields the explanation of phenomena which cannot be accounted for without it. There is, first, the "entrepreneurial" function as distinct from the mere "managerial" function—although they may, and mostly must, meet one another in the same individual—the nature of which only shows up within the process of innovation. There is, secondly, the explanation of entrepreneurs' gain, which emerges in this process and otherwise gets lost in the compound of "earnings of management,"[1] the treating of which as a homogeneous whole is unsatisfactory for precisely the same reason which, by universal consent, makes it unsatisfactory so to treat, say, the income of a peasant tilling his own soil, instead of treating it as a sum of wages, rent, quasi-rent and, possibly, interest. Furthermore, it is *this* entrepreneurs' profit which is the primary source of industrial fortunes, the history of every one of which consists of, or leads back to, successful acts of innovation.[2] And as the rise and

[1] The function in question being a distinct one, it does not matter that it appears in practice rarely, if ever, by itself. And whoever cares to observe the behaviour of business men at close quarters will not raise the objection that new things and routine work are done, as a rule, indiscriminately by the same manager. He will find that routine work is done with a smoothness wholly absent as soon as a new step is to be taken, and that there is a sharp cleavage between the two, insuperable for a very worthy type of manager. This extends far into the realm of what we are wont to consider as automatic change, bringing about external economies and increasing returns. Take the instance of a business letting out motor cars on the principle "drive yourself." A mere growth of the neighbourhood, sufficient to make such a business profitable, does not produce it. Someone has to realise the possibility and to found the firm, to get people to appreciate its services, to get the right type of cars and so on. This implies solution of a legion of small problems. Even if such a firm already exists and further environmental growth make discontinuous extension feasible, the thing to be done is not so easy as it looks. It would be easy for the trained mind of a leading industrialist, but it is not so for a typical member of the stratum which does such business.

[2] It is, as has been said in a previous note, not the *running* of a business according to new plan, but the act of *getting it* to run on a new plan, which accounts

decay of industrial fortunes is *the* essential fact about the social structure of capitalist society, both the emergence of what is, in any single instance, an essentially temporary gain, and the elimination of it by the working of the competitive mechanism, obviously are more than "frictional" phenomena, as is that process of underselling by which industrial progress comes about in capitalist society and by which its achievements result in higher real incomes all round.

Nor is this all. This process of innovation in industry by the agency of entrepreneurs supplies the key to all the phenomena of capital and credit. The rôle of credit would be a technical and a subordinate one in the sense that everything fundamental about the economic process could be explained in terms of goods, if industry grew by small steps along coherent curves. For in that case financing could and would be done substantially by means of the current gross revenue, and only small discrepancies would need to be smoothed. If we simplify by assuming that the whole circular process of production and consumption takes exactly one period of account, no instruments or consumers' goods surviving into the next, capital—defined as a monetary concept—and income would be exactly equal, and only different phases of one and the same monetary stream. As, however, innovation, being discontinuous and involving considerable change and being, in competitive capitalism, typically embodied in new firms, requires large expenditure previous to the emergence of any revenue, credit becomes an essential element of the process. And we cannot turn to savings in order to account for the existence of a fund from which these credits are to flow. For this would imply the existence of previous profits, without which there would not be anything like the required amount—even as it is, savings usually lag behind requirements—and assuming previous profits would mean, in an explanation of principles, circular reasoning. "Credit-creation," therefore, becomes an essential part both of the mechanism of the process and of the theory explaining it.

---

for entrepreneurs' profits, and makes it so undesirable to try to express them by "static" curves, which describe precisely the phenomena of the "running" of it. The theoretical reason for our proposition is, that either competition or the process of imputation must put a stop to any "surplus" gain, even in a case of monopoly, in which the value of the patent, the natural agent or of whatever else the monopoly position is contingent on, will absorb the return in the sense that it will no longer be profit. But there is also a "practical" observation to support this view. No firm ever yields returns indefinitely, if only run according to unchanged plan. For everyone comes the day when it will cease to do so. And we all of us know that type of industrial family firm of the third generation which is on the road to that state, however conscientiously it may be "managed."

Hence, saving, properly so called, turns out to be of less importance than the received doctrine implies, for which the continuous growth of saving—accumulation—is a mainstay of explanation. Credit-creation is the method by which the putting to new uses of existing means of production is brought about through a rise in price enforcing the " saving " of the necessary amount of them out of the uses they hitherto served (" enforced savings "—cp. Mr. Robertson's " imposed lacking ").

Finally, it cannot be said that whilst all this applies to individual firms, the development of whole industries might still be looked at as a continuous process, a comprehensive view " ironing out " the discontinuities which occur in every single case. Even then individual discontinuities would be the carriers of essential phenomena. But, besides, for a definite reason that is not so. As shown both by the typical rise of general prices and the equally typical activity of the constructional trades in the prosperity phase of the business cycle, innovations cluster densely together. So densely, in fact, that the resultant disturbance produces a distinct period of adjustment—which precisely is what the depression phase of the business cycle consists in. *Why* this should be so, the present writer has attempted to show elsewhere.[1] *That* it is so, is the best single verification and justification of the view submitted, whether we apply the criterion of its being " true to life " or the criterion of its yielding explanation of a phenomena *not itself implied in its fundamental principle.*

If, then, the putting to new uses of existing resources is what " progress " fundamentally consists in; if it is the nature of the entrepreneur's function to act as the propelling force of the process; if entrepreneur's profits, credit, and the cycle prove to be essential parts of its mechanism—the writer even believes this to be

[1] " Theorie der wirtschaftlichen Entwicklung," 1911, 2nd ed. 1926. Cp. also " The Explanation of the Business Cycle," *Economica,* 1927. The failure of the price-level to rise in the United States during the period 1923–1926 will be seen to be no objection but a further verification of this theory. It has, however, been pointed out to the writer, by a very high authority, that prices did also fail to rise in the United States in the prosperity immediately preceding the War. It could be replied that the factors which account for the stability 1923–1926 had been active already before the War. But the U.S. Bureau of Labour figures for 1908–1913 are 91, 97, 99, 95, 101, 100. Cp. also Prof. Persons' chart in *Review of Economic Statistics,* Jan. 1927. It may be well to mention that constructional trades and their materials need not necessarily show their activity fully by *every* index. Iron, *e.g.*, being an international commodity, need not rise in price if the phases of the cycle do not quite coincide in different countries. As a matter of fact, they generally do. But the right way to deal with iron and steel is to use the Spiethoff index (production + imports − exports), and this has, so far, always worked satisfactorily.

true of interest—then industrial expansion *per se* is better described as a consequence than as a cause; and we should be inclined to turn the other way round what we have termed the received chain of causation. In this case, and as those phenomena link up so as to form a coherent and self-contained logical whole, it is obviously conducive to clearness to bring them out boldly; to relegate to one distinct body of doctrine the concept of equilibrium, the continuous curves and small marginal variations, all of which, in their turn, link up with the circuit flow of economic routine under constant data; and to build, alongside of this, and *before* taking account of the full complexity of the " real " phenomenon—secondary waves, chance occurrences, " growth " and so on—a theory of capitalist change, assuming, in so doing, that non-economic conditions or data are constant and automatic and gradual change in economic conditions is absent. But there is no difficulty in inserting all this. And it would seem to follow that the organic analogy is less adapted to express faithfully the nature of the process than many of us think; although, of course, being a mere analogy, it may be so interpreted as not to imply anything positively wrong and as to avoid the idea of an equilibrium growth *ad instar* of the growth of a tree, which it may, but need not necessarily, suggest.

Summing up the argument and applying it to the subject in hand, we see that there is, indeed, one element in the capitalist process, embodied in the type and function of the entrepreneur, which will, *by its mere working and from within*—in the absence of all outside impulses or disturbances and even of " growth "—destroy any equilibrium that may have established itself or been in process of being established; that the action of that element is not amenable to description by means of infinitesimal steps; and that it produces the cyclical " waves " which are essentially the form " progress " takes in competitive capitalism and could be discovered by the theory of it, if we did not know of them by experience. But by a mechanism at work in, and explaining the features of, periods of depression, a new equilibrium always emerges, or tends to emerge, which absorbs the results of innovation carried out in the preceding periods of prosperity. The new elements find their equilibrium proportions; the old ones adapt themselves or drop out; incomes are rearranged; prosperity inflation is corrected by automatic self-deflation through the repayment of credits out of profits, through the new consumers' goods entering the markets and through saving stepping into the place of " created " credits. So the instabilities, which arise from the process of innovation, tend to right themselves, and do not go on accumulating. And we may phrase the result we reach in our terminology by saying that there is, though instability of the *System*, no economic instability of the *Order*.

§ 6. The instability due to what we conceive to be the basic factor of purely economic change is, however, of very different importance in the two historic types of capitalism, which we have distinguished.

Innovation in competitive capitalism is typically embodied in the foundation of new firms—the main lever, in fact, of the rise of industrial families; improvement is forced on the whole branch by the processes of underselling and of withdrawing from them their means of production, workmen and so on shifting to the new firms; all of which not only means a large amount of disturbance as an incident, but is also effective in bringing about the result, and to change " internal " economies into " external " ones, only *as far as* it means disturbance. The new processes do not, and generally cannot, evolve out of the old firms, but place themselves side by side with them and attack them. Furthermore, for a firm of comparatively small size, which is no power on the money market and cannot afford scientific departments or experimental production and so on, innovation in commercial or technical practice is an extremely risky and difficult thing, requiring supernormal energy and courage to embark upon. But as soon as the success is before everyone's eyes, everything is made very much easier by this very fact. It can now, with much-diminished difficulty, be copied, even improved upon, and a whole crowd invariably does copy it—which accounts for the leaps and bounds of progress as well as for setbacks, carrying in their wake not only the primary disturbance, inherent to the process, but a whole string of secondary ones and *possibilities*, although no more than possibilities, of recurrent catastrophes or crises.

All this is different in " trustified " capitalism. Innovation is, in this case, not any more embodied *typically* in new firms, but goes on, within the big units now existing, largely independently of individual persons. It meets with much less friction, as failure in any particular case loses its dangers, and tends to be carried out as a matter of course on the advice of specialists. Conscious policy towards demand and taking a long-time view towards investment becomes possible. Although credit creation still plays a rôle, both the power to accumulate reserves and the direct access to the money market tend to reduce the importance of this element in the life of a trust—which, incidentally, accounts for the phenomenon of prosperity coexisting with stable, or nearly stable, prices which we have had the opportunity of witnessing in the United States 1923–1926. It is easy to see that the three causes alluded to, whilst they accentuated the waves in competitive, must tend to soften them down in trustified, capitalism. Progress becomes "automatised," increasingly impersonal and decreasingly a matter of leadership and individual initiative. This amounts to a fundamental change in many respects, some of which reach far out of the sphere of things economic. It means the passing out of existence of a system of selection of leaders which had the unique characteristic that success in *rising* to a position and success in *filling* it were essentially the same thing—as were success of the firm and success of the man in charge—and its being replaced by another more akin to the principles of appointment or election, which characteristically divorce success of the concern from success of the man, and call, just as political elections do, for aptitudes in a candidate for, say, the presidency of a combine, which have little to do with the aptitudes of a good president. There is an Italian saying, "Who enters the conclave as prospective pope, will leave it as a cardinal," which well expresses what we mean. The types which rise, and the types which are kept under, in a trustified society are different from what they are in a competitive society, and the change is spreading rapidly to motives, stimuli and styles of life. For our purpose, however, it is sufficient to recognise that the only fundamental cause of instability inherent to the capitalist system is losing in importance as time goes on, and may even be expected to disappear.

§ 7. Instead of summing up a very fragmentary argument, I wish to emphasise once more, in concluding, that no account whatsoever has been taken of any but purely economic facts and problems. Our diagnosis is, therefore, no more sufficient as a basis for prediction than a doctor's diagnosis to the effect that a man has no cancer is a sufficient basis for the prediction that he will go on living indefinitely. Capitalism is, on the contrary, in so obvious a process of transformation into something else, that it is not the fact, but only the interpretation of this fact, about which it is possible to disagree. Towards this interpretation I have wished to contribute a negative result. But it may be well, in order to avoid misunderstanding, to state expressly what I believe would be the positive result of a more ambitious diagnostic venture, if I may presume to do so in one short and imperfect sentence: Capitalism, whilst economically stable, and even gaining in stability, creates, by rationalising the human mind, a mentality and a style of life incompatible with its own fundamental conditions, motives and social institutions, and will be changed, although not by economic necessity and probably even at some sacrifice of economic welfare, into an order of things which it will be merely matter of taste and terminology to call Socialism or not.

JOSEPH SCHUMPETER

University of Bonn.

MITCHELL'S BUSINESS CYCLES

Reprinted from *Quarterly Journal of Economics,* Nov. 1930, 150-172.

I

As far as it is the primary function of a review to draw to a book the attention of the scientific community and to tell by summary or critique what readers are to expect from it, this review is superfluous. Every economist knows Professor Mitchell's great book of 1913 and also the present instalment of the new monumental work. It does not want any introduction to the public, and is beyond any critic's power to help or to hurt. The only task left, it would seem, would be to enter into a discussion of the vast mass of important points of detail raised — a task to the fulfilment of which this book is fairly entitled both by its merits and by the eminence of its author, but which it is impossible to carry out within the compass of a review.

Yet every book of weight tells us something beyond what it has to say about its particular subject. It conveys necessarily a general message from author to readers about methods, horizons, aims and views, of which the treatment of the subject in hand is but an application or paradigma. If this be true of any book of stature, it is, in the economic field, especially true of books on the problem of business cycles, which by its very nature calls for a display of practically all the powers and acquirements of the author and unavoidably bears, by implication at least, upon every other department of our science. One of the best things said

1. Business Cycles; The Problem and Its Setting, by Wesley C. Mitchell, with a foreword by Edwin F. Gay, New York, National Bureau of Economic Research, Inc., 1928.

in the volume before us, is the suggestion (p. 452), "that ideas developed in the study of business fluctuations may lead to reformulations of economic theory." It is indeed obvious that in dealing with business cycles we are dealing with all the most fundamental elements of the economic life of capitalist society, and are sure to meet practically all our great problems on our way. Rarely, if ever, has any worker in this field made so full a use of the possibilities thus offering themselves as Professor Mitchell has, and it is this aspect of his work on which primarily I shall undertake to comment.

First, we cannot be too grateful to the eminent author for rigorously brushing from his path idle controversy on fundamental principles of "method," which lingers in this field longer than in any other. The reader has but to look at pp. 469–474, where there is a resumé of Professor Mitchell's views on this point, in order to be assured that he will be able to follow the argument without feeling in duty bound to turn from relevant discussion and to send in some grand remonstrance on such topics as the respective merits of collecting facts, of statistical treatment of facts, and of handling them by that kind of refined and systematized common sense, which we have come to call "economic theory." Professor Mitchell's every line is, needless to say, well nourished with every kind of available fact, including his "own store of experiences and observations"; he is "ready to apply the mathematical technique of statisticians"; and he proposes "to guide our statistical investigations by rational hypotheses," repudiating the "error to think that free use of factual materials reduces the need for careful reasoning." Guarded and judicial as these utterances are, they cover in their admirable brevity and simplicity a great deal of ground. They are infinitely valuable, when said ex cathedra by a prominent leader in a field in which they are as yet less universally accepted than in others and which still suffers from a belief, harbored by many ardent workers, that explanation can ever come to us as a by-product of mere collection of facts and that it spells scientific sin to use, in dealing with these facts, any logical tools not at the command of the "man in the street." Nor is this all. *Via facti*, by starting in his first chapter with a survey of the work done since the discovery of the problem as well as of the solutions now current, he testifies to his belief in the continuity of science, thereby condemning implicitly any program of "starting anew" and that attitude which takes a pride in mere lack of scientific training. His teaching on this point may be summed up, I believe, saying that any "New Economics" can come about not by program but only by achievement.

True, Professor Mitchell does not take kindly to what savors of "theoretical construction," and his preferences, while toned down both by scrupulous fairness and by his invariable courtesy and generosity, are yet clear enough. He can hardly help associating the work of theorists with insufficient command over facts and with ways of thinking which seem to him backward. Even in cases in which an author's command of facts was no more backward than his analytic apparatus, he would stress the former and underrate, as it seems to me, the importance of the latter point; just as, on those few and well-timed occasions when he is looking for formal analogy to the procedure of physical science, he seems to overstate the importance of the experimental, and to understate the importance of the theoretic side of their work. In places he forgets or denies that there is such a thing as theoretic proof or disproof of a proposition, and seems to consider "theories" as so many suggestions of which one is really as good as any other before being put to the decisive judgment of statistics. I confess to some doubt, whether every one of the authors considered in the first chapter will recognize themselves in the pictures drawn of them. But this matters little. In spite of it he is leading up to common ground, on which we may hope to work harmoniously towards the common goal, even tho the task being a complex one and calling for very different mentalities, aptitudes, and likings, we may never be able fully to appreciate each other. To quote a colleague of mine, professor of Experimental Physics at the University of Bonn: "If I call in a theorist to hear what he has to say about the results of my experiments, and if my man shows so much experimental aptitude as is implied in being able to switch off the light, I begin to doubt his competence as a theorist." Yet he calls him in.

There is another comment I should like to make upon the work as a whole or its "general message," which extends the importance of the book far beyond the precincts of the mere problem of business cycles. Professor Mitchell, as he has told us somewhere, is no friend to systematic treatises — which most of us will probably agree to be in some respects necessary evils. But as a matter of fact, he has written one or, at all events, sketched out the fundamental contours of one, with such unmistakable clearness, that any competent economist could supply most of the rest without risk of serious error. I think it safe to say that no more than one fifth of the book before us bears specifically on business cycles in the sense that it has not just as much to do with any other group of the great problems of our science — distribution, or pricing, or monopoly. Now, inasmuch as we have before us the work of one of the leading figures of the scientific world of economics and of a leader who has, in former years, often betrayed some displeasure at the state of our science and our ways of dealing with its problems, both in toto and on a number of well-defined headings, it seems but natural, and hardly unfair, to ask what the outstanding features are, which could be pointed to as constituting or implying fundamental differences in results or horizons, and whether the presence of such differences spells revolution or evolution. It is natural, in trying to answer this question, to think of that mighty structure which, tho battered in places by the impact of newer methods and results, still stands broadly in the background of much, if not most, of the best work of our day — Marshall's great treatise.

There is undoubtedly a difference in aim and character. Marshall's fame and influence rest on his mastership in constructing tools of analysis, on his having built, out of the material of the theoretic ideas of his time, an engine of analysis. It is the fifth book of the Principles (and matter placed elsewhere in the treatise which really belongs in that book) which is immortal in the sense in which scientific achievement can ever be called immortal. Now Professor Mitchell, being of the experimentalist type, would never undertake a similar task; he would consider it, as all experimentalists do, of secondary importance; he thinks of theory not as an analytical engine, but primarily either as a store of rational hypotheses, or as a body of doctrine or as an arsenal of generalizations gleaned from arrays of well-digested facts. He even would never, I presume, preface factual analysis by an elaborate theory as, to quote another instance, Professor Taussig has done in his International Trade. He would think theory in the Marshallian or Walrasian sense just as little worth while for its own sake as he would refinements on statistical methods which have no immediate bearing on problems in hand. But, again, just as he is not prepared to forego the use of the tools put at his command by modern statistical methods or to condemn the use of all of them except the elementary ones, so he would not and could not deny — he would in fact have no logical standing ground to do so — that science cannot progress, after a certain stage has been reached, without the construction of tools of thought different from those of every day life, growing up as the result of conscious effort: *id est*, without a theory, which has as little to do with metaphysical speculation or political doctrine as the discussion by the pure theory of mechanics of "possible" forms of movement, and which is not an unscientific or provisional substitute for facts, but an instrument — spectacles, so to speak — needed in order to discern the facts.

This being the case there is a great difference in emphasis, and yet no epistemological gulf between Mitchell and Marshall; not even between Mitchell and Marshall's fifth book (appendix included). If difference there be, it can only be found under one of the following headings, in none of which it spells break or revolution.

(1) It can be held, that, while theoretical tools are a necessary evil, yet all the tools so far devised are vitiated at their root by some initial error, *e.g.* a fundamentally false psychology. To which I should reply, that, however faulty we may think the psychology of economists to be in dealing with such problems as property, taxation, motives of enterprise or saving and so on, our tools of analysis such as quasi-rent, equilibrium, coefficients of production, *even* marginal utility can be interpreted so as to tally with *every* kind of psychology. The psychological background is, so far as any point of this kind is concerned, little more than a façon de parler

and hence cannot possibly be the logical — as distinct from historical — derivate of any particular one.

(2) Without attacking fundamentals there is, of course, plenty of room for difference as to the usefulness or otherwise of any single tool or method — that is, any way of handling a given set of facts for given purposes. For myself, I confess to a strong belief, for example, in the future rôle, both within theory itself and in the practical problems of "Welfare Economics," of the tool called "sum total of consumers' surpluses." Perhaps Professor Mitchell does not share this belief. But if we were to discuss the question, we could not but discuss it as a question of theory and by means of theoretical arguments. Epistemology and methodological creeds would not enter. Such differences, necessarily incident to scientific work, are no cleavages between "schools."

(3) But must the tools of theory not prove useless for the book before us, being constructed without reference to its task — a *numerical* treatment of our problems? But have they been thus constructed? Have those who went before us not all theorized with an eye to quantitative [2] treatment, present or future? In Marshall's case especially, Mitchell, the fairest of critics, surely would not deny that he both saw and worked for, this task. We need not read between the lines in Marshall or dwell on the explicit statement in that great manifesto of his, "The old generation of economists and the new." We need only look at the text, at the treatment of demand or of cost, at the distinction between external and internal economies, the theory of monopoly, the dealing with the element of time, the formula of point elasticity — all opening their arms, as it were, to future masses of statistics. Nor need we speak of his reiterated hints at

2. "Quantitative" and "numerical" are synonymous in Mitchell's book.

the stores of statistics of all kinds already available. It is true that, to take the simplest instance, his demand curve has repeatedly been denied the aptitude to serve as the demand curve of statistics. Yet it has been the beacon to all work in the field, and whether it will or will not prove useful in the end is still *sub judice*.

(4) Finally, our analytic engine, it is held, is bound to undergo continuous change, fully as much as mere "hypotheses" are, under the influence of the results of "factual" study. It can never stand by the side of them as if an immovable organon of hyperempirical canons. Not only must the stream of new fact present to us ever new problems necessitating, to use a phrase of Pigou's, the attaching of new arms to our engine; but also, and much more important, increasing insight into facts necessarily makes some instruments of theory obsolete and creates the need for new ones. As Mitchell says a propos of a special case (p. 54): "But as our knowledge grows wider and more intimate, our attitude toward the discussion of causes undergoes a subtle change." Of course it does. The theoretical part of every science always refers to, and acquires its meaning from, a given state of factual knowledge. The instruments of theory which have been useful, and theorems which, in the sense of pragmatism, have been "true" in one state, may very well, and often *do*, prove bars to progress and even downright wrong in another. New theories and new criteria for the acceptance of theories become inevitable as time and work go on. They would be necessary even if the old ones had been perfect for their day. A single fact à la Michelson may change the face of theory. But *quis negavit*? Difference on this head can arise only if "factual" students deny that the influence of factual study on the apparatus of theory is no greater than the influence of theory on factual study; if they overlook the

necessity of continuously directing part of our collective effort toward improving our theoretic tools as such, independently of the impulse of new facts or problems; if they refuse on general grounds to acquire a working knowledge of them; and if they reject particular instruments in cases in which it is doubtful whether they have fully mastered their meaning.

II

If I have succeeded in scaling down to a difference of what might be termed the scientist's personal equation, what at first sight appears to be a fundamental difference of worlds between the book Marshall *has* written and Mitchell *might* have written, it becomes easier to indicate the other characteristic features of our author's hypothetical "Principles." There are the institutional element, the statistical element and (following Professor Mitchell's caption) what we will call "the contribution of business annals."

The institutional contribution (Chapter II, on Economic Organization), could be incorporated into a general treatise almost verbatim. Its bearing on the particular problem in hand is but indirect. Unless acquainted with the embers of recent controversial flames, no reader would think of the names of Veblen or Schmoller in reading it. It is this to which I want to draw attention. I believe it to be no part of our duty to the memory of those men to try to overlook the serious and even glaring defects in their equipment, both natural and acquired. On the contrary, justice toward them requires us to mention them precisely in order to explain, and thereby to excuse, part of what they said. He who insists upon taking at face value certain tenets of theirs, casts an undesirable imputation on their mental power. Schmoller was undoubtedly a great man. Nobody would like to do without the fruits of his positive work on institutional history. No economist thinks, or ever thought, these things superfluous or secondary. It is with part of his technique of economic argument that we find fault. Here it is impossible to deny either that he was far from perfect or that he exerted an influence which is in part responsible for what everyone — especially every German — admits to be an unsatisfactory state of economic science in Germany. Veblen differed from Schmoller in very many points. But as far as economic reasoning goes, much the same applies to both. Had he been able to have his way, had his teaching not met a phalanx of competent theorists, we should perhaps have to make a somewhat similar statement as to America. Now Professor Mitchell's pages are remarkably free from any tendency to *substitute* institutional investigation to economic theory. They are entitled, here again, to the tribute that while they show an open mind to whatever valuable contributions may be expected from that quarter, they are resolutely shut to the misconceptions which have often impaired their usefulness. In some of the sections of this chapter, conspicuous among which is the one on "guidance of economic activity," there is nothing but matter for cordial endorsement.

Critical comment, then, can only bear on particular points. The prominence given e.g. to the monetary aspect of business phenomena is but natural from either of two viewpoints. One of these, however, implies provable error, which I am far indeed from imputing to Professor Mitchell. Whoever is guilty of the erroneous view that economic life is changed to its very core by the intervening of money, that a money economy must be explained on principles differing *toto caelo* from those applicable to a non-monetary life, or that, finally, when pointing to the difference between making goods and making money, he is pointing to a fundamental cleavage — would obviously be justified from that point of view in so emphasizing that aspect. The other viewpoint is that *calculating in money* gives to our economic behavior a measure of precision which it would not otherwise display, and that it rationalizes economic life, and, further, life in general. The use of money may well be looked at as one of the great moulding influences of civilization, both in the sense of a cause and in the sense of a vehicle of other causal elements. This is correct, but more relevant to sociology than to economics. And if we avoid the error just mentioned, and if the other statement, tho true is one with which economics is little concerned, then it becomes surely more useful to base "The Meaning of Business Economy" (p. 63) on our old friend, the division of labor, of which the practice of "making and spending money" is nothing but a technical consequence.

Again, the section on the system of prices may well be accepted as a translation into non-technical language of part of the fundamentals of theory of the Walrasian type. But it may equally well be accepted as an example of what is lost in the process of translation. Nicer questions, more recondite interrelations are absent. No guiding principle is provided, in the face of the fact, that, the interdependence between *all* prices being recognized, it would be logically impossible for the author to deny the existence of such a principle. The intending "factual" student goes without the help of so much as "elasticity," "cost-curve" or "quasi-rent," which he not only ought to, but in our days actually tries to, fill with numerical material. The forms of interrelations between prices are of many kinds. Theorists, such as

Edgeworth and Fanno, have attempted to work out some of them and the result of their labors is essential for many things, among them an understanding of the details of what happens during business cycles. But we do not hear of them. Nor could it be pleaded that, the interrelation among prices being taken simply as a fact of experience, whatever more may be to it will automatically show itself in the process of enlarging that experience and sifting further data. This hope must fail, for the same reason which makes direct and mere observation of the phenomena displayed by patients inconclusive and untrustworthy — because some of the interrelations among symptoms may be, and generally are, overlaid by others. If there be anything less than admirable in the two highly instructive sections on the monetary mechanism and the flow of money payments, I believe it to be traceable to the eminent author's dislike of the theoretical apparatus. It is, however, more important that there is nothing in this chapter — or in any other — which could be considered as incompatible with the apparatus of theory; nothing which could either be proved to be wrong by it or prove it to be wrong in toto or in part. As in every point of detail, this may be seen in Mitchell's treatment of the fundamental concept of equilibrium (p. 186). We might plead with him as to the justice of calling it a mechanical analogy, and try to win his assent to the view, that the equilibrium of a balance sheet is not, as he holds, "a different conception of equilibrium" but one special case of it, and we should perhaps demur to the statement that we have simply (p. 187) no more warrant for assuming that business processes "tend" to maintain an equilibrium than to assume that they "tend" to get out of balance. To most of us it seems that the one assumption applies to certain business processes and the other to different ones and that it is important, again in the interest of factual study, to distinguish between the two. We should also like to have Professor Mitchell's view on the usefulness or otherwise of some related "tools," among them that called "representative firm." Finally we should have been grateful to learn more than we do (p. 376) about how "equilibrium" stands to that "figment" of a normal state of trade. Yet the idea itself is there and brought into definite relation to factual study, from which we may in future discuss it — and it is this what matters.

III

Fully 170 pages out of the 474 in the book are none too many to deal with the momentous matter of Chapter III, the "Contribution of Statistics." Many of us will echo Professor Mitchell's criticism of the current distinction between statistical and theoretical work. It is here that the economics of the future will differ most significantly from the economics of the past. The salient point is not in the increasing wealth of statistical information or in an increasing readiness to use it. Nobody who weighs the methodological implications of Ricardo's reply to Mr. Bosanquet, can deny that on principle economists have always been ready to use what "factual" information was at their command, or that the difference in this respect is no greater than the difference between the theoretical apparatus of the classic and the modern theorist. The point is rather that we are increasingly learning to *think* in terms of statistical quantities [3] and with a view to the fact that our data offer themselves to us mostly in the shape of time series. And here I beg to echo Mitchell's call for closer coöpera-

3. An important instance of what I mean is the present process of remodeling the Theory of International Trade by means of the concept of the Barter Terms of Trade.

tion from the other side of the fence, or, as I should rather say in view of what Mitchell himself tells us on the subject of trends (pp. 221 and 230), to add emphasis to an element of the case already emphasized by him. It is not only that economics has to learn from the statistician's approach and, incidentally, to struggle with its static fetters, but also that statistical methods will have to be remodelled at the suggestions of economic theory and to get as much as possible over its own static fetters, which are no less stringent than ours.

Some of us still look upon the store of methods in modern statistics as if they were, like Calculus, wholly unconnected with any particular subject and equally applicable to all. There exists a body of general theorems and there are pieces of mathematical technique of which this is quite true. And on the strength of this there is a tendency to proceed to calculating averages, indices, coefficients of correlation, trends, deviations from trends, as if the methods used would, if only correctly applied, of necessity yield significant results, and as if the choice between alternative methods were merely a matter of statistical convenience, or, at best, of applying formal criteria, such as the absence of freakishness in results, sensitiveness to influences obviously relevant, or, again, stability, reversibility, closeness of fit, and so on. But it has long been pointed out that this is entirely inadmissible. Whether we are measuring, as we mostly do in Physics or Astronomy, one and the same magnitude, or a type; whether the type is a constant one or variable in time; whether we do or do not theoretically know something about the form or law of its variation — in every one of these cases we are faced with different problems, to which different rules must apply. Even a mere arithmetical average, or its standard deviation, is perfectly meaningless unless we know beforehand, whether there is some "norm" in the set of data we have to deal with and what the nature of that norm is.[4] I am very far from imputing to Professor Mitchell any errors on this score, yet I confess to a feeling that in perusing Chart 24, Fig. R, which presents the duration of 106 (!) cycles in what looks like a frequency polygon — with standard deviation and all — I have missed any warning to the effect that this figure has no statistical meaning whatever. It has none, because the norm of the phenomenon under consideration has obviously changed and the criteria as to what is to be called a "cycle" are neither definite nor uniform enough to warrant one in speaking in this case of a statistical "universe," of which the 106 cycles could be considered as a sample. "Static" assumptions are no exclusive *privilegium odiosum* of economic theory. What I am concerned with here is the fact that only theory — in the boldest acceptance of the word — can tell us anything about the presence and in the end about the nature of a norm [5] or, more generally, of a "Kollektiv gegenstand" in the sense of H. Bruns. Further, the statistical formula we apply can only grow out of the theory of the subject we have, if it is to have definite meaning. Any example will show this. We have, e.g. been constructing indices of "general prices" these many years and discussing their respective merits and shortcomings without working out their theory, i.e. without settling what it is they are to measure. All the inconclusiveness of the discussion and all the difference

4. It may still be useful to look up what Lexis says on this point, in the article on Anthropologie and Anthropometrie in the Handwörter buch der Staatswissenschaften.

5. To be sure, the theoretical norm is a thing differing in its very essence from the statistical norm. Yet it embodies what may be called the "meaning" of the latter — its theoretical soul, as it were — and this meaning must be settled before we can proceed to construct a statistical norm and to put it to any scientific use.

of opinion about the tests to be applied in judging alternatives, is traceable to this source — and disappears immediately, when we tackle the problem from the theoretical side. It is easy to do this in this case: Writing the Walrasian equations of the equilibrium, we find that we have one less than unknowns. We usually mend the case by putting one of the p's equal to 1. It is better to mend it by giving the Σpq of consumer's goods an arbitrary value. As we could assign it any other value just as well, we may also say that we are introducing an arbitrary "factor of proportionality." This factor is the exact kernel of the vague idea of "level of general prices," and it is its changes we are seeking to extricate from the changes in individual prices when we try to measure changes in general prices. And as soon as this is understood — and no sooner — we derive a formula which has a title to being called *the* correct one.[6]

Again, we have indeed become more critical about the coefficient of correlation, and it is being well nigh universally recognized, that $n = 0.999 \ldots$ is compatible with the absence of any real relation, $r = 0$ with its presence. The relation may be overlaid by other influences or simply have some other form. It is less universally recognized that this tool grew out of a soil very different from ours, and that by using it we are introducing the whole of the assumptions of the theory of errors — of

6. Denoting by E the sum spent on consumers' goods, and by $p_1, p_2 \ldots p_m$ the prices, by $q_1, q_2 \ldots q_m$ the quantities sold at the time t, similarly by $E + dE$, $p_1 + dp_1 \ldots p_m + dp_m$, $q_1 + dq_1 \ldots q_m + dq_m$, expenditure, prices and quantities sold at the time $t + dt$, we have $dE = \sum_1^m pdq + \sum_1^m qdp$. As it is easy to see, the price-level would be constant if $\sum_1^m qdp = 0$, and the deviations from zero of this expression are a measure of its changes. Of course, the formula which we get from this applies only to infinitesimal changes from point to point, but it gives us a standard by which to judge every other one. It is readily seen that Professor Fisher's ideal formula comes out well.

"static" statistics — which may well reduce our results to meaninglessness. To be sure, we need not, and cannot, let the matter rest there. Noteworthy attempts have been made to get over these limits of that important tool — e.g. by Oskar Anderson (*Die Korrelationsrechnung in der Konjunkturforschung*, Bonn, 1929). But it remains true that we must carefully scrutinize the justification we have each time we use it. And, here again, the construction of the statistical tool can only come out of previous theoretic analysis of the case in hand.[7]

Nowhere are considerations of this kind of such importance as in the case of trends. There would be little overstatement in saying that trend-analysis will be the central problem of our science in the immediate future and the center of our difficulties as well. It is here that our contention will be most readily conceded by the statistician. He is so often being forced to discard "unbelievable results" that it is easy — or ought to be — to show that an inspection of results from other than statistical standpoints imposes itself upon us not only in cases of *glaring* absurdity of results, but in *all*. This is only another way of saying that if trend-analysis is to have any meaning, it can derive it only from previous theoretical considerations, which must not only guide us in interpreting results, but also in choosing the method. Failing this, a trend is no more than a descriptive device summing up past history with which nothing can be done. It lacks economic connotation. It is, in fact, merely formal. We can apply the familiar methods just as well to e.g. a few succesive years of a pros-

7. This is my objection to most of those textbooks of statistical method which undertake to give the economist "just what he wants for practical work" and which start with comforting him that they will not lead him into the redoubtable thickets of mere mathematics. They can hardly help misleading him. For there is no understanding of our tools without a full grasp of their mathematical implications.

perity-phase, as to the whole of the material we may happen to have (as, again, to a period of political commotion). The result has the same claim in every case to be called a trend in the statistical sense, and may in each case be decomposed into component elements in an indefinite number of ways which have no rational connection to each other — unless it be supplied by the theory of the subject under research.[8] As soon as we speak of "the" trend of a series, *a fortiori* if we follow Professor Mitchell in dignifying it with the term "secular," we are theorizing by implication; and there is no bolder theorizing than that which works up from impressions or propositions not explicitly stated. We cannot be too grateful to Professor Mitchell for discouraging exclusive reliance on the test of closest fit. The trends we want are very different from those we get by fitting a curve through unanalyzed material.[9] But this opens up a host of questions, for example, the question barely touched in the volume before us, whether it is the trend which is the "generating" phenomenon of cycles or the cycles which generate the trend; whether or not the trend is a distinct economic phenomenon at all, attributable to one factor, or a well-defined set of factors; whether all the points on our raw graphs have on principle equal right to exerting an influence on its slope, and, if not, which credentials we are to ask of everyone point before admitting it. Now, inasmuch as there has been much work on a number of some of these factors — cp., for instance, the string of analyses Professor Pigou presents in his Industrial Fluctuations — we might hope

8. These considerations are entirely independent of — altho practically reinforced by — the shortcomings of the methods actually in use, which it is impossible to enter upon here.

9. To have to change one's trend in the lapse of time is no misfortune, but what we should generally expect to happen. But misfortune there may be in not being able to account for it theoretically.

that "factual study" would step in to grip our data with these newly forged tools. That is what the "experimentalist" worker undoubtedly would do in every other science. Not so on our field; here this blessing seems slow to come. Yet it should not be difficult to show that keeping distinct such things as (*a*) *that element of growth, which is capable of being decomposed into infinitesimal steps* — such as increase in population or savings; (*b*) the effect of industrial and commercial innovation; (*c*) influences from outside the economic system — such as harvests, gold discoveries, wars, changes in social organization or in the attitude of men towards business success — and the working out of theoretical schemata for every one of them, might go a long way towards answering many of the questions alluded to, and give additional definiteness both to the aims and results of "realistic study." It is in this direction that we have special reason to look forward eagerly to what Professor Mitchell is going to tell us in the next volume.

IV

I have the same to say on the Contributions of Business Annals. The National Bureau of Economic Research has put all of us under obligation by offering us so handy a work as Dr. Thorp's. There can be no doubt that the *histoire raisonnée* of cycles is to the student of cycles what "mother earth" was to Antaeus. It is, moreover, a source which opens up aspects inaccessible to mere time-series-analysis, just as it needs, in its turn, reinforcement by monographical research into single industries and, in many cases, individual concerns (such as we may hope to get from the series of monographs Spiethoff is starting at present). But looking at the use made by Professor Mitchell of the material collected under his auspices, I cannot help being struck by what seems to me an excess of caution traceable to a reluctance to let himself be served by theory — not as *hypothesis*, but as a *tool*. He even refrains (p. 450) from attempting to draw up a full catalogue of the factors obstructing the tendency to international synchronization of cycles, which would be one of the main contributions to expect from intensive "factual" study. In such matters as e.g. the cause of difference in cycles in different countries, he does not care to link the difference in the character of the "turning points" in England on the one side, and Germany and pre-war America on the other, with the difference in relative capital-wealth, a relation suggested by theory and signally verified by facts. Surely we have no quarrel with such results as that cycles are becoming increasingly internationalized by "the endless series of actions and reactions among the influences exerted and experienced by all the nations. . . ." (P. 447.) Yet most of us will come to the conclusion that the Annals, while undoubtedly enabling us to see more clearly, have not so far helped us to see farther.[1]

Again, doubts about the fruitfulness of the Annals *without* the aid of theoretical groundwork, as distinguished from their fruitfulness, if used with it, arise occasionally, where the attempt is made to make them yield additional information of significance. Professor Mitchell, in dealing with the duration of cycles, finds, for instance, many more of them than his predecessors used to. But this is simply due to the lack of a sufficiently definite principle in deciding what is to be called

1. Comparison, too, suggests itself with the results of the life-long, tho single-handed, labors of Spiethoff, and doubts arise as to the advisability to confine coöperation with him to a hardly satisfactory reference in the introductory chapter.

a recession. We could easily find still more cycles, and without theoretical aid there is no logical resting-place until we get down to those ripples which everyone knows are common even within a year of clearly marked boom or depression. To quote another instance, Professor Mitchell considers at length, and with qualified and guarded approval, Professor Mills' hypothesis on the changes in the length of cycles. With due respect to Professor Mills and the eminent services rendered by him to our science, I am at a loss to account for this preference except on the ground that that hypothesis is *not* theoretically founded. Else it is hard to understand how the difficulty of verifying it, the arbitrariness incident to it, and such blemishes as that it makes Austria after 1873 rank with old industrial countries saturated with capital, like England or the Netherlands — how these things can have failed to put it out of court, when confronted with the proposition of the "period of gestation," which theory would suggest and which Mr. Robertson has made a promising first attempt to verify — an attempt banished by Professor Mitchell to a modest place in his introductory chapter.

It may be the theorist's egotism or prejudice which accounts for my impression that, to conclude, the main direct contribution of this volume towards the solution of the problem, with the "Setting" of which it deals, suffers from the same cause. This contribution consists in the attempt to establish cycles as a "valid" (= real?) species of phenomena (p. 383). Having very properly followed Juglar in discarding the surface-phenomenon which we loosely call a "crisis," Professor Mitchell defines cycles as recurrences [2] of depression, revival, pros-

2. He might safely have called then "periodic" recurrences. The objection to the adjective has no other foundation than that every day parlance does not recognize "periodicity" except periodicity which displays either a constant period, or a period obeying a definite mathematical law.

perity, recession, and defends them against the attacks of Dean A. B. Adams and Professor Fisher (p. 464 *et seq.*) — with the question of phases to be distinguished he deals as if this were a mere matter of convenience. He even emphasizes their existence as a phenomenon *sui generis* somewhat at the expense of the "Long Waves" and the so-called "40-months cycle," altho the existence at least of the former is not only equally well established as that of the cycles themselves, but may well turn out to constitute the really significant problem, compared with which cycles may move to the background in much the same way as crises had to as soon as the cyclical movement was discovered. He seems, however, forced, by his method of approach, to stress so exclusively the formal requirement of recurrence as such, that the ground gained is largely lost thereby, and that his grip on his subject relaxes to the point of feeling (p. 396) "that we have no warrant for discarding cases in which cycles have been cut short or prolonged by wars . . . *or any other factor* (my italics) unless we believe that such disturbing circumstances will not recur in the future as in the past." Well, even earthquakes recur, and as we should have to extend the principle just quoted to cases which are not only cut short or prolonged, but also *caused* by wars and similar influences, we stand to lose the contours of our phenomenon. Incidentally we should lose much of what is so valuable in Professor Mitchell's separate treatment of irregular fluctuations (p. 249, *et seq.*). In fact, we should be on the road to giving up the idea of the cycles being a "valid" phenomenon.

All this is of secondary importance. Criticism is apt to loom unduly large in a review, and may do so in the present discussion. If so, I apologize and express again gratitude to the eminent author and admiration for his work, which must ever stand out as a landmark within its field and far beyond it. Such difference in outlook as remains between us can be summarized by saying the theory of the cycle is not the last but the first step on the road to our goal.

JOSEPH SCHUMPETER

THE PRESENT WORLD DEPRESSION: A TENTATIVE DIAGNOSIS

Reprinted from *American Economic Review Supplement*, March 1931, 179-182.

Like every other individual phenomenon, a given depression can only be explained by many factors, the number of which depends on the accuracy desired and, therefore, is indefinitely large. In this sense any explanation pointing to one factor only can have no other meaning than that a given situation is so very much dominated by that factor that we may neglect the others in a first approximation.

Yet there is another sense in which it is permissible to look for *the* cause of depressions in general. The meaning of this becomes obvious if we ask: Assuming a perfect absence of disturbing influences acting from without on the economic system, is there, or is there not, reason to expect that there would still be industrial fluctuations or alternating periods of prosperity and depression? "Influences acting from without" must be interpreted to mean not only occurrences such as earthquakes and wars, but also chance occurrences not subject to economic volition, such as gold discoveries or harvests (so far as these are due to accident) and even such things as changes in tariff policy or banking legislation. Although it is that question which constitutes the basic scientific problem, "the other circumstances" may have much more importance in accounting for what actually happens in any given individual case.

Hence the first thing we have to ask is whether the present world depression can be so accounted for; i.e., whether it can be attributed to a number of unfortunate events which interrupted what otherwise would have been continued prosperity or at least an even flow of economic life. The answer is in the negative. Changes in method of production in the widest sense of the word, such as have occurred in the period following upon the post-war crisis, necessarily create disturbances in the economic organism sufficient to produce a period of adaptation or recession. Disturbances of this kind differ among each other not only in intensity but also according to the time which must elapse before the new things created take their full effect; i.e., in most cases, before the products of the new plans reach the consumer's market. Theoretically we should, therefore, expect an indefinite number of waves to be concurrently in motion and to produce different business situations by their interference with each other. So far the existence of three kinds of waves (the "long waves," then what may be termed the Juglar cycle, and finally the forty-month cycle) seem to be established with greater or less certainty. It is probable that 1930 has at least in its second half fallen into the trough of such a forty-month cycle, and certain that the whole of the year forms part of the down-grade phase of a Juglar cycle as well as of a "long wave."

The depression which would have been due anyhow, but which might have been brought home to the nations concerned by no more serious symptoms than decreasing rates of increase, has been and still is under the influence of outside factors, some of which have helped to bring it about while others merely intensified it or made adaptation and recovery more difficult. The industrial depression has undoubtedly been intensified, and in its severity is partly due to the agrarian crisis which we observe in nearly all countries. This phenomenon is complex and of different character with different nations. One element in it, especially in the United States, cannot be separated from the industrial depression, because it is really part of it; namely, important changes in methods of agrarian production which have been one of the outstanding features of the last decade. It would not be easy to find so good an example of the manner in which productive innovation bears hard on those who are unable to adopt it. But for various reasons there would be an agrarian depression quite independent in its nature of the industrial depression. This agrarian depression would, furthermore, have been intensified in any case by the fact that in some countries, especially in Germany, protective tariffs have created an uneconomically large extension of the area under cultivation. As far as the agrarian crisis is an independent phenomenon, it must be listed as an "outside factor" which makes things worse than they otherwise would be.

It is easy to exaggerate the influence of monetary policy in contributing to the present situation. Yet it is obvious that if a monetary system exactly equal in all particulars to the pre-war system were reintroduced, prices would have to come down to a level lower than that of 1913. Although we are not confronted with this case, yet we have an approximation to it, and it is impossible to treat the consequences as negligible. Especially in England, depression is undoubtedly partly due to the policy which culminated in the gold standard act, which for various reasons has taken some time to evolve its full effects.

Related to this are the effects of reparation and inter-allied payments. They are a contributory cause of the deflation policy of the countries concerned, and they create a stream of exports which would not otherwise exist. The effect of reparation payments is in this respect equivalent to a rebate offered by Germany on her goods. In absolute quantity this effect may not be very important, but even a small additional supply disorganizes markets already weak.

Similarly the flight of capital from some countries, acting in the same way, makes for more intensive depression. This flight, which we observe especially in Germany and to a lesser degree in England, is mainly a flight from oppressive taxation and may, therefore, be made to enter under the heading of changes in political structure uncongenial to capitalist activity, or of political disturbances generally.

The depression has not been brought about by the rate of wages, but having been brought about by other factors, is much intensified by this factor. The causes are different in different countries but everywhere wages are higher than is compatible with full employment. This statement does not mean that unemployment in its present extent is due to the rate of wages. But part of it is, as shown by the unusually high figures during the preceding prosperity. Moreover our statement does not mean that the rate of wages is too high in any other sense or that the policy of high wages is a mistaken one. For there may be compensating advantages to it.

The fall in short-time money rates has for various reasons not been followed by a sufficient fall in long-time rates, which fact must delay the emergence of those activities which usually precede general revival. The importance of this element must not, however, be exaggerated. There are wide strata of industry in all countries which in a depression as severe as the present one would not borrow even if credit were offered to them for nothing. It is easier to dampen prosperity by a high rate of interest than to alleviate depression by a low one.

Both level and system of prices have lost some of the elasticity they used to have. All commodities under strict control account for a special class of difficulties both when they fail to adapt themselves and when the control breaks down, as has happened with some of the most important of them. These breakdowns while in some cases due to the depression itself, have in others been independent of it so as to act as additional factors of the situation.

It is believed that these elements of the situation account for 90 per cent of the values of the measureable symptoms. But there are many factors of minor or local importance, which are sometimes unduly stressed and the stressing of which sometimes spells definite economic error, but which it would be wrong to overlook entirely. So breakdowns of stock exchange speculation may intensify a depression or even be the immediate cause of the location of a turning point, although it would be quite wrong to look upon them as a cause. So may the system of installment payments, encouraging as it does the spending of expected income, add to difficulties if a change has occurred. And probably the best authorities in the field would agree that present-day tariff policies, while they may soften in special cases the effects of existing depression, have the tendency to develop strains and untenable positions, and that in this sense they may be counted among the contributory factors of the situation.

Without entering into the problems of remedial policy it may be stated that there is no difficulty in devising on the basis of this diagnosis remedies both for the situation in general and for any particular feature of it. In cases like the one before us economics is not inferior to, say, medicine either in diagnosis or in remedial advice. The difference and the difficulty lies in the fact that our patients will not take what we might be able to prescribe.

THE COMMON SENSE OF ECONOMETRICS

Reprinted from *Econometrica,* Jan. 1933, 5-12.

THE AIMS of this Journal, and of the Society of which it is to be the organ, have been stated above by the Editor with that brevity and precision which are characteristic of every statement of a sound case. What I have to add, by way of comment and amplification, will, I hope, confirm the impression that there is nothing startling or paradoxical about our venture, but that it grows naturally out of the present situation of our science. We do not wish to revive controversies about general questions of 'method,' but simply to present and discuss the results of our work. We do not impose any credo—scientific or otherwise—, and we *have* no common credo beyond holding: first, that economics is a science, and secondly, that this science has one very important quantitative aspect. We are no sect. Nor are we a 'school.' For all possible differences of opinion on individual problems, which can at all exist among economists, do, and I hope always will, exist among us.

Like everything else, economic life may be looked at from a great, strictly speaking an infinite, number of standpoints. Only some of these belong to the realm of science, still fewer admit of, or require, the use of quantitative methods. Many non-quantitative aspects are, and always have been, more interesting to most minds. Fruitful work can be done on entirely non-quantitative lines. Much of what we want to know about economic phenomena can be discovered and stated without any technical, let alone mathematical, refinements upon ordinary modes of thought, and without elaborate treatment of statistical figures. Nothing is farther from our minds than any acrimonious belief in the exclusive excellence of mathematical methods, or any wish to belittle the work of historians, ethnologists, sociologists, and so on. We do not want to fight anyone, or, beyond dilettantism, anything. We want to *serve* as best as we can.

ECONOMICS, THE QUANTITATIVE SCIENCE

There is, however, one sense in which economics is the most quantitative, not only of 'social' or 'moral' sciences, but of *all* sciences, physics not excluded. For mass, velocity, current, and the like *can* undoubtedly be measured, but in order to do so we must always invent a distinct process of measurement. This must be done before we can deal with these phenomena *numerically.* Some of the most fundamental economic facts, on the contrary, already present themselves to our observation as quantities made numerical by life itself. They carry meaning only by virtue of their numerical character. There would be movement even if we were unable to turn it into measurable quantity, but there cannot be prices independent of the numerical expression of every one of them, and of definite numerical relations among all of them.

Econometrics is nothing but the explicit recognition of this rather obvious fact, and the attempt to face the consequences of it. We might even go so far as to say that by virtue of it every economist is an econometrician whether he wants to be or not, provided he deals with this sector of our science and not, for example, with the history of organization of enterprise, the cultural aspects of economic life, economic motive, the philosophy of private property, and so on. It is easy to understand why explicit recognition of this fact should have been so difficult, and why it has taken so long to come about. Philosophers, who have at all times delighted in classifying sciences, have always felt uneasy about the precise place to be allocated to economics as a whole. As it was, they practically followed the empirical dividing line between 'natural' and 'moral' sciences, and classed economics with the latter. And there, of course, the quantitative aspect or sector of our science found but uncongenial ground.

Another reason was that economic problems have most of the time been approached in a practical spirit, either indifferent or hostile to the claims of scientific habits of thought. No science thrives, however, in the atmosphere of direct practical aim, and even practical results are but the by-products of disinterested work at the problem for the problem's sake. We should still be without most of the conveniences of modern life if physicists had been as eager for immediate 'application' as most economists are and always have been. This accounts for the neglect of econometrics, as well as for the unsatisfactory state of our science in general. Nobody who craves for quick and short answers to burning questions of the day will care to entangle himself in difficulties which only patient labor can clear in the course of many years.

Nevertheless, the quantitative character of the subject was bound to assert itself. It is one of the most striking facts about the history of our science, that most—and if we exclude historians, *all*—of those men whom we are justified in calling great economists invariably display a remarkably mathematical turn of mind, even when they are entirely ignorant of anything beyond the quantitative technique at the command of a schoolboy; Quesnay, Ricardo, Böhm-Bawerk, are instances in point.

Nor is this all. If econometricians have any wish to imitate other people and to glory in heroic ancestry, they may with justice claim the great name of Sir William Petty as their own. The second part of the seventeenth century is full of vigorous ventures into the field of econometrics—one has but to point to Gregory King's statistical demand curve. It is a question of some interest how it was possible that such hopeful beginnings could have failed to inspire further work, and how their results could have been left to linger in the dusk, although they were by no means forgotten, the reference to 'King's rule' being part of the stock in trade of almost every stale textbook written ever since.

In the sphere of monetary phenomena and its neighborhood, quantitative and even numerical analysis became established practice as far back as the sixteenth century, mainly in Italy, and this tradition was never lost again; passages in the Italian writers of the eighteenth century, such as Beccaria, Carli, Verri, and others, sounding very familiar to the modern ear. What we have before us there is nothing less than a conscious attempt to weld into one indivisible argument theorems and statistical facts.

And, provided we leave out the word 'conscious,' we find substantially the same tendency in whatever piece of the work of our predecessors we choose to look at. To give but one example; we are accustomed to scoff at the literature of the time-honored controversy on Value. But what else is at the bottom of it, overlaid it is true by heavy masses of speculative verbiage, if not the truly scientific search for an economic unit of measurement, or of several such units adapted to different classes of phenomena? There was no more un-empiric speculation about it than there is about every science in its infancy. Nor is there less connection with such statistical materials as each epoch could command than we are entitled to expect—as everyone will admit who has taken the trouble of perusing Ricardo's reply to Bosanquet.

LATER DEVELOPMENTS

Essentially quantitative analysis, but crippled by the lack both of appropriate technique and of adequate statistical material—this is the diagnosis we arrive at when we study the work of economists up to that time, when Mill's principles were fairly representative of what our science had to give. This, too, is the element of truth which emerges from the hostile phraseology which we are in the habit of using about 'classical doctrine.' Obviously, therefore, what our society stands for is anything but an innovation. It is no more than a conscious endeavor to remove obstructions to the flow of a stream which has been running ever since men began to think and write about economic life.

In order to see in their full significance the conditions which have made it desirable, and indeed necessary, to form, under the banner of Econometrics, a *coalition* of the different types of economists who are to join hands in our society, we must, however, now glance at later developments. The phase that could, until about ten years ago, be called the 'modern' phase of economics, admits of description in terms of three facts and their consequences: first, the rapid growth of our wealth of statistical and other material; second, the progress of statistical technique at our command—which so far as it grew up largely outside our own field and without reference to our needs, was a stroke of good fortune, very much as a lift in another man's car is to the wanderer on a dusty road; and third, the emergence of a theoretical engine very much superior to the old one. True, on none of these heads are we, or can we ever be, satisfied; on every one of them, it seems to me, the real thing is still to come, and present performance calls for apology rather than congratulation. Yet it would not only be ungenerous, but positively false, to deny the importance of what has been achieved, or the possibilities which begin to loom in the future.

In all this the econometric line stands out clearly. It was definitively established that economic theory involves quantity, and therefore requires the only language or method available to deal with quantitative argument as soon as it outstrips its most primitive stage. To W. St. Jevons belongs the honor of having spoken one of those simple messages, which at times seem to focus both past and future history and to become mile-stones visible ever after. It was he who said in the introduction to his *Theory of Political Economy* (1st ed. 1871); "It is clear that Economics, if it is to be a science at all, must be a mathematical one." But still higher tribute is due to A. Cournot who, without encouragement or lead, in what was then a most uncongenial environment, in 1838 fully anticipated the econometric program by his *Recherches*, one of the most striking achievements of true genius, to which we pay respect to this day by nearly always starting out from them. Of course, it would be superfluous to emphasize the paramount importance of that great teacher of ours whose exposition of exact theory sprang from his head as did Minerva from the head of Jove. What I want to stress is that he constructed his analytic apparatus with a clear perception of the ultimate econometric goal, every part of it being thought out so as to fit it to grip statistical fact when the time should come. In this he went much farther than Jevons. This reads like a paradox because Jevons actually worked on figures, as in the matter of index numbers. But within the precincts of pure theory itself, he seems much less concerned with that goal than Cournot, and it is much more difficult for the numerical horse to jump Jevons' fences than it is to trot on Cournot's road.

In our pantheon, J. H. von Thünen's place is side by side with Cournot's. It is not only—indeed not even primarily—the idea of marginal productivity which it is important to mention here, but Thünen's peculiar relation to a set of facts, which is as vital to econometrics as statistics in the narrow sense of the word. Thünen pointed out that cost accounting, bookkeeping, and neighboring headings, cover a mass of material which economists have entirely neglected. This neglect has indeed been so complete that the specialists of 'Business Administration' now actually have begun to build their own theoretical houses which wall them off from 'general theory' as completely as it, in turn, had excluded them, in spite of the fact that both groups of workers to a great extent—a signal instance is the matter of cost curves—till the same ground. It is clear that economists cannot indefinitely do without that vast reservoir of fact, nor cost accountants, bookkeepers, and so on, do without the economists' contribution. And, looking back, we see now that as early as 1826, Thünen's book could have taught us *how theory grows out of the observation of business practice.*

I for one shall always look up to Léon Walras as the greatest of all economists. In his theory of equilibrium he gave a powerful basis to all our work. It is true that while he made the decisive step in the *quantitative,* he failed to move in the *numerical* line, the *junction* of which two is characteristic of econometrics. But we have been taught of late to look more hopefully even on the 'numerical' possibilities of that most general and most abstract part of our science which is equilibrium theory in Walras' sense. And this fact similarly indicates the econometric claims of the work of Auspitz and Lieben, of Knut Wicksell, of Francis Y. Edgeworth, and of Walras' great successor in Lausanne, Vilfredo Pareto.

In a somewhat different sense, we may finally claim as our own that greatest of all teachers of economics, Alfred Marshall. With some of us, it has become a custom to speak of him as the exponent of 'neoclassical' doctrine. This is not the place to show how it came to pass—not without some fault of Marshall himself—that so utterly unjust, and in fact meaningless, a label was affixed to his name. But I wish to emphasize first, that nobody can peruse his address on "The Old Generation of Economists and the New" without discovering, though not perhaps without some surprise, how clearly our program stood before his mind. Nor is it possible for anyone who knows how to read his *Principles* in the light of his *Industry and Trade* to define what he really strove to accomplish in any but econometric terms. Most important of all, he always worked with an eye to statistical application, and he was at his best *as a theorist* when constructing those handy tools, like elasticity, quasi-rent, external and internal economies, and so on, which are so many bridges between the island of pure theory and the terra firma of business practice and business statistics.

I do not wish to speak of any living economists. But the readers would probably not forgive me if I failed to make two exceptions, and to mention the pioneer work of Irving Fisher and Henry L. Moore.

THE PRESENT STATE

All these achievements were, to say the least, enough as a good start and to build up from. And, indeed, work full of promise has been done in our line during the last two decades, work which makes us feel, when we now look at the Walrasian system, very much as we feel when beholding the model of a motor car constructed forty years ago. But still, most of us undoubtedly do agree in finding the present state of our science disappointing, not only in comparison with the achievements of other sciences, but also in comparison with what our science could fairly be expected to perform. There are many reasons for this, but some of them only, having special bearing on the mission of this Society, call for attention here.

Reasoning on economic facts means, and always meant, within a very important sector, quantitative reasoning. And there is no *logical* breach between quantitative reasoning of an elementary character, and quantitative reasoning of the kind involving the use of 'higher mathematics.' But nothing makes a greater *practical* breach in the evolution of a science than the introduction of a habit of thought which has so far been foreign to the recognized equipment of the specialist, and which at the same time is inaccessible except by strenuous effort. When the necessity of proceeding to the use of more refined mathematical methods, both in economic theory and in statistics, became apparent to some, the majority even of those economists who did work the quantitative sector refused to follow. At first they laughed. They do so no longer. Integrals cease by and by to be as hieroglyphs to them. Many of them try to understand and have made their peace with us, while reserving their right to criticize our results and to object to mathematical excesses. But this is not the full cooperation we need. Even in this improved situation, economics lacks that broad expanse of professional common ground which, in the case of physics, transmits acquired results to the general public. Beginners are bewildered by this unsettled situation. Energy is being wasted and the real business of the science hampered. Recent progress, and still more than *actual* progress wide *possibilities* of it, has drawn to our field a most promising host of newcomers. But the old situation being fundamentally changed, we had no uniform training to offer them. Hence the lack of coordination of the work. The new men came to face our problems from very different angles and with very different acquirements, full of impatience to clear the ground and to build entirely anew. The man whom nature had moulded to delight in unadulterated fact, whether he worked in a statistical bureau or did field work on his own, often knew little and cared less for that engine of analysis, which we call 'economic theory,' or for refined statistical technique. On the other hand, the master of this technique, feeling its power and seeing the material to grip with it, tried to rush at his own kind of regularities or generalizations. And the theorist, conscious of his own task, refused more often than was wise to accept the work of the other two types as anything but (possible) verifications of his theorems. But, although uncoordinated, the growth has been tropical. It might be expected to settle down and bear fruit in time, but there is chaos for the present, in which only a very experienced eye can see an underlying tendency working its way slowly though powerfully towards a goal common to all.

THE PROGRAM

The common sense of the program of our Society centers in the question: Can we not do better than this? Surely it would not be a reasonable policy to sit down and wait till, in the end, things find their level by themselves, and meanwhile to allow econometricians of all countries to fight single-handed their uphill battle. What we want to create is, first, a forum for econometric endeavor of all kinds wide enough to give ample scope to all possible views about our problems, yet not wide enough to be hampered by the weight of an audience which keeps discussion in the ante-rooms of the real points at issue, and forces every speaker or writer to go every time over the same preliminaries.

On this forum, which we think of as international, we want secondly to create a spirit and a habit of cooperation among men of different types of mind by means of discussions of concrete problems of a quantitative and, as far as may be, numerical character. The individual problems themselves are, as it were, to teach us how they want to be handled. We want to learn how to help each other, and to understand *why*, and precisely *where*, we ourselves, theorists, statisticians, collectors of facts, or our neighbors, do somehow not quite get to where we want to be. No general discussion on principles of scientific method can teach us that. We have had enough of it. We know it leads nowhere, and only leaves the parties to the contest where they were before, still more exasperated perhaps by those gentle rudenesses it is customary to administer to each other on such occasions. No general arguments of this kind ever carry conviction to the man who means real work. But, confronted with clear-cut questions, most of us will, we hope, be found to be ready to accept the only competent judgment on, and the only relevant criterion of, scientific method, that is the judgment or criterion of the result. There is high remedial virtue in quantitative argument and exact proof. That part of our differences —no matter whether great or small—which is due to mutual misunderstanding, will vanish automatically as soon as we show each other, in detail and in practice, how our tools work and where they need to be improved. And metaphysical acerbity and sweeping verdicts will vanish with it. Theoretic and 'factual' research will of themselves find their right proportions, and we may not unreasonably expect to agree in the end on the right kind of theory and the right kind of fact and the methods of treating them, not postulating anything about them by program, but evolving them, let us hope, by positive achievement.

We should not indulge in high hopes of producing rapidly results of immediate use to economic policy or business practice. Our aims are first and last scientific. We do not stress the numerical aspect just because we think that it leads right up to the core of the burning questions of the day, but rather because we expect, from constant endeavor to cope with the difficulties of numerical work, a wholesome discipline, the suggestion of new points of view, and helps in building up the economic theory of the future. But we believe, of course, that indirectly the quantitative approach will be of great practical consequence. The only way to a position in which our science might give positive advice on a large scale to politicians and business men, leads through quantitative work. For as long as we are unable to put our arguments into figures, the voice of our science, although occasionally it may help to dispel gross errors, will never be heard by practical men. They are, by instinct, econometricians all of them, in their distrust of anything not amenable to exact proof.

Harvard University

DEPRESSIONS

Can We Learn from Past Experience?

Reprinted from *The Economics of the Recovery Program,* 1934, 3-21.

To many people, who today speak of unprecedented disaster, historic precedent is not only inconclusive but distasteful. There is some practical wisdom in this attitude, as far at least as it implies protest against misleading analogies in a world in which nothing ever reproduces itself with the mechanical exactness of a laboratory experiment. But recurrent the depressions are and certain features repeat themselves; and these recurrent features as well as those which are peculiar to any one crisis show some truths, which it would be much more laborious to establish without such illustrative material. Take for instance the crisis which occurred in this country in 1896. Up to this date the crises of the nineteenth century had been international. But the American crisis of 1896 was not. In all other countries 1896 was a year of fair business — of distinct prosperity in some, of moderate prosperity in others. Common sense leads us to look for some cause peculiar to this country. And we have not far to seek. The peculiar cause stands out clearly, and every history of business cycles registers it — the Bryan campaign and the threat of silver inflation. The case is instructive. Many persons, perhaps most, would argue that Americans, expecting inflation, would have rushed into contracts, started building, ordered industrial equipment, "bought now," thereby producing a boom. In fact, they did not. On the contrary, although underlying conditions were by no means unfavorable for an upswing, business went to pieces. But as soon as sound money was assured, the wheels of the economic machine started moving again of themselves. Lesson: our industrial system is sensitive to political, especially monetary, disturbances. The system may be a very imperfect one, to be improved or even quite cast aside. But this is beside the point when we discuss crises and recovery. Nothing prevents recovery as effectively as fear of political action; nothing promotes it as does firm and sober handling of the existing situation under the existing conditions.

1825

The international crisis of 1825 is still more instructive. We must, however, speak of it in terms of English experience, which was in some respects curiously like the course of events in this country since the World War. The Napoleonic Wars were over and so was the postwar crisis (1815). Forty years of what was an unexampled rate of development — that process which is popularly known as the "industrial revolution" and the outstanding feature of which, in the industrial field, was the emergence of a mechanized textile, especially cotton, industry — had established England's industrial, colonial expansion and the capture of the trade of the other belligerent nations, her commercial supremacy. Both these causes, changing the whole of her economic life and her social structure, were bound to bring about a period of painful readjustment to the conditions of a new equilibrium. In international finance, England became a great lending or "creditor" country. As she had not been a debtor country before, the change was less spectacular than the corresponding change in America's position after 1914. Still it was then that she established herself as the financial center of the world. Resumption of specie payments (1819) *did not interrupt her prosperous march at all,* but the Act of 1822, which facilitated the expansion of credit by the provincial banks, produced all the consequences of what is euphemistically called "elasticity of the credit system." A high protective tariff gave an artificial stimulus to profits and to stock exchange speculation. But the price-level from 1814 to 1825 showed a sharply declining trend.

The annals of the period abound with reports of all imaginable symptoms of "prosperity." The progress of the working classes — starting, it is true, from a deplorable level — was considerable. The well-to-do prospered, and that conventional living, which we are accustomed to associate with the English bourgeois, was a much admired achievement of that boom. The agricultural sector had not quite its share, as the increase of capacity in response to the panic demand of the war years had led to depressed prices and rents.

Then came the crash, and reaction and readjustment, both of the most typical kind. The first thing to break down was speculation, which had persisted through 1824 and the greater part of 1825 because of the failure of the rate of discount to rise adequately. Next came a collapse among banks, seventy of them failing within six weeks. Thereafter everything else went on exactly as the usual statistical picture of crises has it.

The financial crisis was over before the year was out, but roughly three years of depression followed. Here is a case which exemplifies how much basis there is for the belief in the recuperative powers of capitalism. For Government did next to nothing beyond permitting, at the height of the financial strain, the issue of one-pound and two-pound notes by the Bank of England. Although the masses did not suffer in silence and their riots, if nothing else, should have been sufficient motive for public action, things were allowed to take their course. And business did recover. Losses had to be taken, South American investments to be written off, prices had to find their levels, what was unable to adapt itself had to be eliminated. All this took time. But as soon as it was done, an upward swing set in by itself. It is true that things were nothing like as serious as they are today, but the catastrophe was of the same kind. Two observations force themselves upon us: first, that the inaction of government, however reprehensible on humanitarian grounds, contributed to recovery at least by not hampering it. Second, that adequate relief would not have been beyond the means of England; had it been provided, the darkest hues would have been removed from the picture without interfering with the process of clearing the ground for revival.

1873

The year 1873 caught the United States while the country was going through the long process from Civil War inflation to the resumption of specie payments in 1879. During the period as a whole, prices sagged continuously. There was a temporary stage of rising prices, about a declining trend, on the back of the vigorous wave of activity and prosperity which, interrupted only by mild recessions in 1866-1867 and 1870, came to an end with the breakdown of 1873. What happened in 1866-1867 and 1870 may fairly be compared with the events of 1924 and 1927; while 1873 and the four years of depression which followed display similarities to 1929 and after. The similarities and the differences are alike illuminating. Both give to the case of 1873 a value almost equal to that of deliberate experiment: Whoever reads the annals of that time becomes conscious of an uncanny feeling to the effect that life itself experiments for us in order to teach us lessons which we nevertheless forget, time after time. Clamor for reckless inflation, for instance, arose at once. An inflation bill was passed by Congress. But President Grant vetoed it (1874). Money eased and prices began to *rise* promptly although slowly.

The center of economic gravity was then in Europe. It was there that the trouble began, and part of the consequences of that world crisis affected this country but indirectly. Everywhere, however, the period 1842-1873 was fundamentally the first railroad age, the age of steam and steel. The expenditure on railroad building was the backbone of the booms of that time. The new facilities of transportation changed the surface of the economic world and were at the bottom of the necessity of readjustment. We may smile now at the opinion of the age that railroads were being overdone, seeing how small a part of what we now know had to be done was accomplished then. But certainly they were in advance of what was then required. Of course they were, for they themselves created the economic world, which was to provide the demand for their services and which never could have developed without them. They also were the center of reckless finance and malpractice of all sorts. It was the business of railroad construction which produced that mentality, half visionary, half criminal, so well expressed by the saying of one of the railroad magnates of the time — not an American, however — who was indicted when things had gone wrong: "You don't build railroads with moral principles."

Railroads were not the only factor, of course. Incident to their construction and independent of it, there is a long list of other ventures, all of which in some countries were facilitated by the removal of the last remaining shackles by which earlier centuries had fettered enterprise — they were of much the same character as those we are about to forge afresh today — and by legislation favorable to the emergence of the modern joint stock companies. Those countries, especially Germany and Austria, lived then through their South Sea Bubbles and in this way laid the foundation of their industrial career. With the exception of France, which did not share fully either that prosperity or the breakdown which followed it, the whole world basked in the sunshine of what to some extent really was a new era.

Again it was stock exchange speculation which broke down first. This always is so and accounts for the fact that the public mind so often looks upon it as the cause of the trouble. But it should be obvious that just as the rise of speculation requires another cause to start it, so the downfall of speculation requires a more fundamental explanation than the speculative excess itself. In 1873 this explanation is not difficult to find. It was the slackening down of construction and equipment due to the increasing difficulty of adapting calculation to situations changing with disconcerting speed. This broke prices, called forth unemployment, but first of all created difficulties in the structure of credit and so brought down speculation. Then only, by way of afterthought, people became critical and started out on a revision of values which turned through the discovery of errors and crimes into a panic outrunning by much the measure of adjustment really required by hard fact.

American speculation collapsed in September, carrying with it, almost immediately, the failure of brokers and many banks. Others had to suspend legal tender payments, to resort to clearing house certificates, and so on. But the monetary system stood firm, the premium on gold touching a new low. It was the market for railroad shares which suffered most, and the speculation in lands which went to pieces most completely. Of course, certain features of the present situation, which are traceable to the World War, were absent then. Apart from them, however, there is *nothing* in what has happened in the capitalist world during the last three years, which was not also present in the picture of 1873. Not even the skyscraper trouble of today was absent then; for although there were no skyscrapers, overbuilding, in Vienna, Berlin, Rome, was one of the features of the situation. And again, it is only the failure to provide adequate relief that can be pointed to with confidence as an obvious matter of reproach. All other measures which, this time, were actually taken by the governments of some countries cannot be credited with any remedial effect on the depression, however beneficial they may have been in other respects. Moreover, it is doubtful whether, given the social and economic structure of industry in 1873, anything really helpful could have been done *after the breakdown.* It would, of course, have been possible to prevent the preceding boom. But this would have strangled also its achievements.

Four years of stagnation followed.

The Problems of Depression.

At the threshold of every sensible diagnosis of any given depression lies a fundamental distinction between two different sets of causes and consequences. The reader is welcome to call it pedantic, but without it there is no hope of clear perception of what happens. *First,* as our examples show, business adapts itself to the new state of things created by the preceding prosperity; it reacts on the upheaval due to the intrusion of new and more efficient methods of production and to the dislocation of everyone's profit and loss account. One needs no more than look around in order to grasp this point: The emergence of mass production of cheap cotton goods from the last decades of the eighteenth century onward spelled elimination of many an old shop. The construction of railroads changed the competitive position of localities and opened up undreamt of sources of supply of all kinds of commodities, necessarily supplanting some old ones. Now we have had combines and dry farming, more efficient methods of producing electricity, rayon and motors and radios, and a thousand similar things. This is really at the bottom of the recurrent troubles of capitalist society. They are but temporary. They are the means to reconstruct each time the economic system on a more efficient plan. But they inflict losses while they last, drive firms into the bankruptcy court, throw people out of employment, before the ground is clear and the way paved for new achievement of the kind which has created modern civilization and made the greatness of this country. It is easy to understand, on the one hand, that all this would happen even if nobody ever made any mistakes and if there were no crooks; but also, on the other hand, that everything that is unsound for either reason shows up when prices break and credit ceases to expand in response to decreased demand for it. Nor is it difficult to see why errors and misbehavior should be abnormally frequent in prosperity. Everyone is a great business man when prices go up, and windfall profits are easily made which obliterate the consequences of errors of judgment and of worse things. When everybody talks of new eras — blissfully unaware of the fact that soon he will be talking of the hopeless failure of capitalism — an increasing volume of business is being done on the assumption that things will continue to boom. A superstructure of such transactions rises above what is substantially sound and comes down with a crash as soon as, under the impact of the new products or increased quantities of products, readjustment sets in.

But, second, there are the consequences of events of quite a different order. Economic life is constantly acted upon by social and political factors. It lives in a social and political environment full of disturbances of its own. In prosperity and while margins are wide, these influences, though present, are obscured. But they show as soon as things cease to boom. It is manifest, that the maladjustments which resulted from the Napoleonic Wars had much to do with what happened in 1825, that the aftermath of the Civil War and especially of the greenback inflation was an important element in the American situation of 1873. It is equally obvious that in trying to understand any given case we must always bear in mind that what we are faced with is never simply a depression but always a depression *moulded and made worse by forces not inherent to the working of the economic engine as such.*

Now it is of the utmost importance to realize that the only distinctive characteristic of the present world's crisis, the only thing, that is, which makes it *fundamentally* and not only quantitatively differ from such crises as those of 1825 and 1873, is the fact that non-economic causes play the dominant rôle in its drama. It is not only such consequences of the war as political payments, the annihilation of Russia, and so on, but also other things which make a catastrophe of what without them would have been mere depression: impediments to the working of the gold standard, economic nationalism heaping maladjustments upon maladjustments, a fiscal policy incompatible with the smooth running of industry and trade, a mistaken wage policy, political pressure on the rate of interest, organized resistance to necessary adjustment and the like. It is beside the point to ask, whether this should induce us to reapportion our blame for what has happened between the business and the political world. Nor is it in order for the economist to take melancholy satisfaction in the truth, that present calamities are, contrary to a common opinion, in the nature of a verification of some of the oldest teachings of his science, which have been consistently ignored ever since 1914. What does matter, however, is to realize that *this* is the cause of the impossibility to forecast. As a doctor is unable to predict whether his patient will be run down by a motor car, so the economist is unable to predict in a situation in which so many political motor cars run about. What we face is not merely the working of capitalism, but of a capitalism which *nations are determined not to allow to function.* This may be, and probably is, inevitable. But it is the great difficulty in the way to recovery.

Hence the problems presented by periods of depression may be grouped as follows:

First, removal of extraeconomic injuries to the economic organism: Mostly impossible on political grounds.

Second, relief: Not only imperative on moral and social grounds, but also an important means to keep up the current of economic life and to steady demand, although no cure for fundamental causes.

Third, remedies: The chief difficulty of which lies in the fact that depressions are not simply evils, which we might attempt to suppress, but — perhaps undesirable — forms of something which has to be done, namely, adjustment to previous economic change. Most of what would be effective in remedying a depression would be equally effective in preventing this adjustment. This is especially true of inflation, which would, if pushed far enough, undoubtedly turn depression into the sham prosperity so familiar from European postwar experience, but which, if it be carried to that point, would, in the end, lead to a collapse worse than the one it was called in to remedy.

Fourth, reforms of institutions not intended to *remedy* the situation but *suggested* by the moral and economic evils of both booms and depressions: The crucial point of these reforms lies in the coincidence of a political atmosphere exceptionally favorable, and an economic situation exceptionally unfavorable to their success. No doubt they will always be carried amidst enthusiastic clapping of hands. But they will also be stigmatized in future by their tendency to prevent or retard recovery. This should not blind us to any merits they may have, but it is a plain and undeniable fact.

The Atmosphere of Periods of Depression

We have seen that the course of events in all periods of depression presents a significant family likeness. So do the attitudes of people. Defeat on the battlefield destroys the prestige of military rulers and their confidence in themselves; crises destroy whatever of both these things business leaders may enjoy. Their cry for help is the more damaging for them the more they disapproved of government interference before. For the time being, the majority of people grows out of humor with the economic system under which they live and becomes inclined to favor what in some cases we call reaction and in others radicalism. In fact, it makes astonishingly little difference which way they move politically. The consequences are much the same in both cases.

The readiest attitude to take is to blame individuals, a blame which is undoubtedly only too justified in very many cases. Just as it was, at some times and with some nations, a habit to clamor for the heads of unsuccessful generals, so there was always, and is today, a disposition to punish both culprits and scapegoats in business. English opinion, after the ignominious breakdown of the speculative craze known to history as the South Sea Bubble (1720) seems to have been to the effect that the most desirable measure to take was the hanging of some people. This bent persists. It is more rational that people should insist on measures for regulating and purifying financial practice. The ways of speculation, the responsibilities of promoters and managers, the methods of banking are the chief objects of such legislation. Broadly we may say that while most of these measures, as the historian surveys them, went too far in some respects, and were ineffective in others, and while many of them made immediate recovery more difficult, they have justified themselves on balance and have succeeded in improving what they were meant to improve.

More important, depression in some cases produces, in other cases materially strengthens, protectionism. People may advocate "self-sufficiency" primarily from non-economic motives. But in prosperity most people realize more vividly what it would cost them; in depression they look upon it as a remedy. It is significant to note that protectionism in England was recalled to life and became a political factor in the prolonged depressions of the eighties but failed to succeed in the boom times that followed. Similarly, English radicalism, although born in the philosopher's closet centuries ago, *emerged* as a power strong enough to count for the politician in the twenties of the nineteenth century, and *established* itself in the eighties. Legislation which Americans would call radical was enacted in the eighties by the conservative governments of Germany and Austria, the first measures of social insurance, for instance, or factory legislation, or restriction of competition, or measures to bridle the rate of technological progress which then took the form of various favors to the small craftsman and so on — some of which lasting achievements, now approved by everyone, others merely due to definite and provable error.

The Upshot

There is no reason to despair — this is the first lesson to be derived from our story. Fundamentally the same thing has happened in the past, and it has — in the only two cases which are comparable with the present one -- lasted just as long. We are more keenly alive now to human suffering, and we are dealing with the situation under political pressure by political methods, but substantially we are confronted only with problems which the world was confronted with before.

In *all* cases, not only in the two which we have analyzed, recovery came of itself. There is certainly this much of truth in the talk about the recuperative powers of our industrial system. But this is not all: our analysis leads us to believe that recovery is sound only if it does come of itself. For any revival which is merely due to artificial stimulus leaves part of the work of depressions undone and adds, to an undigested remnant of maladjustment, new maladjustment of its own which has to be liquidated in turn, thus threatening business with another crisis ahead. Particularly, our story provides a *presumption* against remedial measures which work through money and credit. For the trouble is fundamentally *not* with money and credit, and policies of this class are particularly apt to keep up, and add to, maladjustment, and to produce additional trouble in the future.

Finally, our cases teach unmistakably that, futile as it is to hope for miraculous cures, it is exactly as wrong to believe that the evils of depression are all of them inevitable and that the only sound policy consists in doing nothing. There is no single and simple remedy. The numerous problems which present themselves must be dealt with individually and patiently. The kind of activity which is clamored for in such situations is likely to make matters worse. But all those features of depressions, which spell widespread suffering and needless waste, can yet be taken care of. Especially if a country has steadily improved its public finances during prosperity as the United States did in the decade which preceded the present crisis, enough means are available, and other means can be procured, for an expenditure which will blot out the worst things without injury to the economic organism, *provided only* that action on this line is taken promptly and followed up by equally sound fiscal habits as soon as recovery gets under way.

THE NATURE AND NECESSITY OF A PRICE SYSTEM

Reprinted from *Economic Reconstruction,* 1934, 170-176.

I.

The reason why it may be useful to insert into our considerations a few remarks on the nature of price, highly theoretical though they may seem on the one hand and trivial though they may seem on the other, is simply that recent discussion on fundamental economic reform has shown that some people take the view, not new, of course, in itself, that prices and especially prices plus profits are nothing but an incident in the life of acquisitive society, that they are an obstacle to the full use of existing productive possibilities, and that they might with advantage be done away with. Prices have been compared to tolls levied for private profit or to barriers which, again for private profit, keep the potential stream of commodities from the masses who need them. The writer believes it to be a mistake to consider such views as beneath discussion and thereby to insure their survival. Among the theoretic tools needed in order to deal with this view are some of the oldest of our science, dating back to the seventeenth century and also some of the most recent ones which have been contributed to our theoretic arsenal only in the last few years. As the problems involved are familiar ground to economists, it will be possible to confine the following remarks to a few points, in fact little more than headings which could be worked out more fully.

The writer wishes to point out one thing at the outset: in the course of progress of economic analysis during the last twenty years or so, it has happened repeatedly that views largely held by practical men or amateurs which bygone generations of economists have been in the habit of disposing of as simply foolish have, by newer methods, been shown to contain some element of truth after all, and sometimes quite a large one. In no case that the writer knows of has the reasoning itself which led to such views been rehabilitated. But whilst its errors remained what they were, newer methods of analysis have repeatedly shown by other reasoning that there was yet something to the proposition which the wrong reasoning ineffectually tried to prove. It would be easy to give instances. Our problem is among them, for though as much economic insight as can be got out of an elementary course on economics would seem to be sufficient to refute that view on prices, recent investigations on limited-competition and short-period phenomena have yielded results which will go a long way toward justifying in some measure the practical implications involved in that view.

2.

In order to show that price is a phenomenon incident to all forms of organization of society and to economic action in general, it is sufficient to look upon it as a coefficient of economic choice. That is to say, by paying a price for any commodity, buyers show a preference for that commodity as compared with other commodities which they could also buy if they wanted to, for the same money. At the point at which they stop buying, the price will exactly measure that preference for every one of them, and this is what is meant by calling price a coefficient of choice.

Now if we take the organization of a centralized socialist state as an example of non-capitalist forms of society, it stands to reason that the central management would have nothing to go by in its decisions on the questions of the what and how of production unless it gave the comrades an opportunity to express their preferences with quantitative precision. This is equivalent to saying that the coefficient of choice of the members of such a society would have to be found out somehow, for instance, by assigning to them a certain number of claims to units of product in general and allowing them to express their preferences for the various commodities by means of those units. If then prices can be considered to be coefficients of choice, then the coefficients of choice of the comrades would be essentially prices. Moreover, in order to choose between the various possible methods of production, it would be necessary for the managers to attribute values to the means of production at their command which it would be possible to deduce from the coefficients of choice expressed by the comrades. These values would be essentially the same thing as the prices of the means of production in a capitalist organization.

The last sentence already shows that the phenomenon of price covers in fact the whole range of economic action. If a man produces whisky rather than bread from his rye, then what he does can be interpreted as bartering bread for whisky, and at the point at which he stops doing this we shall again be able to obtain a quantitative expression of his preferences and again get a coefficient of choice which in all respects is the same thing as price in a market. It is obvious that the choice between these two alternatives is not determined by technical considerations. It should be equally obvious that economic considerations of precisely the same kind enter into the choice of the method of producing either bread or whisky, and that it would be incorrect to say that the decision about the what of production is an economic matter and the rest, namely, the decision about the how of production, a technological matter. For whenever there is more than one way of producing a thing, and methods of production differ as to the relative quantities of the means of production they require, it will be necessary to take account of their relative scarcity, or to put it in another way, to consider how valuable the other products are which could also be produced by the individual units of the means of production which the producer contemplates using for a given purpose. These values of alternative production show themselves in capitalist society in the money price of the means of production and would show themselves in equivalent expressions in any other form of society. This explains why technically backward methods of production may still be the most rational ones provided the more perfect methods would require less of a plentiful factor and more of one which is less plentiful, and why the technically most perfect method of production is so often a failure in economic life. Hence rational production can never rest on exclusively technological considerations, at least not as long as all means of production are not at the command of a society in unlimited quantities. An economic dimension is, therefore, always necessary for the guidance of production, and this economic dimension at all times and under all circumstances finds expression in coefficients of choice which are fundamentally the same thing as prices in capitalist society. Of course, this does not mean that these coefficients would be numerically the same under all circumstances and in all forms of society, but they would always be of the same nature and fulfill the same purpose from which it follows that any attempt to do without them would be devoid of sense.

3.

Well-known arguments of very different degrees of scientific rigor have been put forward to show that a régime of perfect competition would invariably result in a maximum of welfare and also in a maximum of total product. The first proposition is wrong but the second is correct, or at least nearly so, provided we define competition as a state of things in which no buyer and no seller of any commodity or productive service is big enough to exert by his own action any influence on the price of the product he sells or the price of the means of production he buys. For this case it can also be shown, at least as a matter of broad practical probability, that the sources of waste inherent in such a society are smaller than those inherent in others, that the process of saving would not create disturbances and, incidentally, that if free competition prevailed absolutely unfettered *all over the world*, the gold standard, although not functioning ideally, would yet not be the cause of any great or violent disturbances. But the great scientific interest of all those and many other conclusions is for practical purposes very much reduced by the fact that competition in that sense not only does not exist but under modern conditions of large-scale production could not exist. It is here that the practical man and the amateur score. For it is not true that what can be proved for the case of perfect competition holds approximately for the case of imperfect competition, as the older theory uncritically assumed. On the contrary, it has been proved of late that in important respects imperfect or monopolistic competition will produce exactly the opposite of those results which might be expected from free competition in the theoretic sense. Without going into the matter I refer to the literature of the subject, especially to the new book by Edward Chamberlin entitled *The Theory of Monopolistic Competition*. As the man in the street never meant anything else by competition but the absence of agreements or interference from outside, and as he certainly visualized monopolistic competition when he talked about competition in general, he is perfectly right in attributing to it all sorts of waste as well as a systematic tendency to stop short not only of any technical but also of the economic optimum of quantity of product. We need only go on to insert into our picture various kinds of inertia and friction in order to realize that whatever gain in life-likeness we thereby attain is exactly proportional to the distance we travel from the assumptions of rationality and free competition. We may add that under the conditions of limited competition profits emerge of a kind unknown to the system of free competition and that, however wrong it may be to consider the fact of profits as such, as an obstacle to economic progress, and however true it may be that some kinds of profits have been the prime movers of progress actually achieved, yet the profits of limited competition are precisely of the kind of which the first of these two statements would be true. Of course, factual investigation and analysis of the results obtained would still be necessary before we could compare those wastes and lags of the system we have with those of every one of the alternatives, all of which have sources of waste and lags of their own.

The diagnostic value of the theory of free competition in the pure sense is, however, not impaired by these considerations. It is still worth while not only to work it out but to present it in a simplified form to the public because it shows where the sources of trouble do *not* lie and therefore by implication where we are to look for them. We may indeed sum up by pointing to the more important possibilities:

(1) It can be shown that the mere fact of turning coefficients of choice into prices by expressing them in units of money does not alter their nature or the way in which they function. But this has nothing to do with the question whether the monetary and credit mechanism which determines the unit of price-accounting harbors sources of disturbance or not.

(2) The proof that competitive equilibrium is stable does not admit of extension to the case of limited competi-

tion. And all deviations from an unrealizable ideal state of competition may be so many causes of instability and disturbance.

(3) Even a perfectly competitive state of things would be exceedingly sensitive to disturbance from outside. Such disturbances, which obviously are very plentiful at present, must primarily be looked to if we are to understand the instabilities and troubles of the day. Among them we must not forget to glance at the general humor of the social environment which, quite apart from specific measures resulting from it, may injure the efficiency of the capitalist machinery in a thousand subtle ways by its general hostility to the forms of life and methods of business with which capitalist society works.

REVIEW OF ROBINSON'S ECONOMICS OF IMPERFECT COMPETITION[1]

Reprinted from *Journal of Political Economy,* April 1934, 249-257.

IT CANNOT be repeated too often that the case of perfect competition owes the fundamental importance which it always had and still has in economic theory to certain properties characteristic of it and neither to any tendency in the facts to conform to it nor any "desirability" of the state of things it depicts. From the beginning of scientific analysis of economic phenomena until comparatively recent times most economists would, it is true, have based the claims of free competition on the latter two grounds, the first of which we now all agree to be untenable, while the second is simply another illustration of how difficult it is in our field to acquire a scientific habit of mind. Their work, however, is not invalidated by these facts. For by virtue of those properties the theory of perfect competition still remains a useful and almost indispensable background with which to compare, and therefore by which to understand, any other situation, however far removed it may be from it. In view of the fact that some of our institutionalist friends are still known to harbor a belief that a typical theorist believes in free competition as a fact or, still worse, that he "advocates" it, it may even not be superfluous to point out that the theory of free competition is the only avenue to a rational theory of planning and of centralistic socialism.

In the course of the nineteenth century the theory of another case emerged with the slowness characteristic of a science which has proved so little attractive to true scientific talent: the "model" of free competition was supplemented by a "model" of perfect monopoly. That is to say, the two were set up side by side without much connection between them, the implication being that monopoly was in the nature of an exception. This is not true of Cournot, the great father of the theory who, on the contrary, made it the starting-point from which to proceed towards the other limiting case. But it is eminently true of Marshall and Edgeworth, who also afford examples of the common practice of the time of looking at the whole stretch of ground between the two limiting cases as rather unsafe and incapable of yielding determinate results. As the majority of practical cases lie on that stretch

[1] *The Economics of Imperfect Competition.* By Joan Robinson. London: Macmillan and Co., Limited, 1933. Pp. xii+352. 18*s*. (New York: Macmillan Company, $7.20).

of ground, this position was of course highly unsatisfactory. Things look still worse as soon as we realize that the case of free competition cannot be looked upon as an approximation, and that it becomes a distortion of what it is meant to describe if its assumptions are not fulfilled exactly. To complete our discomfiture, analysis of these assumptions and the resulting correct formulation of them reveal the fact that they are much farther removed from reality and much less likely to be fulfilled than even Marshall probably thought.

Two things had to be done and have been substantially accomplished during the last decade. For any science or part of a science, the first task always consists in establishing the logical autonomy of its field, or rather the conditions under which there is logical autonomy. In economics this involves the question of determinateness of equilibrium. The position arrived at in the nineteenth century and vigorously voiced by Edgeworth had to be revised. This was done by starting anew from Cournot's treatment of duopoly, "oligopoly" (the latter term is Chamberlin's), and bilateral monopoly. As the reader knows, the result was that various classes of important cases do, and others do not, yield determinate equilibria in a sense similar to that in which the monopoly-price is determinate: for we must never forget that the equilibrium of perfect monopoly does not carry guarantees for its realization as stringent as those inherent in the mechanism of perfect competition.

Not all of the economists, however, who have worked in this field started primarily with the question of determinateness of equilibrium in imperfect competition, but some directly proceeded to forge tools for, and to establish propositions about, the behavior of firms in imperfect competition, without first settling the question of equilibrium. Practice has shown this to be possible to a larger extent than we should expect, so that we may class this kind of work as a special type fulfilling, along with the first type of investigation, a function of its own. Both kinds of contributions together contain the elements of a very complete picture which the time has probably come to put into a systematic form. But even without having it before us as an architectonic whole, we can see how many important problems this new body of analysis will have to face, and how powerfully our general outlook on the economic process will be affected by it. To mention but one instance, as soon as we realize the implications of imperfect competition all presumption vanishes for some of those effects to emerge which we used to attribute to the normal working of an economic society which in common parlance would still be called "competitive." Our theorems about maximum satisfaction or maximum national dividend cease to hold true and the list of cases in which collective political action can increase both of them becomes so extended as to make these cases the rule rather than more or less curious exceptions. Views which our predecessors smiled at and which they considered as slips of the untutored mind turn into established theorems. And if it be part of our business to advise on questions of economic policy, then this advice would in very many cases have to be the exact opposite of what it was twenty years ago. Perhaps it is but natural that this should be interpreted as a breakdown of scientific economics, by a public (which term here covers many professional economists) which never got out of the habit of associating economic theory with liberalism in the nineteenth-century sense. The public always does so interpret any striking development in any science. On the other hand, some of the best economists of our times display a tendency towards committing in their turn the Ricardian error of rushing prematurely to practical applications and stand a good chance of again discrediting our science thereby. It is nevertheless but fair to state that we owe substantial progress to the works of all the theorists of imperfect competition, among whom Mrs. Robinson in this book establishes a claim, certainly to a leading, and perhaps to the first, place.

The book is indeed an admirable performance, both by virtue of its pioneer achievement and by the energy and straightforwardness of its exposition which eminently qualify it for classroom use, at least for such teachers as do not think it their duty to deal with their students as if they were feeble-minded. It is remarkably free from the blemishes (and flourishes) which so often disfigure and impair exposition of theoretical work. Its results, never irrevelant, mostly interesting, often novel, are presented in a thoroughly workmanlike way. It is an excellent example of what serious theory should be and well lives up to the standard of rigor set by the author in a pamphlet entitled *Economics Is a Serious Subject* (1932). As in the case of E. H. Chamberlin's book, the delay in publication has deprived it of some of the formal claims to priority which it would otherwise have had, but we are gainers thereby. For we have now before us in addition to the individual gifts we owe to Chamberlin, Harrod, Robinson, Schneider, Shove, Sraffa, Stackelberg, Zeuthen and others, also what they contributed jointly in the settings peculiar to their different mentalities, and this is much more useful and stimulating than the results of a "planned economy" would have been in this case. Mrs. Robinson's genuine originality stands out from the whole perhaps better than it would if her book stood alone.

The discovery which was to be the master key to a well-stocked store of tools of analysis is as simple and was as overdue as most useful discoveries are. It consists in recognizing that the derivative of total money expenditure on a commodity with respect to the quantity of the commodity may serve as well as does the derivative of total money cost with respect to quantity, our old friend marginal cost, and that it was quite illogical behavior on our part to work with the latter and to ignore the former, the marginal revenue, as Mrs. Robinson calls it. The demand function or, as its new and less honorific title is, the average revenue function, dropped back into its proper place and the whole demand-supply schema gained in symmetry. Much more important than this, the whole analysis of the pricing process acquired an unexpected unity covering the limiting cases of perfect competition and perfect monopoly, and ceased to be the patchwork it was for such a time. A single formula now gives the price for all cases (price equal to marginal revenue times $\frac{\eta}{\eta - 1}$). Anybody at all familiar with the history of theoretical physics will agree that the typical performance it records is exactly of this kind.

To this instrument the author adds many others of lesser but still great importance, one of which may be mentioned here. If $y=f(x)$ be the equation to the demand curve, then $\frac{xf'(x)}{f(x)}$ is the expression of the flexibility, the reciprocal of Marshallian elasticity. As it stands to reason that the behavior of the second derivative enters into the solution of many important problems, it is obviously desirable to have a similar expression which contains it. By a simple argument (p. 40 n.) the author arrives at the expression $\frac{xf''(x)}{f'(x)}$ which practice proves to be very useful indeed, for instance in dealing with problems of discrimination (Book V), a subject which Mrs. Robinson may justly be said to have put on a new footing. She calls it by the self-explanatory name of "adjusted concavity."

In justice to the book we must always bear in mind, first, that besides being very much more it is also a textbook, the work of a mind eminently gifted for, and almost passionately fond of, teaching. To this are due many simplifying assumptions which, looked at from another standpoint, would be unnecessary, and which in some points seriously impair the generality of the argument. Great sacrifices are cheerfully made by the author to secure elementary treatment and to avoid anything beyond the reach of very scanty acquirements. But if the reader be tempted to complain occasionally about those two-variable functions, lending themselves to illustration by plane curves, he should not forget that they teach certain fundamental truths just as well as, and better than, more complicated methods would and that this is probably all that can efficiently be put across to the beginner. We probably get fewer and less perfect results than the author could have derived by more advanced technique, but we also owe to her severe self-denial one of the best textbooks ever written.

Second, justice requires us to bear in mind that the book is Marshallian to the core. Everything about it is Marshallian: the approach, the fundamental "conceptual scheme," the manner of reasoning, the starting-points[2] as well as the goals, even the general social vision (although somewhat "modernized") which floats about it. The author steps out of the Cambridge circle only as far as the marginal revenue curve makes it necessary to do so by virtue of the fact that it was simultaneously discovered by a number of economists outside of Cambridge. But on no other occasion. She even fails to pay her respects to Cournot. Excepting her recognition of Mr. Harrod's work in her special field, she found even Oxford too far off—for she does not mention or use the indifference curve. And Walras and Pareto have not written for her. Hence her analysis is strictly an analysis of partial equilibria of single firms or industries.[3] The complement of it is not general equilibrium in the Walrasian sense but analysis of "total output" which, as we know from her interesting article in the first number of the *Review of Economic Studies*, is made to coincide with the theory of money. This is not meant to imply adverse criticism. I am too strong an admirer of Marshall's teaching to mean that. I also admire too much the vigorous contour lines of the analytic system

[2] Including the famous blades of the scissors—than which there is no better example of how perfectly even a great man can misunderstand what he does not like.

[3] These industries must be "small" ones for some purposes though not for all. But although the requirement of smallness is not absolutely stringent, it is a delicate question how far it may be stretched.

which I conceive to be Mrs. Robinson's. For part of our way her machine works more efficiently than any other would, but it is none the less true that it stops of itself after a certain point and that it does so not only, as Mrs. Robinson herself emphasizes, because its parts are as yet imperfect, but because of imperfections inherent to its fundamental design.

The author, primarily wishing to teach a technique, relegates to digressions (chaps. viii, x, xvii, and xx, to which we must add the important Appendix) the many contributions she makes to general theory. We cannot enter here into the numerous merits of these digressions or into the few points in them which seem less satisfactory, such as the placing of a capital measured in monetary units side by side with labor and land both measured in "corrected natural units" (p. 332), or the handling of the concept of normal profit, which cannot but form a center of difficulties in any theory of imperfect competition.[4] Instead, I beg leave to make a more general remark. The author's positive mind is averse to controversy about fundamentals, and the very excellence of her achievement shows how much more useful this attitude is for our science than the exasperating slant of some of us towards "Grundlagenforschung"—so out of place in a science still in the pioneer stage. But in some points it limits the scope of her work, and it needlessly exposes it to objections in others. To give examples of both: Mrs. Robinson keeps up (rightly, I think) the Marshallian tradition with respect to marginal utility. It would be highly unwise to do entirely without a concept which every day proves its vitality in spite of its critics by readily appealing and carrying meaning to the unsophisticated mind of the beginner. But being aware of all the objections leveled against it, she brushes it aside as much as possible. Recent developments in certain lines primarily associated with the name of Ragnar Frisch lend some support to the belief that the concept may prove again in future the heuristic value it undoubtedly has had in the past. The problems which may arise are precisely of the sort for which Mrs.

[4] In perfect competition, normal profits are of course zero, excepting wages of management or returns to any other factors a business man may own. Some of Mrs. Robinson's arrangements—reward of the entrepreneur to be independent of output, normal profits to be an element of cost—would lend themselves to interpretation in the sense of "earnings of management." But this would not do, and so far Mr. Harrod (*Economic Journal*, June, 1933) seems right in taking an entirely different line. The surpluses incident to imperfect competition raise, however, problems to which his analysis is not entirely adequate.

Robinson seems to have a special aptitude. And some parts of her work could have acquired additional interest by a less cautious reserve.

Again, it has been said above that in the field of imperfect competition it is possible to proceed very far without settling the questions surrounding determinateness of equilibrium in oligopoly and bilateral or even universal monopoly. But a stage is reached at which these questions become vital and further progress begins to imply a definite opinion about them. This is brought home to the reader at some points in the otherwise excellent chapters on the demand for labor and especially in the chapter on "A World of Monopolies," where the argument does not get as far as it easily could.

The first chapter, entitled "The Assumptions," affords instances of the second group of dangers which beset the path of a workmanlike mind impatient of any loss of time and energy in the midst of questions of burning interest. If in spite of the presence of more urgent tasks we do want to look at our tools before using them, we must do so more thoroughly than it is done here, or we shall make existing misunderstandings still worse. Mrs. Robinson says that her fundamental assumption is "that each individual acts in a sensible manner in the circumstances in which he finds himself from the point of view of his own economic interests." This is surely defining *ignotum per ignotius* and is hardly up even to Marshall's normal business man, unsatisfactory though the latter construction is. The whole array of institutionalist objections is fully justified if set on this definition. As in the sentence immediately following the author contrasts the behavior which her definition is to characterize with "neuroses" and "confused thinking," it is difficult to resist the suspicion that she considers sensible action to be an unique and clear-cut type, of the nature of a statistical norm and invariant as to time, race, and place. Besides, her monopolist does not act up to her own standard, for he maximizes immediate gains, which can be "sensible," even in the author's sense, only in the rarest of cases. It would be easy, however, to apply adequate corrections, and all that it is necessary to say is that none of her positive results are invalidated by that infelicitous turn of phrase which after all may perhaps even have some pedagogical virtues.

Similarly the work has a claim to defense against its own author in the matter of considerations of social desirability and reflections of a moral character. The author is quite frank about them and pleads guilty in a very straightforward way. It almost looks in places as if she had set up her high ideal of scientific rigor for the very purpose of faltering conspicuously in the face of it. Of course the case is not mended in the least and such reflections are not made any more scientific by being called "ethical" in accordance with another Cambridge tradition. For scientific ethics could itself be nothing else but descriptive and explanatory. But here again it is only the language and not the thought of the author that is unscientific. And it is easy to put things right by inserting at the threshold of the critical passages some such declaration as this: "I am the product of a certain time and place. As such I have certain ideas about what is desirable which any sociologist can satisfactorily explain in terms of my situation and personal and ancestral experience. It is my will now to reason as if those ideas had general validity, and then such and such consequences would follow."

A book of such range and power always leaves our minds with a question. Having been carried so far by this Virgil, where shall we go now? We may see "il sol ch'in fronte ci reluce," but what are the things we have to do immediately? The answer seems to lie ready at hand.

First, the element of time must be got hold of in a much more efficient manner, if for no other reason because what people try to maximize is certainly gain *over time*. And, as we know, this line of advance leads very soon to expressions admitting of periodic integrals.

Second, the element of money cannot any longer remain in the background to which long and good tradition has relegated it. We must face the fact that most of our quantities are either monetary expressions or corrected monetary expressions, a fact which puts the index problem to the fore.

Third, we probably all agree that our equilibrium analysis is really a tool for the analysis of chronic disequilibria. But if this be so we shall not be able to rest content with an analysis for which the shifting of a demand or supply curve is a thing which just happens and with which we can do no more than investigate its consequences. Certain kinds of shifts are amenable to rule or law and can be handled with relative ease just as movements along a curve, and this means that we must build the economic cycle into our general theory.

Fourth, in some lines of advance the time has probably come to get rid of the apparatus of supply and demand, so useful for one range of problems but an intolerable bearing-rein for another. This should, incidentally, prevent us from forcing it on the theory of money, where it can in any case do but little good.

JOSEPH A. SCHUMPETER

HARVARD UNIVERSITY

THE ANALYSIS OF ECONOMIC CHANGE

Reprinted from *Review of Economic Statistics,* May 1935, 2-10.

EVER since, in the sixties of the past century, Clement Juglar definitely established the existence of wave-like movements which pervade economic life within the institutional framework of capitalist society, the work of finding, linking-up, measuring relevant fact, has been steadily progressing. Although much hampered by needless controversy and inadequate technique, this work has yielded results which, it is believed, need only be properly coördinated and developed in order to enable economics to offer a substantially satisfactory and reasonably exhaustive picture of the phenomenon, and thus to make what would certainly be its most immediately practical contribution to human welfare. Coördination is particularly necessary of the historical, statistical and analytical modes of approach which are each of them thwarted by that reluctance to coöperation incident to the differences in training, tastes and horizons of individual workers. The purpose of this paper is to explain the main features of an analytic apparatus which may be of some use in marshaling the information we have and in framing programs for further research.

Outside Factors. If we survey, for instance, the course of economic events in England from the beginning of the French Wars in 1792, through the suspension of specie payments, the Peace of Amiens, the trade war with America, up to the crisis in 1809–1810, it becomes obvious that we could without any glaring absurdity account by political "disturbances" for all the fluctuations we observe in our material. Or if we follow the course of the world crisis through the spring of 1931, we may trace the breakdown of the distinct upward movement observable at the beginning of that year to a string of events arising out of the flutter caused by the reopening of the question of the union of Austria to Germany and the movements of short balances incident thereto.[1] Common sense immediately suggests that here we have discovered an obviously important source of economic fluctuations. From the ubiquity of such events it follows that practically every economic fluctuation must be a historic individual and cannot be made amenable to explanation but by minute historical analysis of the innumerable factors actually at work in each case. In other words, in order to understand business cycles we must first of all acquire what may be termed historical experience of the way in which economic life reacts to such disturbances, and this is one of the reasons why every conquest of past fact is of paramount practical importance, in some respects of greater importance than additions to our stock of contemporaneous fact which can increase our knowledge over time only by infinitesimal steps. The statistical and analytical description of the various mechanisms of reaction (with a hope in our minds that we may ultimately get as far as to be able to measure the effects attributable to every such disturbance) seems thus to be the most urgent task before us. It should be observed in passing that for various reasons any influence acting on the economic process is practically sure to produce not a single dent but a wave-like motion extending over a longer time than it takes to reach the next disturbance, as well as, if it impinges on a particular spot, a vibration throughout the whole system. Moreover, with adaptation proceeding almost always with a lag and very often with reference to the rate of change of prices rather than to their absolute magnitude, our attempts at exact description are more than likely to result in expressions admitting of periodic integrals.

This being so, the question arises whether there are any fluctuations at all which arise out of the

[1] If we further ask how it was that that particularly sensitive short-balance situation arose in Germany, we find, following events from 1924 to 1929, that the steadily increasing public expenditure, and the methods by which it was financed, amounted to taxing away what would otherwise have been an annual average increase of working capital of about one billion marks. If we deduct from the figure of foreign short-term indebtedness as it stood in 1930 not only the four billions of counterclaims of German banks on short capital account, and the four to five billions which simply were revolving credits financing Germany's foreign trade and which, therefore, were not dangerous, but also the, roughly, five to six billions, which could and would have been accumulated but for that fiscal policy, it is easily seen that the interest rate would have been lower and that that part of foreign short indebtedness, the proceeds of which replaced the formation of domestic working capital, would have been so small as to be no major factor in the situation. We are thus enabled to account for some of the darkest hues of the situation of 1931–1932 by what was not only on the surface, but also in a more fundamental sense, a political cause. Cf. the last two sentences of this section for a defense of this way of reasoning.

behavior of business communities as such and would be observable even if the institutional and natural framework of society remained absolutely invariable. Although disturbance of the kind glanced at and reaction thereto may in individual cases be much more important, yet the presence or absence of a fluctuation *inherent* to the economic process in time is practically and scientifically the fundamental problem and the only one to be considered here. In order to make headway with it, we shall proceed as physical sciences do in those cases in which it is impossible actually to isolate a phenomenon by producing it in a laboratory: from our historic and everyday knowledge of economic behavior we shall construct a "model" of the economic process over time, see whether it is likely to work in a wave-like way, and compare the result with observed fact. Henceforth, therefore, we shall disregard not only wars, revolutions, natural catastrophes, institutional changes, but also changes in commercial policy, in banking and currency legislation and habits of payment, variations of crops as far as due to weather conditions or diseases, changes in gold production as far as due to chance discoveries, and so on. These we shall call *outside factors*. It will be seen that in some cases it is not easy to distinguish them from features of business behavior. All we can do about this here is to recommend to the reader to hold tight to the common sense of the distinction and to consider that every business man knows quite well that he is doing one kind of thing when ordering a new machine and another kind of thing when lobbying for an increase of the import duty on his product. It will also be seen that many of the things we list as outside factors are, when considered on a higher plane and for a wider purpose, the direct outcome of the working of the capitalist machine and hence no independent agencies.[1] This is surely so but does not reduce the practical value of the distinction on our plane and for our purpose.

Cycles, Trends, Equilibria, Growth, Innovation. For shortness' sake, we assemble in this section a few necessary definitions and propositions, which are really quite simple, although we cannot help adding here and there somewhat pedantic formulations which are necessary in order to make our meaning perfectly precise to the specialist.

Statistically, the term "cycle" means two things: first, that sequences of values of economic quantities in historic time (as distinguished from theoretic time) do not display monotonic increase or decrease, but (irregular) recurrence of either these values themselves or their first or their second time-derivatives; and secondly, that these "fluctuations" do not occur independently in every such time series, but always display either instantaneous or lagged association with each other.

Statistically, we mean by the word "trend" the fact that in many, although not in all, such time series it is possible to divide the whole interval covered by our material into sub-intervals such that the mean values of the time integrals over these sub-intervals are monotonically increasing or decreasing as we go along in time, or that they display recurrence only once.

If we study, say, the economic state of things in all countries in 1872 and behold the wild excesses of that boom, we shall have no difficulty in assigning very realistic meaning to the terms "want of balance" or "disequilibrium." Nor is it difficult, if we look at things one year after, to recognize that however much the then situation differed from that of 1872 it was similar to it in that it was about equally unbalanced. Again, if we analyze the course of events in, say, 1897, we may well sum up the result by speaking of a comparatively equilibrated state of things. This common sense distinction between compara-

[1] Professor W. C. Mitchell, in his review of Professor L. Robbins' recent book (*Quarterly Journal of Economics*, May, 1935), objects to the latter's attributing part of the phenomena of the depression 1929–1934 to "politics." Sociologically, he is of course quite right not only for this case, but generally. The action, e.g., of Sir Robert Peel's administration in repealing the corn laws in 1846 undoubtedly arose out of, and is to be accounted for by the economic pattern of the time and place, itself created by the working of the *whole* social system, of which the capitalist mechanism was a part. But this is relevant only for *some* purposes, for instance, if we wish to *judge* the action of politicians. As far as this is done on predilections of the scientist for certain types of social institutions, it is certainly extra-scientific as well as extra-economic. We should, in this case, have to disagree with *both* the eminent authors mentioned, as they both of them display such predilections. The argument is, however, not relevant if the question is merely what of observable effects may have been due to the Peel policy: for an investigation of the course of English cycles in the 1840's that policy is as much of an outside factor as an earthquake would have been. For the sake of clearness it is essential to keep both standpoints strictly separate. The same reasoning applies, of course, to the distinction of an economic process and its institutional setting in general. The distinction is, in a sense, quite unrealistic. But if we do not make it, we shall never be able to say more than that everything depends upon everything.

tively balanced and comparatively unbalanced states of the economic system is of utmost importance for the description and measurement of cyclical phenomena. In order to bring out the exact skeleton of such observations we define: (Marshallian) *particular equilibrium* exists in an individual industry if this industry as a whole displays no tendency either to increase or decrease its output or to alter the combination of the productive factors it employs. *Aggregative equilibrium* exists if the sum total of receipts of business as a whole, expressed in current dollars, equals the sum total of costs similarly expressed and including as much profit as will induce everybody to keep on doing what he is actually doing. This kind of thing, which is compatible with plenty of disequilibrium as between industries and within industries, is the basic concept in Mr. Keynes' analysis of the monetary process. *General equilibrium* exists if every household and every firm in the domain under research is individually in a state of equilibrium in the sense of Léon Walras. It is only this last concept that matters for us. To give it statistical meaning, we must link it up with certain points on the graphs of our time series. These we call "normal points." As in reality such states can never be perfectly realized we can be concerned only with states which are nearer to, or farther from, them than other states. Hence we further define: *neighborhoods of equilibrium* are time intervals in which normal points occur in the graphs of our time series excepting those which in that interval are deflected by a definite and provable individual circumstance. (The word "neighborhood" is therefore not used here in its strict mathematical sense.) Discussion of the question how we are to locate these neighborhoods cannot be entered upon in this article.

By "growth" we mean changes in economic data which occur continuously in the sense that the increment or decrement per unit of time can be currently absorbed by the system without perceptible disturbance. Increase of population, resulting in an increase of the supply of labor of at most a few per cent per year (historically an increase of three per cent per year is already high), is the outstanding example. If the factors which enter into this category were the only ones at work, there would be obvious economic meaning to the concept of trend and to its determination by least squares or other methods resting on similar assumptions. In what follows we shall, however, not deal with the problems arising out of mere growth, nor with the very complicated questions of their relation to the other types of factors involved in economic change. In fact we shall, for clearness' sake, disregard it altogether, which, as in the case of outside factors, does not imply any view about its importance.

It stands to reason, finally, that outside factors and growth factors do not exhaust the list of the influences which produce and shape economic change. Obviously the face of the earth would look very different if people, besides having their economic life changed by natural events and changing it themselves by extra-economic action, had done nothing else except multiply and save. If it looks as it does, this is just as obviously due to the unremitting efforts of people to improve according to their lights upon their productive and commercial methods, i.e., to the changes in technique of production, the conquest of new markets, the insertion of new commodities, and so on. This historic and irreversible change in the way of doing things we call "innovation" and we define: innovations are changes in production functions which cannot be decomposed into infinitesimal steps. Add as many mail-coaches as you please, you will never get a railroad by so doing.

It is a question of some interest why the old type of economist, Marshall included, should, while recognizing this element and taking account of it in special cases, yet have persistently refused to face it squarely and to build an analytic apparatus fully descriptive of its mechanism and consequences. For our purpose it is both necessary and sufficient to list innovation, however much it may be linked to the other two, as a third and logically distinct factor in economic change, and to submit the propositions: The kind of wave-like movement, which we call the business cycle, is incident to industrial change and would be impossible in an economic world displaying nothing except unchanging repetition of the productive and consumptive process. Industrial change is due to the effect of outside factors, to the non-cyclical element of growth, and to innovation. If there be a purely economic cycle at all, it can only come from the way in which new things are, in the institutional conditions of capitalist society, inserted into the economic process and absorbed by it. In fact, the cycle seems to be the statistical and historical form in which what is usually referred to as "economic progress" comes about. This is why any serious attempt at analytic and even at practical control of the business cycle must be an historical one in the sense that the key to the solution of its fundamental problems can only be found in the facts of industrial and commercial history.

Prosperity and Depression. To simplify argument we will in this section make the hypothesis, presently to be discarded, that there is sense in speaking of only *one* "cyclical movement" in our material.

We can of course never expect to discover a definite date when the first cycle arose out of a state of perfect equilibrium, but it is essential, in order to avoid circular reasoning, to make our model describe such an event and, as far as historical and statistical description goes, to make it start from what has first to be identified as a neighborhood of equilibrium. We then get the picture of the system of economic quantities drawing away from this equilibrium or neighborhood under the impact of innovations which would supply, barring outside factors, the only possible "force." Let us visualize this by thinking of any of those booms in this country or in England which everyone would label as railroad booms. The new thing in this case takes years to get into working order and still longer to exert its full effects on the location of industry and agriculture, agglomerations of population, the evolution of accessories and subsidiaries, and so on. During this time there would, in strict logic and if the preceding equilibrium had been a perfect one, be little or no increase in the stream of commodities and services (there may in fact be a *decrease* in the output of consumers' goods), while producers' and consumers' expenditures would increase in consequence of credit creation and in other ways. The realistic complement of this is that, during this period, expenditure regularly expands more than output and that the non-innovating sectors of the economic system adapt themselves to this state of things. It is not possible to show here by the historical interpretation of the behavior of time series (neither should it be necessary to show, for it must be obvious to everyone who has ever, e.g., studied the charts published in this REVIEW) how perfectly this accounts for everything we mean when identifying a given interval as a time of business prosperity. After a period of gestation, which of course must be distinguished from what we may also designate by this term in the case of an individual firm, the products or services of the new business structures reach their markets, displacing either other such products and services, or methods of production and enterprises linked to them which have now become obsolete, and enforcing a process of liquidation, readjustment, and absorption. This would be so even if nobody ever made any errors and nobody ever misbehaved, although there is no difficulty whatever in understanding that the consequences of error and misbehavior will show up during this period in which the system struggles back to a new neighborhood of equilibrium. On the side of money and credit, the fundamental element which induces all others is the fact that as soon as the receipts stream in from the sale of the new products and as far as they are used to pay back bank loans, deposits will have to contract, in strict logic, down to the point of the previous neighborhood and, in reality, some way towards it. Again, there is no difficulty in inserting into this picture, as understandable consequences of this fundamental chain of events, all the accidental phenomena which experience tells us are usually associated with it. This not only gives a truer picture of the nature and the organic functions of cyclical down-swings, but also accords satisfactorily with statistical evidence.

Whatever starts a deviation of the system from equilibrium always, although not with logical necessity, gives rise to secondary phenomena which are mainly due to the fact that business men will act on the rates of change they observe. The sum total of these induced phenomena which are the center of the mass psychology of cycles and greatly intensify their amplitudes, we call "secondary waves." The expression, first used in 1911, is misleading and is kept only because Mr. Keynes has taken it up. But the thing is very important, so much so that the majority of students of the business cycle see nothing else. Whilst this accounts for many errors in diagnosis and remedial policy, it also helps to explain and partly to justify a large group of "theories" which, though missing the essential phenomenon, are yet perfectly satisfactory when viewed as descriptions of part of the mechanism of the secondary waves superimposed on the primary ones.

The units of the cyclical movements, then, lie necessarily between neighborhoods of equilibrium. In the simplest form of the model of economic change they have only two phases. But because of the fact that depressive forces gather momentum on the way back from the prosperity-excursion of the system, notably owing to the phenomena incident to the breakdown of the secondary wave, the system outruns usually the first neighborhood of equilibrium it strikes on its way back, and embarks upon a depression-excursion, from which it is forced up by the action of the equilibrium *ligamina* which bring it up again to another neighborhood from which the prosperity of the next cycle starts. Hence we have as a rule four phases: prosperity, recession, depression, and revival. This is almost generally recognized, but it is important to note that for purposes of fundamental analysis we are not free to count cycles from any point or phase we please, for instance, from peak to peak or trough to trough, but must always begin after the revival and at the beginning of a prosperity. It is, moreover, essential to distinguish these two, although it may be difficult to do so owing to the fact that they are both positive. The failure to do so, and especially to recognize that the "forces" at work in revival are entirely different from the "forces" at work in prosperity, is one of the main sources of faulty analysis.

The fundamental question still remains unanswered. Why should the carrying into effect of innovations (as distinguished from "invention" or experimentation which are quite another matter and do not in themselves exert any influence on business life at all — which is the reason why so little has come out of the Marshallian recognition of the element of invention) *cluster* at certain times, and not be distributed in so continuous a way as to be capable of being just as continuously absorbed as the current increase in the supply of labor is? One answer suggests itself immediately: as soon as the various kinds of social resistance to something that is fundamentally new and untried have been overcome, it is much easier not only to do the same thing again but also to do *similar* things in different directions, so that a first success will always produce a cluster. (See, e.g., the emergence of the motor-car industry.) This is indeed the method of *competitive* capitalism which has not as yet died out in *trustified* capitalism, to spread an improvement and to reap the social harvest — in the succeeding depression. But to carry full persuasion it would be necessary to go much deeper into this phenomenon, the roots of which stretch far beyond the economic field, than is here possible. However, as it has been the unfortunate experience of the present writer that even a very elaborate exposition has failed at times to convey to critics the picture he desired to convey, he prefers to ask the reader to consider the clustering of innovations as a postulate or hypothesis made to fit the facts in the same way as hypotheses are made in physics, irrespective of what might be adduced for or against their objective truth. Yet he feels entitled to say to anyone who doubts this proposition: Look around you in industrial life and see for yourself whether it is not so. Other writers have quite independently stressed the fact that it is possible to associate historically every business cycle with a distinct industry, or a few industries, which led in it and, as it were, applied the torch to what after becomes a flare-up covering a much wider surface.[1] The well established fact that fluctuations in investment goods are so much more marked than fluctuations elsewhere points, by virtue of its being explainable on the postulate mentioned, in the same direction.

It should be added that the above analytic model supplies an interpretation of economic trends which also bears on the technique of their determination. It follows, e.g., that barring the element of growth the trends of our time series are not due to influences distinct from those that create the cyclical fluctuations but simply embody the results of the latter. To these "result-trends," as the writer calls them in his workshop, it is entirely unwarranted to apply formal methods of the type of least squares. For extrapolation there is, of course, no warrant in any case. But there are certain general characteristics which may be used in developing

[1] The first author to do this consciously was, as far as the present writer knows, Mr. D. H. Robertson (*A Study of Industrial Fluctuations*, published in 1915, and an earlier paper in the *Journal of the Royal Statistical Society*), who, equally independently, also developed a schema of the working of the credit mechanism, similar in many respects to the one implied above and developed in 1911, in his *Banking Policy and the Price Level* (1926).

formal methods as more or less rough approximations. No general proposition is possible as to the relative or absolute lengths of the four phases, even apart from the fact that they will be influenced by outside factors. Partly but not wholly for the latter reason no great significance attaches to the mere height or depth of a peak or a trough, although we shall presently find a reason for expecting that certain depressions will be much more severe than others.

The Three-Cycle Schema. The above analysis not only accounts for the fact that waves of prosperity always do arise whenever a neighborhood of equilibrium is reached "from below," and that they always do taper off into a new neighborhood of equilibrium, but, as far as the present writer is able to make out, also accounts for every single fact or characteristic ever proved to be associated with either up-swings or down-swings not provably due to the action of outside factors. The reader is invited to make the experiment of testing this assertion by drawing up a list of what he considers these characteristics to be and observing whether they fit into the model offered. But there is no ground to believe that there should be just *one* wave-like movement pervading economic life. On the contrary, it stands to reason that some processes covered by our concept of innovation must take much longer time than others to have full effect. The railroadization or electrification of a country, for instance, may take between one-half and the whole of a century and involve fundamental transformations of its economic and cultural patterns, changing everything in the lives of its people up to their spiritual ambitions, while other innovations or groups of innovations may arise and disappear within a very few years. Moreover, the former will generally be carried out in distinct steps and thus give rise both to shorter fluctuations and longer underlying swells. Under these circumstances it is not the most natural thing to assume the existence of a single cycle and to postulate that it will display any very marked regularities. This is in fact a very bold hypothesis which could be justified only if clearly imposed upon us by our material. But as this is not the case, even apart from what we may reasonably attribute to the outside disturbances to which our material is subject, it seems much more realistic (and also likely to do away with some spurious irregularities, that is to say, irregularities which are only due to the single-cycle hypothesis) to admit that there are *many* cycles rolling on simultaneously, and to face squarely the problem of analyzing their interference with each other. As, however, it is necessary for the purpose of handling our time series to settle on a moderate number of distinct movements which may be thought of as superimposed on each other and as passing their normals or neighborhoods of equilibrium *near* the points where they cross the path of the next higher cycle underlying them, the three-cycle schema is here suggested as a fairly useful working hypothesis. Nothing more than descriptive merits are claimed for it, but manifestly it fulfills the one condition which a device of this kind may reasonably be required to fulfill, the condition of carrying historical meaning, which — with material as exposed as ours is to disturbances by outside factors which are not small, independent, or "numerous" in the probability sense — is much more important than fulfillment of any formal criterion.

Historical knowledge of what actually happened at any time in the industrial organism, and of the way in which it happened, reveals first the existence of what is often referred to as the "Long Wave" of a period of between fifty-four and sixty years. Occasionally recognized and even measured before, especially by Spiethoff, it has been worked out in more detail by Kondratieff, and may therefore be called the Kondratieff Cycle. Economic historians of the nineteenth century have unconsciously and independently testified to the reality of the first of these waves our material allows us to observe, viz., the cycle from about 1783 to 1842, and they have also borne out in advance our interpretation of the phenomenon by coining the phrase of the "industrial revolution," which really implies everything we mean. The phrase is infelicitous and justly considered obsolete by now, but it pictures well how the happenings of the period struck entirely unprejudiced observers. The years 1842–1897 are readily interpreted as the age of steam and steel, particularly as the age of the railroadization of the world. This may sound superficial, but it can be shown in detail that railroad construction and work incident to it, connected with it, or consequential upon it, is the dominant feature both of economic change and of economic fluctuations during that time, and of every one of the four phases into which it is possible to divide it. Future historians finally will find no difficulty in recognizing the initiating importance of electricity, chemistry and motor cars for both the up-swing and the down-swing of the third Long Wave, which rose about 1897. Of course, if we prefer a more usual way of expressing the same thing, we may put these processes also into terms of "investment" and the expansion and contraction of credit: this is certainly a very important part of the mechanism. Unfortunately, this description is not only more usual but also more superficial, and opens the door to all the crudities and errors of the various monetary theories of the cycle. Any satisfactory analysis of causes must start with what induces that credit expansion, as every satisfactory analysis of effects must start by investigating what is done with the increased monetary resources — after which we immediately cease to wonder why the mere increase of credit facilities in or before a depression proves as ineffectual as we know it does. If, however, we stop at the process of investment and postulate that it has a mechanism of its own, we not only fail to get at the core of the matter but we also find it difficult to avoid such desperate logic as is implied in the conclusion that because increase of investment and expansion of credit are associated with a prosperity phase, we therefore can produce prosperity by expanding credit.

The majority of students of the business cycle does not consider the evidence alluded to sufficient to establish this particular cycle. But what does that mean? The term Kondratieff Cycle is for us but a name for a certain set of facts (a certain long-time behavior of the price level, the interest rate, employment, and so on), none of which is open to doubt. It is true that the term also implies an interpretation to the effect that this behavior of our series is amenable to interpretation on the same lines as their behavior in shorter cycles. But this again is merely an inference from historical facts, which have not so far been called in question either. Of course, experience of about two and three-fourths units of a phenomenon does not warrant much generalization, and still less prediction.

It is therefore *only as a statement of fact* that we venture to say that the two complete Kondratieff units within our range of statistical vision contain each of them six cycles of from nine to ten years' duration, equally well established by industrial history, though less clearly marked in our time series, which correspond as a matter of fact roughly to that cyclical movement which was the first to be discovered. Following the same procedure as in the earlier case, we may call them Juglar Cycles. As pointed out by D. H. Robertson,[1] it is possible in every instance to indicate the particular industry and the particular innovations which are responsible for the up-swing and the process of readjustment.

Finally, every Juglar so far observed (those of the present Kondratieff included) is readily, in most cases and in this country already by inspection, divisible into three cycles of a period of roughly forty months. The existence of this shorter cycle has been pointed out repeatedly these hundred years or more, and still oftener has it been felt and recognized implicitly, but one may remark that it was the two studies by Mr. Kitchin and Professor Crum in this REVIEW that were chiefly instrumental in establishing it.[2] Evidence about the commercial paper rate, this series being the most purely cyclical of all, is of course particularly important. That this cycle, as well as the others, is more clearly marked in this country than in any other and notably more marked than in England, is easily accounted for by the fact that cycles in most series will tend to be toned down or even ironed out the more a country's economic life is interwoven with international influences and the more its policy approaches Free Trade. The question of the statistical methods which arise out of this analysis (for statistical methods must arise out of our understanding of the phenomenon they are to be applied to) will be taken up at another time. It is, of course, admitted not only that non-cyclical changes also create wave-like movements but that besides the three just mentioned there are other cyclical waves.[3] It is held, however, that the three-cycle schema works sufficiently well for the purposes of the stage of rough approximations in which we are, and are likely to remain for a considerable time.

A Research Program. If we coördinate available information, statistical and historical, in the light of the principles sketched out, we get not so much a picture as indications which give us an idea of what the real picture would be like. These principles do enable us to link up in a general way the behavior of those of our series which are most

[1] Cp. previous note, p. 6.

[2] This REVIEW, vol. v (1923), pp. 10–16 and 17–29.

[3] As pointed out by Wardwell, Kuznets and others.

symptomatic of the pulse of economic life as a whole. These "systematic" series may be either "synthetic," as, for instance, series of price levels or of physical volume of production, or "natural," as, for instance, series of interest rates, clearing-debits, unemployment, pig-iron consumption, at least for the pre-war time, or the sum total of deposits. They all, also in a general way, behave as they would have to if the view outlined above were true to life. In the case of what, by way of distinction from "systematic," we may call "individual" series, such as the prices and quantities of individual commodities, our analysis becomes more complicated and perfect knowledge is necessary of the particular conditions in every branch of industry and commerce, of its lags, frictions and inertias, of the mentality of its men, of the particular random influences to which it is exposed, and especially of its active or passive rôle in any given cycle. As the outside factors impinge upon some phase of a process consisting of a number of superimposed wave-like movements, and as every one of these movements itself impinges upon a particular phase of some other movement underlying it, so all of this impinges on a particular resonator in the case of every individual industry or firm, *which responds according to its own structure*. This is perhaps the best way of stating the problem in its full complexity. It also helps us to understand the many "special cycles" which some students have found or think they have found in various individual industries.

Now first, as regards a research program, it may be suggested that not a single one of the "systematic" series above spoken of represents adequately what it is meant to represent. And in no case is our historical or contemporaneous information adequate to account quantitatively for the fluctuations of the systematic series. It is only one side of the problem that this makes convincing verification of the result of any analysis impossible, and that all we can do at present is to say that the testimony of such facts as we have is compatible or incompatible with it. The other side is that many questions are not questions of principle and analysis at all, but simply of relative quantitative importance. The statement, e.g., that in the down-grade of any cycle inertia of wages counts for something in determining the amount of unemployment, is too obvious to require proof; but not only for practical but also for scientific purposes this is entirely irrelevant as long as we are unable to say whether this element accounts for one per cent or for ninety per cent of the unemployment figure observed in a given place at a given time. No wonder, therefore, that, if we are unable to be more precise than this, economics is considered as entirely useless by the practical man. Yet our analytic apparatus would turn out a definite answer all right, provided the necessary factual information were inserted into it, the assembling of which is, of course, much beyond the means of any individual worker or private group of workers.

Secondly, there is no reliable information at all on a number of subjects which are obviously of primary significance. Two examples must suffice. Waiving our objection to the present tendency to overstress the importance of price levels and monetary magnitudes in general, we may say that the stream of expenditure by households on consumers' goods is one of the most indispensable elements in the analysis of the business cycle. We have acceptable though far from satisfactory indicators for the post-war time but, owing to the exceptional circumstances present in this period, these are almost valueless for a fundamental understanding. And for the pre-war time we have to be content with pay-roll figures and the like, which might easily mislead even if they went further back than they do. Yet there is plenty of stray information stretching over centuries, which, if it could be brought together, would definitely clear up many pressing practical problems such as this one.

Again the process of investment and the corresponding process of credit contraction in down-grades can never, whatever the theorist may say, be fully grasped in its importance and consequences until we know more about the relative importance of its sources and the actual behavior of borrowers and lenders. The decisive figure here is the sum actually spent on the production of durable producers' goods *for new purposes*. It is in these last three words that our chief difficulty lies, which has so far been overcome only in a very few cases: we can follow up, for instance, how much was spent on railroad construction in England in the 'forties. It is difficult enough to find out how great the sum total is that newly enters industry and trade every year. It is still more difficult to find how much of this is spent on equipment. And even this would not be enough. However, an investigation lighting up this very important side of the past and present of capitalist society would be perfectly feasible.

Although, thirdly, the phenomenon of the cycle cannot be defined and understood as a sort of average between independent changes in individual industries, yet the behavior of individual industries, on the one hand causing and on the other hand responding to the sweep of changing business situations, requires a special study for each of them. Plenty of work has been done in this direction, but, as the decisive questions have hardly ever been in the minds of the writers to whom we owe that literature of industrial monographs, the evidence is incomplete and inconclusive. There is hardly any event, or peculiarity of structural pattern, in any industry which would be irrelevant to the question why the business cycle is what it is. Besides, if it be true that industrial change is at the bottom of the cyclical phenomenon, its mechanism can be established only by covering in detail all recorded cases of such change. To the thoughtful observer, for instance, a striking similarity reveals itself immediately between such different processes as the development of the English iron industry from the sixteenth to the end of the eighteenth century, and the rise of the motorcar industry in our time. In these, as in many other cases, we have even now advanced much beyond general impressions. There is, however, a long way between this and the goal of establishing the validity of the schema of innovation and showing how innovation produces, together with its monetary complement, the particular kind of waves inherent to the economic life of capitalist society and paralleled by similar phenomena in other fields of human activity.

Joseph A. Schumpeter.

Harvard University.

PROFESSOR TAUSSIG ON WAGES AND CAPITAL

Reprinted from *Explorations in Economics,* 1936, 213-222.

I

THERE IS more logic in the history of those tools of analysis which we have come to call economic theory than either its friends or its foes admit. The former are generally theorists themselves and mostly prone to underline the distinctive elements of their work rather than those which they take from their predecessors. The latter discuss theory almost exclusively in terms of "systems" and "schools" and "hypotheses," which they associate with social philosophies and attitudes toward questions of economic policy rather than with methods of handling the facts of economic life. But underneath the controversies with which both cover the surface that is all the layman sees, theoretical work goes on with a consistency truly astonishing under the circumstances. There are of course ups and downs, times when some major piece of the analytic engine is exchanged for a new one and times when effects are directed toward making the new device work, occasions when results, accumulated in comparative obscurity, burst spectacularly into extra-professional publicity and other occasions when the onward march halts and falters. But each situation grows out of the preceding one by logical development of new truth latently present in the latter, and even the most violent attempts at revolution seem powerless to deflect the process from its course.

The "classical" period of English economics, 1776–1848, illustrates this. However much injustice to many good men this implies, it will ever be characterized by the names of Smith, Ricardo, and the younger Mill. It dates from a most conspicuous "burst into publicity"—the *Wealth of Nations* was not more than this—to Mill's *Principles,* which were less than this but which, by their careful restatements and by opening their doors to all relevant currents of their times, were no less effective in molding young minds and in transmitting to them the more obvious results achieved in the half century that preceded them. Within that period Ricardo's work affords the best example of the logic with which economic thought unfolded itself. His basic construction was the result of an attempt to straighten out the difficulties and haziness in Adam Smith's first two books, and followers as well as opponents in turn tried to straighten out the difficulties and to fill the gaps he left. In this sense there is some warrant for speaking of a classical body of doctrine in spite of all the differences of opinion and of vision which make it impossible to attribute to the "classical" economists either the same scientific or the same political creed. Nor is it very wrong to say that that impulse substantially spent itself with Mill's effort at systematizing, and that but little headway was made during the twenty years that followed upon it. Heartily disgusted, economists turned away in order either to build a new body of concepts and theorems or to take up non-theoretical pursuits of which the work of the German Historical School is the outstanding example. Such was the intention, but such was not the result. Exactly as M'Culloch and Mill were not in the least less socially minded than any of the Socialists of the Chair that rated them for their "liberalism" while really carrying on their tradition, and exactly as the institutional investigations of the Historical School only continued work of the same type done under the auspices of the "classics," so Jevons, Walras, and Menger are easily seen, at this distance of time, to have continued rather than revolutionized. This is not intended to belittle their achievement or to deny that our science, like any other, changes and rejuvenates itself from time to time. Only, preceding stages are not, as immediate successors invariably think, really cast away to make room for new structures; they remain like geological layers carrying and conditioning the ever new ones that overlay them and are in turn destined to be overlaid. In this sense, although in no other, any scientific achievement is immortal, at least within the civilization that gave birth to it.

If, on the strength of this, we count a new era from the dusk of the classical one, we should bear in mind that the two are not strictly comparable. Looked at from the standpoint of theoretical workmanship only, classical theory has no other claim to its epithet than pristine simplicity. Whoever means unsurpassed masterpieces when he speaks of classic works should never think of applying the term to the economic—or, perhaps, any other technically so-called—classics. Part of that pristine simplicity was a naïve belief that a few rather primitive generalizations were sufficient to settle once and for all the political and cultural problems of humanity, to the satisfaction of Caroline and everybody else. That belief fell away from the following generations, as so many other beliefs did, and theory appeared to them in a much less brilliant light. Theorists began to concentrate on their technical job, and to draw away from direct practical application and from the primitive methods that were intended to be, and presumably actually were, understandable to any intelligent reader. This precluded any such popular successes as fell to the lot of Smith or Ricardo or Mill and fatally restricted outlook and purpose, although theorists were, as some of them are even now, reluctant to realize it and never ceased to yearn for the past splendors of "Political Economy." But as soon as we resign ourselves to this unavoidable sacrifice, and compare theoretical achievement of that era with what was truly theoretical achievement in the doctrine of the classics, we may speak of considerable progress—in the limited sense in which it is possible to speak of progress at all—and of the superiority of the new work to the old. Waves of scientific activity are as international as waves of business activity are, but conditions differ sufficiently in different countries to keep both of them from moving exactly in step. Confining ourselves to England, where uniformity at a time and continuity over time was and is more obvious than anywhere else, we see at the first glance that practically everything centers around one man and one work, Alfred Marshall and his *Principles*. More careful scrutiny no doubt qualifies this and discloses the presence of other peaks, yet it substantially confirms that first impression. All that was done in England in the field of economic theory before 1890 leads up to Marshall's *Principles*, and almost all good work that has been done in England since proceeds from them: a truly marvelous success, fully as great as that of Smith or that of Ricardo, perhaps even greater if we strip these of the non-theoretical and the extra-scientific elements of their fame. Good luck and merit both had their share, as they had in Adam Smith's case, in what was substantially the same kind of achievement. Marshall undoubtedly had the ball at his foot but he played it *en maître*. It was good fortune not only that he had before him an excellent group of rising talents to mold but also that the times were ripe and called for precisely that work which he was himself molded to do. It was merit and personal force that he accomplished it in such a way as to make it difficult to this day to point to anything in English theory which, *in nuce* at least, is not present in his great treatise. This even extends to its very faults Moreover, he constantly pointed beyond himself, visualizing clearly future developments: as he led up to his own ground gently, stressing continuity and avoiding breaks, so he smoothed transition to the ground that lies beyond, in particular transition from qualitative to quantitative analysis. Whether worshiped beyond reason or criticized beyond decency, he still leads.

Elsewhere, environments did not permit any such single peak to emerge or evolution to proceed on such clear and simple lines. But nevertheless, though by much more devious routes, through many more halts and setbacks, and over ground that if rougher is also much richer in possibilities and much more varied in outlook, things moved in substantially the same directions. In all countries the foundations of present work in economic theory had been laid before 1900. Modern theorists may not be aware of it. As a matter of fact most of them are not, the outstanding exceptions being the direct followers of Marx, of the early Austrians, and of Walras. They may even resent the idea and defend themselves against it by violent criticism and by disclaiming any affinity. But a subconscious background is still a background and disclaimed obligation still obligation. There is, however, an important difference between this situation and the situation of theoretical economics in the time of John Stuart Mill and immediately after. As pointed out above, classical theory was, by the public as well as by most economists, understood to be a body of doctrine. It interested primarily because it was so understood, that is, because it was taken to pronounce general truth about economic policy. This meant, on the one hand, that the reaction against *laisser faire* that set in in the seventies and steadily gathered force was almost as serious for that "science" as it was for the political prospects of old-fashioned liberalism. And it meant, on the other hand, that the genuinely scientific elements in the teaching of the classics never really "caught on" with economists as a body. Now the theory that was worked out in the seventies and eighties was no longer a doctrine—although often and even to this day mistaken for it—either of *laisser faire* or of anything else. It had, at last, become what scientific theory is in any field, a tool of research that elicited interest and gathered devotees as such. Hence it did not peter out as soon as the foundations were laid, but on the contrary served as the basis for further operations which had nothing epigonic about them and neither rehashed nor broke off but simply went on.

We cannot here do more than illustrate this by a few examples. The most general features of modern economic theory—they really are fundamentally one—are, first, the attempt to make theory which from the nature of the field has always been quantitative more rigorously so by using the forms of thought appropriate to dealing with relations between sets of quantities, that is, the methods of the calculus, and, secondly, the attempt to make that quantitative theory numerical by fitting it to take hold of statistical material. Either attempt is anything but new and can be followed right into the seventeenth century, but the decisive impulse was given by those who built the theory that was called "new" and "modern" in the eighties, Marshall and Walras in particular. In this, then, we are merely following their suggestion, fulfilling their program. Nor is this all. We are not only following a general hint but we are advancing on the lines chalked out by them. Walras' marginal utility theory was followed by Pareto's equilibrium theory. Pareto was none too generous to his predecessor but at this hour of the day it is obvious that the latter was—and as soon as a science has once found its feet, there is no longer any derogatory implication of want of originality in this: *all* originality is thenceforth of this kind only—nothing but a more rigorous formulation of the former. And H. L. Moore's synthetic economics—he, however, was not wanting in generosity, and emphasized what Pareto suppressed—was nothing but a step toward making Walras' system numerically workable. Again, statistical demand curves, which for a time absorbed so much of the labors of theorists, were originally thought of as numerical forms of Marshallian demand curves, and if they are becoming something else this is so by the logic of achievement and not by virtue of new methodological principles previously adopted. The theory of imperfect competition grew out of, and is an improvement on, the Marshallian apparatus; introduction of rates of change, expectancy, and fluctuations of various kinds grew out of, and are improvements on, the Walrasian apparatus.

II

Those two features of the theoretical work of our own day—which, let us hope, mark the definitive advent of an "exact" science of economics—are nowhere more obvious than in the United States. Part of that work is purely American in the sense that it proceeds from American initiative, another part has carried foreign suggestions much beyond what came of them in the countries of their origin. It is interesting to glance at the antecedents of this work and to ask whether it links up with earlier American achievement in the same way that, though perhaps not so obviously as, modern English work links up with Marshall's teaching.

When Rae's book was rediscovered more than thirty years ago, some of us may have wondered whether the general opinion that American economics did not, during the classic period, produce anything original was quite true after all. However, the very fact that so powerful a piece of analysis could pass unnoticed is in itself a verification of that opinion, which more careful research is not likely to alter. There has been of course plenty of fresh discussion of current questions ever since Colonial times. The level of it has been what the level of such discussion always is and hardly below what it has been (or is) in Europe. In fact several ideas seem to have first emerged in this country which were to have considerable vogue elsewhere—the standard instance is the infant industry argument of which Europe heard so much subsequently. But purely scientific pursuits do not prosper in communities that struggle for control over a new environment. Daniel Raymond may serve, although larger claims have recently been made on his behalf, as an example from a list of writers who hardly got beyond Adam Smith, however useful their service in applying his teaching to American conditions or modifying it in the light of American experience. Carey does not alter the picture.

But things changed rapidly during the decades of decline in ardor and achievement that in England and elsewhere followed upon the period of the classics. They must have changed more rapidly than Americans give themselves credit for, because the new current could otherwise hardly have been running as strongly as it did in the eighties. Although, agreeably to the spirit of those times, scientific economics was more concerned with other lines of advance than with the theoretical one, discussion of theoretical problems was then on a level distinctly higher than in Europe. Simon Newcomb's *Principles*, the original contributions of which have never been properly appreciated, is probably the best book of the "principles-type" written between Mill and Marshall. Francis A. Walker's indefatigable energy prepared the ground for John B. Clark and Frank W. Taussig.

To appraise Taussig's *Wages and Capital* at its true value and to see its place in the history of American theory is much easier today than it would have been twenty years ago, because the lead it gave was not immediately followed up, not at any rate by the main body of theorists. The Jevons-Walras-Menger reform meant primarily a new theory of price or, to use more up-to-date terminology, a theory of the logic of economic choice. Marginal utility and marginal productivity were its pillars. It is clear that the fundamental principle which was coined into those two concepts is not by itself sufficient to describe even the simplest patterns of the economic process. If we compare the latter to a machine which "emits" consumers' goods and "absorbs" original means of production—the machine itself consisting of intermediate products, plant, equipment, raw materials, and half-finished products or, to use Taussig's phrase, of Inchoate Wealth—we discover immediately that scarcity of means is not the only "objective" fact to take account of in framing our maximum theorems. The structure of the machine, in particular the time relations or "periods" inherent to it, constitute another set of conditions to which the economic system must conform. Now, the classical theory of that structure or of those time relations or, as we may also say of (real) capital, being entirely independent of the pure logic of choice, was not directly affected by the reform of the theory of value. Jevons, Walras, and Menger all realized that something had to be done about it. All made a move in this direction without however accomplishing anything at all comparable to their work on value. Decisive achievement in this field is associated with the names of Boehm-Bawerk and Taussig. But although much useful work was immediately done on their line, especially by Wicksell and some of his followers, advance on the other line—the line of marginal analysis—monopolized the interest of the majority of theorists. Of late however the situation has changed. Difficulties encountered in handling the production function have turned attention toward the problems incident to the structure of capital. An important discussion on the concept of the period of production has ensued. And Taussig's contribution is thus coming into its own.

It amounts to a theory of production and distribution, for it would be easy to insert, either from the range of ideas available at the time or from Taussig's own papers on subjects of pure theory, those elements of such a theory that are missing. But he allowed his exposition to grow out of contemporary American discussion—as shaped primarily by Walker—on a particular point, the wages fund doctrine. The additional service he thus rendered, while at the time it drew attention away from the much more important fundamental idea of the book, which could have stood by itself, was an important one. Although a dozen or more theorists claimed, or were held by others, to have given the *coup de grace* to that unfortunate proposition it was Taussig who definitively disposed of it by straightening out the muddle that went under that caption and putting something else in its place, neither of which had been done by any of the numerous objectors that preceded him. All of them had offered more or less reasonable grounds for rejecting it. Many of them had, dimly at least, perceived that behind it or, rather, behind some of the things it can be made to mean, there were substantial elements of truth. But none of them had really settled the question and a most curious situation had dragged on for three quarters of a century.

The reason why this was so unfortunate and so discreditable to our science is intimately connected with what I like to call the Ricardian Vice, although many less brilliant economists sinned and still sin fully as much as that eminent man did. To construct tools of analysis and to try them out on simplified models of reality is not only the right but the duty of the theorist. But if he cannot resist the temptation to present results thus derived without qualification to the public at large, he betrays the cause of science. This is what happened in the instance before us. The "fund that rigidly limits wages" was promptly made to show, sometimes with a sigh of relief, sometimes with regret, that it was "scientifically impossible" to raise wage rates beyond the amount thus determined. Such nonsense may succeed for a time, if the public to which it is neatly presented likes the practical implication. But retribution visits the guilty and the guiltless economist alike, as soon as the public taste changes and that type of critic gets the floor who understands nothing but slogans. The case shows well how valueless such successes and how unnecessary such discomfitures are. For what that doctrine really meant could have been formulated quite harmlessly: with invariant production functions and under conditions of perfect competition forced or voluntary saving, if so invested as to increase the stock of capital goods, will tend to increase the (real) rate of wages; this way of increasing it is, under the same assumptions and excepting reduction in the number of hands, the only one which does not entail also other effects that in turn tend to deprive workers—partly, wholly, or even more than wholly—of the benefit of the increase.

In perfect equilibrium of perfect competition the sum total of wages paid is, no doubt, as uniquely determined as is everything else. But this is so by virtue of the general conditions that determine each individual wage and not by virtue of an independent relation *sui generis* subsisting between a given fund and the number of wage earners. Both Boehm-Bawerk and Taussig stressed the analogy between the latter idea and the quantity theory of money. In fact, the two can be made identical by expanding the wage fund into an income fund, the equality between which and a properl defined *PT* in Fisher's equation of exchange then turns into a condition of monetary equilibrium. The confusion of monetary and "real" concepts, of which many exponents of the wages fund doctrine were guilty, suggests the possibility that that analogy had something to do with their reasoning. This suspicion is strengthened by the fact that both quantity and wages fund theorists argued in terms of supply and demand without recognizing that these concepts *lose* or, at all events, *change* their ordinary meaning if applied to money or to so comprehensive an aggregate as the total wage bill of a country. Perhaps they looked upon both cases as presenting no greater peculiarity than an elasticity of demand equal to unity, and a shift of the demand curve describable in terms of a single parameter.

Of course this condemns them quite irrespectively of the cheap fun to which they laid themselves open. Yet Taussig's verdict was not quite so adverse as this. Having proved step by step both the major and the minor of the syllogism he yet refrained from drawing the conclusion, and it was only in the preface of the 1932 edition of the book that he definitively discarded the term "wages fund." That was because he had invested it with another meaning of his own. Returning to our machine that absorbs productive services and emits consumers' goods, we readily see that there actually is a non-monetary relation between those services and these goods. This of course raises problems which we must here avoid by postulating that there is only one kind and quality of each, say man-hours and bread. Now if the relation between labor "absorbed" and bread "emitted" were merely technological, nothing more need be said. But the machine can be constructed in technologically different ways which differ *economically* on the one hand in results, that is, in the quantities of bread per man-hour and, on the other hand, in the length of time a man-hour has on the average to stay in the machine. In other words, there are different periods of production or turnover to choose between, hence their duration enters as an economic variable, which is characteristic of the structure of capital and provides the link between two genuinely "objective" quantities, present work available and present bread available. This opens an avenue which leads much nearer to the facts of production and distribution than we could ever hope to get by means of the marginal productivity idea alone.

In various papers on subjects of pure theory and in his *Principles* Taussig rounded off the building to which *Wages and Capital* laid the foundation. But a complete survey of all he did for American theory would have to include many contributions made in the course of "applied" arguments particularly in the *Tariff History*, in *Some Aspects* and in *International Trade*. It is, for instance, in these rather than in the theoretical book that we find his message on the meaning of economic theory and its relation to statistical and historical fact. The treatise on international trade especially teaches the methodological lesson all the more impressively because it does so by example and not only by bald precept. However, even such a picture would be inadequate. For it could not contain the lead given to rising generations, and the influence exerted on academic practice, on research, and on scholarly standards, by one of the greatest teachers in the history of our science.

JOSEPH A. SCHUMPETER

Harvard University

REVIEW OF KEYNES'S GENERAL THEORY

Reprinted from *Journal of the American Statistical Association*, Dec. 1936, 791-795.

The General Theory of Employment, Interest and Money, by John Maynard Keynes. London: Macmillan and Company. 1936. xii, 403 pp. $2.00.

A book by Mr. Keynes on fundamental questions which are right at the heart of the practical discussions of the day is no doubt an event. Those who had the opportunity to witness the expectations of the best of our students, the impatience they displayed at the delay in getting hold of their copies, the eagerness with which they devoured them, and the interest manifested by all sectors of Anglo-American communities that are up to this kind of reading (and some that are not) must first of all congratulate the author on a signal personal success, a success not in the least smaller in the cases of negative reaction than in those in which the book elicited fervent admiration. The unfavorable reviews in a sense but testify to the reality of that success, and I for one, being about to write another of those unfavorable reviews, heartily rejoice in this implication and wish it to be understood that what I am going to say is, in its own unconventional way, a tribute to one of the most brilliant men who ever bent their energies to economic problems. Expression of a teacher's gratitude should be added for the gift of what is, in its vigorous exposition and extreme simplicity, an invaluable starter of discussions. Speaking to us from the vantage ground of Cambridge and from its author's unique personal position, defended by a group of ardent and able disciples, the book will undoubtedly dominate talk and thought for some time.

In his preface Mr. Keynes underlines the significance of the words "General Theory" in his title. He professes to address it primarily to his fellow economists and seems to invite purely theoretical discussion. But it is not quite easy to accept that invitation, for everywhere he really pleads for a definite policy, and on every page the ghost of that policy looks over the shoulder of the analyst, frames his assumptions, guides his pen. In this sense, as in another, it is Ricardo all over again. The advice offered implicitly and the social vision unfolded explicitly, do not concern us here. That advice (everybody knows what it is Mr. Keynes advises) may be good. For the England of today it possibly is. That vision may be entitled to the compliment that it expresses forcefully the attitude of a decaying civilization. In these respects, this book invites sociological interpretation in the Marxian sense, and nothing is more certain than that such interpretation will be administered to it before long.

It is, however, vital to renounce communion with any attempt to revive the Ricardian practice of offering, in the garb of general scientific truth, advice which—whether good or bad—carries meaning only with references to the practical exigencies of the unique historical situation of a given time and country. This sublimates practical issues into scientific ones, divides economists—as in fact we can see already from any discussion about this book—according to lines of political preference, produces popular successes at the moment, and reactions after—witness the fate of Ricardian economics —neither of which have anything to do with science. Economics will never have nor merit any authority until that unholy alliance is dissolved. There is happily some tendency towards such dissolution. But this book throws us back again. Once more, socialists as well as institutionalists are right in judging economic theory as they do.

Ricardian as the book is in spirit and intent, so it is in workmanship. There is the same technique of skirting problems by artificial[1] definitions which, tied up with highly specialized assumptions, produce paradoxical-looking tautologies, and of constructing special cases which in the author's own mind and in his exposition are invested with a treacherous generality. In one fundamental point it actually falls short of the line already reached by those writers who in the sixties of the past century criticized some of the tenets of what *to them* was "classical" doctrine,[2] notably Longe and Thornton. These knew perfectly that the old supply and demand apparatus renders its very limited service only if applied to individual commodities, strictly speaking to individual commodities of relatively small importance, and that it either loses or changes its meaning if applied to comprehensive social aggregates. This was in fact their foremost objection to the wage fund theory. Mr. Keynes' fundamental construction (which is all we can consider here) rests on a contraposition of expected[3] net "proceeds," equal to expected profits plus expected current payments to factors (for definition see page 24), and *those* proceeds the expectation of which would be sufficient and not more than sufficient to induce entrepreneurs to decide on producing the corresponding output. Two schedules or functions are imagined in order to describe the behavior and the relation to one another of these two funda-

[1] The definition of involuntary unemployment, page 15, may serve as an example. Taken literally (which of course it would be unfair to do) it would mean that there is no practically conceivable case in which workmen are not partially unemployed by definition. For if prices of wage goods rise a little, other things being equal, it is clear that both the demand for, and the supply of, labor will increase under competitive conditions, the latter at least as long as the flexibility of the marginal utility of income to the workmen is what present statistics lead us to believe.

[2] Mr. Keynes' definition of the word "classical," which is made to include Professor Pigou, who cannot be counted among classics by virtue of any criterion except the one of outstanding achievement, reminds me of a little experience I had in a group of students. I observed that one of the members kept on referring to a highly unconventional proposition as "orthodox." I asked him why he did so, seeing that the proposition was no part of received doctrine. His answer was, "I simply call orthodox everything I don't like." Protest should be filed in passing against Mr. Keynes' methods of criticism. But beyond that it is regrettable that so brilliant a leader should set so bad an example of utter absence of *verecundia*. I am no Marxian. Yet I sufficiently recognize the greatness of Marx to be offended at seeing him classed with Silvio Gesell and Major Douglas. Mr. Keynes is unjust even to Major Douglas for there is no warrant whatever for thinking little of that writer once one has accepted the views of this book. Certainly Marx and the classics (in the proper sense of the word) were grievously at fault in very many points as it is natural that pioneers should be. Yet they are right as against Mr. Keynes. His attitude toward Marshall's teaching is for Marshallians to judge.

[3] The emphasis on *expected* as against *actual* values is in line with modern tendencies. But expectations are not linked by Mr. Keynes to the cyclical situations that give rise to them and hence become independent variables and ultimate determinants of economic action. Such analysis can at best yield purely formal results and never go below the surface. An expectation acquires explanatory value only if we are made to understand *why* people expect *what* they expect. Otherwise expectation is a mere *deus ex machina* that conceals problems instead of solving them.

mental variables. The analogy of the first with the ordinary Marshallian demand curve and the analogy of the second with the ordinary Marshallian supply curve are obvious. In fact, Mr. Keynes speaks of Aggregate Demand in the one case and Aggregate Supply in the other and makes them yield a unique "point of intersection." There is as little justification for this extension of the "Marshallian cross" as there is for its application to the case of money, which has remained a besetting sin of the Cambridge group to this day.

Transition to the central theme of the book is effected by relating those two fundamental variables not to output but to employment, and not to employment of resources in general but to employment of labor. Mr. Keynes is as careful to point out that number of workmen employed is not proprotional to output as Ricardo was to point out that value cannot be proportional to quantity of labor. But exactly as Ricardo reasoned as if it were, so Mr. Keynes assumes that employment of labor is an "adequate" index of the output resulting from it. The arguments offered by both authors, in support of what is a procedure obviously inadmissible in anything that pretends to be a "general" theory, are curiously alike. In particular both display a desire to banish the variations of output—or, in Ricardo's case, of "riches"—from the realm of theory.

It should be clearly realized what that means Readers of this *Journal* will shrug their shoulders at a theory which deserts the statistician in his struggle with the momentous problems surrounding the Index of Production. But disregarding this, reasoning on the assumption that variations in output are uniquely related to variations in employment imposes the further assumption that all production functions remain invariant. Now the outstanding feature of capitalism is that they do not but that, on the contrary, they are being incessantly revolutionized. The capitalist process is essentially a process of change of the type which is being assumed away in this book, and all its characteristic phenomena and problems arise from the fact that it is such a process. A theory that postulates invariance of production functions may, if correct in itself, be still of some use to the theorist. But it is the theory of another world and out of all contact with modern industrial fact, unemployment included. No interpretation of modern vicissitudes, "poverty in plenty" and the rest, can be derived from it.

The central thesis that under-employment can exist in a state of stable equilibrium and that saving is responsible for it is then made to follow from two additional hypotheses. The one—embodied in the concept of Propensity to Consume—is that "when aggregate real income is increased aggregate consumption is increased, but not by so much as income" (page 27). This Mr. Keynes dignifies, in the worst style of a bygone age, into a "Psychological Law." The question of fact apart—statistics of installment selling and other forms of consumers' credit obviously suggest the possibility of doubt—such a "propensity" is again nothing but a *deus ex machina*, valueless if we do not understand the mechanism of the changing situations, in which consumers' expenditure alternatively increases and contracts, and redundant if we do. Postulating, however, an independent and systematic tendency to that effect, Mr. Keynes finds a "gap" in expenditure resulting from it which may or may not be filled by investment and tends to widen as communities grow more wealthy. This amounts to introducing another hypothesis: the hypothesis of failing "Inducement to Invest."

Since Mr. Keynes eliminates the most powerful propeller of investment, the financing of changes in production functions, the investment process in his theoretical world has hardly anything to do with the investment process in the actual world, and any proof, even if successful, that (absolutely or relatively) falling "Inducement to Invest" will produce under-employment would have no greater practical importance than a proof that motor cars cannot run in the absence of fuel. But that proof, even under its own assumptions and granting that in Mr. Keynes' world there would be a systematic tendency for Inducement to Invest to grow weaker,[4] meets the obvious objection that Propensity to Consume and Inducement to Invest are not independent of each other. In some passages (for example, page 30) Mr. Keynes seems indeed to hold that they are. We can absolve him, however, from the grave error this would spell, because each time (for example, page 31) he in fact admits the existence of an equilibrating mechanism. But then the whole *theoretical* case, that is, the case in terms of fundamental features of the economic process, collapses, and we are *practically* left with friction, or "stickiness," institutional inhibitions, and the like, which in particular may prevent the rate of interest from reacting promptly or, in general, prevent the whole of that equilibrating mechanism from functioning adequately.

Space forbids our entering into a discussion of the Multiplier, its relation to the Propensity to Consume, the system of Wage Units, and other tools by means of which Mr. Keynes works out his basic ideas. I wish however to welcome his purely monetary theory of interest which is, as far as I can see, the first to follow upon my own. Unfortunately, I must add that the similarity stops there and that I do not think my argument open to the objections which this one is sure to meet. Some differences would vanish, if the concepts of a demand for money stocks and of "liquidity preference"—which is another *deus ex machina;* there is a whole Olympus of them—were replaced by concepts drawn from the economic processes that lie behind the surface phenomena denoted by those two. But then many of the striking inferences would also vanish. The whole vision of the capitalist process would change. Interest would lose the pivotal position which it holds in Mr. Keynes' analysis by virtue of the same technique which made it possible for

[4] To many people statement of such a tendency will sound "realistic." This is however entirely due to recent experience and would have equally been the case after, say, 1720 or 1825 or 1873. No support of the theory in question can be derived from this, since it rests exclusively on observation of the surface mechanism of a deep depression *already in progress*, the explanation of which must be worked out independently of it.

Ricardo to hold that profits depend upon the price of wheat. And a completely different diagnosis of modern difficulties would follow.

The less said about the last book the better. Let him who accepts the message there expounded rewrite the history of the French *ancien régime* in some such terms as these: Louis XV was a most enlightened monarch. Feeling the necessity of stimulating expenditure he secured the services of such expert spenders as Madame de Pompadour and Madame du Barry. They went to work with unsurpassable efficiency. Full employment, a maximum of resulting output, and general well-being ought to have been the consequence. It is true that instead we find misery, shame and, at the end of it all, a stream of blood. But that was a chance coincidence.

JOSEPH A. SCHUMPETER

Harvard University

PREFACE TO JAPANESE EDITION OF THEORIE DER WIRTSCHAFTLICHEN ENTWICKLUNG

Reprinted from tr. by I. Nakayama and S. Tobata, Tokyo, *Iwanami Shoten,* 1937.

For so ardent an admirer of the Japanese nation and its culture as I am, it is a particular pleasure to welcome this translation and to express a hope that it may contribute to the vigorous stream of Japanese thought in the field of economic theory and stimulate further advance, at least by provoking criticism. The pleasure I feel is much enhanced by the fact that the translation has been done by such brilliant economists. I would not have advised them to undertake it. For, from the impression I had of Professors Tobata and Nakayama, when about ten years ago it was my privilege to welcome them to the University of Bonn where I was then teaching, I conceived so high an opinion of what our science might expect from them, that the decision to put their talents into the service of another man's work would have hardly seemed justified to me. But since they made that generous and self-denying decision, and now the translation is done, I feel free, in tendering them my sincere thanks, to enjoy the conviction that my book could not have been in better hands.

If my Japanese readers asked me before opening the book what it is that I was aiming at when I wrote it, more than a quarter of a century ago, I would answer that I was trying to construct a theoretic model of the process of economic change in time, or perhaps more clearly, to answer the question how the economic system generates the force which incessantly transforms it. This may be illustrated by a reference to two great names: Léon Walras and Karl Marx. To Walras we owe a concept of the economic system and a theoretical apparatus which for the first time in the history of our science effectively embraced the pure logic of the interdependence between economic quantities. But when in my beginnings I studied the Walrasian conception and the Walrasian technique (I wish to emphasize that as an economist I owe more to it than to any other influence), I discovered not only that it is rigorously static in character (this is selfevident and has been again and again stressed by Walras himself) but also that it is applicable only to a stationary process. These two things must not be confused. A static theory is simply a statement of the conditions of equilibrium and of the way in which equilibrium tends to re-establish itself after every small disturbance. Such a theory can be useful in the investigation of any kind of reality, however disequilibrated it may be. A stationary process, however, is a process which *actually* does not change of its own initiative, but merely reproduces constant rates of real income as it flows along in time. If it changes at all, it does so under the influence of events which are external to itself, such as natural catastrophes, wars and so on. Walras would have admitted this. He would have said (and, as a matter of fact, he did say it to me the only time that I had the opportunity to converse with him) that of course economic life is essentially passive and merely adapts itself to the natural and social influences which may be acting on it, so that the theory of a stationary process constitutes really the whole of theoretical economics and that as economic theorists we cannot say much about the factors that account for historical change, but must simply register them. Like the classics, he would have made exceptions for increase in population and in savings, but this would only introduce a change in the data of the system and not add any new phenomena. I felt very strongly that this was wrong, and that there was a source of energy within the economic system which would of itself disrupt any equilibrium that might be attained. If this is so, then there must be a purely economic theory of economic change which does not merely rely on external factors propelling the economic system from one equilibrium to another. It is such a theory that I have tried to build and I believe now, as I believed then, that it contributes something to the understanding of the struggles and vicissitudes of the capitalist world and explains a number of phenomena, in particular the business cycle, more satisfactorily than it is possible to explain them by means of either the Walrasian or the Marshallian apparatus.

It was not clear to me at the outset what to the reader will perhaps be obvious at once, namely, that this idea and this aim are exactly the same as the idea and the aim which underly the economic teaching of Karl Marx. In fact, what distinguishes him from the economists of his own time and those who preceded him, was precisely a vision of economic evolution as a distinct process generated by the economic system itself. In every other respect he only used and adapted the concepts and propositions of Ricardian economics, but the concept of economic evolution which he put into an unessential Hegelian setting, is quite his own. It is probably due to this fact that one generation of economists after another turns back to him again, although they may find plenty to criticize in him. I am not saying this in order to associate anything that I say in this book with his great name. Intention and results are much too different to give me a right to do so. Such similarities in results as undoubtedly exist (compare, for instance, the thesis of this book that in perfect equilibrium interest would be zero, with Marx's proposition that constant capital does not produce any surplus value) are not only obliterated by a very wide difference in general outlook, but also reached by such different methods, that stressing parallelisms would be highly unsatisfactory to Marxians. But I wish to point to their presence because readers trained in Marxian economics may find the reading of the book facilitated by this reference and also may be interested in comparisons.

In concluding, I beg leave to return for a moment to Walras and to the developments in economic doctrine which in him find their ultimate source. I will mention a few of the latter in order to state the relation in which the argument of this book stands to them. There are, first, the improvements which stand to the credit of his direct successors, Pareto being the most eminent among them. As an example I may mention the elimination from the system of general equilibrium of the concept of utility. Whatever we may think of this, it was certainly a gain in scientific elegance and rigor. If I worked out systematically the ideas presented in this book I should have, of course, to take account of this progress as I should of the progress achieved in the theory of the production function, of costs and of many other points, but my own argument would not be affected. Secondly, it might be asked how I should deal with the new theory of imperfect competition. The answer is that this theory proves particularly useful in working out the details of the process which this book attempts to describe. Practically every innovation, especially if it consists in the introduction of a new commodity, at first creates that kind of situation which is designated by the term Monopolistic Competition. The behavior of the entrepreneur, the reaction of the system to him, can very well be described in terms of that theory. The third line of advance which is relevant in this connection, is of particular interest because of its "dynamic" character. Economists have always been in the habit of mentioning frictions and lags and they have probably always been aware of the fact that businessmen do not react to *given quantities* only but also to their rates of change and not to *actual quantities* only but to expected ones. However, during the last ten years exact theories have been worked out of the effects due to lagged adaptation, to action on expectation, and so on. New techniques have been worked out or adapted from other fields. Among the latter, the most remarkable event was the intrusion into economics of the functional calculus, developed by Vito Volterra about fifty years ago. The reader finds nothing of all this in this volume and may well ask how it affects what he will read, and especially how it affects the theory of the business cycle presented in the last chapter, considering that the new methods seem to show the possibility of a vast variety of wavelike movements in economic life which may be used to explain cycles without any reference to the principle of innovation. Again, as in the case of the theory of imperfect competition, I believe that these new tools of analysis will greatly enhance our power of dealing with the patterns of reality and that they will render service also to the process described in this book. But it should be observed that the results due to these new methods (the reader could inform himself about some of them by reading Professor Tinbergen's Suggestions on Quantitative Business Cycle Theory in Econometrica, Volume 3, Number 3) do not constitute an alternative theory of the business cycle or the process of economic change in general. They describe repercussions and propagations without saying anything about the forces or causes that set them into motion. Whatever those causes, the way in which they operate and in which the system reacts to them is elucidated by the new methods. But they do not touch the question whether the force actually at work is correctly described by the principle of innovation or not.

Harvard University
Cambridge, Massachusetts
June, 1937.

THE INFLUENCE OF PROTECTIVE TARIFFS ON THE INDUSTRIAL DEVELOPMENT OF THE UNITED STATES

Reprinted from *Proceedings of the Academy of Political Science,* May 1940, 2-7.

I

I FEEL strongly that nothing but confusion and misunderstanding can result from any analysis of the effects of protective tariffs from purely economic considerations and without reference to the wider ambitions of the nation concerned and to the particular world situation into which its lot is cast. Hence I must devote time, which I sorely need for that purely economic aspect, to what I may term the political setting in which the practical question of protection always has presented, and is now presenting, itself to the people of this country.

First and last, what the American people wanted to accomplish, when they decided to stake their all on independence, was to be a world unto themselves, to work out their own destiny, to be rid of the vicissitudes of Europe and, most important of all, to be no longer pawns on the English chessboard; and this has, in the economic as well as in every other sphere, remained all along the only truly American foreign policy. I will say at once that this accounts for the fact that, though protection immediately creates protectionist interests that will clamor for additional protection for very obvious business reasons, the people at large, with an exception to be noticed presently, have given consistent support to a policy of protection and that they have all along refused to listen to what mere economists might have to say about it.

Attempts at protection, thwarted by the vetoes of colonial governors, were made even before the War of Independence. From the struggle for independence, the country emerged in a protectionist mood that asserted itself before long in the face of many anti-protectionist interests. Protection—or nonintercourse acts and so on—then was simply the economic complement of political independence or of the will to buttress that independence. Anti-protectionist interests, particularly those of wheat growers and cotton planters, were strong enough to put a brake on that fundamental tendency until the Civil War, and even succeeded in enforcing a strategic retreat of the protectionist high command from the "tariff of horrors"—the high-water mark of its success. But when, after the Civil War, it became clear that the immigration of European capital would for an indefinite time solve the problem that protection would otherwise have created, the protectionists had their way, with but minor setbacks, right up to the threshold of the World War. In the discussion of American post-war policy, especially of the Fordney-McCumber Act and of the famous "refusal to accept the implications of the country's new creditor position," it has been persistently overlooked, how much that policy of protection—as far as its popular support went—was part and parcel of the unequivocal verdict passed by the American people upon the Wilson policy, the League of Nations idea or anything that would perpetuate European entanglements. To be sure, it was illogical to embark at the same time upon a policy of forcing exports; but that was no more than a ransom paid to a restricted, if vocal, group.

This argument, however, does not apply to deviations from the principle of protection that aim at extending the country's economic sphere of influence on the continent of America, although such a policy may be the source of problems of a different kind. But barring that, the fundamental rationale of American protectionism is as strong today as it ever was. It may well gather additional strength in the near future.

It will be seen that what I have said so far is not likely to please the economist. In fact, it does not take account at all of the balance of purely economic advantage and disadvantage. Though the economic case for free, or less restricted, trade is not so strong and the economic case for protection not so weak as a bygone generation of economists believed, I do not wish to identify myself with any of the popular arguments that are being adduced for protection in general, or for certain types of protective measures in particular. I readily admit that they are, on the whole, much below the old free-trade argument.

I also admit that, if we lived in a peaceful world, the costs of the economic independence of this country might easily outweigh its advantage. But I submit that, since we do not live in a peaceful world, even the purely economic balance, both from the standpoint of industrial development and from the standpoint of the standard of life of the masses, may well be in favor of protection.

II

The industrial development of the United States, in the early stages of the growth of the industrial organism as a whole, as well as in the early stages of each individual industry, presents an almost ideal case for the application of the (Hamilton-List) infant-industry argument. There is no doubt a considerable list of instances—from watches to motor cars—in which industries either from the outset were, or very quickly became, so superior to any actual or potential foreign competition that nothing could have stopped, or even retarded, their success. But in the majority of instances, nascent American industries found foreign producers in possession. That the emergence of those industries and their conquest of the American market—also the development of certain factors, such as water power—were materially facilitated by protection is obvious.

It should be added that, in the American case, *some* of the most serious disadvantages that are usually associated with a policy of fostering industrial development in this way do not show at all, or do so in a much milder form than we should expect them to show in any other country. To begin with, the country soon grew so large as to make it possible to reap within its frontiers practically all the benefits that are usually attributed to a free-trade policy—benefits that are (like other things) now threatened by recent developments. If the restrictions that are now being placed on interstate and even interlocal commerce should continue to increase, more pressure on the people's standard of life may result than could ever be exerted by any amount of protection.

Moreover, protection usually overdevelops the protected industries, thus creating maladjustments for the future. The history of European protection abounds with instances of that. They are not entirely wanting in the history of this country. The depression following upon the peace of 1814 (just as serious, proportions guarded, as the one following upon 1929) was characterized by the breakdown of many firms that owed their sickly life to the " protection " extended to them by the war, and conditions akin to war, with England. But on the whole, that phenomenon has been conspicuous by absence. The size and natural wealth of the country always absorbed whatever may have been due to the stimulus of protection, and little loss has been incurred *on that account.* To put it differently, protection did not lead to major distortions in the industrial structure. On the contrary, American protection on the whole resulted in a better balanced organism and in all-round, instead of one-sided, development.

That does not mean, of course, that losses of another kind were entirely avoided or that the protectionist policy was costless. A number of industries, of which wool and sugar are conspicuous instances, always remained, for a considerable part of their output, *dependent* on protection. It is those cases of " high-cost industries " which, though they demonstrate, still better than any other, the power of the tariff to increase the size of a country's industrial apparatus, are particularly exposed to well-founded objections on purely economic grounds. As a matter of general theory, it is indeed difficult to find any justification for the cost principle in tariff making, however strongly it may appeal to the untutored mind.[1] But in times like the present one, in which conditions of underutilization of resources prevail, there is reason to believe that, even in those cases and in the long run, a policy of protection does more good than harm, while it is clear that in the short run discontinuance of protection would create most serious difficulties of adjustment.

[1] There is, however, a purely economic argument for protection even in those cases. The differences between domestic and foreign costs that are to be equalized by tariffs are, of course, differences in terms of money. Now differences in money costs may be due either to differences in real costs—it may for instance take more man hours to produce a certain commodity in this country than it does to produce it abroad—or simply to the fact that money values all round are higher in this country than they are abroad. The theoretical argument referred to in the text fully applies to the first case only. In the latter case the tariff only prevents adjustment of values and in particular of money incomes to world-market standards. That may be desirable or not, but is in any case an entirely different matter—in fact, a question of the monetary policy to be pursued.

In *any* case, however, protection increases the rate of profit. Whatever we may think about this from other standpoints, in a rapidly progressing country it will have the effect of accelerating the pace of that progress by propelling investment and making it easier to face risks. After a state of maturity has been reached and especially in a prolonged period of depression such as the one that set in toward the end of 1929—whatever its causes and nature may be or have been—this argument would of course not apply. But obviously, in so far as protection reduces losses, keeps markets from being disorganized by foreign distress sales and so on, another argument takes its place. Also, independently of either booms or depressions, the fiscal interest in profit margins is an important consideration.

Taking this country's industrial organism as a whole, and with qualifications that should be obvious from what has been said above, we may thus conclude that, as far as the past is concerned, the main effect of protective tariffs has been to speed up industrial developments that would have come about in any case, rather than to induce developments that would never have come about without them. As far as this goes, their effect may well be likened to the effect of that kind of inflationism that has been characteristic of this nation from its origins to the present day. *Always*, and even during periods that are commonly dubbed deflationist, the American people were bent on monetary or credit expansion, and on "liberal" financing that did not look too closely at the purpose to be financed — from Franklin to Roosevelt that attitude has not changed except as to techniques and phraseology. And it must be admitted that, in the conditions of this country, our judgment on this practice cannot be quite what it would have to be in the case of any other country. As regards industrial development in particular, there cannot be any doubt but that it *was* accelerated beyond the rate that stricter practice would have allowed.

Of course, I do not mean to defend inflationism or, when it comes to that, the rate of industrial development itself. For instance, it is certain that the violence of American booms and breakdowns has partly been the consequence of loose finance and protection. It might well be argued that this country would today be a healthier and happier place, and that its problems would be much more manageable, if industrial progress had been less rapid and if there had been less of monetary expansion, of protection, of immigration. Our result, however, stands nevertheless. If size of industrial apparatus or amount of wealth is what we focus our attention on, then the effect of those three factors has been clearly positive — the country is now much richer than it would be without them.

But whereas, at the present stage of the country's economic evolution, there is *no* argument for further immigration, and whereas inflationary policies can henceforth have no function except that of palliatives in extreme cases of depression, the protectionist policy has not yet outlived its usefulness.

Even if there should never again arise a case in which protection could play the rôle it used to play in the past — and there is no warrant for assuming this—it will continue to be one of the simplest means of safeguarding the existing industrial structure. Given present conditions, situations will unavoidably arise in which temporary vicissitudes in other parts of the world might cause permanent damage to American industries. Of course these considerations exclude neither bargaining for advantages in individual cases (introduced, as a principle, in 1897) nor occasional resort to reciprocity agreements. But if we have got to live in a mercantilist, nationalist, bellicose world dominated by a few great empires, on the one hand, and if the domestic policy of this country is to remain free to shape its own destiny, on the other hand, I do not see the possibility, and I should very much doubt the wisdom, of any major deviation from the policy of protection.

CAPITALISM IN THE POSTWAR WORLD

Reprinted from *Postwar Economic Problems,* 1943, 113-126.

I

For the purposes of this essay capitalism will be defined by three features of industrial society: private ownership of the physical means of production; private profits and private responsibility for losses; and the creation of means of payments—banknotes or deposits—by private banks. The first two features suffice to define private enterprise. But no concept of capitalism can be satisfactory without including the set of typically capitalistic phenomena covered by the third. Where it is absent we might speak of commercial society. By socialism we shall mean an institutional arrangement that vests the management of the productive process with some public authority.[1]

In trying to forecast the role, if any, that capitalism in the sense defined may be expected to play in the postwar world it is well to remember that its fate is not a question of the merits or demerits we may individually see in it. Our judgment about these is a matter of personal or groupwise preference that depends on interests and ideals largely determined by our personal or groupwise location in the social organism. What we mean when we say that we are for or against capitalism is that we like or dislike a certain civilization or scheme of life which is historically associated with the three economic features mentioned. But civilizations are incommensurable. Even if we agreed to neglect those cultural aspects which are what really matters to us, and to make the "desirability" of retaining or eliminating capitalism turn on some purely economic

[1] It should be noted that this definition of socialism is not only purely economic but also purely formal. It says nothing about the structure and character of a socialist society, *e.g.*, whether it is equalitarian or not, warlike or pacific, democratic or authoritarian. Friends and foes of socialism are in the habit of endowing their concept of it with additional traits and hence in general mean by it something much more specific.

criterion—such as comparative productive efficiency—we should never agree about the result. For even if those extraeconomic and largely extrarational preferences did not prevent us from admitting that any criterion could ever tell against the alternative we have chosen to espouse—which they no doubt would in most cases—we should immediately challenge a criterion that did. No amount of honest intention to place oneself on the standpoint of the public welfare or of the nation's interest avails against that. For the point is precisely that these words carry different meanings for different minds. The only thing we can do in something like a scientific frame of mind is therefore to try to visualize, irrespective of our wishes, the actual situations which may be expected to emerge and the relative power of the groups which will be in a position to assert their interests and ideals in handling those situations.

Another point should be borne in mind. No social system is ever pure either in its economic or in its political aspects. As regards the former, structural principles, such as, in the case of commercial society, private management of the process of production and free contracting, are never fully carried to their logical consequences. People were at no time allowed to do with their own quite as they pleased, and society at all times limited the range within which they might freely contract. In the epoch of intact capitalism, law, custom, public opinion, and public administration enforced a certain amount of public planning, while in a society that had adopted the structural principles of socialism there was such a thing as Lenin's New Economic Policy that left room for a certain amount of *laissez faire*. It follows that, public management or planning being never either absent or complete, our question concerning the immediate future should not be couched in terms of "capitalism or socialism": there is a great variety of intermediate possibilities.

Still more important for social diagnosis and prognosis is, as we shall presently see, the fact that no society is ever homogeneous. By this I do not merely mean that the political sector of every society grows out of, and hence reflects, all the different interests and attitudes of the various groups and classes that the prevailing social system produces. I mean something much more fundamental: every society contains, at any given time, elements that are the products of different social systems. Thus, feudal society harbored, besides the lords and peasants and artisans that constituted the essential elements of its system, also other elements—traders, for instance, and certain classes of producers—that did not belong to the feudal organism and dwelt in towns which that organism failed to subjugate or to assimilate. In the capitalist epoch, the classes that are the products of the capitalist process are hardly ever found alone. Practically always they exist in symbiosis with an aristocracy and a peasantry of noncapitalist origin. And this fact is not only, as one might think, responsible for frictions and other secondary phenomena. It is of the essence of the social process. A purely capitalist society—consisting of nothing but entrepreneurs, capitalists, and proletarian workmen—would work in ways completely different from those we observe historically, *if indeed it could exist at all.*[1]

II

Both in its international and in its domestic aspects, capitalist economy is adapted to the requirements and habits of a normally pacific world. "Total war" under modern conditions calls for a concentration of effort much more stringent than the mechanism of capitalist markets can achieve. Wartime planning by government in fact suspends the normal operation of capitalist processes. In doing so it develops, on the one hand, economic structures and situations and, on the other hand, new social organs and positions of power which do not automatically disappear with the emergency that brought them into existence. They have to be liquidated, if at all, by a series of distinct measures which naturally meet resistance. We have seen that the outcome of the ensuing struggle will not depend on any abstract desirability of a return to prewar ways but on the political forces marshaled for and against it.

The strength of these forces in turn will depend, first, on the duration of the war in question and, second, on the vitality of the capitalist system independently of the war. Thus, in 1919, the United States emerged from a spell of wartime planning that had been both mild and short. The various war boards and their bureaucracies had not had time to get into full working order, let alone to settle into positions which they would have looked upon as permanent. The business world and the public in general had not had the time to get accustomed to their rule and to accept them as

[1] Many readers will feel that while this might apply to European and Asiatic countries, it could not possibly apply to the United States. But it would be easy to enumerate the very particular conditions—now rapidly passing—which explain why a purely bourgeois regime was in this case able to hold its own for so considerable a time.

parts of the normal scheme of things. Moreover, all the groups that counted politically were fully determined to stand for private enterprise and in fact did not clearly perceive an alternative—which fact indicates precisely that the vitality of American capitalist society then was not yet substantially impaired.

This historical instance should not blind us to the possibility that events such as total war may influence social evolution more profoundly than words like "catastrophe" and "conflagration" imply. They may create situations so compelling as to impose permanent departures from the lines previously followed, and attitudes greatly at variance with any observed before. They may change the distribution of political power in unpredictable ways. The bolshevist regime is obviously of more than passing importance; yet it could never have established itself without the First World War and the largely accidental ways in which that war affected Russia. We may indeed succeed in interpreting the break as the result of existing tendencies that were merely accelerated by the war, and thus formally salvage historical determinism as a philosophy. But this does not increase its value as a working hypothesis.

There cannot be any doubt but that, in all countries concerned, the present war effort will put existing social structures under severe strain which may result in breakdown or fundamental transformation. The chances for this to happen are presumably greater in vanquished countries, but the victor countries are by no means exempt from this possibility. All the more important is it to raise the question of what we may term the tensile strength of the social systems that are being exposed to that strain.

It is a commonplace that capitalist society is, and for some time has been, in a state of decay. But there is no agreement about the precise nature of that decay. Differences of opinion on this point can be conveniently described in terms of two theories.

There is, first, the familiar theory of Vanishing Investment Opportunity.[1] It starts from an undeniable truth, more or less explicit recognition of which constitutes its chief merit. Unlike other economic systems, the capitalist system is geared to incessant economic change. Its very nature implies recurrent industrial revolutions which are the main sources of the profit and interest incomes of entrepreneurs and capitalists and supply the main

[1] The outstanding exponent of this theory is Prof. Alvin H. Hansen; see, *e.g.*, his *Fiscal Policy and Business Cycles* (New York, 1941), Ch. I, and his essay in this volume.

opportunities for new investments—such as railroad building or the construction of electric-power plants—and the main outlets for new savings. Whereas a stationary feudal economy would still be a feudal economy, and a stationary socialist economy would still be a socialist economy, stationary capitalism is a contradiction in terms. This becomes evident when we survey its most characteristic types, processes, and institutions, all of which would become atrophic in a stationary world.

Now the theory in question holds that this is happening in our day. That process of economic conquest is exhausting its possibilities. No very great innovations are in prospect, and those minor ones that may be said to be in the offing fail to stimulate entrepreneurship and investment either because they are capital-saving rather than capital-consuming or else because they are more suited to public than to private management. Moreover the great impetus given to investment in the nineteenth century by the opportunity of opening up new countries and sources of raw materials has spent itself. Finally the falling birth rate and the consequent slackening of the rate of increase in population tend to dry up a source of particularly calculable investments. For all these reasons the saving-investment process, which is of obviously vital importance to capitalist society, works with increasing friction. Thrift, instead of being the means of expanding the industrial equipment becomes a cause of falling prices and of unemployment. Hence the necessity of injecting into an anemic system new purchasing power: the first and foremost application of this theory was in fact to provide a rationale for the fiscal policies of the past decade. Hence also—so we may continue for our purpose—progressive paralysis of the political organs of capitalist society and reduced ability to withstand shocks or to defend itself against attack.

This theory cannot be adequately discussed here.[1] It must suffice to state that there does not seem to be any good reason for believing that, except as a temporary effect of the world crisis, the opportunity for great innovations in the economic process has been exhausted; that the tendency of innovations to become capital saving to the required extent has been illustrated by examples but has not been established convincingly; that the opening up of new countries, even if we assume it to be completed, was but one of many opportunities and might be replaced by others—in fact has

[1] I refer the reader to the discussion in my *Business Cycles* (New York, 1939), Vol. II, Ch. XV.

been replaced by others during the twenties; that the falling birth rate, both through its direct effects on demand and through its indirect effects on motivation, may become economically significant in the future but that it could hardly be used in an explanation of the course of events in the thirties, even if the relation between the rate of increase in population and economic progress were less complex than it actually is.

The theory of vanishing investment opportunity obviously invokes the factors mentioned in order to deduce from them a state of perennial inadequacy of profit expectations or, to use Lord Keynes's term, of the marginal efficiency of capital. It is only by this effect on profit expectations that those factors can be held to account for insufficient investment and, in turn, for underemployment. But, surely, if profit expectations are the operative link in the deduction, it is natural to stress another element the reality of which cannot be called into question and which acted on profit expectations much more obviously, *viz.*, the anticapitalist policies adopted, in most European countries, ever since the First World War and, in the United States, since 1933. The fact that both in Europe and in the United States the capitalist process displayed unmistakable symptoms of strain exactly since the break in the legislative and administrative attitudes of public authority occurred may be significant. This element constitutes the pivot of the other theory.[1] It also starts from the proposition that capitalism is essentially a process of economic change and then goes on as follows.

One of the most familiar phenomena of that process of change, the full importance of which was first recognized by Karl Marx, is the emergence of large-scale business, which to some extent tends to compete out of existence—or, to use the Marxian phrase, to "expropriate"—small or medium-sized firms. It stands to reason that, especially under conditions of democratic politics, this process weakens the political position of the industrial bourgeoisie, for a numerous stratum of businessmen owning and managing small or medium-sized firms is obviously much less exposed to political attack and in a much better position to withstand it than is a small number of salaried executives and large shareholders,[2] *quite irrespec-*

[1] I have developed it at length in my *Capitalism, Socialism, and Democracy* (1942), Part II.

[2] Here, any adequate exposition of that theory would have to digress into political sociology in order to show that the behavior of a society toward a particular interest is primarily determined by the inducement and the opportu-

tive of comparative economic performance or "service." Moreover, within the big concern the pungent sense of property and the will to fight for it tooth and nail withers away: the big concern thus not only "expropriates" some of its competitors but also its own capitalist interest. Those executives and shareholders are not only in a less favorable position to defend their ground than were the owner-managers of old but they meet attack in a much weaker spirit. Big business is in fact but a midway house on the road toward socialism.

The capitalist process undermines the structure of capitalist society in many other ways. I shall mention two only. First, it tends to destroy, economically or socially, the position of what may be termed the protective strata. The rise of the bourgeoisie ousted from political leadership the old aristocracies who knew so much better how to rule than does the businessman. The factory destroyed the old crafts and the department or chain store destroys the small traders who counted at the polls. It also reduced, relatively at least, the number of farmers and peasants. And so on. Second, capitalist civilization is a rationalist civilization. It tends to eliminate extra- or hyperrational sanctions and habits of mind without which no society can exist.

Though the argument cannot be adequately developed, it should be clear that we have now before us the elements of a more realistic substitute for, or of a more realistic version of, the theory of vanishing investment opportunity and of the decay of capitalist society. The capitalist process itself produces, as effectively as it produces motorcars or refrigerators, a distribution of political power, an attitude of the public mind, and an orientation of the political sector that are at variance with its own law of life. It produces anticapitalist policies, *i.e.*, policies that, regardless of individual intentions, prevent it from functioning according to its logic, the implications of which increasingly meet moral disapproval. Modern principles of taxation, although only one among many manifestations of the disintegration of capitalist society, afford perhaps the most telling illustration.

It is a nice question, on which it is much easier to differ than to agree, how far this decay has gone in any given case. Some symp-

nity for attacking it and only to a minor degree by what the observer according to his own standards may consider justifiable reasons for approving or disapproving of it. These reasons, so far as produced by political or intellectual agents, are simply rationalizations in the psychological sense.

toms showed in Europe before the First World War, but without it the majority of observers might have taken a long time in becoming aware of them. In the United States, the first unmistakable symptom of decay was perhaps the lack of spirit displayed by the bourgeoisie toward the end of the world crisis when the modal business-man proved that he was no longer up to the tests imposed by his own order of things. That the decay of capitalist society is very far advanced by now—everywhere—is not open to doubt. However much we may approve of some or all of the policies of the New Deal, we cannot fail to be struck by the absence of any serious resistance to them. A bourgeois society that meekly accepts the vast transfer of wealth accomplished in the United States during the thirties—I am not speaking of war taxation—thereby testifies to its readiness to surrender, though it may not be ready to surrender to every type of conqueror. It is in such conditions that events like world wars may acquire an importance in shaping the history of institutional patterns which they could never acquire if they impinged on an intact social system.

III

We are now in a position to form an idea about the various possibilities concerning the capitalist order's survival in the postwar world. It is first necessary to visualize the economic and political situation that will confront the dominant political groups at the end of the war. In what follows we shall confine ourselves to the United States and consider no other case but that of complete victory.

Everybody is afraid of a postwar slump, threatening from a drastic reduction of military expenditure financed by inflationary methods as well as from mere reorientation of production. The all but general opinion seems to be that capitalist methods will be unequal to the task of reconstruction. This opinion in itself will be a political factor of first-rate importance. All the more essential is it to understand its rationale.

Viewed as a purely economic problem, that task might well turn out to be much easier than most people believe. It may happen that peace will be preceded by a period of decreasing military expenditure and of gradually increasing production for civilian consumption and also that the former will continue, though at a reduced rate, on a level much beyond that of prewar times. Either or both of these possibilities would greatly facilitate transition.

But in any case, the wants of impoverished households will be so urgent and so calculable that any postwar slump that may be unavoidable would speedily give way to a reconstruction boom. Capitalist methods have proved equal to much more difficult tasks.

Nevertheless the opinion that the capitalist solution of the problem will prove unworkable or, at all events, unsatisfactory, may well be true. For, like any other system, capitalism cannot be expected to function efficiently except on its own terms, that is to say, in a social atmosphere that accepts its responsibilities and incentives and allows it sufficient freedom of action. As we have seen, however, such an atmosphere and the corresponding attitude of public authority have not existed for some time, do not exist now, and are obviously unlikely to exist in future. Capitalist management would hence have to solve the problems of reconstruction at home and abroad in the face of public antagonism, under burdens which eliminate capitalist motivation and make it impossible to accumulate venture capital, with risks of borrowing greatly increased,[1] without authority in the plant, and under the close control of a hostile bureaucracy. Deadlock so complete as to practically impose socialism as the only alternative is not inconceivable, but even conditions far removed from deadlock may preclude performance comparable to that of the past.

To be sure, a temporary revulsion of public sentiment in favor of *laissez faire* is not unthinkable. I need hardly stay however in order to show how very improbable it is. The public mind has renounced allegiance to the capitalist scheme of values. Private wealth is under a moral ban. All those bars to the effective functioning of capitalism embody what to most of us are cherished achievements. In particular, reduction of the fiscal burdens imposed upon the high income brackets and upon large-scale business and removal of administrative fetters would be highly unpopular and could hardly be carried to the requisite extent in a situation in which high rates of taxes on all incomes will continue to be necessary. Intellectuals and organized labor will emerge from the war in a radical frame of mind. Nobody will dare and, what is more, nobody will care to advocate what would have to be a return not only to prewar conditions but—substantially—to the conditions of 1929.

[1] High or highly progressive taxation of profits increases the risks of borrowing for purposes of long-run investment, because it absorbs profits the accumulation of which might be counted on to take care of subsequent losses.

Nor will there be a motive for any of the political groups of significant importance to influence the public mind in a procapitalist direction. Any regime that may be established will have to court the farm group and to present attractive schemes of agricultural "planning." Farmers therefore might not be actively hostile to partial reversal of anticapitalist policies—especially if their views about railroads were taken account of—but they will see little reason why they should go out of their way for the sake of it. Organized labor will find it impossible to abandon any of the positions it has conquered even if some labor leaders should entertain doubts as to their economic value. The strata of small and medium-sized business still constitute a factor which no regime can afford to neglect. But they can be satisfied without making any concessions to big business which embodies the achievements and the vital energies of the American economy.

Thus there is a reasonable chance that the bureaucratic apparatus of the Federal administration will hold its own. At the end of the war it will first of all be in possession. It will have outgrown initial difficulties and be in something like working order. It will have consolidated its position and have acquired enormous power. It will be a factor in its own right and stand ready to deal with the postwar emergency as it dealt with the war emergency. Political forces strong enough to liquidate the organs of the war economy as they were liquidated in 1919 are not in sight. There seems to be no reason why these organs should not succeed in establishing themselves as permanent institutions, especially as they will be in a position to serve the immediate interests of agriculture and of labor and hence derive support from these quarters. In this case a sort of *classe dirigente* may develop.

The nature, structure, and ideology of this managing class is not determined as yet. Many mutually exclusive possibilities exist both as to what it will eventually turn out to be and as to what it will eventually do. Disregarding all other aspects and placing ourselves on a purely economic standpoint, we may, however, out of a mash in full process of fermentation, select a few typical possibilities each of which corresponds to the views and interests of some existing subgroup.

1. The most obvious possibility is that the economic principles of the period immediately preceding the war will be applied to postwar problems—being consolidated and developed, revised and extended, according to circumstances. In this case the policy of

income-generating public expenditure would be continued, first in order to prevent or mitigate the postwar slump and after that as a permanent device for regulating the pulse of the nation's economic life. As the reader knows, this policy commands widespread support. The fear of the postwar slump may well silence such opposition as may be said to exist. And groups with completely different ultimate aims may agree on it because it is the easiest way toward all of them and carries the further advantage that none of them need be mentioned in advocating it.

Theorists are in the habit of dealing with this policy in the abstract. But its nature and consequences depend upon the complementary policies with which it is linked. In the case under discussion, these are taxation high enough and progressive enough to prevent private accumulation and in consequence the possibility that large-scale business should ever again, financially speaking, stand on its own feet and become independent of government; labor legislation that shifts questions of wages, hours, and factory discipline to the political sphere; and strict regulation, enforced by the threat of prompt prosecution, of the behavior of big business in every respect. Under these conditions, public income generation will automatically become permanent, quite irrespective of the factors stressed by the theories framed to prove its necessity from causes inherent in the saving-investment process of capitalist society.

Such a system will no doubt still be called capitalism. But it is capitalism in the oxygen tent—kept alive by artificial devices and paralyzed in all those functions that produced the successes of the past. The question why it should be kept alive at all is therefore bound to be put before long. Such concessions about relief from war rates of taxation and so on as are within practical politics, may temporarily change details of the picture and postpone the putting of that question, but cannot be expected to change essentials.

2. It will therefore be perfectly natural—in fact it may be a practical necessity—to take further steps toward state management.

To begin with, it is difficult to see what role will be left for non-public banking and finance in an economic world thoroughly dependent on government financing that is itself entirely independent of private voluntary saving. Government, to be sure, still goes through the motions of "borrowing" and "lending," pays and receives interest and so on. But the life has gone out of these forms and an administrative rationalization of what is actually being done could easily eliminate them. If we assume that capitalist methods will disappear gradually there will be a narrowing sphere of activity for banks as we know them also in the future. They may continue to keep accounts and to fill administrative functions for an indefinite time. But though this may facilitate transitions it does not alter the fact that, if we must stick to old words, government will develop into the sole banker.

Again, government spending as a permanent policy cannot fail to develop into governmental planning of investment. In fact, its failure to do so would be quite uneconomical. If government expenditure is to be the pivot of the economic process it stands to reason that the productive efforts propelled by that expenditure will in the end have to be directed by public authority. The government will from time to time have to proclaim a national goal which its expenditure is to serve—such as housing for the masses, completion of the electrification of the household, reorganization of the transport system and of urban life to make them fit the conditions created by the airplane—and to define the ways in which and the extent to which each particular goal is to be approached.

There is still another reason for this. Whatever the outcome of the war, the postwar world will hardly be a place for privately controlled trade and industrial venture. As to the first, it is not easy to see how private enterprise could cope with the conditions created by the immense differences as between countries in monetary and real cost of production that have developed of late.[1] From a purely commercial standpoint, and taking account of all the "rigidities" that will prevent adaptation, the United States might well be unable to export at all.[2] Quite apart from the political considerations that are bound to complicate the problem still further, international trade in commodities and services will have to be cut off from its old background of commercial calculation and have to be managed by political treaties, bilateral and multilateral. But this implies domestic public management just as the latter implies the public management of international economic relations.

As to the second, international industrial venture involving long-term investment, the need for government leadership, per-

[1] This position is not inconsistent, however, with the theory of comparative costs.

[2] The roots of this difficulty are in the prewar situation. One of the most curious contradictions in New Deal policy was its attempt to "liberalize" foreign trade while erecting a rigid economic structure at home.

haps on lend-lease lines, in an expansion that will inevitably carry imperialist features, is still more obvious. The spacious possibilities that open up under these heads should be noted not less than the sources such a system harbors of waste surpassing anything ever charged to the account of capitalism. It should also be noted that such a system leaves the managing bureaucracy free to allocate to private business as much or as little room as may be desired. Just as the TVA, a national venture, let contracts to private firms, so a similar national venture on the Yangtze, though initiated by government and controlled by it, may parcel out individual jobs to capitalist firms. Therefore, on the understanding that the essence of the bourgeois economy will be absent from the picture, we may call this system Guided Capitalism.

3. Some measures of nationalization will almost inevitably suggest themselves in a system of the type just discussed. Moreover, other measures—perhaps the nationalization or municipalization of utilities, of insurance, of mines—will be rendered easy by public support. It is difficult to foretell how far this tendency will go. The term "nationalization" does not sound well to every ear and it may be that other means of establishing no less complete public control, even if less rational and fraught with more friction, will be preferred by the political groups in power. But if the Federal government should follow this line to a significant extent, and if it should try to run the nationalized industries according to the principles of business rationality, Guided Capitalism would shade off into State Capitalism, a system that may be characterized by the following features: government ownership and management of selected industrial positions; complete control of government in the labor and capital market; government initiative in domestic and foreign enterprise.

4. It will always be a matter of taste whether a given way of running the economic engine be called socialist or not. On the one hand, disgruntled bourgeois spoke of socialism when the first municipal gas works and the first progressive income taxes put in appearance; on the other hand, socialist groups that are not "in on it" will never admit that anything not sanctified by Marxian doctrine can possibly be genuine socialism. Moreover, people care so much more for words than they do for things, that acceptance or avoidance of the term socialism may be dictated by tactical considerations. In this country, these considerations seem to tell against rather than for it so long as no violent break is on the cards.

If, however, we agree that advance on any of the lines we have briefly surveyed comes within the definition of gradual socialization, the problem narrows down considerably. Any approach to socialism other than by continued extension of government control and expropriation of the upper strata by taxation would no doubt meet resistance from the farm interest and from small and medium-sized business. Neither would put up a life-and-death fight in order to prevent the nationalization of big business—say, the corporations owning assets amounting to $50 million or more. But they presumably would fight against anything much more radical than this, particularly against anything which they recognized as a "revolution." Barring such a revolution which, while never impossible, cannot be expected to be successful, an amphibial state for the calculable future is certainly the most probable one. From a purely economic standpoint this may be regrettable. Such a state will suffer from a lot of frictions and inefficiencies that a return to the capitalist alternative or a resolute adoption of the socialist one would save, and it will not command the full motive power of either. On the other hand, amphibial states conserve many human values that would perish in others. Thus there may be as little reason for the fears of some as there is for the hopes of others.

CAPITALISM*

Reprinted from *Encyclopaedia Britannica,* 1946, Vol. IV, 801-807.

A society is called capitalist if it entrusts its economic process to the guidance of the private businessman. This may be said to imply, first, private ownership of nonpersonal means of production, such as land, mines, industrial plant and equipment; and, second, production for private account, *i.e.,* production by private initiative for private profit. But, third, the institution of bank credit is so essential to the functioning of the capitalist system that, though not strictly implied in the definition, it should be added to the other two criteria. Common parlance applies the adjective "capitalist" to almost all the phenomena of modern society, particularly when envisaged with reference to the socialist alternative. This article first presents an outline of historical developments (sections 1-4), then a summary of the economics and the sociology of capitalism (sections 5 and 6), followed by a brief survey of some of the principal topics usually discussed in connection with capitalism (sections 7 and 8); and by comments on the problem of the future of the capitalist order (section 9).

1. Early Capitalism.—Most of the features that define the capitalist order may be found in the ancient world, and particularly in its Graeco-Roman sector. There were factories producing for markets; there were bankers; and merchants that traded internationally. The upheavals and devastations that accompanied the fall of the western Roman empire never destroyed this capitalist trade and manufacture entirely. The warrior society and warrior civilization that rose from those ruins (feudalism) greatly differed, of course, from the businessman society and businessman civilization of the 19th century. But the former also contained elements of, and partly subsisted on, economic activities that differed from those of capitalist times only in technique and importance. Surveying the course of economic history, we find no sharp break anywhere, but only slow and continuous transformation. Need for protection largely accounts for the growth of fortified towns and for the concentration in them of industrial production and trade. The craft guilds —

corporations of the arts and trades — that had no facilities for trade at a distance, found their complement in the early trading companies — also primarily the products of the need for protection — and both developed together. The individual of supernormal energy who was irked by the strict regulations of the craft gilds moved out of the towns controlled by them, and either set up a workshop in his home where, with the assistance of apprentices and journeymen he was able to produce with more freedom and on a somewhat larger scale, or confined himself to furnishing raw materials to such "masters" and specialized in the commercial and financial task (domestic industry).

Interlocal and international trade was, however, by far the most important line of early capitalist endeavour. It was often associated with the business of providing for the financial needs of spiritual and temporal princes — the earliest form of international finance — and with the exploitation of the privileges or "concessions" — exclusive rights to mine, to trade, or to produce — that were sometimes granted in return. Fighting its way through the resisting framework of feudal society, this process of economic change slowly evolved greater freedom of property and lending and also the institutions of typically capitalist hue, such as the joint-stock company, the salable share, the bank and the bank deposit, the negotiable paper, the stock exchange. All these institutions and practices, including speculation, were well developed, at least in a number of business centres, by the middle of the 16th century, but none of them were then entirely new. Moreover, the public mind then reacted to the phenomena of capitalism in much the same way as it does in our time; it cried out against usury, speculation, commercial and industrial monopolies, cornering of commodities and other abuses, and the arguments used were, both in their common-sense content and in their one-sidedness, neither much worse nor much better than are the popular arguments of the 20th century. Governments reacted in sympathy. They dealt with the practical problems that presented themselves by means of regulations, the technical and administrative shortcomings of which must not be allowed to obliterate a fundamental similarity of intention with those of more recent times. This applies also to the extensive labour legislation of that epoch such as the Elizabethan Statute of Apprentices and Poor Law (*q. v.*) which, on the one hand, continued an old tradition and, on the other hand, embodied ideas so "modern" as index wages and arbitration.

Some economists, among whom it must suffice to mention Max Weber (*q. v.*), have felt the need of explaining the rise of capitalism by means of a special theory. But the problem such theories have been framed to solve is wholly imaginary and owes its existence to the habit of painting unrealistic pictures of a purely feudal and a purely capitalist society, which then raises the question what it was that turned the tradition-bound individual of the one into the alert profit hunter of the other. According to Weber, it was the religious revolution that, changing humanity's attitude toward life, produced a new spirit congenial to capitalist activity. We cannot go into the historical objections that may be raised against this theory. It is more important that the reader should realize that there is no problem. Nothing but proper attention to the details of the social and economic structure of the middle ages and of the economic history from the 8th to the 16th century is necessary in order to understand that transformation. Far from being stationary or tradition-bound or hostile to economic activity, the medieval world offered plenty of opportunity for rudimentary entrepreneurial venture. Success and failure taught their lessons. And each lesson produced an increment of capitalist practice and capitalist spirit alike. Thus, merely by functioning, the world of Charlemagne developed into the world of Luther and Calvin, of the Chigis (*q.v.*) and Fuggers (*q.v.*), of Charles V and Elizabeth. It still remains necessary, of course, to take into account all the particular events and circumstances that accelerated, retarded and shaped the process.

2. Mercantilist Capitalism.—Of particular interest are those events and circumstances which are extraneous to the logic of the capitalist process and must, from the standpoint of the latter, be considered as accidental. Such an accident was, for instance, the inflow of American silver and gold that superimposed silver and gold inflation on pre-existing inflationary tendencies and accelerated capitalist developments in one very obvious way and retarded them in another less obvious way. Much more important, however, was the circumstance, purely fortuitous though it was, that these capitalist developments impinged upon a social structure of extraordinary vitality whose ruling stratum, the feudal artisocracy headed by the families of sovereign positions, was able to harness the new wealth into the service of its own interests, traditions, and political goals. This symbiosis of two different social worlds was the dominant factor in European history from the 16th to the end of the 18th century and an important factor even during the 19th. In

particular, it accounts for the well-known economic policies of the so-called age of mercantilism (*see* MERCANTILE SYSTEM) which, roughly speaking, lasted until the end of the 18th century.

We behold the struggle of the rising national states. They all fostered domestic industry and supported it in its conquest of foreign markets; they mostly — though not so generally as has been often asserted — sided with employers against the workmen; those of them that were in a position to do so embarked upon careers of rival colonial enterprise and vied with one another in trying to secure the biggest possible share in the slave trade; and all this was geared to the one pivotal purpose of asserting and expanding national power by military force. These traits were indeed blurred and mitigated by many other issues, but on the whole the picture may be summed up in the phrase "doing business sword in hand." The finishing touch is supplied by our impression, though it is not uniformly borne out by such fragments of statistical information as we possess, that, while the wealth of the business class fairly rapidly increased, at least in western Europe, extreme poverty was widespread among the masses.

This pattern lends itself to the interpretation that has in fact been put upon it, viz., that the rising business class or, to use the Marxist term, the *bourgeoisie,* acting on the spur of its economic interest, was the propelling force behind mercantilist policy and, in particular, mercantilist aggressiveness. But the presence, in a position of supremacy, of a nonbourgeois stratum suggests another interpretation; the wars were often, and the incident taxation was always, contrary to the bourgeoisie's interest; the mercantilist state regulated industry and trade with a heavy hand; the rule of a growing bureaucracy was not congenial to the businessman's mind. The bourgeoisie indeed accepted that supremacy. It no doubt endeavoured to use to the full the profit possibilities offered by mercantilist policy and itself acquired in doing so something of the prevailing spirit of aggression. But its role is perhaps more truly described as that of a servant than that of a master. The importance of this question of interpretation is obvious: it makes all the difference to our view of the capitalist process whether we attribute observed tendencies toward economic nationalism and political aggression to its very nature or to a distortion of this nature by extra-capitalist factors. The history of the subsequent epoch when the business class really enjoyed ascendancy supports the later view.

3. INTACT CAPITALISM.—Accelerated change in technology and

organization that revolutionized first agriculture and then industry (*see* THE INDUSTRIAL REVOLUTION; last quarter of the 18th, first quarter of the 19th centuries) produced a significantly different social pattern which may be termed Intact Capitalism and prevailed substantially from the Napoleonic wars to the end of the 19th century. The familiar features of its political complement, liberalism, were laissez-faire (*q.v.*), in particular free trade (*q.v.*), and "sound money" (meaning unrestricted gold currency), or at least tendencies toward these goals; a pacific, though far from pacifist, attitude toward foreign nations and, though with many relapses, toward colonies; unprecedented respect for personal freedom not only in economic but in all matters; increasing "democratization," meaning extension of the suffrage and the secret ballot. For a time, the state and its bureaucracy were in full retreat. But nothing is more characteristic of the spirit of that age than its fiscal policy of which William E. Gladstone (*q.v.*) was the most representative as well as the most brilliant exponent. The principle of leaving individuals to themselves and of trusting their free interaction to produce socially desirable results cannot be better expressed than it was by the three rules which sum up that policy: that public expenditure should be limited to the minimum required for the essential services ("retrenchment"); that budgets should not only balance but display a surplus to be applied to the reduction of the national debt; and that taxation should serve no other purpose than that of raising the necessary revenue, and exert as little effect as possible on the distribution of income and on the channels of trade, from which it followed that it must be light. The income tax was an essential part of this program; but it was not less essential that it should be so low as to constitute a minor item in the taxpayer's total expenditure. We cannot enter into the question whether the social legislation of the period — protection to women and children, hours acts, factory acts, social insurance, the recognition of trade unions and of collective bargaining, etc. — was in accord with these policies or spelled deviation from them. We merely note that it was not absent.

This system, though well-defined and logically coherent, must of course be understood as a system of tendencies only. The heritage of the past and other obstructions prevented the full realization of its principles except in relatively few cases, of which English free trade is the most important instance. The adverse judgment passed upon these principles by conservative and socialist critics alike must be considered in the light of this fact and, let us add at once, in the light of the further fact that the economic history of that epoch, owing to its brevity, is unduly loaded with records of its childhood diseases, most of which were rapidly passing within its span. Such as they were, however, both tendencies and realizations bear the unmistakable stamp of the businessman's interests and still more of the businessman's type of mind. Moreover, it was not only policy, but the philosophy of national and individual life, the scheme of cultural values, that bore that stamp. Its materialistic utilitarianism (*q.v.*), its naïve confidence in progress of a certain type, its actual achievements in the fields of pure and applied science, the temper of its artistic creations, may all be traced to the spirit of rationalism that emanates from the businessman's office. For much of the time and in many countries the bourgeoisie did not rule politically. But even noncapitalist rulers espoused its interests and adopted its views. They were what they had not been before, its agents.

More definitely than in any other historical case these developments can be explained by purely economic causes. It was the success of capitalist enterprise that raised the bourgeoisie to its position of temporary ascendancy. Economic success produced political power, political power produced policies congenial to the capitalist process, and the latter in turn responded to these policies by further success. Thus the English bourgeoisie obtained free trade, and free trade in turn was a major factor in a spell of unprecedented economic expansion. The same example serves to show that the bourgeoisie was not the only or even the principal beneficiary of these developments. The much-derided "free breakfast table," more accurately, the untaxed exchange of industrial products for the raw materials and foodstuffs of newly opened countries, meant more for labour than did many spectacular reforms of later times. And labour was quite aware of the fact: though many individuals and minority groups challenged the capitalist system, the large majority of the manual workers of all countries accepted it, and was content to improve its position within it, through the period. For the rest, it was the age of steam and steel, of another industrial and agrarian revolution that, following upon the preceding one, once more transformed the economic world and subsided into a period of readjustment, 1873-97, that is, misleadingly, known as the Great Depression. There is a note of admiration for the performance of the system even in Karl Marx's and Friedrich Engels' (*q.v.*) *Communist Manifesto.* Looking back, however, we should be less impressed by the actual performance of that epoch than by the performance it rendered possible for the future.

4. THE MODERN PHASE (1898 and later).—Upon the Great Depression followed a period of intense prosperity, interspersed with short depressions, that was associated with the new electrical, chemical, automotive and rubber industries. It lasted until about 1912 and, indeed, amounted to yet another industrial revolution. Like the two preceding ones, this period issued into a period of predominantly depressive character interspersed with spells of prosperity, the longest and most intense of which occurred in the United States, 1923-29. In order to exclude at least those disturbances that were directly due to actual warfare, this period should be dated 1919-39. So far there was, except the *absolute* values of statistical figures, nothing new or unprecedented in the sequence of events. On the whole, the behaviour of industrial output, price levels, interest rates, profits, monetary and real wage rates, income and employment repeated the pattern made familiar by previous experience, and peculiar features are amply accounted for by war effects. It is important to note that, contrary to a widespread impression, this also applies to the world crisis, 1929-32: like every crisis, it was, of course, an historical individual, but its general features did not differ substantially from those of the comparable instances, 1826-30 and 1873-78.

Nevertheless, it is undeniable that this epoch witnessed a complete reversal of the attitude toward capitalism and of almost all the tendencies of the liberal epoch. The best method of showing this is to visualize the expectations that an observer might have formed in 1870 and to contrast them with what actually happened. He might have expected steady progress toward universal free trade; more and more peaceful foreign relations; reduction of armaments; decreasing tax burdens, removal of such obstacles to free enterprise as still remained; internationally unrestricted gold currencies; gradual development of security and other labour legislation within the increasing means provided by growing wealth. Instead, we find revival of protectionism from the first; growing antagonism between nations; expansion of armaments; rising public expenditure and taxes; increasing regulation of economic activity; increasing strain in the system of international gold monometallism that eventually resulted in its abandonment in favour of strictly managed national currencies; security and other labour legislations that did indeed develop according to expectation until 1914, but displayed a new spirit and acquired a new significance in Germany during the 1920s and in the

United States during the 1930s. Again, all this may be linked with corresponding changes in social structures, philosophies of life, schemes of values. The fundamental explanation, however, is much more complex and difficult than is generally realized, and cannot be attempted here. Instead, we shall briefly notice two important doctrines concerning the change that has come upon, or is supposed to have come upon, the economic process itself, the doctrine of the maturity of capitalism and the doctrine of imperialism.

The first, which may also be called the doctrine of vanishing investment opportunity, is not intended to explain the economic and political pattern of modern capitalist society as a whole. It limits itself to the propositions: (1) that the capitalist system has reached maturity in the sense of having substantially exhausted its possibilities of growth, particularly its opportunities for new investments on a large scale, both for technological reasons and because of the decreasing rate of increase of population; (2) that the whole scheme of capitalist society, particularly its saving habits, being geared to the task of exploiting such opportunities, the permanent depression of anaemia will result from their gradual disappearance; (3) that in this state of maturity or stagnation, the capitalist process can be kept going only by incessant injections of purchasing power by means of government deficit spending. This theory, mainly framed to account for the unsatisfactory conditions that prevailed in the United States (and in France) during the 1930s, is unsupported by any facts prior to 1932. Its wide appeal is, however, understandable: the public and the economic profession are equally apt to be more impressed by the real or supposed peculiarities of their own problems and troubles than by any analogies with conditions half a century ago.

The second explanation is the orthodox socialist theory, according to which "imperialism" is the last phase of capitalism. It has been developed, on a Marxist basis, by O. Bauer, R. Hilferding, V. I. U. Lenin, L. D. Trotsky, F. Sternberg and others. Competition among capitalist firms tends to eliminate all of them except a small number of giant concerns; these find themselves unable to use the productive capacity they have built up owing to the falling, or inadequately increasing, purchasing power of the masses; they are therefore driven to invading foreign markets and to excluding foreign products from their own markets; this state of things produces aggressive colonial and foreign policies and "imperialist" wars, which the proletariat then turns into the civil war of socialist revolution. This doctrine, even if stripped of its most obviously ideological elements, is open to serious objections. Three points, however, must be recorded in its favour: first, it does attempt what no other theory has attempted, viz., to subject the whole of the economic, political, and cultural pattern of the epoch that began in 1898 to comprehensive analysis by means of a clear-cut analytic schema; second, on the surface at least it is strikingly verified by some of the outstanding features of this pattern and some of the greatest events of this epoch; third, whatever may be wrong with its facts and interpretations, it certainly starts from a fact that is beyond challenge, the tendency toward industrial combination (*see* COMBINATION IN INDUSTRY) and the emergence of largest-scale concerns. Though both cartels (*q.v.*) and trusts (*q.v.*) antedate the epoch, the role of what is popularly called big business has so much increased in its course as to constitute one of its outstanding economic characteristics.

5. THE ECONOMICS OF CAPITALISM.—It must be borne in mind that capitalism cannot, any more than any other form of organization, be judged by economic results alone. Account must also be taken of the social and cultural achievements for which the capitalist process provided both the means and the psychological prerequisites. Moreover, as has been pointed out, any final appraisal really involves appraising an attitude toward life, a scheme of life's values, in short, a civilization. It is this fact which precludes agreement even among those who agree about the economic facts and their interpretation.

Not even the purely economic results of the capitalist process, however, are capable of exact measurement, still less of measurement by a single figure. The nearest approaches to such a figure, the various indices of total, agrarian, and industrial output that are available for the leading countries, over varying periods and in varying degrees of perfection, tend to understate actual performance by giving too little weight to new industries, taking insufficient or even no account of improving quality, and are inadequate also for other reasons. However, the often-repeated estimate of a 3% average annual rate of increase of total output, 1850-1910, may serve to give at least a vague idea. For the output of the U. S. *manufacturing* industries alone, a careful investigation (*see* Fabricant, *Output of Manufacturing Industry,* National Bureau of Economic Research, 1940) yielded, for 1899-1937, in spite of the world crisis and its aftermath, an increase of 276% (3.5% in the annual average) which, after various corrections, corresponds roughtly to a *per capita* increase of 100% in all finished processed goods produced by factories. While appraisal of such figures is not a simple matter, it is safe to assert that a repetition of this performance would eliminate anything that could reasonably be called poverty, *even if no part of capitalist incomes were, by means of taxation, diverted to purposes directly benefiting labour.* This conclusion presupposes, of course, that the relative share of labour in national incomes remains constant. But so far back as our statistical information carries us, this relative share, though fluctuating with cyclical phases, has in fact, contrary to Marxist prediction, displayed remarkable stability. On the absolute share and the course of real wages, *see* WAGES.

Few observers are in fact inclined to find fault with capitalism considered as an engine of production. Criticism usually proceeds either from moral or cultural disapproval of certain features of the capitalist system (*see* below, section 7), or from the short-run vicissitudes with which long-run improvement is interspersed (*see* below, section 8). At the moment, however, we are concerned with the problem how far the economic achievements of the capitalist *epoch* should be attributed to the capitalist *system.* For instance, it is often argued that observed developments were the fruits, *not* of capitalist enterprise *but* of the technological progress. It is true that the historical increase in output of commodities and services is not only or even primarily due to the increase of capital or of the working population, still less to increased skill or effort of the individual operative, but principally to improvements in technology and organization. But these are not independent of the capitalist system that, on the contrary, tends to call them forth by concentrating human energy upon economic tasks, by creating the rational attitude favourable to technological development, and by setting high prizes upon success in this field. For the rest, owing to the impossibility of experimental variation of conditions, we must look to economic theory in order to derive such answer as we can to the question whether observed results may reasonably be ascribed to the capitalist system.

The first thing to be noticed about the capitalist process is its evolutionary character. Stationary socialism would still be socialism but stationary capitalism is impossible, is, in fact, a contradiction in terms. For the central figure on the capitalist stage, the entrepreneur (*q.v.*), is concerned not with the *administration* of existing industrial plant and equipment but with the incessant *creation* of new plant and equipment, embodying new technologies that revolutionize existing industrial structures. This is the source of his profits (*see* PROFIT), so far as they exceed interest on owned capital and the remuneration of routine management and salesmanship, as well as the typical source of private capitalist fortunes. The other sources, ownership of appreciating natural resources, especially urban land, speculation, financial piracy, and saving from current income are of but secondary importance. The financing of this activity is the essential function of bank credit, which removes from the path of the industrial innovator the requirement of ownership of capital. All the typical phenomena of capitalism, all its achievements, problems and vicissitudes, including the trade cycle (*q.v.*), derive from this process. Nevertheless traditional theory is primarily a theory of the current management of resources. The points most relevant to our subject may be summed up as follows:

If in all markets of products and services sellers and buyers be so numerous that none of them is able to influence price perceptibly by his own individual action (hypothesis of perfect competition. [*see* COMPETITION IN INDUSTRY]) then it can be proved that there will be a tendency towards a determined state of the economic organism, the so-called equilibrium state, in which: (1) all firms will expand their production to the point at which the current price just covers the cost of producing an additional increment of product; (2) all resources including labour are fully employed; and (3) a competitive rate of interest and a competitive rate of earnings of management being counted as costs, all profits above costs vanish. These propositions do not establish, as many 19th-century economists believed, that competitive capitalism tends to produce ideal results. But they do serve to dispel certain gross errors, such as that an economic process which is not consciously planned by a central agency must necessarily be chaotic; or that action guided by the profit motive must, because of this fact alone, be less efficient in satisfying consumers' wants than would be action by an agency guided by their interest alone. The fact that a perfectly competitive capitalist system would tend, in the sense defined by proposition (1), to maximise total output, together with certain corollaries concerning distribution, has induced the best theorists among modern socialists not only to drop the Marxist objections but also to frame their own plan for the socialist form of society upon this model and to base their criticism of capitalism, so far as it is not directed against the effects of private thrift (*see* below, section 8), upon the deviations of capitalist practice from perfect competition. It is indeed obvious that none of those three propositions applies to monopoly (*q.v.*) or even to monopolistic competition, *i.e.*, to cases where firms are in a position to fix their prices at will within a certain range instead of being constrained to accept a current market price. In these cases which are, of course, much more frequent than are cases of perfect competition, outputs are not maximized, excess capacity (*see* below, section 8) and surplus profits appear even in equilibrium, and existing industrial positions are exploited and protected by quasi-monopolistic practices.

Criticism on these scores derives support from the public's impulsive aversion to anything to which the label monopoly can be affixed and has, mainly for this reason, met with considerable political success. But it has no general validity, as distinguished from validity in individual instances. The proposition that monopolists will sell smaller quantities of product at higher prices than will firms in conditions of perfect competition is true only under the proviso that other things — cost structures in particular — be strictly equal, and therefore has but little practical importance. Almost without exception, largest-scale concerns do alter the cost structure of their industry, by introducing new methods of production and in other ways that are beyond the reach of numerous competing concerns of medium size. Therefore it does not follow that their outputs are actually smaller and their prices actually higher than would be the outputs and prices with the methods within the reach of perfectly competitive business. In fact, the behaviour of indices of manufacturing output in the era of mergers and big concerns lends some support to the opposite view. Also it is clear that the potentialities of mass production can be fully realized only by concerns that are beyond the size compatible with perfect competition. Finally, the wages paid in the largest concerns are, more often than not, higher than the wages paid elsewhere for comparable work.

6. THE CLASS STRUCTURE OF CAPITALIST SOCIETY.—The classes of traditional economic theory, such as landowners, capitalists, workmen, are functional categories, not living and acting sociological entities. Classes in the latter sense, and the corresponding concepts of class consciousness, class action, class war were introduced by Karl Marx. Choosing ownership of means of production for sole criterion, he recognised two classes only, capitalists and proletarians. But this scheme, though it served his purpose and though it had the further advantage of linking up with the popular distinction between haves and have-nots, rich and poor, is next to valueless for purposes of analysis. On the one hand, even if we disregard

the presence of non-capitalist strata — the "symbiosis" emphasised above — and confine ourselves to the classes created by the capitalist process, it still spells distortion and not simplification to reduce them to two. In order to understand the economics and politics of the capitalist epoch, it is essential to see the co-operative and antagonistic interactions of, at least, the classes associated with the control of large, medium and small business; the farmers who differ so significantly from the other business classes that there is no point in including them with one of these; the *rentier* class ("capitalists" in a narrower but more useful sense); the professional class; the clerical ("white collar") class; the skilled workers; the unskilled workers. On the other hand, it is equally essential to realise that these classes, and still more such classes as rich and poor, by virtue of their very nature, do not admit of clearly defined border *lines,* but shade off into each other across broad border *zones.*

Class distinctions are perhaps inevitable in any social group of any size and complexity. They have already developed in soviet Russia. They produce, and are in turn buttressed by, what is usually referred to as "connection." But in capitalist society they are further buttressed by the presence or absence of inherited wealth and therefore present, to the casual observer, a misleading impression of stability: because there are always industrialists, bankers, farmers, labourers, etc., and because the corresponding economic and social positions are as a rule passed on from father to son, we are apt to think of these classes as if they consisted of a self-perpetuating set of families and as if rise into a "higher" class, and fall from it into a "lower," were exceptional occurrences. This opinion, though implied in widely accepted social ideologies, is the exact opposite of the truth. It is one of the outstanding characteristics of the social structure of capitalism that its "higher" strata incessantly lose members to, and incessantly recruit themselves from, its "lower" strata and that this incessant rise and fall in general proceeds relatively quickly: the slogan "three generations from overalls to overalls" expresses a great deal of truth.

While this is rarely denied explicitly, no agreement seems possible on another question that is not less important for our general picture of capitalism, viz., whether the kind of business success that spells ascent in capitalist society is causally related to the presence of personal qualities that the observer believes to be socially desirable or undesirable or, to put it differently, whether social ascent and descent through success or failure in business spells positive or negative social selection. Partisans of the capitalist system almost invariably attribute success in business, in the broad average, to superior moral stamina and ability, opponents not less regularly to either "luck" or absence of moral inhibitions. Although industrial and family history, as well as other sources, afford sufficient material for arriving at an answer, the question has not received from serious scholars all the attention it deserves. In the special case — which is not unimportant quantitatively — where ascent through successful enterprise starts from a working class environment, it is safe to assert that supernormal will power and intelligence constitute the most important of all ascertainable causal factors. Other cases, while frequently suggesting a similar inference, present greater difficulties of interpretation. Unrealistic ideas about the size and nature of what is commonly called the "leisure class" are another obstacle to arriving at a life-like picture of capitalist society as it really is.

7. Exploitation and Inequality.—As we have seen above (section 5), to evaluate capitalism is to evaluate a civilization in all its aspects. The complexity of such a task is, however, not the only reason why agreement is not to be expected. Another is that moral and cultural *judgments* presuppose moral and cultural *standards* that are matters of individual preference and beyond the range of scientific proof or disproof. All that can be done about them from a scientific standpoint is (1) to establish the truth or falsity of such statements of fact as may enter into those judgments and (2) to point out the economic and cultural consequences to be expected from giving effect to them. The two topics of this section illustrate this truth.

In itself, the statement that capitalism involves exploitation of man by man conveys nothing except ethical disapproval. Recognising this, Marx tried to give it more definite content by means of his theory of exploitation: starting from the propositions that economic values of commodities tend to be proportional to the number of hours of labour that enter into their production (labour-theory of value, derived from David Ricardo [*q.v.*]) and that in capitalist society labour is a commodity, he went on to argue that the workmen will receive wages equal to the value of their labour, which is proportional to the number of hours of labour that enter into the production of their labour force (or of the commodities and services required in order to rear, train, feed, clothe, house . . . the workmen) and, further, that the product of their work will similarly sell at its value, which is proportional to the numbers of hours the workmen are constrained to work. Since workmen can work more hours than it takes to produce their labour force, there is a positive difference between the value of products and the value of the labour force, the surplus value, which goes to the capitalist employer. This is what constitutes exploitation. The argument is open to fatal objections and is no longer upheld by any economists except the Marxists of strictest observance. The other attempt at giving meaning to the term has been made by a group of English theorists. Whereas Marx's theory also applies to the case of perfect competition, there is, according to these theorists, no exploitation in this case; and whereas Marx's theory applies only to labour, any factor of production may suffer exploitation. This will happen whenever, owing to deviations of practice from the competitive model, the share of a factor falls short of what it would receive if perfect competition prevailed. It should be observed that, even if it were possible to agree on what constitutes exploitation, this would not necessarily determine the judgment to be pronounced. For exploitation, even if admitted, might still be the means of providing for economic or cultural needs that we may not be prepared to sacrifice.

The general problem of social inequality cannot be considered in this article. We must confine ourselves to a single type of inequality, the inequality of income (for illustrative figures, *see* WEALTH AND INCOME, DISTRIBUTION OF). In capitalist society this inequality is due to the facts (1) that incomes are the result of pricing processes and reflect the market values of products and productive services (this, as is easy to see, also has an important *equalizing* effect), and (2) that, once acquired, wealth may be transmitted by inheritance. The first fact is essential in the sense that a society from which it were completely eliminated could no longer be called capitalist; the second is not inherent in the logic of the capitalist plan, but so deeply rooted in the structure of capitalist society as to be practically inseparable from it. Again, it should be borne in mind that, in itself, disapproval of this inequality from the standpoint of equalitarian ideals expresses nothing beyond the critic's personal feelings of fitness or justice. These differ widely. The critic may disapprove, on religious or other grounds, of any inequality whatever; or he may reserve disapproval for particular kinds or aspects of inequality, such as "inequality of opportunity," inequalities of income due to inheritance, all inequalities not due to inequality of effort, etc. Errors of fact or reasoning may, however, enter into statements of particular reasons for ethical disapproval. One of the most common ones is the belief that the majority of people is poor *because* a minority is rich.

Appraisal of the purely economic effects of inequality depends mainly, though by no means wholly, upon our views (1) on the relation of inequality to economic motives, and (2) on private thrift. Looking back into the past, we can hardly fail to perceive the prime importance of the stimulating atmosphere of inequality. The lure of big prizes coupled with the threat of complete destitution no doubt produced a scheme of motivation of perhaps unique effectiveness. The importance of inequality *within* the highest income brackets should be particularly noticed. A single spectacular success may draw far more brains and means into an industry than would be attracted to it by the same sum if more equally divided. To this extent current views about unnecessarily or even absurdly high rewards and about the total cost to society of entrepreneurial performance should be modified. Under modern circumstances this argument has lost some of its importance, and there is room for difference of opinion on the question what weight should be attached to it for the future. But in any case it should not be forgotten that, whatever its weight, this argument also covers the case of inequality through inheritance: the privileged position of the entrepreneur's family may be more important as a motive than any desire for personal position or enjoyment.

So long as economists were practically unanimous in considering thrift or saving as the principal requisite for the expansion of the physical apparatus of industry (capital formation), or even for all economic progress, the most important, and indeed a decisive, economic argument for inequality was that the bulk of saving is done by the higher incomes and that equalisation by share-the-wealth policies would hence paralyse the very process that operates to raise the standard of life of the masses. But that practical unanimity does no longer exist. The classical theory of the role of saving, much too absolutely stated by its sponsors, was bound to lose ground, as it had repeatedly done before, in times of prevalent unemployment. During the 1930s, an increasing number of economists adopted the opposite view, viz., that saving, withholding income elements from being expanded on consumers' goods, has a depressing effect on the economic process and thus impedes, instead of fosters, the expansion of plant and equipment. It ought to have been admitted from the first that the persistence of saving habits during a depression may make things worse than they otherwise would be. Larger claims on behalf of the newer theory are of doubtful validity. The support it lends to prevalent political attitudes toward capitalism should, however, be noticed.

8. Unemployment and Waste. Planning by a central agency, whatever else it may or may not be able to accomplish, can certainly be expected to mitigate the trade cycle. Therefore, so far as involuntary unemployment (*q.v.*) is an inevitable concomitant of cyclical depressions, it may with justice be placed to the debit of capitalism's account. This also covers technological unemployment irrespective of whether or not we include it with cyclical unemployment, on the ground that the investment characteristic of prosperity in part finances labour-saving technologies: in either case, a central agency is in a position to plan technological advance in such a way as to minimize unfavourable effects it may have on employment. However, in order to see this fact in the proper perspective, it must be borne in mind that in many important instances the introduction of new technologies has directly increased employment opportunities; that where it did not, the resulting unemployment has been but temporary, though often severe; and that, so far as we know, the unemployment *percentage* has not, until 1929, displayed any tendency to increase over time, that is to say, that the capitalist process has always absorbed, *at increasing real wage rates,* not only the unemployment it generated but also the increase in population. Interpretation of the persistent unemployment, 1933-39, that was particularly severe in the United States and France, is the subject of a controversy ("reform *vs.* recovery") greatly influenced by political preferences. No scientifically reliable conclusions can in any case be based on the experience of seven years.

The above argument in favour of a centrally planned economy may be extended, with varying degrees of confidence, to other types of involuntary unemployment as well as to the numerous cases that may be called voluntary or involuntary with equal justice. An example will illustrate the most conspicuous of these. If a trade union succeeds in keeping wage rates abnormally high within its jurisdiction, this will cause unemployment among its members but may nevertheless draw newcomers to its waiting list who will also be unemployed. Both members and newcomers are involuntarily unemployed from the standpoint of the individual workmen, but their unemployment is caused by the voluntary policy of their directing agency. It may be argued that such unemployment would possibly be nonexistent in a perfectly planned society. These cases, however, serve to bring out an aspect of planning which is more or less present in all. In part, unemployment is the price workmen and their organizations pay for the freedom they enjoy in capitalist society. In order to be fully effective in eliminating the one, the planning authority would have also to eliminate the other and to adopt the principle enunciated by Trotsky: who does not obey, *i.e.*, undertake the work assigned to him at the wages fixed by the authority, shall not eat.

In the past, criticism of unemployment primarily emphasized the sufferings of the unemployed. For the future this aspect has lost much of its importance, because the capitalist process may be expected to produce adequate means for supporting them. But there still remains the loss to society of the potential products of their services and also of the services of other factors of production that may be unemployed or underemployed along with labour. This loss, largely attributable to the trade cycle, is indeed the most important element in the indictment of capitalism on the score of waste ("poverty in [potential] plenty"). But there are others. Thus, excess capacity is not entirely avoidable in any form of economic organization, but certain types of it are peculiar to monopolistic competition (*see* above, section 5); even perfect competition does not exclude wasteful multiplication of service; much of the energy of some of a nation's best brains is absorbed by struggles — between concerns and against regulating bureaucracies — that do not serve, or serve only remotely, productive efficiency; in important instances natural resources have been used uneconomically and without regard to the more remote future. Facts may be adduced in support of all these and other headings. The obvious inference, however, should not be drawn without due attention to the following points: (1) against some of those types of waste must be set compensating advantages; for instance, multiplication of service may be the best guarantee of excellence of service; excess or reserve capacity may have its uses in national emergencies; (2) some of the wastes observed are not due to the logic of the capitalist process but to the prevailing hostility to it, which produces protective behaviour often harmful to efficiency; (3) *all* those sources of waste must be viewed in connection with the evolutionary character of capitalism; much that appears as unrelieved waste if considered as an incident of a stationary economy, ceases to do so when viewed as an incident of a rapidly progressive one; (4) no machine being 100% efficient, appraisals of efficiency are essentially relative to the quality of available substitutes; it is a serious as well as common mistake to overlook the sources of waste that may be inherent in alternative arrangements and, in particular, to compare the *reality* of capitalism with an *ideal* picture of bureaucratic socialism.

9. The Future of Capitalism.—This problem, naturally first raised by socialist writers, Karl Marx in particular and, partly under Marxist influence, by the economists of the German historical school, has become a standard topic of popular discussion. This fact greatly increases the difficulty of stating it with precision and of distinguishing the various issues involved. The following comments may, however, assist the reader in forming his opinion.

(a) In most writings on the subject, there is an obvious association between prognosis and preference: there cannot be any doubt but that, in this as in other matters, people are apt to foresee what they desire. This tends not only to vitiate argument and presentation of facts but also to confuse two issues that should be carefully kept distinct. It is one thing to believe that the survival of capitalist institutions is desirable or undesirable; and quite another thing to believe that they will or will not survive. The first is a matter of personal preference; only the second constitutes a problem that may be attacked by scientific methods.

(b) Karl Marx was the first to realize the importance of this distinction and to formulate correctly the fundamental scientific question involved, viz., whether or not there are observable tendencies, inherent in the capitalist process as we know it, which, if allowed to work themselves out fully, will destroy the capitalist and produce the socialist system. Scientific prognosis — medical or other — can never mean more than the assertion or denial of the presence of such tendencies, and it is in this sense only, not in the sense of a prophecy, that the term "inevitable" must be understood. In Marx's affirmative answer to that question, it is necessary to separate the arguments, drawn from his analysis of the capitalist process, by which he supported his answer and the answer itself. *All* his arguments, but in particular the one that asserts that labour will be goaded into revolution by steadily increasing misery, can be proved to be untenable. But this does not dispose of the answer itself, because it is possible to arrive at a correct result by faulty methods. The case for the affirmative answer is in fact strong. We observe that, as the capitalist epoch wears on, the individual leadership of the entrepreneur tends to lose in importance and to be increasingly replaced by the mechanized teamwork of specialized employees within large corporations; that the institutions and traditions that sheltered the structure of capitalism tend to wear away; that the capitalist process by its very success tends to raise the economic and political position of groups that are hostile to it; and the capitalist stratum itself, mainly owing to the decay of the bonds of family life that in turn may be traced to the "rationalizing" influence of the capitalist process, tends to lose some of the grip and part of the scheme of motivation which it formerly had. Other arguments, such as the one from exhaustion of the objective possibilities of private enterprise (*see* above, section 4), may be unconvincing. But the ones just glanced at are quite sufficient. It should be noticed, however, that they establish no more than the presence of a tendency toward the shifting of economic activity from the private to the public sphere, or, as we may also put it, toward increasing *bureaucratisation* of economic life, coupled with an increasing dominance of the labour interest. So far as the tendency in question is concerned, transitional states might be in prospect which, while greatly differing from the economic and cultural pattern of intact capitalism, would yet fail to attain full-fledged socialism for an indefinite time. In fact, they might equally well be called the one or the other, according to the requirements of political warfare. The only reason why Marx used to stress sudden transition by revolution was that, as was natural in his time, he greatly overrated the bourgeoisie's power and will to resist gradual changes that are contrary to its interest or uncongenial to its scheme of life.

(c) We have had occasion, however (*see* above, section 2), to emphasize the importance, for the interpretation of social processes, of circumstances that are extraneous to what may be termed the inherent logic of an economic system. Applying this principle to prognosis, we cannot fail to realize that World War I is an instance in point. Whether or not economically conditioned, it visibly accelerated, in Europe at least, existing tendencies unfavourable to the survival of capitalist institutions. On the one hand, it produced situations of stress that, though due to a chance combination of factors, caused permanent breakdown of social patterns which without such stresses might have persisted indefinitely; this is strikingly exemplified by the case of the U.S.S.R. On the other hand, it caused a permanent change in the distribution of political weights that produced policies which prevented the capitalist engine from working according to design and thus further undermined allegiance to the system; this is exemplified by the case of England. A similar argument applies, of course, to the war that broke out in 1939: in the 1920s some competent observers used to qualify a prognosis otherwise favourable to the survival of capitalism by the proviso "unless there be another world war."

(d) Much light may be shed (1945) on the *immediate* future by visualizing how far the process of transformation has advanced already. Government control of the capital and labour markets, of price policies and, by means of taxation, of income distribution is already established and needs only to be complemented systematically by government initiative in indicating the general lines of production (housing programs, foreign investment) in order to transform, even without extensive nationalization of industries, *regulated,* or *fettered,* capitalism into a *guided* capitalism that might, with almost equal justice, be called socialism. Thus, prediction of whether or not the capitalist order will survive is, in part, a matter of terminology. If it is to be more than that, it depends upon the likelihood of a reversal not only of existing tendencies, but also of an established state of things, and therefore upon the answer to the question where the political forces are to come from that will be able and willing to effect such a reversal.

Bibliography.

Practically the entire economic literature deals with problems of capitalism. The general reader's best approach to a vivid and realistic view leads through historical works, such as P. Mantoux, *La Révolution Industrielle* (1906, rev. transl. 1928); J. H. Clapham, *Economic History of Modern Britain* (1926-38); V. Clark, *History of Manufactures in U. S.* (1929); H. See, *Les Origines du Capitalisme Moderne* (1926, transl. 1928); W. Sombart, *Der Moderne Kapitalismus* (1924-27) W. Meakin, *The New Industrial Revolution* (1928). For Weber's theory of the rise of capitalism, *see* R. H. Tawney, *Religion and the Rise of Capitalism* (1926). For the Marxist theory of capitalism, *see* P. M. Sweezy, *The Theory of Capitalist Development* (1942). On the *"Recruiting of the Employing Classes from the Ranks of the Wage-Earners in the Cotton Industry," see* the study by Chapman and Marquis, *Journal of the Royal Statistical Society*, vol. 72; on a cognate subject, F. Redlich, *History of American Business Leaders* (1940). Also *see* E. J. Benn, *Confessions of a Capitalist* (1925); M. H. Dobb, *Capitalist Enterprise and Social Progress* (1925); F. D. Graham, *Social Goals and Economic Institutions* (1942); F. A. V. Hayek, *The Road to Serfdom* (1944); E. M. Queeny, *The Spirit of Enterprise* (1943); J. A. Schumpeter, *Capitalism, Socialism and Democracy* (1942); B. and S. Webb, *The Decay of Capitalist Civilization* (1921).

(J.A. Sr.)

THE DECADE OF THE TWENTIES

Reprinted from *American Economic Review Supplement,* May 1946, 1-10.

Discussion of a span of past history is one of the best methods for testing what economic analysis can and cannot do and for shedding light both on the common ground and on the differences of opinion between us. In order to serve these purposes, I am going to ask two questions with reference to the economic history of the United States in the twenties of this century: Do we agree as to the facts? How far can we agree as to interpretation? In the third part of my paper it will be convenient to sum up separately about the causation of the "world crisis" 1929–32.

I

The statistical contours of the economic process are given by a number of time series that are familiar to everyone. Debits outside of New York City are perhaps the most important *single* index of the pulse of economic life. But most of us will, I think, agree that we cannot make much headway without considering the following "fundamental" series: total output; employment; price level; interest (commercial paper rate, bond yield, customers' line of credit rate, Federal Reserve bank rates); deposits (minus interbank deposits); income, wages (rates and pay roll, both monetary and real), and profits (dividends); consumption and investment expenditure; and that, for a variety of purposes, we also need series on: stock and bond prices, brokers, business and consumers' loans; issues; government income generating expenditure; net foreign balance (gold movements, foreign lending); LCL (or department store sales); residential and other building (separately); individual and group prices. This is by no means all, of course, but I submit that this list includes the bulk of the statistical information which most of us will require for purposes of diagnosis and which is analogous to the information a doctor assembles in the course of his investigation when we go to him for a check-up. I further submit, first, that a large amount of difference of opinion exists between us concerning the value and statistical merits and demerits of those items as well as concerning the relative merits of different series for the same item; the very meaning being controversial in the case of total output.

Second, I submit that these differences of opinion do not, in general, cause corresponding differences of opinion as regards the processes these series are intended to measure. For instance, we all agree substantially on the general features of the actual movements of commodity prices at wholesale no matter what our opinion is about the degree of excellence of the particular commodity-price index used.

And, third, I submit that, so far as I can see, there are only two major exceptions to this statement. First, we disagree as to whether or not the bulk of time deposits was, *during the twenties*, "the same thing" as demand deposits so that we should be nearer the true facts of the monetary process if we work with demand plus time deposits than if we exclude the latter and connect them with "saving." Myself, I hold the former opinion. Second, we disagree as to the amount of savings. This, however is largely a matter of definition which should be settled according to the purpose in hand. If this purpose is to ascertain whether household receipts that are costs to firms were or were not "withheld" from the stream of expenditure, then it seems to me to be proper to exclude from the estimate of savings, realized but unspent capital gains; and to consider sums spent (however financed) on the acquisition of homes simply as part of household expenditure for this is what they actually are. To say that these sums were saved and that this saving was "offset" by "investment" in the homes seems to me to be needlessly circuitous at best, and suggestive of erroneous theories at worst. If, then, we define household expenditure on the lines suggested by these comments, it is the undeniable fact that, during the twenties, households habitually overspent their current receipts from firms[1] or that the algebraic sum of household savings was negative throughout, the deficit being covered by borrowing and by drawing upon speculative gains. This fact must be seen in connection with the other fact that income-generating expenditure by public bodies was positive and nonnegligible throughout, except in 1929.

Time series never tell the whole tale and must be supplemented by a detailed historical account of what actually happened in the economic organism. The economic history of the twenties has been written by very many authors. Since it is difficult to write history without implying some theory about causal relations between the phenomena reported, we shall not be surprised to find that much of that work is vitiated by preconceived notions of the authors. But I submit, first, that the essential facts have nevertheless been stated with adequate accuracy and, second, that we substantially agree about them. They are indeed familiar to all of us. For instance, we know all of us about the essential features of the various downturns and upturns and their different impacts upon different industries and parts of the country; the actual

[1] In the case of noncorporate business these receipts have been put equal to Professor Kuznets' figures for "entrepreneurial withdrawals." The rest of the net income of noncorporate business has been allocated to business savings.

behavior of the Federal Reserve System and of all banks; the booms in residential building, in utilities, in state and municipal public works; the developments in the new industries and in the "old new industries," especially the automobile industry and its satellites; the ups and downs in the agrarian sector and in foreign investment and trade; and so on.

II

The highest ambition an economist can entertain who believes in the scientific character of economics would be fulfilled as soon as he succeeded in constructing a simple model displaying all the essential features of the economic process by means of a reasonably small number of equations connecting a reasonably small number of variables. Work on this line is laying the foundations of the economics of the future and should command the highest respect of all of us. A few immediately valuable results it has produced already. In this paper I shall not, however, avail myself of any opportunities offered by this type of research[2] because, with the same frankness with which I have expressed my high opinion of its future, I must confess to a feeling that at present the premature and irresponsible application to diagnosis, prognosis, or recommendation, of what of necessity are as yet provisional and flimsy constructions can produce nothing but error and can only result in discrediting this pioneer work.

Nor shall I avail myself of any of the theories that attempt to explain economic processes in terms of monetary mechanics; that is, theories which attribute a dominant role in the economic process to such items as interest rates, deposits ("supply of money"), and the like. Take, e.g., the almost ludicrously exaggerated opinions many economists held in the twenties concerning the power of open-market operations over business situations. We then entered upon a period of reaction against the opposite views that had prevailed before and some will even today expect from a paper on that period nothing but a discussion of the play of monetary quantities. But I hope and believe that we are growing out of this and I expect, with more confidence than I should have felt ten years ago, assent to the proposition that analysis of the economic phenomena of any given period must proceed from the economic facts that produce them and not from the monetary aggregates that result from them.

Beyond this, I have only one general principle to posit. No decade in the history of politics, religion, technology, painting, poetry and what not ever contains its own explanation. In order to understand the religious events from 1520 to 1530, or the political events from 1790 to 1800, or the developments in painting from 1900 to 1910, you must

[2] The most important opportunity of this kind is afforded, I think, by the theory of inventory cycles; see, e.g., the remarkable work done by L. Metzler.

survey a period of much wider span. Not to do so is the hallmark of dilettantism. Evidently the same applies to economic history. The quickest way to give effect to this principle is to take our clew from the felicitous phrase, "the Economic Revolution of the Twenties." Only we must interpret it in the same sense in which Sir John Clapham maintained that an earlier economic revolution occurred, not in the last decades of the eighteenth century but in the first decades of the nineteenth. This is true if it means that *effects* did not fully manifest themselves—especially in the cotton textile and machinery industries—until the twenties and thirties of the nineteenth century. It would not be true to locate the *sources* of these effects in those two decades: the decisive industrial events did occur in the last quarter of the eighteenth. Similarly, everyone knows that towards the end of the ninteenth century and in the first decade of the twentieth a number of industrial events occurred that were bound to change the world's economic structure fundamentally but, partly owing to the "first" World War, did not take full effect until the twenties. To mention but one instance, it was not until then that the technological changes in agriculture that had occurred from the nineties on disclosed their power to dislodge eventually the majority of farmers in all industrialized countries. The response of the business organism to the impact of changes of this type adequately explains the general features of that period in the United States. For other countries, England in particular, this explanation must be supplemented by appeal to additional factors specific to their individual historical patterns.

History, if we would but listen, would teach us all the essentials about those processes. Response to the consequences of industrial revolutions has never meant undiluted depression. If we had time, it would be possible to show how and why it also produces spells of prosperity. But it always meant a depressive undertone, a tendency for prices, profits, and interest rates to fall, for output (real incomes) and, owing to the incident dislocations, unemployment to rise, and so on through a familiar list. And it meant precisely these things in the twenties: history—compare, for instance, the seventies and eighties of the nineteenth century—substantially repeated itself, even the booms in residential building and in public works duly putting in appearance as they had done in similar conditions before. In Europe, particularly unfavorable conditions, *fiscal policy among other things*, accentuated the depressive tendency. In the United States, particularly favorable conditions, *fiscal policy among other things*, accentuated—as they had in the eighties—the spells of prosperity, so much so that people lost sight of that tendency—though it was visible enough below a surface dominated by the speculative craze; and indulged in talk about prosperity plateaus—

though we may sense suppressed uneasiness in the applause that invariably greeted stabilization programs. Nevertheless, the economists who wrote the report of the President's Conference on Unemployment were not so wrong as it might seem when they declared (1929!): "Our situation is fortunate . . . we have a boundless field before us." They only forgot that the road into this boundless field leads through a succession of valleys.

Of all the points that should be made, two only can be mentioned. First, throughout the twenties, as always, prosperity as well as recession was essentially "spotty." That is to say, for no year is it possible to render a lifelike picture only by means of national totals or averages. Conditions always differed in different industrial and geographical sectors, and it is an essential feature of the process that they did. If, in a given year, one industry makes 100 millions and another loses 100 millions, these two figures do not add up to zero or, to put it less paradoxically, the course of subsequent events generated by this situation is not the same as that which would follow if both had made zero profits. This is one of the reasons why theories that work with aggregates only are so misleading and why they bid fair to achieve what institutionalist arguments have failed to achieve; namely, to convert all of us to institutionalism. The few general features by which I tried to characterize what I have called the depressive tendency of the twenties must be understood in this sense: they impinged upon different sectors of the economy in entirely different ways; no diagnosis of what actually happened can be derived from them alone.

Second, it is not only lack of time which motivates my silence on Federal Reserve policy. In a detailed picture it would have its place, of course. But I do not think that, speaking broadly, it made much difference one way or another. Federal Reserve policy is not entitled to such praise as we may feel disposed to bestow on maintaining the "Coolidge prosperity"; on the other hand, it seems to me plainly absurd to blame it for "not having prevented the depression." The Board was in no position to do either and its policy turns out, on analysis, to have been but little affected by the theories forged in glorification or criticism of its policy. The wider questions whether more resolute inflation or else more resolute deflation would have been indicated call for completely different answers according to the scheme of values of the man who asks them. The various "rigidities" in the system, real and alleged, seem to me to have been of minor causal importance in the economic processes of the twenties. Before going on, I shall briefly present a set of supplementary facts that will indicate the lines on which a fuller analysis would proceed.

1. *The Monetary Process.* Total demand plus time deposits (including

those in savings banks) minus government deposits plus currency in circulation which amounted to 20.3 billions in 1914 and to 38.5 billions in 1920 rose to 54.5 in 1929 (about 141 per cent of the 1920 figure). Note that the so-called "deflation" in 1921 produced, for the yearly figure, a fall of only 0.36 billion. Total income payments to individuals rose from 68.5 billion in 1920 to 82.4 billion in 1929, or by about 20 per cent. Bank debts of corporations fell throughout (especially in 1924), though the reduction was mostly well below the increase in other items of "outside funds." Nineteen twenty-nine shows the familiar phenomenon of substitution of stock to long-term debt particularly clearly. The long interest rate was on the downgrade and so was, *properly interpreted*, the tendency of short rates, though this tendency was obscured by the abnormal events of 1927–29 which also pushed up rates on customers' loans. Cash balances of nonfinancial corporations, 1926–29, were fairly stable at about 7 billions, with a moderate tendency to rise. All this must be seen in connection with the behavior of consumers' credit and the habit of households to spend part of their speculative gains, especially on homes. The picture is perfectly clear: if a loose monetary rein and liberal spending were all that is needed to insure prosperity, we should indeed have had a "prosperity plateau." But large-scale business certainly used the monetary ease in order to consolidate its financial structure and to gain independence from banks. The suggestive increases in 1922, 1924, 1927 in the investment item of banks outside of New York City should be particularly noticed as indicative of an important structural change in banks' assets.

2. *Prices and production.* After the downward revision of prices in 1920–22, which was relatively uniform (41 per cent for finished products, 45 for raw materials, 48 for farm products), the falling tendency remains perceptible under a fluctuating surface, but there can be as little doubt that it was not what it would have been under a stricter monetary management as that it could have been counteracted by additional government income-generating expenditure. Stricter management would have dampened prosperities, though in terms of dollar indices much more than in terms of real indices, and mitigated the subsequent depression. Deficit spending would have accentuated prosperities, though in terms of dollar indices much more than in terms of real indices, and might have avoided the depression. The latter proposition, of course, does not mean more than that inflation may turn *any* situation into one that will display the usual features of prosperity and does not, in itself, constitute any argument for it. But the opposite argument is much too complex to be presented in the available space. All I want to draw attention to is, first, that a period which everyone will associate with prosperity rather than depression did run its course on a price

level that was falling in the above sense, though in the short-run *waves* of prosperity prices turned up each time; and that, so far as these short-run cycles are concerned, prices played, statistically, a distinctly secondary role: things recovered in 1921, when prices were still falling; the downturn of 1920 set in when they were still rising.

Output of manufacturing industry, 1920–29, increased by about 50 per cent; man-hours per unit may have fallen by as much as 40 per cent (Fabricant); the corresponding figures for 1899–1907 (to avoid the crisis figure of 1908) were 61 and (about) 15. We have the picture of rapid though not unheard-of development in the output figure and one that may have been unparalleled in industrial efficiency. Friends and foes of the policies of the thirties should agree that it was these developments that raised the hopes associated with those policies above the level of chimeras. Also, most features of the period under discussion—movements of dollar figures in particular—find their chief explanation in them.

3. *Profits and Wages.* The tendency of profit rates to fall, obscured as it is by the events of 1928 and 1929, requires substantiation although it should not surprise anyone familiar with the statistics of the period. Impressions to the contrary result from the habit to concentrate attention only on corporations reporting profits or even, in some cases, on samples that contain the peak successes. The decisive fact stands out in any analysis of the obviously prosperous interval 1924–26, when the earnings ratios ran roughly between 2 and 3 per cent (1.98 for 1926) and "a considerable share of the total gross corporate business was done at a loss" (W. L. Crum).

The income distribution of the period displays the familiar invariants, both as to shares going to "factors" and as to the relations between income brackets. What appears to be a tendency for the relative share in national income going to the top 1 per cent of income receivers to increase seems to be accounted for by capital gains.

During the twenties the United States economic system taken as a whole absorbed, at rising monetary and real wage rates, substantially more labor than was displaced by technological improvement—in fact almost, though not quite, the simultaneous increase in the job-seeking population. In the over-all picture, that rise looks smaller than it really was owing to the sharpness of the rebound from the downward revision in 1921 that occurred in 1922–23. Detailed analysis of national as well as sectional movements lends more support to theories that aver than to theories that deny the existence of an inverse relation, other things being equal, between money wage rates and employment, though it is no doubt possible to make too much of the historical association of the prompt recovery in 1922 with the prompt fall in money wage rates and of other facts that point in the same direction and tally well with the opposite experience of the thirties. "Mere facts" are never decisive per se. But neither should we neglect them. Any theory to the effect that the unemployment of the twenties had anything to do with any excessive propensity to save is in any case patently wrong.

III

One of the most common indictments leveled at economists is their alleged inability to offer a satisfactory explanation of the world crisis of 1929–32. I submit that this indictment is without foundation. We cannot —any more than can any physician or anyone else who deals with organic processes—prove the adequacy of our explanation numerically, but we can point to facts which will plausibly account for everything that happened. In order to do so, it will be convenient to distinguish between facts that explain why there should have been a "depression" and facts that turned this "depression" into "disaster." Both the validity and the practical usefulness of this distinction will presently become evident.

When we behold the face of a man in early middle age, we are to some extent able to form an idea of how he will look in old age. Performing an analogous operation on the pattern of the twenties, we have no difficulty in realizing that certain traits in it, merely by accentuating themselves as they were bound to do, would gradually turn it into a pattern answering to our idea of a depression, particularly if we attach proper weights to some of the features of the "Coolidge prosperity" that were obviously destined to fade out for the time being, such as the booms in residential building and in utilities. That is to say, the prevailing tendencies, such as the tendency of prices and profits to sag—quite normal phenomena for periods of the character indicated—had only to go further in order to submerge, temporarily and in some cases definitively, increasing *sectors* of the economy—the most defenseless of all being the agrarian sector—and to develop *sectional* difficulties or breakdowns from which downward "vicious spirals," attended by widespread unemployment, were increasingly likely to start. And this is the fundamental fact about both the depression (1929–32) and the subsequent recovery, although it would take elaborate analysis to display the full strength of this argument. It explains in this case exactly what it explains in all previous historical instances of the same kind. It does not explain, however, any more than it does in these previous instances, any "disaster" but only the supernormal sensitivity of the economic system to adverse occurrences and to the weaknesses in the institutional setup of the country.

I submit that, given what we have just described as depressive tendency and supernormal sensitivity, the following facts constitute adequate explanation of the "disaster" in the United States though the list would, at least in part, look different for other countries. In thus invoking individual historical facts that are in a sense accidental we do not more confess failure of our analytic apparatus than does the physician who in his diagnosis takes account of facts that are in the same sense accidental or extraneous to the organism of his patient such as, for instance, drinking or the effects of a motor accident.

The first fact is the speculative mania of 1927–29. In itself, of course, stock and land speculation is a "natural" and even "necessary" concomitant of every business prosperity. But those wild excesses and the attendant financial practices were clearly abnormal; they can be explained only by a specifically American mass psychology and could not have been foretold from anything within the range of statistical fact or reason. They were bound to issue in catastrophe and, once this catastrophe had occurred, in distortion of the course of subsequent events particularly owing to the annihilation of that part of consumers' demand that had been financed from capital gains—and, in many cases, unrealized ones.

The second fact was the weakness of the United States banking system. There was, of course, no reason why, by 1929, a small number of giant banks, as impregnable to the impact of depression as were the English "Big Five," should not have evolved from the nebula of inefficient pigmies and why, incidentally, extensive branch banking should not have provided much better banking facilities for the public than actually existed in that year. It seems safe to say that without the obstacles set up by an irrational attitude of the public mind this would have been the case. Now I do not see how it could be denied that it was the—avoidable—three bank epidemics that occurred during the years of the crisis which broke the morale of the public, spread paralysis through all sectors of the business organism, turned retreat into rout and thus were the most important reasons, speaking quantitatively, for the prevailing distress and unemployment which would not have been half as bad without them, and for the prevalence of a feeling that the world had come to an end.

Third in importance was the mortgage situation, both urban and rural. Again I maintain that its most serious features were entirely due to reckless borrowing and lending; that is to say, to avoidable deviations from normal business practice. Two points should be particularly noticed. First, direct effects upon business and banks were serious enough; but still more serious were the psychological effects upon the community, for nothing is so apt to get on a man's nerves as will a threat to the roof over his head. The explanatory value for the crisis of this element is ten times as great as that of the most elegant difference equation. Second, it is not always recognized that it was *only* the mortgage situation that made the plight of the farmers so serious. On the unencumbered farm, people will, of course, live less comfortably when prices break than when prices rise, but they are able to weather any economic storm without permanent injury.

These items do not, of course, exhaust the list. But I refrain from lengthening it because I wish to focus attention on what seem to me the cardinal points, and because the importance of some of the additional disturbers—such as the state of foreign trade and foreign investment which was fundamental, for instance, to England's difficulties—is smaller than it may look at first sight in the case of the United States.

I beg to add in concluding, first, that, however great the gulf between "stagnationists" and "antistagnationists" may be, they must largely agree in the analysis of any given situation. I am not a stagnationist—at least not in the sense that I believe in a future of permanent stagnation irrespective of political sabotage—but if I were, I should not have had to paint a greatly different picture of the conditions in the twenties. Second, that the difficulty of making practical recommendations—ex post—as to "what should have been done about it" at any point of time consists entirely in the fact that, unlike doctors, we hopelessly differ in aims, preferences, valuations. So soon as people sincerely tell us what it is they really want, we can tell them—and not more than the above analysis, rudimentary though it is, is needed for it—what should have been done at any moment in the past or, for that matter, what should be done now.

THE CREATIVE RESPONSE IN ECONOMIC HISTORY

Reprinted from *Journal of Economic History,* Nov. 1947, 149-159.

I

ECONOMIC historians and economic theorists can make an interesting and socially valuable journey together, if they will. It would be an investigation into the sadly neglected area of economic change.

As anyone familiar with the history of economic thought will immediately recognize, practically all the economists of the nineteenth century and many of the twentieth have believed uncritically that all that is needed to explain a given historical development is to indicate conditioning or causal factors, such as an increase in population or the supply of capital. But this is sufficient only in the rarest of cases. As a rule, no factor acts in a uniquely determined way and, whenever it does not, the necessity arises of going into the details of its *modus operandi,* into the mechanisms through which it acts. Examples will illustrate this. Sometimes an increase in population actually has no other effect than that predicated by classical theory—a fall in per capita real income;[1] but, at other times, it may have an energizing effect that induces new developments with the result that per capita real income rises. Or a protective duty may have no other effect than to increase the price of the protected commodity and, in consequence, its output; but it may also induce a complete reorganization of the protected industry which eventually results in an increase in output so great as to reduce the price below its initial level.

What has not been adequately appreciated among theorists is the

[1] Even within the assumptions of classical theory this is not necessarily true; but we need not go into this.

distinction between different kinds of reaction to changes in "condition." Whenever an economy or a sector of an economy adapts itself to a change in its data in the way that traditional theory describes, whenever, that is, an economy reacts to an increase in population by simply adding the new brains and hands to the working force in the existing employments, or an industry reacts to a protective duty by expansion within its existing practice, we may speak of the development as *adaptive response*. And whenever the economy or an industry or some firms in an industry do something else, something that is outside of the range of existing practice, we may speak of *creative response*.

Creative response has at least three essential characteristics. First, from the standpoint of the observer who is in full possession of all relevant facts, it can always be understood *ex post*; but it can practically never be understood *ex ante*; that is to say, it cannot be predicted by applying the ordinary rules of inference from the pre-existing facts. This is why the "how" in what has been called above the "mechanisms" must be investigated in each case. Secondly, creative response shapes the whole course of subsequent events and their "long-run" outcome. It is not true that both types of responses dominate only what the economist loves to call "transitions," leaving the ultimate outcome to be determined by the initial data. Creative response changes social and economic situations for good, or, to put it differently, it creates situations from which there is no bridge to those situations that might have emerged in its absence. This is why creative response is an essential element in the historical process; no deterministic credo avails against this. Thirdly, creative response—the frequency of its occurrence in a group, its intensity and success or failure—has obviously something, be that much or little, to do (a) with quality of the personnel available in a society, (b) with relative quality of personnel, that is, with quality available to a particular field of activity relative to quality available, at the same time, to others, and (c) with individual decisions, actions, and patterns of behavior. Accordingly, a study of creative response in business becomes coterminous with a study of entrepreneurship. The mechanisms of economic change in capitalist society pivot on entrepreneurial activity.[2] Whether we emphasize opportunity or conditions, the responses of individuals or of groups, it is patently true that in capitalist society objective opportunities or conditions act through

---

[2] The function itself is not absent from other forms of society; but capitalist entrepreneurship is a sufficiently distinct phenomenon to be singled out.

entrepreneurial activity, analysis of which is at the very least a highly important avenue to the investigation of economic changes in the capitalist epoch.[3] This is compatible with widely different views about its importance as an "ultimate cause."

Seen in this light, the entrepreneur and his function are not difficult to conceptualize: the defining characteristic is simply the doing of new things or the doing of things that are already being done in a new way (innovation).[4] It is but natural, and in fact it is an advantage, that such a definition does not draw any sharp line between what is and what is not "enterprise." For actual life itself knows no such sharp division, though it shows up the type well enough. It should be observed at once that the "new thing" need not be spectacular or of historic importance. It need not be Bessemer steel or the explosion motor. It can be the Deerfoot sausage. To see the phenomenon even in the humblest levels of the business world is quite essential though it may be difficult to find the humble entrepreneurs historically.

Distinction from other functions with which enterpreneurship is frequently but not necessarily associated—just as "farmership" is frequently but not necessarily associated with the ownership of land and with the activity of a farm hand—does not present conceptual difficulties either. One necessary distinction is that between enterprise and management: evidently it is one thing to set up a concern embodying a new idea and another thing to head the administration of a going concern, however much the two may shade off into each other. Again, it is essential to note that the entrepreneurial function, though facilitated by the ownership of means, is not identical with that of the capitalist.[5] New light is urgently needed on the relation between the

---

[3] Arthur H. Cole has opened new vistas in this area in his presidential address before the Economic History Association, "An Approach to the Study of Entrepreneurship," THE TASKS OF ECONOMIC HISTORY (Supplemental Issue of THE JOURNAL OF ECONOMIC HISTORY), VI (1946), 1–15.

[4] An exact definition can be provided by means of the concept of production functions. On this, see Oscar Lange, "A Note on Innovations," *Review of Economic Statistics,* XXV (1943), 19–25.

[5] It is sometimes held that entrepreneurship, although it did not require antecedent ownership of capital (or very little of it) in the early days of capitalism, tends to become dependent upon it as time goes on, especially in the epoch of giant corporations. Nothing could be further from the truth. In the course of the nineteenth century, it became increasingly easier to obtain other people's money by methods other than the partnership, and in our own time promotion within the shell of existing corporations offers a much more convenient access to the entrepreneurial functions than existed in the world of owner-managed firms. Many a would-be entrepreneur of today does not found a firm, not because he could not do so, but simply because he prefers the other method.

two, especially because of the cant phrases that are current on this topic. In the third place, it is particularly important to distinguish the entrepreneur from the "inventor." Many inventors have become entrepreneurs and the relative frequency of this case is no doubt an interesting subject to investigate, but there is no necessary connection between the two functions. The inventor produces ideas, the entrepreneur "gets things done," which may but need not embody anything that is scientifically new. Moreover, an idea or scientific principle is not, by itself, of any importance for economic practice: the fact that Greek science had probably produced all that is necessary in order to construct a steam engine did not help the Greeks or Romans to build a steam engine; the fact that Leibnitz suggested the idea of the Suez Canal exerted no influence whatever on economic history for two hundred years. And as different as the functions are the two sociological and psychological types.[6] Finally, "getting new things done" is not only a distinct process but it is a process which produces consequences that are an essential part of capitalist reality. The whole economic history of capitalism would be different from what it is if new ideas had been currently and smoothly adopted, as a matter of course, by all firms to whose business they were relevant. But they were not. It is in most cases only one man or a few men who see the new possibility and are able to cope with the resistances and difficulties which action always meets with outside of the ruts of established practice. This accounts for the large gains that success often entails, as well as for the losses and vicissitudes of failure. These things are important. If, in every individual case, the difficulties may indeed be called transitional, they are transitional difficulties which are never absent in the economy as a whole and which dominate the atmosphere of capitalist life permanently. Hence it seems appropriate to keep "invention" distinct from "innovation."

The definition that equates enterprise to innovation is a very abstract one. Some classifications that are richer in content may be noticed because of their possible use in drawing up plans for specific pieces of research. There is the obvious classification—historical and systematic—of the phenomena of enterprise according to institutional forms, such as the medieval trading company, the later "chartered companies," the partnership, the modern "corporation," and the like, on all of which

---

6 The relation between the two has attracted interest before. See, e.g., F. W. Taussig, *Inventors and Money-Makers* (New York: The Macmillan Company, 1915).

there exists a vast amount of historical work.[7] The interaction of institutional forms and entrepreneurial activity, the "shaping" influence of the former and the "bursting" influence of the latter, is, as has already been intimated, a major topic for further inquiry. Closely connected with this classification is the old one according to fields of activity—commerce, industry, finance[8]—which has been refined by the following distinctions: enterprise that introduces "new" commodities; enterprise that introduces technological novelties into the production of "old" commodities; enterprise that introduces new commercial combinations such as the opening up of new markets for products or new sources of supply of materials; enterprise that consists in reorganizing an industry, for instance, by making a monopoly out of it.[9]

But there are other classifications that may prove helpful. We may classify entrepreneurs according to origins and sociological types: feudal lords and aristocratic landowners, civil servants—particularly important, for instance, in Germany after the Thirty Years' War, especially in mining—farmers, workmen, artisans, members of the learned professions, all embarked upon enterprise as has often been noticed, and it is highly interesting from several points of view to clear up this matter. Or we may try to classify entrepreneurial performances according to the precise nature of the "function" filled and the aptitudes (some may even add motivation) involved. Since all this presumably changed significantly in the course of the capitalist epoch, economic historians are particularly qualified for work on this line.

Though the phrase "getting a new thing done" may be adequately comprehensive, it covers a great many different activities which, as the observer stresses one more than another or as his material displays one

---

[7] Gustav von Schmoller introduced the subject into his general treatise (*Grundriss*) of 1904. But the novelty consisted only in the systematic use he made of the result of historical research. Less systematically, the subject had entered general treatises before.

[8] Financial institutions and practices enter our circle of problems in three ways: they are "auxiliary and conditioning"; banking may be the object of entrepreneurial activity, that is to say, the introduction of new banking practices may constitute enterprise; and bankers (or other "financiers") may use the means at their command in order to embark upon commercial and industrial enterprise themselves (for example, John Law). See the recent book by Fritz Redlich, *The Molding of American Banking—Men and Ideas* (New York: Hafner Publishing Company, 1947).

[9] This case emphasizes the desirability, present also in others, of divesting our idea of entrepreneurial performance of any preconceived value judgment. Whether a given entrepreneurial success benefits or injures society or a particular group within society is a question that must be decided on the merits of each case. Enterprise that results in a monopoly position, even if undertaken for the sole purpose of securing monopoly gains, is not necessarily antisocial in its total effect although it often is.

more than another, may, locally, temporarily, or generally, lend different colors to entrepreneurship. In some cases, or to some observers, it may be the activity of "setting up" or "organizing" that stands out from the others; in other cases, or for other observers, it may be the breaking down of the resistances of the environment; in still other cases, or for still other observers, simply leadership or, again, salesmanship. Thus, it seems to me, there was a type of entrepreneur in early capitalist industry that is best described as a "fixer." Modern history furnishes many instances of entrepreneurship vested in a company promotor.[10] The typical industrial entrepreneur of the nineteenth century was perhaps the man who put into practice a novel method of production by embodying it in a new firm and who then settled down into a position of owner-manager of a company, if he was successful, or of stockholding president of a company, getting old and conservative in the process. In the large-scale corporation of today, the question that is never quite absent arises with a vengeance, namely, who should be considered as the entrepreneur. In a well-known book, R. A. Gordon has presented much interesting material bearing upon this question.[11]

II

The economic nature, amount, and distribution of the returns to entrepreneurial activity constitute another set of problems on which investigation may be expected to shed much-needed light. Conceptual difficulties confront us here even before we come up against the still more formidable difficulties of fact finding. For the "profit" of the English classics, which was analyzed by J. S. Mill into wages of management, premiums for risk, and interest on owned capital, was a return to normal business activity and something quite different from, though influenced by, the gain of successful enterprise in our sense of the term. What the latter is can best be explained by considering a special case. Suppose that a man, realizing the possibility of producing acceptable caviar from sawdust, sets up the Excelsior Caviar concern and makes it a success. If this concern is too small to influence the prices of either the product or the factors of production, he will sell the

[10] In a sense, the promotor who does nothing but "set up" new business concerns might be considered as the purest type of entrepreneur. Actually, he is mostly not more than a financial agent who has little, if any, title to entrepreneurship—no more than the lawyer who does the legal work involved. But there are important exceptions to this.

[11] Robert A. Gordon, *Business Leadership in the Large Corporation* (Washington, D.C.: The Brookings Institution, 1945).

former and buy the latter at current prices. If, however, he turns out the unit of caviar more cheaply than his competitors, owing to his use of a much cheaper raw material, he will for a time, that is, until other firms copy his method, make (essentially temporary) surplus gains. These gains are attributable to personal exertion. Hence they might be called wages. They may with equal justice be attributed to the fact that, for a time, his method is exclusively his own. Hence they might also be called monopoly gains. But whether we elect to call them wages or monopoly gains, we must add immediately that they are a special kind of wages or monopoly gains that differ in important respects from what we usually mean to denote by these terms. And so we had better call them simply entrepreneurial gains or profit. However, it should be observed that if this venture means a "fortune," this fortune does not typically arise from the actual net receipts being saved up and invested in the same or some other business. Essentially, it emerges as a *capital* gain, that is, as the discounted value of the stream of prospective excess returns.

In this simple case, which, however, does constitute a type, the investigator is not confronted with difficulties other than those involved in fact finding. Also, it is clear what happens with that surplus gain: in this case the entrepreneurial gain goes to the entrepreneur,[12] and we can also see, if we have the facts, how, to use a current phrase, the "fruits of the progress involved are handed to consumers and workmen." The speed of this process of "handing on" varies widely, but it would always work, in isolated cases like the one under discussion, through a fall in the price of the product to the new level of costs, which is bound to occur whenever competition steps up to the successful concern. But even here we meet the practice of innovators striving to keep their returns alive by means of patents and in other ways. The gains described above shade off into gains from purposive restriction of competition and create difficulties of diagnosis that are sometimes insurmountable.[13] Cumulation of carefully analyzed historical cases is

[12] It should be obvious that this does not mean that the whole social gain resulting from the enterprise goes to the entrepreneur. But the question of appraisal of social gains from entrepreneurship, absolute and relative to the entrepreneurial shares in them, and of the social costs involved in a system that relies on business interests to carry out its innovations, is so complex and perhaps even hopeless that I beg to excuse myself from entering into it

[13] Still more difficult is, of course, responsible appraisal, that is to say, appraisal that is not content with popular slogans. Measures to keep surplus gains alive no doubt slow up the process of "handing on the fruits of progress." But the knowledge that such measures are available may be necessary in order to induce anyone to embark upon certain ventures. There

the best means of shedding light on these things, of supplying the theorist with strategic assumptions, and banishing slogans.

If innovations are neither individually small nor isolated events, complications crowd upon us. Entrepreneurial activity then affects wage and interest rates from the outset and becomes a factor—the fundamental factor in my opinion—in booms and depressions. This is one reason, but not the only one, why entrepreneurial gains are not net returns (1) to the whole set of people who attempt entrepreneurial ventures, (2) to the industrial sector in which innovation occurs, (3) to the capitalist interests that finance entrepreneurial activity and to the capitalist class as a whole.

Concerning the first point, I might have made my special case more realistic by assuming that several or many people try their hands at producing that caviar but that all but one fail to produce a salable product before the success of this one presents an example to copy. The gains of the successful entrepreneur and of the capitalists who finance him—for whenever capital finances enterprise the interest is paid out of the entrepreneurial gains, a fact that is very important for our grasp of the interest phenomenon—should be related not to his effort and their loan but to the effort and the loans of all the entrepreneurs and capitalists who made attempts and lost. The presence of gains to enterprise so great as to impress us as spectacular and, from the standpoint of society, irrational is then seen to be compatible with a negative return to entrepreneurs and financing capitalists as a group.[14]

It is similarly clear that entrepreneurial gain is not a net accretion to the returns of the industrial sector in which it occurs. The impact of the new product or method spells losses to the "old" firms. The competition of the man with a significantly lower cost curve is, in fact, the really effective competition that in the end revolutionizes the industry. Detailed investigation of this process which may take many forms might teach us much about the actual working of capitalism that we are but dimly perceiving as yet.

---

also may be other compensating advantages to such measures, particularly where rapid introduction into general use of new methods would involve severe dislocations of labor, and where entrepreneurial gains are important sources of venture capital.

14 Whether this actually is so in any particular case is, of course, extremely difficult to establish. The successes stand out, statistically and otherwise; the failures are apt to escape notice. This is one of the reasons why economists seem so much impressed by peak successes. Another reason for faulty appraisal is neglect of the fact that spectacular gains may stimulate more effectively than would the same sum if more equally distributed. This is a question that no speculation can decide. Only collection of facts can tell us how we are to frame our theory.

Concerning the third point, while we have a fair amount of information about how the working class fares in the process of economic change, in respect to both real wages and employment, we know much less about that elusive entity, capital, that is being incessantly destroyed and re-created. That the theorist's teaching, according to which capital "migrates" from declining to rising industries, is unrealistic is obvious: the capital "invested" in railroads does not migrate into trucking and air transportation but will perish in and with the railroads. Investigation into the histories of industries, concerns, and firms, including surveys of sectors in order to point out how long a typical firm stays in business and how and why it drops out, might dispel many a preconceived notion on this subject.

III

Finally, I should like to touch one more set of problems on which we may expect light from historical analysis, namely, the problems that come within the range of the question: does the importance of the entrepreneurial function decline as time goes on? There are serious reasons for believing that it does. The entrepreneurial performance involves, on the one hand, the ability to perceive new opportunities that cannot be proved at the moment at which action has to be taken, and, on the other hand, will power adequate to break down the resistance that the social environment offers to change. But the range of the provable expands, and action upon flashes or hunches is increasingly replaced by action that is based upon "figuring out." And modern milieus may offer less resistance to new methods and new goods than used to be the case. So far as this is so, the element of personal intuition and force would be less essential than it was: it could be expected to yield its place to the teamwork of specialists; in other words, improvement could be expected to become more and more automatic. Our impression to this effect is reinforced by parallel phenomena in other fields of activity. For instance, a modern commander no doubt means less in the outcome of a war than commanders meant of old, and for the same reasons; campaigns have become more calculable than they used to be and there is less scope for personal leadership.

But this is at present only an impression. It is for the historian to establish or to refute it. If, however, it should stand up under research, this would be a result of the utmost importance. We should be led to expect that the whole mechanism of economic development will change significantly. Among other things, the economy would progressively bureaucratize itself. There are, in fact, many symptoms of this. And consequences would extend far beyond the field of economic phenomena. Just as warrior classes have declined in importance ever since warfare—and especially the management of armies in the field—began to be increasingly "mechanized," so the business class may decline in importance, as its most vital figure, the entrepreneur, progressively loses his most essential function. This would mean a different social structure.

Therefore, the sociology of enterprise reaches much further than is implied in questions concerning the conditions that produce and shape, favor or inhibit entrepreneurial activity. It extends to the structure and the very foundations of, at least, capitalist society or the capitalist sector of any given society. The quickest way of showing this starts from recognition of the facts that, just as the rise of the bourgeois class as a whole is associated with success in commercial, industrial, and financial enterprise, so the rise of an individual family to "capitalist" status within that class is typically [15] associated with entrepreneurial success; and that the elimination of a family from the "capitalist" class is typically associated with the loss of those attitudes and aptitudes of industrial leadership or alertness that enter our picture of the entrepreneurial type of businessman.

Now these facts, if they are facts, might teach us a lot about such fundamental problems as the nature of the class structure of capitalist society; the sort of class civilization which it develops and which differs so characteristically from the class civilization of feudal society; its schema of values; its politics, especially its attitudes to state and church and war; its performance and failures; its degree of durability. But a great deal of work needs to be done in order to arrive at scientifically defensible opinions about all these and cognate things. First of all, these "facts" must be established. How far is it really true, for instance, that entrepreneurs, while not forming a social class themselves but originating in almost all existing strata, do "feed" or renew the capitalist stratum? To put it differently, does the latter recruit itself through entrepreneurial successes? Or, to put it still differently,

[15] That is to say, successful entrepreneurship is that method of rising in the social scale that is characteristic of the capitalist blueprint. It is, of course, not the only method. First, there are other possibilities within the economic sphere, such as possession of an appreciating natural agent (for example, urban land) or mere speculation or even, occasionally, success in mere administration that need not partake of the specifically entrepreneurial element. Secondly, there are possibilities outside the business sphere, for business success is no more the only method of rising in capitalist society than knightly service was in feudal society.

does the "typical" history of industrial families lead back to entrepreneurial performances that "created" a concern which then, for a time, yielded capitalistic surpluses by being merely "administrated" with more or less efficiency? How much statistical truth is there in the slogan: "Three generations from overalls to overalls"? Secondly, what is, as measured by observable results, the economic and cultural, also political, importance of the further fact that, though the entrepreneurial function cannot be transmitted by inheritance, except, possibly, by biological inheritance, the financial or industrial position that has been created can? How much truth is there in the contention that the industrial family interest is, in capitalist society, the guardian of the nation's economic future?

These questions, which could be readily multiplied, have often attracted attention. Every textbook of economic history contains some material about the origins of entrepreneurs of historical standing, and a number of studies have been inspired by full awareness of the importance of the answers for our understanding of capitalist society and of the ways in which it works.[16] But these studies are few and that attention has been desultory. We do not know enough in order to form valid generalizations or even enough to be sure whether there are any generalizations to form. As it is, most of us as economists have some opinions on these matters. But these opinions have more to do with our preconceived ideas or ideals than with solid fact, and our habit of illustrating them by stray instances that have come under our notice is obviously but a poor substitute for serious research. Veblen's—or, for that matter, Bucharin's—*Theory of the Leisure Class* exemplifies well what I mean. It is brilliant and suggestive. But it is an impressionistic essay that does not come to grips with the real problems involved. Yet there is plenty of material. A great and profitable task awaits those who undertake it.

Harvard University JOSEPH A. SCHUMPETER

---

[16] An example is the study by F. J. Marquis and S. J. Chapman on the managerial stratum of the Lancashire cotton industry in the *Journal of the Royal Statistical Society*, LXXV, Pt. III (1912), 293–306.

THEORETICAL PROBLEMS OF ECONOMIC GROWTH

Reprinted from *Journal of Economic History Supplement,* 1947, 1-9.

IT is with some diffidence that I submit the following notes which I have not been able to work up into a fully developed argument. The inartistic use of numerals has been resorted to in order to mark off clearly the various problems touched upon.

1. It will be understood, I trust, that in this paper the term theory means nothing that in any way transcends the domain of empirical analysis, that is to say, nothing that is in any way dependent upon "philosophical" or "metaphysical" or "speculative" premises. In particular, so far as philosophies of history imply anything extraempirical, the paper has nothing to do with philosophy of history. However, it is more important to emphasize that in this paper the term theory has also nothing to do with ethical or cultural evaluation of facts or tendencies, such as the term progress suggests, and is not simply synonymous with the term explanatory hypothesis. I want to emphasize the instrumental role of theory. It shall be considered exclusively as a tool of research or rather a "box" of such tools that are to help us in the task of describing facts and relations between facts. Sometimes the historian finds that the "theoretical" apparatus—in this sense—of common experience suffices for his purpose and then he feels that he is not using any "theory" at all. At other times, this common-sense theory proves inadequate. Our topic belongs to the latter class.

2. The first part of the analysis of economic growth consists, then, in deriving concepts of economic growth and in devising means of measuring it or, at least, of establishing criteria by which to judge whether there was, at any given period, growth or contraction. Historians and economists seem to know well enough what they mean by economic growth or contraction. But this is so only because, in most cases, it is not necessary to be very precise about it. If we do wish to be precise, especially numerically precise, we run at once into a series of difficulties:

even if we agree to take total output as the criterion, to which there are many objections, we find it difficult to present an acceptable "theory" of the index of output; moreover, we may prefer total output per head of population, or per gainfully employed person, or per consumption unit, or per man hour, or total output of consumable goods and services per consumption unit (perhaps plus imports minus exports). Or we may wish to correct for cases in which contraction of output does not carry the usual implications, if, for example, as very well might happen in the future, contraction in total output is due to changes in fashion or technology or to preference for increased leisure. Leaving this set of problems to Mr. Kuznets, I want merely to state the theses that there is no all-purpose concept of economic growth or contraction; that this concept must be defined—just as must other concepts, for example, the concept of income—separately for every purpose; and that the concept, in each case, is defined by the index or other criterion that is chosen by the investigator.

For the purpose of this paper, it will be sufficient to adopt the following definition, highly unsatisfactory though it is in some respects: I speak of economic growth during any stated period if the trend values of an index of per capita total output of goods and services have increased during that period.[1]

3. The second part of the analysis of observed growth is the study of the factors that economists and historians have adduced in explanation. These factors are too numerous for enumeration, especially if we take account not only of factors that are mentioned in discussions of economic growth per se [2] but also of factors that are incidentally mentioned in other investigations.[3] Here are a few of the most familiar ones, partially overlapping: physical environment, including commercial location and maritime opportunities; social organization, including the whole of the institutional pattern (contracts, property, inheritance, credit systems, taxation, labor relations, public or corporative regula-

[1] This is to convey an idea of a "concept." It is not required that available statistics permit actual evaluation of a figure. For periods in which adequate statistics are not available the definition simply reads: if available indications justify the belief that the trend values . . . .

[2] Good examples are afforded by the third book of the *Wealth of Nations* and by Chapters 2 and 3 of the first book of Marshall's *Principles*. These examples are "good" in the sense that they represent well what economists have had and have to say on the subject in general—but not otherwise. I fancy that historians will read both with a smile, good-natured or not.

[3] Such incidental comments on what caused positive or negative growth in individual cases, for example, in the history of an individual industry, are all the more valuable when they are proferred unintentionally, that is, if their bearings upon a *general* theory of growth is not perceived by the writer. For in this case the writer's opinion is not vitiated by his philosophies or preconceptions.

tion of economic activity, and so on, together with the immediate consequences of all this for either "freedom" or "security" or "planned" action); "politics" by which I here mean the way in which these institutions are worked by the political sector of a society (administrative personnel and its actual practice, quality and practice of the legal profession and the courts of law) including such things as wars, inflations, revolutions, violent or otherwise, and expectations of all this; technology in a very wide sense, including techniques of business organization, accounting, banking, and commerce; and the human material, not only its quantity and the rate of change of numbers, but also its quality, moral and intellectual, innate[4] or acquired, and the portion of total "ability" or "energy" that in a given social situation goes to economic as distinct from other pursuits. Finally, in connection with all this but in a connection that differs materially according to a writer's philosophies is the factor "national spirit," which term is to denote not only prevalent systems of ideas or beliefs, religious or other, but also prevalent attitudes, especially to such matters as parsimony, pecuniary gain, risk-bearing, physical and intellectual work, and the like. The theory of Max Weber affords a conspicuous instance. This incomplete list is offered without any intention either to commit myself to, or to criticize, any or all of the items it contains per se. The only comment I offer for the moment concerning the analytic use made of them is that they are frequently ill-defined, sometimes ideologically caparisoned, and mostly taken for granted without being—in regard to existence, relevance, and importance—established by anything that can pass muster as a scientific method. Historians stand first among all the groups of research workers whose task it is to change this state of things. In connection with analysis of these factors I submit three theses.

Economic growth is not an autonomous phenomenon, that is to say, it is not a phenomenon that can be satisfactorily analyzed in purely economic terms alone. This conclusion imposes itself from a glance at the items of our list and can be avoided only if we adopt the Marxist hypothesis (economic interpretation of history) which achieves this

[4] This does not necessarily imply emphasis upon "race." For it is possible to hold that the range of variation in "ability" (for definiteness, think of the Spearman factor) among individuals is very great and even that "ability runs in stocks" (K. Pearson) without attaching importance to the racial aspects of these stocks (that is to say, without believing that this ability of human stocks is differentiated racially). It is, however, interesting to note that prominent economists, especially English ones, have been in the habit of emphasizing race. Nobody thinks of J. S. Mill—the utilitarian radical!—and A. Marshall as "racialist." Yet the racial note is unmistakable in the general introductions to both their *Principles*.

Marx didn't make everything economic.

autonomy, in a sense, by making economic evolution the prime mover of history in all its aspects so that all other factors become functions of this prime mover, with the exception of some, though not all, elements of the physical environment, such as earthquakes. It is part of my thesis that this is inadmissible.

Since, then, economic growth is not autonomous, being dependent upon factors outside of itself, and since these factors are many, no one-factor theory can ever be satisfactory. That is to say, such theories as that economic growth is a function, chiefly, of the objective opportunities of the environment, of increase in population, of the "spirit" of a nation's civilization, of technological progress (increasing "control over nature") can never be adequate. Such statements may hold true approximately in special cases where, as a matter of fact, no great change has occurred in any of the factors of growth but one. I do not know of any historical instance of this. But I do know many instances in which the number of factors may be reduced because some of them have in the period under research not changed significantly. Thus the period from 1871 to 1914 in the United States was certainly not free from political disturbances and institutional changes; on the whole, however, when describing the economic growth of the country in that period, we may neglect them on the ground that they were not important enough to influence the economic process very greatly. Also, some statements provide schemata for the purely theoretical purpose of working out the *modus operandi* of a single factor, the others remaining constant by assumption. Such schemata have their uses. But they must not be expected to fit historical reality.

Refusal to accept the Marxist theory of history must not be interpreted to imply denial of the obvious fact that economic growth influences, in turn, all the factors (with the same exception concerning certain properties of the physical environment) "on which it depends": this is precisely the reason why these factors should not be called "causes." But, in addition to being in turn dependent upon economic growth, these factors are, as is easily seen, also dependent upon each other. This involves, of course, no circular reasoning but simply recognition of the fact that, in principle, we have to deal with a system of interdependent factors of which economic growth is just one. Certain mathematical notions might be useful in order to explain the logic of such a system. But if we tried to use mathematics, we would immediately run up against the difficulty that some of the most important of these interdependent factors cannot be quantified,[5] not, at all events, beyond what is implied in calling them "important" or "unimportant" or "more important" or "less important" than others.[6]

The third task in the analysis of economic growth I shall call "describing mechanism." Logically, the distinction between "describing mechanisms" and "indicating factors of growth" is not bombproof. But nevertheless it is useful because it emphasizes the necessity, which is so often overlooked, of inquiring carefully into the *modus operandi* of every factor that observation may suggest as significant. For instance, to say that during a stated period a war or an increase of population through immigration or an inflation through gold discoveries, wildcat banking, or government paper was a factor of change is saying next to nothing, besides being in most cases obvious: all the really valuable results come into view only when we try to answer the question precisely *how* the war, the increase of population, or the inflation effected whatever it is it is supposed to have effected. In particular, I want to draw attention to two classes of these results. First, analysis of the *modus operandi* of a factor is frequently the best and sometimes the only method for establishing the significance of a given candidate for the role of factor and for forming a rational opinion regarding its comparative weight. Second, analysis of the *modus operandi* of factors is the most obvious remedy in cases where no definite effect, not even sign (direction), can be predicated of a factor for once and all. Wars, increases of population, inflations are examples. They may affect growth favorably as well as unfavorably.[7] Everyone will agree that actual effects depend upon the "circumstances" of each case. But this remains a loose and unenlightening phrase unless we specify *a schema of possible modi operandi* that tells us which are the "circumstances"

---

[5] This difficulty must not be confused with mere inability, owing to lack of figures or methods, to express our factors numerically. The difficulty is much more fundamental than that.

[6] An interesting intermediate case of partial quantification should be noticed in passing. When trying to form an opinion about the effects on economic growth in the United States of a reduction of the income tax in the higher brackets we have to distinguish two things: the effect upon investment ("saving") and the effect upon motivation. The first effect, given adequate data and also given agreement on certain points of theory (which seems unattainable just now) could be calculated to a nicety. But the second effect cannot; it must be left to (highly prejudiced) hunches or impressions that hardly deserve to be called "estimates." More precisely, however, this is true only with respect to the net of this effect. Certain elements in it are also quantifiable. It need hardly be added that, giving in to human weakness, economists are prone to treat as nonexistent what is not quantifiable and sometimes even what is not measurable.

[7] The problem is, of course, further complicated by the fact that unfavorable effects are compatible with positive observed rates of growth and favorable effects with negative ones.

to watch and which will produce which effects. This is where economic theory might come in to serve the historian—and not by offering sweeping explanatory hypotheses.

The importance of this could be made to stand out only by discussing many and complicated cases. I shall, however, merely to illustrate my meaning, mention a single case only and one that does not call for any complicated theory at all. I take the case of the precious-metal inflation in sixteenth-century Spain, taking my stand on the year 1560 or thereabouts, that Earl J. Hamilton has done so much to elucidate. I further simplify by confining myself to one strand in the pattern, namely, to that part of the metal imports into Spain that was directly transformed into an access of purchasing power in the hands of the government.[8] This amount being spent promptly on consumers' goods and services, soldiers' services among them, we have here an ideal case for the application of the quantity theorem in its crudest form. In fact, commodity prices did react nearly, though not exactly, as this theorem would lead us to expect. The illustration expresses what I mean by (a piece of) mechanism. But it does so in a peculiar manner, namely, by stating what will be the ultimate outcome of the working of the mechanism that it presupposes rather than by describing this mechanism itself. A more perfect theory would have, on the one hand, to show the various steps (transitional states) that lead up to the outcome,[9] and, on the other hand, to include many more possibilities than just that one: the possibilities, for instance, that the new money is not promptly spent at all; or that it gets into hands that will spend it on economic enterprise; or that it will induce an additional credit inflation; or that it impinges upon an economic process that expands so readily that, in the limiting case, prices fall instead of rise, a possibility recognized by certain seventeenth-century writers and then again by Pietro Verri.

5. Instead of developing this instance of the nature and importance of "mechanisms" or adducing others, I shall advert to an argument

[8] To repeat, this is, of course, not the only phenomenon to watch. Moreover, processes in other countries were much more complex. And this was not overlooked by contemporaneous writers. Bodin, for example, did criticize the one-sided view of Malestroit but included the element stressed by the latter in his own analysis. He also included others. It would be quite wrong to aver that he propounded a strict quantity theory. All he did was state that the impact of the precious metals was the first item to consider in an explanation of that price revolution. Not even the late Lord Keynes or Mrs. Robinson would deny that.

[9] That is to say, the quantity theorem is essentially static; in the equation $MV = PT$, all four quantities refer to one and the same point of time. Its contents may be enriched by "dynamizing" it, that is, by giving appropriately different time subscripts to the several quantities.

that comes near to being a general theory of economic growth. It proved extremely durable for we find it first in Adam Smith and, with but unessential developments and improvements, in J. S. Mill and Alfred Marshall. Briefly, it may be stated like this. Taking institutional, political, and natural factors for granted, these economists, and most others, start from the assumption that a social group—we may just as well call it "nation"—will, unless periodically plundered, experience a certain rate of economic growth that is accounted for by increase in numbers and saving. This induces a "widening of markets" which, in turn, increases division of labor and thus increases "productivity." With Smith, division of labor is a catchall for changes in methods of production of all kinds, but with Mill and more explicitly with Marshall, "induced inventions" appear as a separate factor of growth, whereas inventions that are not induced by previous increase in production (so-called revolutionary inventions) are outside the theoretical picture—they just happen, as manna might fall from heaven—and break the line of growth, establishing a new one. Growth is therefore reduced substantially to increase in the quantities of means of production, on the one hand, and increase in effective demand for their potential products, on the other. I cannot, and perhaps need not, stop to point out the weaknesses of this theory. But there is one feature that it has in common with certain, largely subconscious, conceptual schemata that historians sometimes use in describing both processes of economic growth and individual economic developments. This feature is its impersonal automatism.

In the Smith-Mill-Marshall theory, the economy grows like a tree. This process is no doubt exposed to disturbances by external factors that are not economic or not strictly so. But in itself it proceeds steadily and continuously, each situation grows out of the preceding one in a uniquely determined way, and the individuals, whose acts combine to produce each situation, count individually for no more than do the individual cells of the tree. This passivity of response to given stimuli extends in particular to accumulation of "capital": in a mechanical way, households and firms save and invest what they have saved in given investment opportunities. The same passivity of response is also implied in many historical descriptions of the development of countries or industries: they are descriptions of objective opportunities created, perhaps by protective duties, victorious wars, discoveries, or "inventions"; and it is tacitly assumed that people react to them in a uniquely determined manner than can be taken for granted and does not offer any problems. I submit that this is not so and that response to objective opportunity is not uniquely determined and cannot be predicted: accumulation or investment may indeed be on existing lines, but it also may create something entirely new; response to a protective tariff may indeed consist in expanding production (at higher prices) on existing lines, but it also may consist in complete reorganization of the industrial structure on new lines; a victorious war may have no other consequence than that the victorious country exploits a conquered colony just as the vanquished country had done before, but it also may result in making something new of the colony; and so on. I suggest that we take account of this by recognizing two, instead of only one, types of responses and that we may label them, respectively, adaptive and creative. I further suggest that we have no choice but to admit that, from our information in the observed situation before the fact (of creative response), we cannot foresee it, and that thus an element of indeterminateness inevitably enters the analysis of economic growth whenever there is creative response. We may bring this element within the range of our list of factors of growth by observing that it links up with "quality of the human material" and in particular with "quality of leading personnel." And since creative response means, in the economic sphere, simply the combination of existing productive resources in new ways or for new purposes, and since this function defines the economic type that we call the entrepreneur, we may reformulate the above suggestions by saying that we should recognize the importance of, and systematically inquire into, entrepreneurship as a factor of economic growth.[10]

6. To sum up: I entirely sympathize with the historians' aversion, which I have often observed, from "theories" or "philosophies" of history that have been produced in quantity ever since the seventeenth century; they were, at best, premature attempts at exploiting inadequate historical information and, at worst, rank dilettantism, the products of preconceived ideas—of ideological fantasy even—rather than of serious research. Personally, I am prepared to include in this verdict even the peak performances of this genus, such as Condorcet's theory in the

[10] This is, after all, but a special case of a problem of general historical methodology of which historical determinism is the other side. It is, so it seems to me, just as "speculative" and "unscientific" to equate the undetermined or at least undeterminable personal element to zero as it is to overemphasize it in the way of Carlyle. Only unbiased historical research can reveal its true contours. Had I time, I might suggest particular methods for doing this. But the real difficulty is in getting that unbiased research. For it is inevitable that, at present more than ever, individual research workers should emotionally like one type of result and dislike another.

eighteenth, Marx's theory in the nineteenth, and Max Weber's theory in the twentieth century. But the task that those writers have attacked with such equivocal success remains. It is the task of improving our grasp of historical processes, the process of economic growth among them. This task is for historians themselves to attack. As a matter of fact, historians are, and have been for a century or more, attacking it with increasing success: an economic historian is actually doing this when he defines his work not in terms of country or period, but in terms of some historical *problem,* such as the origin of towns, the disintegration of manor and village, the rise of capitalism, the development of deposit banking, medieval forms of enterprise, and so on. The time may have come (that is not for me to judge) to co-ordinate and to organize this work by means of comprehensive "programs" and to provide, for the use of the individual research worker, orderly schemata of possibilities and problems. It is here, and in its instrumental capacity, not as a master but as a servant of historical research, that theory may prove useful. As an example, I wish to recommend to the critical attention of the economic historians of the country the program for the study of the role in economic growth of "entrepreneurship" that has been worked out recently by Arthur H. Cole.

Harvard University JOSEPH A. SCHUMPETER

THERE IS STILL TIME TO STOP INFLATION

Reprinted from *Nation's Business,* June 1948, 33-35, 88-91.

I have been a close observer of the inflations that ran their courses in and after World War I in Austria, France, Germany and Italy. If I were asked what it is that strikes me about them more than does anything else, my answer would be this:

Those inflations were simple processes. There was nothing mysterious about them or about the remedies that could have been applied before they got out of hand. All of them were the results of war finance and could have been stopped within a year or two. But they were not stopped because the people who counted politically did not *want* to stop them.

The new Austria that emerged in 1918 was a leftover from the old Austro-Hungarian monarchy, and completely disorganized. It is perhaps not difficult to understand that a government without authority should have grappled with its difficulties by handing out ever-increasing masses of paper money until the currency broke down (1919-23). Nor is it difficult to understand that Germany, crushed by defeat and revolution, should deal with every difficulty by pouring upon it new billions of paper marks, as long as the mark retained any value at all (1919-24).

But, it was the absence (however understandable) of political stamina, not any *economic* impossibility of stabilization or any lack of knowledge as to what remedies would have been effective, that caused the ultimate catastrophe. Politicians, preoccupied with the problems of the day, farmers and industrialists who were not sorry to get rid of their debts, and other groups who put the sham profits of inflation above their permanent interests, pussy-footed the issue of inflation until it was too late.

Italy is another example. The governments in office between the close of the war and the advent of fascism did the same thing as Germany for the same reason (1919-23). But Mussolini wanted to stop inflation. So he stopped it.

The most interesting case, however, is France, because the French franc emerged from the war in a somewhat better condition than the other currencies. In fact, as late as 1923, there was no *economic* reason why it should not have been stabilized — at the 1923 level of purchasing power — by the same measures by which Poincaré actually did stabilize it, at a much lower level, in 1926.

But most of the politicians who sat in the many cabinets of those years were of no mind to tackle the problem seriously. Each cabinet felt that this task might be more fitly undertaken by its successors who were welcome to spoil their electoral chances by doing so.

It is common knowledge that something of this kind is now going on in America. Our inflation problem is serious only because neither politicians nor the politically important interests take it seriously. In itself it is relatively easy to solve because the most trying of all the difficulties that beset European countries — difficulties about foreign exchange — do not exist for us. But, as we shall see, all really effective measures are unpopular.

Any cure will inevitably produce what is more unpopular still, a temporary depression, because, so soon as inflation ceases, there will be readjustments in prices and production that will mean losses and unemployment, though neither need be serious. Everyone feels this and is afraid of it, especially in an election year. So inflation runs on by common consent.

We shall first try to form an idea of the nature of the inflationary process and then discuss the means by which it could be made to die out.

Causes of Inflation: We have inflation whenever means of payment increase more rapidly than the total output of goods and services. This may be due to many causes — for instance, the "wildcat" banking of old, or gold discoveries — but the only one we need to consider is government expenditure financed by newly created "money," such as the greenbacks of the Civil War.

Modern governments, indeed, do not issue greenbacks but "borrow" from banks. This comes to the same thing because such borrowing implies that new deposits are created instead of greenbacks. Observe, furthermore, that even if governments borrow from the public instead of from banks, this still comes to the same thing so far as subscribers to the public loans *do not reduce their expenditure* in order *to pay their subscriptions but borrow from banks in order to do so.* What happens in this case differs from an issue of greenbacks only in technique.

We shall divide the inflationary process into three phases: Incipient Inflation, Advanced Inflation, and Wild Inflation. This division is somewhat arbitrary, devised to facilitate exposition, because, in practice, these phases shade off into one another.

Incipient Inflation: Newly created money affects prices, incomes and production only by being spent. The government which creates the money can be relied on to spend it promptly. But the firms and households whose receipts are increased by the government's spending react to this increase in ways that differ characteristically in the three phases of the inflationary process. In Incipient Inflation they are likely to use the money for repaying debts or for strengthening cash positions.

So long as this lasts we have latent inflation.

Moreover, if the government expenditure impinges upon an underemployed industrial organism, firms may react to the new demand by expanding output rather than by raising prices. In this case, part of the inflationary impulse is being absorbed. For both reasons, Incipient Inflation may make little impression on prices and on the sum of individual incomes paid out. Thus, the fact that the government deficits of the 1930's and the consequent increase in deposits had but little effect on either should not have surprised anybody.

Advanced Inflation: If government expenditure, financed by newly created money, proceeds beyond the situation just described, we enter the phase of Advanced Inflation. Industry is then fully employed and prices and incomes rise all round if they are allowed to do so. Cash holdings are no longer greater than is necessary to do business at the higher costs and are therefore currently spent.

But there will be something else.

Not all concerns are able to finance their expanding operations by the new money that, directly and indirectly, they get from the government. They have to borrow from banks.

Moreover, there will be an additional demand for goods because everybody wants to strengthen his inventories in anticipation of further increases in prices and costs and because new investment becomes necessary to meet the new demand for products.

Hence, there will be an additional demand for bank credit. These increased borrowings produce further increases in deposits that are promptly spent. A secondary inflation, therefore, superimposes itself on *the primary inflation induced by government spending.*

Before we go on to consider the third phase of the inflationary process, Wild Inflation, it will be well to insert two comments on what has been said so far:

The first refers to an error of diagnosis frequently made by business men and especially by bankers. A banker who experiences an increasing demand for credit is likely to say that his customers need more money because prices, hence their costs, have risen. This is true as regards what we have called the secondary inflation. It is even true for part of the government expenditure itself as it develops during Advanced Inflation. The previous rise in prices does, in fact, account for additional expenditure. But, if the banker further says that he is doing nothing to "inflate prices" in granting those increasing loans, then he is wrong. His loans increase deposits and this increase in turn acts on the price level.

Moreover, the true chain of causation must not be lost sight of. It is government expenditure financed by new money — in a state of full employment of resources — which raises prices in the first place. Once prices have risen, they become an intermediary cause of further creation of means of payment. But that increase in prices is never the ultimate cause of credit expansion.

The other comment refers to a way of describing the mechanism of inflation that at first sight seems to differ from mine. I have stated that the creation of new money has no effects unless this money is *spent,* and that the extent of these effects will depend on how it is used. It is not likely to percolate throughout the economy and to raise prices all round unless the payments which it finances become incomes of private individuals.

On the strength of this, many economists prefer to say that it is not the newly created money (deposits) as such, but the increase in incomes which "inflates prices." This opinion may be accepted because it serves to bring out the role that the increase in wages plays in inflation. Even the increase in incomes does not "inflate prices" unless these increased incomes are promptly spent, and it is only wage incomes which are being promptly spent because a large portion of the incomes in the higher brackets is either saved or taxed away.

For this reason and because of its importance as a cost factor, the national payroll is by far the most important conductor of inflationary effects.

The thing to be noted about this proposition is that it is not peculiar to any group of economists but the common property of all.

Wild Inflation: This differs from Advanced Inflation by a characteristic change in people's way of handling their money — often expressed by saying that they are losing their confidence in the national currency. But this phrase lends itself easily to misunderstanding. We shall, therefore, state the individual facts that are meant by it. People no longer want to hold cash. They seek safety in "flight into real values"; they buy whatever they can get whether they want it or not, and borrow as much as they can in order to do so.

Normal business habits are upset. Increasing paper profits are paralleled by increasing real losses. The familiar race starts between wages and prices which often ends in the adoption of index wages.

So soon as this system is adopted, wages increase automatically because prices increase, and prices increase automatically because wages increase: there is no logical limit to this process except zero value of the monetary unit. Economies in public budgets become impossible. And the currency is being further inflated by far more than such economies could compensate for through the irresistible demand for redemption of the short-term government debt.

In the end, bondholders and policyholders are expropriated as effectively as any bolshevist revolution could expropriate them. The monetary system and production cease to function.

We are far removed from all this. Yet two of the characteristics of this phase are observable: the race between wages and prices has started; and the Federal Reserve system has had to meet a growing demand for redemption of maturing government issues, as well as to support the market for governments to an extent that may not exceed what we should expect in the normal course of managing a public debt of $250,000,000,000 but it is a danger signal all the same.

How to Stop Inflation: Measures to stop or mitigate inflation differ according to the phase the process has reached. Measures that promise success at a given moment may be futile a few months later.

We are in a stage of Advanced Inflation, with the race between prices and wages in full swing, though as yet far from Wild Inflation.

It is to this stage that the following survey of possible remedies refers. We shall consider them under four headings: 1, direct controls, 2, reducing the volume of means of payment, 3, credit restriction, 4, public finance.

But two things should be kept in mind.

First, there is no single remedy for the disease.

Second, it is not possible to stop Advanced Inflation without producing some symptoms of depression.

This puts the idea of a "rollback" of the price level out of court. Individual prices that are out of line will correct themselves if allowed to do so or may, in certain cases, have to be corrected by special action. But any attempt to reduce the price level as a whole would intensify the inevitable depression and cause widespread unemployment. The partial expropriation of bondholders, policyholders and other groups is no doubt regrettable. But we shall be lucky if we succeed in salvaging for them what they have left.

1. Direct Control of Prices, Consumption and Production: Such measures aim at suppressing the symptoms of the disease. Moreover, by suppressing the symptoms, they prevent necessary adjustments. But the public understands them readily and they afford opportunity for hitting unpopular scapegoats. Hence such measures always appeal to politicians. Three bills before Congress sponsored by Senators Capehart, Barkley and Taylor, bear witness to this. From Roman times on, such measures have been tried out in innumerable cases, never with success.

In our case, the public's growing impatience with bureaucratic vexations and the difficulty of extending the "freeze technique" to wages constitute obstacles that make these proposals hardly worth discussing.

This is not to say, however, that allocation, price control, and even rationing may not do more good than harm in individual cases, particularly when the Marshall plan gets under way. It is true that this plan will absorb no more than about three per cent of the nation's output and that it may not raise exports above the 1947 level. But it is at this level that inflation threatens to get out of hand and that a public demand for direct controls must be expected to develop.

The measure for European rehabilitation that has been recently passed, whatever we may think of it from other standpoints, must be considered as the most serious individual feature in our financial situation, especially if we fail to adjust to it our policies of taxation and of wages. There is no justification for hiding from the people how serious the burden is which it is bound to impose upon all classes of society. The relation of the measure to the revival of plans for direct control is obvious.

2. *Reducing the Volume of Means of Payments:* Since it is the creation of new money, no matter whether greenbacks or deposits, which causes the trouble, the natural remedy seems to be to eliminate it again. This can be effected by converting the inflated mass of money into a smaller amount which is what the Austrian Government did in 1811 and what has been done recently in Russia.

Or it can be effected by a capital levy the proceeds of which are to be destroyed. This was tried in several countries after World War I, always without success. With rigid price and wage rates, such an experiment would be much like trying to make a man stand up by pulling his chair from under him. It is difficult to see what difference it makes whether a man has more dollars with a lower level of purchasing power or fewer dollars with a higher. Stalin's measure would have been meaningless but for the levy on the peasants which it achieved.

3. *Credit Restrictions:* Those of us who believe that return to the principles of private enterprise will most speedily repair the ravages of the war realize, of course, that this implies the reestablishment of a normal money market. Accordingly, some advocate that cheap-money policies should be abandoned, that interest rates should be allowed to find their level, and that the Federal Reserve system should rely on discount policy, open-market operations, and the other methods of traditional money-market control.

This is in fact an important part of any program of long-run normalization and should be kept in view as the ultimate goal. Every business man and especially every banker should also realize, however, that the inflationary process has by now gone beyond the range within which orthodox banking policy can be expected to be effective and that, especially in a country with 14,000 banks, additional methods of credit control are necessary in order to reach that ultimate goal.

The argument that establishes this necessity runs as follows: The normal functioning of our credit system, as it established itself at the beginning of the 1920's, requires that the banks' ability to lend be regulated by the Federal Reserve system through its control over commercial bank reserves. No serious economist has ever denied that such regulative powers are necessary if excesses of lending and the consequent breakdowns are to be avoided.

But at present these regulative powers of the Federal Reserve system are paralyzed. Moderate increases in discount rates have little effect in inflation. Moreover, commercial banks hold about $70,000,000,000 of government securities which they can sell to Federal Reserve Banks thereby creating additional reserves and increasing their ability to lend, under present conditions, by six times the amount sold.

Even if we disregard the further increase of reserves that results from gold imports, this is a potential source of inflation compared with which the existing degree of inflation is as nothing. Nor is this all. Further expansion of credit must lead to further depreciation of the dollar in terms of commodities and services. This is bound to set in motion the mass of government and other bonds in the hands of non-bank holders. If the Government and the Federal Reserve system refuse to take up this supply, they may make matters still worse, because holders will then be even more eager to get rid of depreciating assets.

The poorest credit restriction scheme is in such circumstances better than none. Most of the proposed schemes, however — such as further increases in reserve requirements, limitation of the right of commercial banks to hold securities against deposits, establishment of special reserves to be held in Treasury bills and certificates — would do something to improve the situation.

It is true that such restrictive measures carry disadvantages and dangers. Those who advocate restrictions on industry's ability to borrow for plant improvement advocate sacrificing the nation's future to the present. Those who advocate withholding credit to an industry faced with incessantly increasing wages are advocating unemployment. But we have no choice except as between evils.

There is something that may be done, however, to minimize undesired effects of those controls. The most obvious danger points lie in the fields of consumers' credit and of mortgage credit on housing. Both have increased during the past few years, and are increasing still, at a rate that is incompatible with sound principles of credit management. Credit restriction might be chiefly directed against them. This would mitigate inflation and at the same time take account of the truth that the best remedy for inflation is increase in production.

However, if this increase in production is to have any positive effect, the volume of credit must not rise in the same proportion. In other words, an increase of production that is to counteract inflation involves more hours and better quality of work. It has been argued that our production is at or near its practical peak and that hence no significant increase in output can be expected from an increase in hours of work.

But production is at or near its peak only relative to the actual labor conditions. With more work available, different and more productive arrangements of processes would be possible, and any shortages of equipment or raw materials that might obstruct increase of output would be quickly eliminated. At present, any suggestion of an increase in hours is sure to be styled as an attack on labor. It should be obvious, however, that under actual conditions labor would almost immediately experience an increase in the purchasing power of wages.

4. Public Finance: Curtailment of public expenditures sufficient to produce a substantial budgetary surplus is the most orthodox of all means to fight inflation. But ordinarily it is also the most difficult to adopt because no other measure encounters an equally determined opposition and because inflation inevitably increases the cost of public administration.

As a rule, effective retrenchment involves rationalization of the whole apparatus of the federal, state, and local governments and restriction of many government activities, both of which are sure to be resisted.

Worst of all, many people who pay lip service to public economy go on advocating expensive schemes for European aid, increased GI benefits, extended social insurance, housing subsidies, universal military training, education and so on without bothering to specify how they propose to finance them. However, something may be achieved with comparative ease. The importance of the recent investigation of the National Association of Manufacturers that resulted in its proposed $31,000,000,000 federal budget lies precisely in its having established the fact that the elimination of the wastes of war finance would suffice to produce an impressive surplus even without rationalization of normal public administration, without restrictions on normal government activities, and without renouncing some of those expensive schemes entirely—in other words, without attacking at once the really hard part of the task before us.

We are also in the position of being able to discuss tax relief against the background of a budgetary surplus. But even if we are so optimistic as to take a substantial surplus for granted — a net surplus of all public bodies, not of the federal Government alone — this question is likely to divide economists.

Many of them oppose the use of economies to reduce taxes on the ground that this would neutralize the anti-inflationary effect of these economies: what governments economize, so they argue, would then be simply spent by individuals. So far as this is true we are, it seems, left with a result that is similar to that reached in the case of credit restriction.

However necessary tax reform might be as a part of a long-run scheme of normalization, we should have to conclude that, in order to create the conditions for it, the abnormal load has to be carried until the danger of inflation is past. But how far is it true that tax relief neutralizes the anti-inflationary effects of a budget surplus?

It is true so far as the sums by which tax reduction increases disposable incomes are actually spent on consumers' goods. It is not true so far as they are saved and invested. If it were possible to canalize them into industrial investment, they would exert an anti-inflationary effect because they would finance, in a non-inflationary manner, those industrial requirements that are at present financed by the inflationary method of borrowing from banks.

This can be achieved to a considerable extent. An old proposal comes to mind. This was to exempt savings from income taxes. To reduce the rates of the corporate and individual income taxes on the saved part of corporate and individual income without creating a deficit is in fact the best way of using available surplus, not only from the standpoint of long-run considerations about capital formation, but also from the standpoint of anti-inflationary policy.

This idea shouldn't offend economists who in the 1930's advocated tax policies that were hostile to saving.

On the contrary, it should appeal to them. For if they believed that measures hostile to saving — such as the undisturbed-profits tax — were indicated in a deflationary situation, they must, by the same token, expect favorable effects from opposite measures in an inflationary situation.

As regards the recent tax measure, economists are, I believe, unanimous or nearly so. If it creates a deficit, it is clearly inflationary. Even if it does not, it is at best neutral.

Relief to Europe and rearmament can only mean more taxation and not less. Tax remission in the lower income brackets is, of course, particularly dangerous. Illogical though this may seem, it will produce additional demands for increases in wages because it will first produce an additional increase in prices.

To sum up: It is not possible to stop inflation in its tracks, without creating a depression that may be too much for our political system to withstand. But it *is* possible to make the inflationary process die out, and in such a way as to avoid a depression of unbearable proportions.

Direct controls are futile, except as temporary measures in individual cases.

Reduction in the mass of money, by Stalin's method or by a capital levy, is out of the question.

Credit restriction is necessary to the extent indicated but not sufficient by itself. It must be supplemented by a pro-saving fiscal policy and by an attitude to public expenditures that is prepared to fight for every dollar.

If we add the proviso "except for emergencies" then all we shall achieve is that politicians will style any occasion to spend as an emergency. This attitude implies that for the time being the inflation issue should dominate national policy. Whoever else may object to this, it should not be the defender of our social system. For inflation undermines allegiance to that system, and demoralizes labor and the salaried class as does nothing else. One of the best things Lenin ever said was: "In order to destroy bourgeois society you must debauch its money."

Some readers may welcome a few words on the question of how far the recent fall in individual prices affects the argument of this article. Two things must be distinguished:

1. Certain prices had reached levels that were far out of line with the rest. It is as easy to account for this, by the conditions peculiar to them, as it is to account for their (partial) return to the general level even though this affects the cost of living index in a way that creates the misleading impression of a fall all around.

2. In addition to this, there is a reaction of the general level itself. But this fact lends no support to the belief that "inflation is over." Such setbacks, attended by unemployment, occur in every inflationary process.

The mechanism of these setbacks is not difficult to explain: it is akin to the breaks owing to profit-taking that we observe during booms on the stock exchange although, in our case, matters are not quite as simple.

The importance of the recent weakness of markets reduces to this: it affords an opportunity for carrying measures that will put a brake on inflation when pressure resumes. But that it will resume is not open to doubt although, owing to the political factor, it would be hazardous to say when.

ECONOMIC THEORY AND ENTREPRENEURIAL HISTORY

Reprinted from *Change and the Entrepreneur,* 1949, 63-84.

In the areas of economic theory and entrepreneurial history, I propose to deal with three topics. First, I shall present a brief survey of the history, within economic literature, of the notions that economists have formed at various times on the subject of entrepreneurship and economic progress (I). Secondly, I shall deal with some aspects of enterprise as it actually evolved through the ages (II). And, thirdly, I shall briefly comment on the possibilities of what might be termed "general economic history" as viewed from the standpoint of the phenomenon of economic enterprise (III). The first topic will also provide the conceptual apparatus to be used in the treatment of the other two.

I

In the field to be discussed, as in others, early economic analysis started from the notions evolved by common experience of everyday life, proceeding to greater precision and refinement of these notions as time went on. From the first, the businessman was a familiar figure that did not seem to call for elaborate explanation at all. The particular forms of business enterprise that every particular environment produced — the artisan, the trader, the money-lender, and so on — took a long time in merging into the general concept of businessman. But by the end of the 17th century this modest generalization was pretty much accomplished. It is, however, worth noting that at least from the beginning of the 15th century on, the scholastic doctors in their economics had a very definite idea of the businessman and his functions, and that in particular they distinguished clearly between the specific *industria* of the merchant and the *labor* of the workman. The same applies to the laic successors of the scholastic doctors, "the philosophers of natural law," and still more to all those pamphleteers of the "mercantilist" age that laid the foundations of classic economics. Cantillon's work, which is usually, though not quite correctly, described as the first systematic treatise on economics, then introduced the term "entrepreneur." It is worth our while to note that Cantillon defined this entrepreneur as the agent who buys means of production at certain prices in order to combine them into a product that he is going to sell at prices that are uncertain at the moment at which he commits himself to his costs. I think that this embryonic analysis was not infelicitous. Besides recognizing business activity as a function *sui generis,* it emphasizes the elements of direction and speculation that certainly do enter somehow into entrepreneurial activity. Like most of Cantillon's ideas, including the idea of the *tableau économique,* this one was accepted by the physiocrats as a matter of course. Since directly and through the physiocrats Cantillon's teaching continued to be known in France, it seems fair to say that J. B. Say only continued the French tradition by developing this analysis further. In this he was greatly helped by the fact that, knowing from experience what business practice really is, he had a lively vision of the phenomenon which most of the other classic economists lacked. With him, then, the entrepreneur is the agent that combines the others into a productive organism. It could be shown both that this definition might be expanded into a satisfactory theory of entrepreneurship by analyzing what this combining of factors really consists in, and that Say himself did not do much with it beyond stressing its importance. Let us note in passing, however, that he put the entrepreneur into the center of both the productive and the distributive theory which, though it is disfigured by many slips, first adumbrated the analytic structure that became fully articulate in the hands of Walras, Marshall, Wicksell, Clark, and the Austrians. Still more clearly the nature and importance of entrepreneurship were perceived by Jeremy Bentham. It is a curious fact (curious, that is, considering the tremendous influence that Bentham exerted in other respects) that his views on this subject — which were not fully given to the public until the posthumous publication of his collected works — remained almost unnoticed by professional economists.

In spite of the great influence of the physiocrats and of Cantillon upon Adam Smith, English thought took a quite different line. To be sure, Adam Smith repeatedly talked about the employer — the master, the merchant, and the undertaker — but the leading or directing activity as a distinctive function played a surprisingly small role in his analytic scheme of the economic process. His reader is bound to get an impression to the effect that this process runs on by itself. Natural law preconceptions led Adam Smith to emphasize the role of labor to the exclusion of the productive function of designing the plan according to which this labor is being applied. This shows characteristically in his turn of phrase that asserts that "capitalists" hire "industrious people," advancing them means of subsistence, raw materials, and tools, and letting them do the rest. What the businessman does in the system of Adam Smith is, therefore, to provide real capital and nothing else: the identification of the capitalist's and the entrepreneur's function was thus accomplished. Let us note: first, that this picture of the industrial process is entirely unrealistic; but that, considering the prevalence at Adam Smith's time of the putting-out system, and also for other historical reasons, this identification was then less absurd than it became fifty years later; and that Smith's authority explains why it survived so well into times that presented different patterns. Since capital, according to Adam Smith, is the result of saving, and since providing capital is the only essential function of the businessman, the latter's profits was essentially interest to be explained on the lines of either an exploitation or an abstinence theory. Adam Smith elaborated neither, but no doubt suggested both.

With Ricardo and Marx the processes of production and commerce are still more automatic. The designing, directing, leading, co-ordinating function has practically no place at all in their analytic schemata. To avoid misunderstandings, let me emphasize that there is no doubt but that, if pressed, both Ricardo and Marx (and this goes for a majority of the writers of the classic period) would certainly have recognized the importance of entrepreneurship or business management or however they would have called it, for the success or failure of the individual concern. But it is possible to recognize this and to hold, nevertheless, that for the social process as a whole individual differences in this respect are of no great moment. John Stuart Mill who, at an early age, had experienced the influence of Say, abandoned Ricardianism in this as he did in other points. He emphasized the function of direction in the productive process and went out of his way to say that very often it required "no ordinary skill." His perception of the importance of entrepreneurial activity shows among other things in the fact that he regretted that there is no good English word for the French "entrepreneur." But this was all. When we observe that he analyzed the entrepreneur's profits into wages of management, interest on owned capital, and premium of risk, we wonder why he should not have been content with the perfectly good English term "business management," which was in fact to satisfy Marshall. For, after all, his entrepreneur does a type of non-manual work that does not essentially differ from other types, and therefore reaps a return that is analogous to wages. There should be no need for a distinctive term.

Just as the understanding of the phenomenon of rent of land was facilitated by the English land system that showed up the distinction between the owner of land and the agricultural producer with unmistakable clearness, so the distinction between the entrepreneur and the capitalist was facilitated in the second half of the 19th century by the fact that changing methods of business finance produced a rapidly increasing number of instances in which capitalists were no entrepreneurs and entrepreneurs were no capitalists. Though the owner-manager remained for a time still the ruling type, it became increasingly clear that a link between owning and operating the physical shell of industry is not a necessary one. Economists accordingly began to emphasize distinctions between the two functions and to devote more attention to the specifically entrepreneurial one. Fundamental change in the analytic set-up was very slow, however. Among other things, this shows in the survival of the risk theory of entrepreneurial profit. If providing the capital is not the essential or defining function of the entrepreneur, then risk bearing should not be described as an essential or defining function either, for it is obviously the capitalist who bears the risk and who loses his money in case of failure. If the entrepreneur borrows at a fixed rate of interest and undertakes to guarantee the capitalist against loss whatever the results of the enterprise, he can do so only if he owns other assets with which to satisfy the creditor capitalist when things go wrong. But, in this case, he is able to satisfy his creditor because he is a capitalist himself and the risk he bears he bears in this capacity and not in his capacity of entrepreneur. To this point I shall return below. The economists, therefore, who went on to emphasize the entrepreneurial function more and more, such as Francis A. Walker in the U. S., Marshall in England, Mangoldt and others in Germany, added very little to its analysis.

Two lines of thought that issued in distinctive theories of entrepeneurial profits as distinguished from interest should not go unmentioned. Mangoldt, following up a generalization of the rent concept that may be traced to Samuel Bailey, defined the particular element of total receipts that goes to the entrepreneur as a rent of ability. The underlying idea is very plausible. All current disturbances of the economic process, the whole task of adaptation to ever changing situations, impinges primarily upon the heads of business concerns. Obviously this is a very personal task of which some people acquit themselves very much better than others. There is a common-sense impression to the effect that there is such a thing as a distinct business ability, which includes aptitude for efficient administration, for prompt decision, and all that sort of thing; and it is very generally recognized in spite of some votes to the contrary (in this country, mainly from economists of Veblenite persuasion) that successful survival of difficult situations and success in taking advantage of favorable situations is not merely a matter of luck. The concept of a rent of ability expresses the element involved quite well. Again the cognate idea that business decisions in a world that is full of uninsurable risks ("uncertainty") will in general produce results that diverge more or less widely from the expected ones and thus lead sometimes to surplus gains and sometimes to losses, is one that common experience presses upon us very strongly. This idea may be but need not be added to the element of business ability and is of course, still more obviously, not quite the same as the element of risk: but we need not stress these relations. So far as I know, Böhm-Bawerk was the first to make use of this notion for the purpose of explaining entrepreneurial profits as distinct from interest. But this line of thought culminates in the work of Professor Knight.

It does not seem far-fetched, however, to analyze the entrepreneurial function in a different direction which moreover leads to a result that comprises also some of the elements of other theories. I shall try to convey this analysis by starting from two different standpoints. The first standpoint to start from is given by Say's definition of the entrepreneurial function. If production in the economic, as distinguished from the technological, sense consists essentially in transforming or combining factors into products, or as I have put it above, in providing the design of production, then we certainly have in this combining or planning or directing activity a distinct function before us. But this function would be an exceedingly simple matter and essentially a matter of administration if the combinations that have been carried into effect in the past had to be simply repeated or even if they had to be repeated subject to those adaptations which common business experience suggests in the face of conditions that change under the influence of external factors. Administrative or managerial activity of this kind, however necessary, need not be distinguished from other kinds of non-manual labor; but if we confine Say's definition to cases in which combinations that are *not* inherited from the past have to be set up anew, then the situation is obviously different and we do have a distinctive function before us. Naturally, to some extent, even current decisions contain elements that have not been contained in inherited routine. There is, therefore, no sharp dividing line between entrepreneurial activity in this restricted sense and ordinary administration or management, any more than there is a sharp dividing line between the *homo neanderthalis* and the types which we recognize as full-fledged human beings. This does not, however, prevent the distinction from being possible and useful. And the distinctive element is readily recognized so soon as we make clear to ourselves what it means to act outside of the pale of routine. The distinction between adaptive and creative response to given conditions may or may not be felicitous, but it conveys an essential point; it conveys an essential difference.

The other standpoint from which to get a realistic understanding of the entrepreneurial function comes into view when we try to analyze the nature and sources of the gains that attend successful entrepreneurship. This can be done in many ways, for instance, by analyzing the sources of a sufficient number of industrial fortunes. We find immediately that industrial activity in established lines and by established methods hardly ever yields returns that are much greater than is necessary to secure the supply of the factors required. Furthermore, we find that the earning capacity of almost any industrial concern peters out after a time that varies from a few months to a few decades. And, finally, we find that the great surplus gains are in general made in new industries or in industries that adopt a new method, and especially by the firms who are the first in the field. These propositions await scientific investigations in order to be fully established, but are strongly suggested by universally known facts.

If then we have, on the one hand, a distinctive function and, on the other hand, a distinct return on the exercise of this function, we can start with the task of conceptualization. First, we need a word. I have myself suggested that the word "entrepreneur" be harnessed into service, but it is quite clear, of course, that since this "entrepreneurial function" is not a neologism other meanings are bound to creep in. I should, therefore, have no objection to some such expression as "business leader" or simply "innovator" or the like. The essential thing is the recognition of the distinct agent we envisage and not the word.[1] Secondly, in applying our conception to reality we find, as we do in other such cases, that real life never presents the function in and by itself. Even the English landlord is not merely the owner of a natural agent but does various other things besides. In the case of the entrepreneur it is even difficult to imagine a case where a man does nothing but set up new combinations and where he does this all his life. In particular an industrialist who creates an entirely new set-up will, in a typical case, then settle down to a merely administrating activity to which he confines himself more and more as he gets older. On the other hand, the entrepreneurial element may be present to a very small extent even in very humble cases and in these the entrepreneurial function may be all but drowned in other activities. It will be seen, however, that while this makes it difficult to deal with entrepreneurship irrespective of the other types of activity of the same individual and while Professor Cole is therefore quite right in emphasizing the necessity of considering business activity as a whole, the distinctive element and its *modus operandi* should not and need not be lost from sight.

Thirdly, since entrepreneurship, as defined, essentially consists in doing things that are not generally done in the ordinary course of business routine, it is essentially a phenomenon that comes under the wider aspect of leadership. But this relation between entrepreneurship and general leadership is a very complex one and lends itself to a number of misunderstandings. This is due to the fact that the concept of leadership itself is complex. Leadership may consist, as it does in the arts, merely in doing a new thing, for instance, in creating a new form of pictorial self-expression, but in other cases it is the influencing of people by methods other than example that is more important. Take, for instance, the phenomenon that we call the ability of being obeyed. Here it is not so much

[1] The difficulty of naming our function is of course greatly increased by the fact that such words as "management" or "administration" from which we are trying to distinguish our function have with many authors also caught some of the meanings that we wish to reserve for the term "entrepreneur."

example as a direct action upon other people that matters. The nature and function of entrepreneurial leadership, its causes and effects, therefore constitute a very important subject of investigation for our group.

Fourthly, the distinctive return to entrepreneurship presents difficulties of its own. It is certainly a return to a personal activity. In this sense we might be tempted to call it a form of wages as has in fact been done in the past by many economists. Furthermore, it is clear that if all people reacted in the same way and at the same time to the presence of new possibilities no entrepreneurial gain would ensue: if everybody had been in a position to develop the Watt condenser, prices of products to be produced with the new steam engine would have adjusted themselves instantaneously and no surplus over costs would have arisen for the firm of Boulton and Watt. Therefore, entrepreneurial gain may also be called a monopoly gain, since it is due to the fact that competitors only follow at a distance.[2] But if we called it either wages or monopoly gains we should be obscuring very important characteristics that do not apply to other wages or to other monopoly gains. Moreover, the entrepreneurial gain does not typically consist, and in any case does not necessarily consist, in a current surplus *per se*. If a man, for instance, sets up a new industrial organization such as United States Steel, the value of the assets that enter into this organization increases. This increase no doubt embodies, at least ideally, a discounted value of the expected surplus returns. But it is this increase in asset return itself rather than the returns that constitute the entrepreneurial gain, and it is in this way that industrial fortunes are typically created — another subject to be investigated.

Finally, as has been often pointed out, the entrepreneurial function need not be embodied in a physical person and in particular in a single physical person. Every social environment has its own ways of filling the entrepreneurial function. For instance, the practice of farmers in this country has been revolutionized again and again by the introduction of methods worked out in the Department of Agriculture and by the Department of Agriculture's success in teaching these methods. In this case then it was the Department of Agriculture that acted as an entrepreneur. It is

[2]The rate of speed at which competitors follow is another very important point for our research program, as are the means at the disposal of the successful entrepreneur for holding his own against would-be competitors (patents and other practices)

another most important point in our research program to find out how important this kind of activity has been in the past or is in the present. Again the entrepreneurial function may be and often is filled co-operatively. With the development of the largest-scale corporations this has evidently become of major importance: aptitudes that no single individual combines can thus be built into a corporate personality; on the other hand, the constituent physical personalities must inevitably to some extent, and very often to a serious extent, interfere with each other. In many cases, therefore, it is difficult or even impossible to name an individual that acts as "the entrepreneur" in a concern. The leading people in particular, those who carry the titles of president or chairman of the board, may be mere co-ordinators or even figure-heads; and again a very interesting field of research opens up into which I do not wish to go, however, since this problem is in no danger of being forgotten.[3]

We have now briefly to advert to the relation that exists between economic change (usually called economic progress if we approve of it) and the entrepreneurial activity. At present there is, as has been stated above, a whole range of differences of opinion on this subject that extends from a complete or almost complete denial of any importance to be attached to the quality of leading personnel to the equally reckless assertion that the creative individual is nothing less than everything. It need hardly be pointed out that most of these opinions carry the stamp of ideological preconception. It is no doubt part of our work to put provable results into the place of such ideologies. The fundamental question is one of fact, but the necessity of a theoretical schema to start with is nevertheless obvious. I submit that the material under observation may be classed into two masses: on the one hand, there are the given data of the physical and social (including political) environment and, on the other hand, there are the observable reactions to these environmental conditions. But it is better perhaps to include those

[3]It is extremely interesting to observe that for a long time and occasionally even now economic theorists have been and are inclined to locate the entrepreneurial function in a corporation with the shareholders. However little the individual small shareholder may have to do with the actual management or else with the entrepreneurial function in the corporation, they hold that ultimate decision still lies with them to be exerted in the shareholders' meeting. All I wish to say about this is first, that the whole idea of risk-taking in this way takes on a further lease of life and, second, that such a theory is about as true as is the political theory that in a democracy the electorate ultimately decides what is to be done.

facts that may be independently observed concerning the quality of leading personnel among the conditions in order to display the interrelation between this and the other factors and to emphasize from the first that on principle there are never any causal chains in the historical process but only mutual interaction of distinguishable factors.

We can then attempt to construct an analytic model of the mechanism of economic change or else, for different countries and periods, different such schemata or models. Let us, in order to visualize this method, consider for a moment the situation that existed in England around 1850. A unique set of historical conditions had produced a uniquely able political sector, the bulk of the members of which hailed from a distinct social class. This sector, while very efficient in certain respects, was entirely unfit and unwilling to undertake anything that we now call economic public management or economic planning. Neglecting for the rest the agrarian sector, we find industry, trade, and finance substantially left to themselves; and if we add a number of other unique historical circumstances we are pretty much able to draw the picture of economic change that is in fact drawn in the ordinary text-book of economic history. In this process of change it is possible to identify a number of factors and events that are entirely impersonal and in some cases random. But looking more closely we see not only that these factors do not determine outcomes uniquely but also that they do not tell us how the actual changes such as the tremendous increase in exports actually came about. In order to make headway with this problem we must investigate how the thousands of individuals actually worked whose combined action produced these results. And for this purpose it is useful as a first step to assume all the environmental factors to be constant and to ask the question what changes we might expect under this assumption. We immediately see that simple increase of population and of physical capital does not constitute the answer. It is not simply the increase of the existing factors of production but the incessantly different use made of these factors that matters. In fact much of the increase in factors and particularly of physical capital was the result rather than the cause of what we may now identify as entrepreneurial activity. What we observe is rather a behavior pattern, possibly supplemented by a schema of motivation; a typical way of giving effect to the possibilities inherent in a given legal and social system both of which change in the process; the effects of entrepreneurial activity upon the industrial structure that exists at any moment; the consequent process of destruction and reconstruction that went on all the time. All these things may be conceptualized in a more or less complicated schema, every item of which has to be nourished with facts and corrected and amplified under their influence. And this is all.

I shall add, however, that in investigations of this kind the notion of an economic process that merely reproduces itself and shows neither decay nor progress has been found to be of considerable use. It is called the stationary state, and plays two distinct roles in economic theory. On the one hand, economists, ever since Adam Smith and perhaps earlier times, have envisaged the possibility that the energetic advance they were witnessing would some day subside into what we now call a stagnating or mature economy. John Stuart Mill differed from Ricardo not in his expectation that a stationary state would one day emerge but in the optimistic view he took of its features — a world without what he considered an unpleasant bustle, a world much more cultured and at ease than the one he observed. Now, as everybody knows, this "stagnationist thesis" has emerged once more, but it has emerged with two differences. First, the stationary state is by some authors not looked upon as something that looms in the far future but as something on which we are actually about to enter. Let us note in passing that the experiences of the crises 1929-1932 may have a lot to do with the emergence of this frame of mind. Secondly, a problem has arisen which did not worry the classics at all. Smith or Ricardo did not anticipate any particular difficulties that would arise from the very process of settling down into stationality: rates of change would converge towards zero in a slow and orderly way. But our modern stagnationists anticipate difficulties in this process of settling down. Keynes in particular anticipated that habits of saving to which equally strong or still stronger propensities to invest corresponded would run on in spite of the fact that there would be no longer any investment opportunities left. With everything indicating now that a new period of unheard-of "progress" is at hand it might be thought that we need not greatly worry about this. But I do not think that we can entirely overlook the problem and history's contribution to it.

II

Whether we define the entrepreneur as an "innovator" or in any other way, there remains the task to see how the chosen definition works out in practice as applied to historical materials. In fact it might be argued that the historical investigation holds logical priority and that our definitions of entrepreneur, entrepreneurial function, enterprise, and so on can only grow out of it *a posteriori*. Personally, I believe that there is an incessant give and take between historical and theoretical analysis and that, though for the investigation of individual questions it may be necessary to sail for a time on one tack only, yet on principle the two should never lose sight of each other. In consequence we might formulate our task as an attempt to write a comprehensive history of entrepreneurship.

So far as the institutional framework is concerned we are, comparatively speaking, well off. The social, legal, technological, and other conditions in which entrepreneurship has run its historical course, from the primitive tribe to the modern large-scale corporation, have been on the whole satisfactorily worked out already. But until relatively recent times it is this framework only that is really known: the actual activity of the entrepreneur, what he really was and did at various stages of historical development, is largely construction. It is true that this construction is in many cases quite safe. For instance, when we know the trade routes in the Near East during the first ten centuries A.D., the commodities that were transported, the political history of the territories through which they were transported, it is not very difficult to imagine the kind of tasks and difficulties that the trader met on these routes and the kind of chap he must have been in order to overcome them. When we know the history of the later trading companies such as the Trading Company of Ravensburg, we again have little difficulty in complementing this by a picture of the kind of man that a member of this company must have been. And to a certain extent we might hope to answer the question directly how environment, public authority, corporate action, and individual initiative must have co-operated and what relative weight we are to attach to each. However, these are favorable cases. In others, much digging may have to be done before we arrive at reliable results. Let us then note that the forms of organization of trade and later on of manufacturing are an acquired asset all along. The same applies largely to the fields and methods of what provisionally we should call entrepreneurial activity. That is to say we know or readily understand that at some times under certain conditions entrepreneurial activity must have consisted largely in trading and transporting, in manufacturing and organizing and financing at others. Finally, the history of entrepreneurial types and of the nature of entrepreneurial performance, the action of these types on the social organization and the reaction of the social bodies on the entrepreneurial impulse should not be too difficult to analyze. Having thus adumbrated my ideas about what that history of entrepreneurship should do, I want now briefly to touch upon a number of problems and stumbling blocks that will inevitably be met with on this road.

The first of all these stumbling blocks is that most of us do not approach the material with a perfectly unbiased mind. In other words, every age and every social organization approaches these problems from an *apriori* of its own, that is to say, from a conviction (all the more dangerous if subconscious) that individual initiative in the matter of economic development counts for almost everything or else for almost nothing, and it is easy to see how such a conviction supplies the basic colors of the picture. For some of us the problem of economic development is all but solved so soon as natural and social conditions and political measures are stated — the rest follows automatically, and if entrepreneurs have anything to do with what actually happens they are a sort of beast of prey who withhold the fruits of technological advance from the community and sabotage progress in their own interest. It is needless to point out that this attitude is very prevalent in this country and that any attempt to take another view is for many a modern economist stigmatized as apologetics. Nevertheless, it should be clear from even a superficial survey of facts that this view is as wrong as is the exactly opposite one and that careful discussion of ever more numerous situations is the only method of arriving at a more tenable one.

Secondly, in connection with this we frequently meet with an attitude that is indeed a necessary prerequisite for the "theory" just alluded to. This attitude may be expressed by saying that the entrepreneur or money-maker simply does nothing but take advantage of technological progress, which therefore appears, implicitly or explicitly, as something that goes along entirely independently of entrepreneurial activity. Now how far is this true? It is perhaps not difficult to understand that technological progress, so obvious in some societies and so nearly absent in others, is a phenomenon that needs to be explained. For instance, it is necessary to find out whether the rational or rationalist attitude to life has or has not been formed by the type of mind that pervades bourgeois society. In this case technological progress would be related to entrepreneurial action in a way that may not always be obvious but would be very important all the same. I have always emphasized that the entrepreneur is the man who gets new things done and not necessarily the man who invents. As a matter of history, the entrepreneur is almost as often an inventor as he is a capitalist but it seems to me that analysis shows that neither of these capacities are essential to him. I can adduce plenty of examples by which to illustrate what seems to me to be the true relation, but only extensive research can present really reliable results.

Thirdly, let us consider a very old problem that has played more of a role in economic literature than it does now under the title of "original accumulation." Some command over physical and personal factors is no doubt necessary in order to start any enterprise: but how is such command acquired in the first place? The old classical answer, that resources came from savings, was understandably unpopular with socialists and is equally unpopular with modern radicals. And it is quite true that, however great the role of self-financing may be in the course of the development of an enterprise, the original nucleus of means has been but rarely acquired by the entrepreneur's own saving activity — which in fact is one of the reasons, and a significant one, for distinguishing the entrepreneur as sharply as I think he should be distinguished from the capitalist. One important source of the means for early enterprise is no doubt to be found in the fact that such means were available in the hands of extra-bourgeois strata and in particular in the hands of temporal and spiritual lords. As everybody knows, this source has been particularly stressed by Sombart and drew so much critical fire that Sombart himself practically surrendered it. But the last word has certainly not been spoken on this affair and if we command co-operation from medieval historians we might well ask them to go into the matter. Another explanation is in the fact that for many types of enterprise the minimum of means to start with was very small: a shack which a man could put up with his own hands, very simple tools, and very few assistants were sometimes all that was required. Means of that order of magnitude many people would possess for a variety of reasons. A third source was tapping the savings of other people and "created credit." The roles of these two last-mentioned sources, though in a general way obvious, also deserve further research. "Credit creation" introduces banks and quasi-banking activities. Here we meet with the difficulty that orthodox banking theory, emphasizing as it does current financing of current trade transactions as the main function of banks, did its best to obliterate all that banks had to do with bringing into existence new industries. French and German experience offers a rich field for the study of this phenomenon, and the common saying that in the United States enterprise developed so well because its banking system was so bad also indicates an important truth: after all, we should not simply shut our eyes or sanctimoniously disapprove when we find that in certain cases even railroad building was financed by the issue of bank notes. Fourthly, it stands to reason that a bank which finances the overhead of a new enterprise must at the very least supervise very closely the behavior of the enterprise founded. That is to say, the necessity of supervising customers which exists to some extent even for the most ordinary routine business acquired in the case envisaged a novel importance. In consequence, two phenomena are observable which are so essential for capitalist life that they are well worth our attention. On the one hand, banks have, though to a very different extent in different countries, established themselves as a social organ of entrepreneurial activity. What this supervision actually consisted in, what the means were by which it was actually carried out, and the success with which it was exerted, has been frequently discussed but quite inadequately, even if we neglect the fact that many social critics have seen nothing in this institution (and it is an institution of later capitalism) but abuse. On the other hand, entrepreneurs and industrialists generally have fought against the restrictions imposed upon their freedom of action by bankers' interference, and important features of modern industrial policy are precisely explainable by the wish of industrialists to free themselves from it. For instance, this has been an important feature of industrial policy in this country during the first World War and in the 1920's. But an entrepreneur can also gain freedom from interference by bankers by turning into a banker himself. John Law and the brothers Pereire are outstanding examples. They illustrate also something else, namely, the fact that the economic and social meaning of this kind of activity has been almost invariably misunderstood.

However, if we could poll business leaders, we should, I am convinced, establish that according to their opinion it is self-financing from earnings which constitutes the soundest method of providing the means for raising an enterprise to its full size. This method, too, is highly unpopular with modern economists and its investigation is a matter of urgent necessity — as is, by the way, the opposite phenomenon, namely, the phenomenon that expenditure on current replacement of equipment is very often financed on credit. The actual results of the method of self-financing, for instance, the question whether or not it involves malallocation of resources, are so much blurred by preconceptions that a reopening of the case promises to add considerably to our knowledge of how modern business works.

III

In the enterprise economy the entrepreneur will inevitably exert some influence on things in general; hence the study of his interests, positions, and so on necessarily constitutes one of the possible approaches to an understanding of economic history or even of history in general. A recent paper by Professor Cochran may be referred to for the general philosophy of this approach as against the approach embodied in what he calls the "presidential synthesis."[4]

It has been emphasized above that when we speak of the entrepreneur we do not mean so much a physical person as we do a function, but even if we look at individuals who at least at some juncture in their lives fill the entrepreneurial function it should be added that these individuals do not form a social class. They hail from all the corners of the social universe. For instance, if we list all the entrepreneurs mentioned in Mantoux's work on the Industrial Revolution we find among them the Duke of Bridgewater and we may, starting from him, go through practically the whole extent of the social ladder until we reach men who rose to entrepreneurship from the ranks of manual labor. This seems to me a very important fact. How important precisely it is can again be only said after extensive research. However, all the men who actually do fulfill entrepreneurial functions have certain interests in common and, very much more important than this, they acquire capitalist positions in case of success. The modern corporation has not entirely done away with inheritance of this capitalist position and so we may say that entrepreneurs do in the end land in the capitalist class, at first as a rule in its most active sector until they wind up in its less active and finally in its decaying sector. I believe that this statement can be supported successfully but I do confess to a wish to see it established.

Now the man whose mind is entirely absorbed by a struggle for

[4]Cochran, Thomas C., "The presidential synthesis in American history," American Historical Review, vol. 53 (1948), pp. 748-59.

entrepreneurial success has as a rule very little energy left for serious activity in any other direction — some philanthropy and some more or less well-advised collectors' interests usually fill the bill. What then does the influence or the power consist in which most economists and historians attribute to him? I shall state frankly that I consider power to be one of the most misused words in the social sciences, though the competition is indeed great. So firmly entrenched in our popular psychology is the idea that entrepreneurs or else the capitalist class into which they merge are the prime movers of modern politics that it is very difficult to make headway against it and to point out how very little foundation there is to this opinion. Let me take an example that is far enough removed from us to be looked at with something like detachment: Ehrenberg's book on the Fuggers.[5] There, the rise and decline of that industrial, commercial, and financial family is in my opinion described in a perfectly responsible way. Among other things, the report itself clearly shows that in the time of Charles V the two Fuggers who came into contact with the imperial policy and especially its financial needs exerted no influence on this imperial policy other than is implied in their getting various concessions, especially mining concessions, in the Emperor's Latin territories. For the rest, however, they were ruthlessly exploited, so much so in fact that their wealth declined in consequence, and there is no sign whatever that they influenced the Emperor's policy in such matters as his attitude toward the Protestants, toward France, toward the Turks, and so on. Although all this is quite clear from Ehrenberg's own report, he is, nevertheless, so imbued with the idea that in a capitalist age the capitalists rule as to emphasize repeatedly what he considers to be the proud position of power of that family. Now this instance could be multiplied as everyone knows and at the end of a long list of instances, if I could present it, I should mention a conversation I had with an otherwise quite intelligent lawyer who defended the legislation that was to subject the insurance companies to federal control on the ground that "we cannot allow the insurance companies to run the country."

It seems to me that at the outset it is necessary to distinguish two entirely different things. Naturally, as has been pointed out above, the mere emergence of a quantitatively significant number of entrepreneurs presupposes, and its existence contributes to, a certain type of civilization and a certain state of the public mind. En-

[5] Ehrenberg, Richard, "Das Zeitalter der Fugger" (Jena, 1896), 2 v.

trepreneurs will be few and without great importance in situations where this activity is despised and frowned upon, and entreprenurial success in turn will tend to change such a situation. If I had space to develop this point, I should end up by saying that to some extent entrepreneurial activity impresses the stamp of its mentality upon the social organism. In any cultural history, therefore, the entrepreneurial factor will have to come in as one of the explaining elements, but this is not the same as saying that the wishes and interests of entrepreneurs or even of the capitalist class into which they merge is a political factor that counts by direct influence or else at the polls. It is quite true that in individual cases, for reasons of self-defense primarily, individual entrepreneurs need to acquire and do acquire political positions of their own. But the importance of these positions seems to be limited, and the way to show this is to analyze the means at their disposal in order to exert influence, such as contributions to politicians' war chests, or ownership of newspapers, and so on. I think it can be shown that the influence that can be acquired in these and other ways is much smaller than it is usually supposed to be. In fact, little more is necessary in order to convince one's self of this than to look at the modern situation in practically all countries. Methodological questions of great interest arise in the course of an attempt to investigate these matters. To begin with, we should have to have a much more realistic theory of politics than any that has been developed so far, but this is not enough. In order to see what entrepreneurs or the capitalist class as a whole can and cannot do, it is necessary to establish facts which are extremely difficult to get at and the appraisal of which requires a kind of experience of life which, even in those cases in which it is present in a research worker, is confined to individual environments, inferences from which may easily mislead.

The attitude of the state to entrepreneurial activity is a most fascinating study and raises questions of interpretation such as these: what was the nature of that amphibial condition of society that culminated in the state of Louis XIV? The court and the bureaucracy which ruled that state were no doubt alive to the fact that in order to spend as they did they needed adequate objects of taxation and that the most promising of these objects was a powerful community of traders and manufacturers. Thus a large group of measures find a ready explanation in the wishes to further the wealth and taxable capacity of the bourgeoisie. But what precisely does this mean and how would all parties concerned fare as a result?

Colbert has had among historians his fervent admirers. To my immense amusement, I have also found that Sir John Clapham described him as a big, stupid, brutal fellow, who never had an idea in his life. Whatever else such judgments prove or do not prove they certainly establish one thing: that the nature and amount of influence exerted by public administration in the period in question really is no more than a big question mark; and if we leave the time of Louis XIV and transfer ourselves into our own I feel that the question mark is still bigger.

IV

Students interested in the history of economic thought and in the writings upon economic development will draw two important, though variant conclusions from their inquiries as far as entrepreneurship and entrepreneurial history are concerned. First, I believe that they would be justified in the view that theories of past economists relative specifically to entrepreneurship will not form a very firm support for future investigations of facts. New hypotheses and the marshalling of factual data, old and new, must proceed together.

Secondly, I would commend to economic historians — and, for that matter, to economic theorists, if they will interest themselves in the problem — that they examine the already available secondary literature for data upon entrepreneurial characteristics and phenomena. A miscellany of such writings — from general economic histories to biographies of businessmen, and from local histories to studies of technological change — all hold information, which sifted and arranged with definite hypotheses in mind will carry us a goodly distance toward our goal. New facts will doubtless be needed in the end, but already we have a multitude that have as yet not been digested.

In the handling of old and new facts, the historian will gain from keeping in touch with theorists. Neither group should ever be distant from one another — but here the promise from collaboration is particularly great for both parties. As I have said before, the study of economic change is an area of research where "economic historians and economic theorists can make an interesting and socially valuable journey together, if they will."[6]

---

[6]Cf. my "Creative Response in Economic History," Journal of Economic History, vol. 7 (1947), p. 149.

SCIENCE AND IDEOLOGY*

Reprinted from *American Economic Review,* March 1949, 345-359.

I

A hundred years ago economists were much more pleased with their performance than they are today. But I submit that, if complacency can ever be justified, there is much more reason for being complacent today than there was then or even a quarter of a century ago. As regards command of facts, both statistical and historical, this is so obviously true that I need not insist. And if it be true of our command of facts, it must be true also for all the applied fields that for their advance mainly depend upon fact finding. I must insist, however, on the proposition that our powers of analysis have grown in step with our stock of facts. A new organon of statistical methods has emerged, to some extent by our own efforts, that is bound to mean as much to us as it does to all the sciences, such as biology or experimental psychology, the phenomena of which are given in terms of frequency distributions. In response to this development and in alliance with it, as well as independently, our own box of analytic tools has been greatly enriched: economic theory, in the instrumental sense of the term—in which it means neither the teaching of ultimate ends of policy nor explanatory hypotheses but simply the sum total of our methods of handling facts—has grown quite as much as Marshall and Pareto had foreseen that it would.

If this is not more generally recognized and if it is etiquette with economists—let alone the public—to pass derogatory judgment on the state of our science, this is owing to a number of causes that, though known all too well, should be repeated: a building plot on which old structures are being torn down and new ones erected is not an esthetic thing to behold; moreover, to a most discouraging extent the new structures are being currently discredited by premature attempts at utilitarian application; finally, the building area widens so

* Presidential address delivered at the Sixty-first Annual Meeting of the American Economic Association, Cleveland, Ohio, December 28, 1948.

that it becomes impossible for the individual worker to understand everything that is going on beyond his own small sector. It would indeed be difficult to present in systematic form, as the Smiths, Mills, and Marshalls have been able to do with more or less success, a comprehensive treatise that might display some measure of unity and command all but universal approval. Thus, though the workers in each sector are not at all displeased with how they are getting on themselves, they are quite likely to disapprove of the manner in which those in all the others go about their tasks, or even to deny that these other tasks are worth bothering about at all. This is but natural. Many types of mind are needed to build up the structure of human knowledge, types which never quite understand one another. Science is technique and the more it develops, the more completely does it pass out of the range of comprehension not only of the public but, minus his own chosen specialty, of the research worker himself. More or less, this is so everywhere although greater uniformity of training and greater discipline of endeavor may in physics reduce the tumult to something like order. As everyone knows, however, there is with us another source of confusion and another barrier to advance: most of us, not content with their scientific task, yield to the call of public duty and to their desire to serve their country and their age, and in doing so bring into their work their individual schemes of values and all their policies and politics—the whole of their moral personalities up to their spiritual ambitions.

I am not going to reopen the old discussion on value judgments or about the advocacy of group interests. On the contrary, it is essential for my purpose to emphasize that *in itself* scientific performance does not require us to divest ourselves of our value judgments or to renounce the calling of an advocate of some particular interest. To investigate facts or to develop tools for doing so is one thing; to evaluate them from some moral or cultural standpoint is, *in logic*, another thing, and the two *need* not conflict. Similarly, the advocate of some interest may yet do honest analytic work, and the motive of proving a point for the interest to which he owes allegiance does not in itself prove anything for or against this analytic work: more bluntly, advocacy does not imply lying. It spells indeed misconduct to bend either facts or inferences from facts in order to make them serve either an ideal or an interest. But such misconduct is not necessarily inherent in a worker's arguing from "axiological premises" or in advocacy *per se*.[1] Examples abound in which economists have estab-

[1] The above passage should be clear. But it may be as well to make its meaning more explicit. The misconduct in question consists, as stated, in "bending facts or logic in order to gain a point for either an ideal or an interest" *irrespective of whether a writer*

lished propositions for the implications of which they did not have any sympathy. To mention a single instance: to establish the logical consistency of the conditions (equations) that are descriptive of a socialist economy will seem to most people equivalent to gaining a point for socialism; but it was established by Enrico Barone, a man who, whatever else he may have been, was certainly no sympathizer with socialist ideals or groups.

But there exist in our minds preconceptions about the economic process that are much more dangerous to the cumulative growth of our knowledge and the scientific character of our analytic endeavors because they seem beyond our control in a sense in which value judgments and special pleadings are not. Though mostly allied with these, they deserve to be separated from them and to be discussed independently. We shall call them Ideologies.

II

The word *idéologie* was current in France toward the end of the 18th and in the first decade of the 19th century and meant much the same thing as did the Scottish moral philosophy of the same and an earlier time or as our own social science in that widest acceptance of the term in which it includes psychology. Napoleon imparted a derogatory meaning to it by his sneers at the *idéologues*—doctrinaire dreamers without any sense for the realities of politics. Later on, it was used as it is often used today in order to denote systems of ideas, that is, in a way in which our distinction between ideologies and value judgments is lost. We have nothing to do with these or any other meanings except one that may be most readily introduced by reference to the "historical materialism" of Marx and Engels. According to this doctrine, history is determined by the autonomous evolution of the structure of production: the social and political organization, religions, morals, arts and sciences are mere "ideological superstructures," generated by the economic process.

We neither need nor can go into the merits and demerits of this conception as such[2] of which only one feature is relevant to our purpose. This feature is the one that has, through various transformations, developed into the sociology of science of the type associated with the

---

states his preference for the cause for which he argues or not. Independently of this, it may be sound practice to require that everybody should explicitly state his "axiological premises" or the interest for which he means to argue whenever they are not obvious. But this is an additional requirement that should not be confused with ours.

[2] In particular, its acceptance is no prerequisite of the validity of the argument that is to follow and could have been set forth also in other ways. There are, however, some advantages in starting from a doctrine that is familiar to all and that needs only to be mentioned in order to call up, in the mind of the audience, certain essential notions in a minimum of time.

names of Max Scheler and Karl Mannheim. Roughly up to the middle of the 19th century the evolution of "science" had been looked upon as a purely intellectual process—as a sequence of explorations of the empirically given universe or, as we may also put it, as a process of filiation of discoveries or analytic ideas that went on, though no doubt influencing social history and being influenced by it in many ways, according to a law of its own. Marx was the first to turn this relation of interdependence between "science" and other departments of social history into a relation of dependence of the former on the objective data of the social structure and in particular on the social location of scientific workers that determines their outlook upon reality and hence what they see of it and how they see it. This kind of relativism—which must of course not be confused with any other kind of relativism[3]—if rigorously carried to its logical consequences spells a new philosophy of science and a new definition of scientific truth. Even for mathematics and logic and still more for physics, the scientific worker's choice of problems and of approaches to them, hence the pattern of an epoch's scientific thought, becomes socially conditioned—which is precisely what we mean when speaking of scientific ideology rather than of the ever more perfect perception of objective scientific truths.

Few will deny, however, that in the cases of logic, mathematics, and physics the influence of ideological bias does not extend beyond that choice of problems and approaches, that is to say, that the sociological interpretation does not, at least for the last two or three centuries, challenge the "objective truth" of the findings. This "objective truth" may be, and currently is being, challenged on other grounds but not on the ground that a given proposition is true only with reference to the social location of the men who formulated it. To some extent at least, this favorable situation may be accounted for by the fact that logic, mathematics, physics and so on deal with experience that is largely invariant to the observer's social location and practically invariant to historical change: for capitalist and proletarian, a falling stone looks alike. The social sciences do not share this advantage. It is possible, or so it seems, to challenge their findings not only on all the grounds on which the propositions of all sciences may be challenged but also on the additional one that they cannot convey more than a writer's class affiliations and that, without reference to such class affiliations, there is no room for the categories of true or false, hence for the conception of "scientific advance" at all. Henceforth we adopt

[3] I should consider it an insult to the intelligence of my readers to emphasize that in particular this kind of relativism has nothing to do with Einsteinian relativity were it not a fact that there actually are instances of this confusion in the philosophical literature of our time. This has been pointed out to me by Professor Philipp Frank.

the term Ideology or Ideological Bias for this—real or supposed—state of things alone, and our problem is to ascertain the extent to which ideological bias is or has been a factor in the development of what—conceivably—it might be a misnomer to call scientific economics.

In recognizing the ideological element it is possible to go to very different lengths. There are a few writers who have in fact denied that there is such a thing in economics as accumulation of a stock of "correctly" observed facts and "true" propositions. But equally small is the minority who would deny the influence of ideological bias entirely. The majority of economists stand between these extremes: they are ready enough to admit its presence though, like Marx, they find it only in others and never in themselves; but they do not admit that it is an inescapable curse and that it vitiates economics to its core. It is precisely this intermediate position that raises our problem. ***For ideologies are not simply lies;*** they are truthful statements about what a man thinks he sees. Just as the medieval knight saw himself as he wished to see himself and just as the modern bureaucrat does the same and just as both failed and fail to see whatever may be adduced against their seeing themselves as the defenders of the weak and innocent and the sponsors of the Common Good, so every other social group develops a protective ideology which is nothing if not sincere. *Ex hypothesi* we are not aware of our rationalizations—how then is it possible to recognize and to guard against them?

But let me repeat before I go on: I am speaking of science which is technique that turns out the results which, together with value judgments or preferences, produce recommendations, either individual ones or systems of them—such as the systems of mercantilism, liberalism and so on. I am not speaking of these value judgments and these recommendations themselves. I fully agree with those who maintain that judgments about ultimate values—about the Common Good, for instance—are beyond the scientist's range except as objects of historical study, that they are ideologies by nature and that the concept of scientific progress can be applied to them only so far as the means may be perfected that are to implement them. I share the conviction that there is no sense in saying that the world of ideas of bourgeois liberalism is "superior" in any relevant sense to the world of ideas of the middle ages, or the world of ideas of socialism to that of bourgeois liberalism. Actually, I further believe that there is no reason other than personal preference for saying that more wisdom or knowledge goes into our policies than went into those of the Tudors or Stuarts or, for that matter, into Charlemagne's.

III

So soon as we have realized the possibility of ideological bias, it is not difficult to locate it. All we have to do for this purpose is to scrutinize scientific procedure. It starts from the perception of a set of related phenomena which we wish to analyze and ends up—for the time being—with a scientific model in which these phenomena are conceptualized and the relations between them explicitly formulated, either as assumptions or as propositions (theorems). This primitive way of putting it may not satisfy the logician but it is all we need for our hunt for ideological bias. Two things should be observed.

First, that perception of a set of related phenomena is a prescientific act. It must be performed in order to give to our minds something to do scientific work on—to indicate an object of research—but it is not scientific in itself. But though prescientific, it is not preanalytic. It does not simply consist in perceiving facts by one or more of our senses. These facts must be recognized as having some meaning or relevance that justifies our interest in them and they must be recognized as related—so that we might separate them from others—which involves some analytic work by our fancy or common sense. This mixture of perceptions and prescientific analysis we shall call the research worker's Vision or Intuition. In practice, of course, we hardly ever start from scratch so that the prescientific act of vision is not entirely our own. We start from the work of our predecessors or contemporaries or else from the ideas that float around us in the public mind. In this case our vision will also contain at least some of the results of previous scientific analysis. However, this compound is still given to us and exists before we start scientific work ourselves.

Second, if I have identified with "model building" the scientific analysis that operates upon the material proffered by the vision, I must add at once that I intend to give the term "model" a very wide meaning. The explicit economic model of our own day and its analoga in other sciences are of course the product of late stages of scientific endeavor. Essentially, however, they do not do anything that is not present in the earliest forms of analytic endeavor which may therefore also be said to have issued, with every individual worker, in primitive, fragmentary, and inefficient models. This work consists in picking out certain facts rather than others, in pinning them down by labeling them, in accumulating further facts in order not only to supplement but in part also to replace those originally fastened upon, in formulating and improving the relations perceived—briefly, in "factual" and "theoretical" research that go on in an endless chain of give and take, the facts suggesting new analytic instruments (theories) and these in turn carrying us toward the recognition of new facts. This is as true when the object of our interest is an historical report as it is when the object of our interest is to "rationalize" the Schrödinger equation though in any particular instance the task of fact finding or the task of analyzing may so dominate the other as to almost remove it from sight. Schoolmasters may try to make this clearer to their pupils by talking about induction and deduction and even set the one against the other, creating spurious problems thereby. The essential thing, however we may choose to interpret it, is the "endless give and take" between the clear concept and the cogent conclusion on the one hand, and the new fact and the handling of its variability on the other.

Now, so soon as we have performed the miracle of knowing what we cannot know, namely the existence of the ideological bias in ourselves and others, we can trace it to a simple source. This source is in the initial vision of the phenomena we propose to subject to scientific treatment. For this treatment itself is under objective control in the sense that it is always possible to establish whether a given statement, in reference to a given state of knowledge, is provable, refutable, or neither. Of course this does not exclude honest error or dishonest faking. It does not exclude delusions of a wide variety of types. But it does permit the exclusion of that particular kind of delusion which we call ideology because the test involved is indifferent to any ideology. The original vision, on the other hand, is under no such control. There, the elements that will meet the tests of analysis are, by definition, undistinguishable from those that will not or—as we may also put it since we admit that ideologies *may* contain provable truth up to 100 per cent—the original vision *is* ideology by nature and may contain any amount of delusions traceable to a man's social location, to the manner in which he wants to see himself or his class or group and the opponents of his own class or group. This should be extended even to peculiarities of his outlook that are related to his personal tastes and conditions and have no group connotation—there is even an ideology of the mathematical mind as well as an ideology of the mind that is allergic to mathematics.

It may be useful to reformulate our problem before we discuss examples. Since the source of ideology is our pre- and extrascientific vision of the economic process and of what is—causally or teleologically—important in it and since normally this vision is then subjected to scientific treatment, it is being either verified or destroyed by analysis and in either case should vanish *qua* ideology. How far, then, does it fail to disappear as it should? How far does it hold its own in the face of accumulating adverse evidence? And how far does it vitiate our analytic procedure itself so that, in the result, we are still left with knowledge that is impaired by it?

From the outset it is clear that there is a vast expanse of ground on which there should be as little danger of ideological vitiation as there is in physics. A time series of gross investment in manufacturing industry may be good or bad, but whether it is the one or the other is, normally, open to anyone to find out. The Walrasian system *as it stands* may or may not admit of a unique set of solutions but whether it does or not is a matter of exact proof that every qualified person can repeat. Questions like these may not be the most fascinating or practically most urgent ones but they constitute the bulk of what is specifically scientific in our work. And they are in logic although not always in fact neutral to ideology. Moreover, their sphere widens as our understanding of analytic work improves. Time was when economists thought that they were gaining or losing a point for labor if they fought for the labor-quantity and against the marginal-utility theory of value. It can be shown that, so far as ideologically relevant issues are concerned, this makes as little difference as did the replacement of the latter by the indifference-curve approach or the replacement of the indifference curves by a simple consistency postulate (Samuelson). I dare say that there are still some who find something incongruous to their vision in marginal-productivity analysis. Yet it can be shown that the latter's purely formal apparatus is compatible with any vision of economic reality that anyone ever had.[4]

IV

Let us now look for ideological elements in three of the most influential structures of economic thought, the works of Adam Smith, of Marx, and of Keynes.

In Adam Smith's case the interesting thing is not indeed the absence but the harmlessness of ideological bias. I am not referring to his time- and country-bound practical wisdom about *laissez-faire,* free trade, colonies and the like for—it cannot be repeated too often—a man's political preferences and recommendations as such are entirely beyond the range of my remarks or rather they enter this range only so far as the factual and theoretical analysis does that is presented in support of them. I am exclusively referring to this analytical work

[4] The contrary opinion that is sometimes met with is to be attributed to the simplified versions of the marginal-productivity theory that survive in textbooks and do not take into account all the restrictions to which production functions are subject in real life, especially if they are production functions of going concerns for which a number of technological data are, for the time being, unalterably fixed—just as in elementary mechanics no account is taken of the complications that arise so soon as we drop the simplifying assumption that the masses of bodies are concentrated in a single point. But a marginal-productivity theory that does take account of restrictions which, even in pure competition, prevent factors from being paid according to their marginal productivities is still marginal-productivity theory.

itself—only to his indicatives, not to his imperatives. This being understood, the first question that arises is what kind of ideology we are to attribute to him. Proceeding on the Marxist principle we shall look to his social location, that is, to his personal and ancestral class affiliations and in addition to the class connotation of the influences that may have formed or may have helped to form what we have called his vision. He was a *homo academicus* who became a civil servant. His people were more or less of a similar type: his family, not penniless but neither wealthy, kept up some standard of education and fell in with a well-known group in the Scotland of his day. Above all it did *not* belong to the business class. His general outlook on things social and economic reproduced these data to perfection. He beheld the economic process of his time with a cold critical eye and instinctively looked for mechanical rather than personal factors of explanation—such as division of labor. His attitude to the land-owning and to the capitalist classes was the attitude of the observer from outside and he made it pretty clear that he considered the landlord (the "slothful" landlord who reaps where he has not sown) as an unnecessary, and the capitalist (who hires "industrious people" and provides them with subsistence, raw materials, and tools) as a necessary evil. The latter necessity was rooted in the virtue of parsimony, eulogy of which evidently came from the bottom of his Scottish soul. Apart from this, his sympathies went wholly to the laborer who "clothes everybody and himself goes in rags." Add to this the disgust he felt—like all the people in his group—at the inefficiency of the English bureaucracy and at the corruption of the politicians and you have practically all of his ideological vision. While I cannot stay to show how much this explains of the picture he drew, I must emphasize that the other component of this vision, the natural-law philosophy that he imbibed in his formative years, the product of similarly conditioned men, influenced the ideological background from which he wrote in a similar manner—natural freedom of action, the workman's natural right to the whole product of industry, individualistic rationalism and so on, all this was taught to him ere his critical faculties were developed but there was hardly need to teach him these things for they came "naturally" to him in the air he breathed. But—and this is the really interesting point—all this ideology, however strongly held, really did not much harm to his scientific achievement. Unless we go to him for economic sociology,[5] we receive from him sound factual and analytic teaching that no doubt carries date but is not open to objection on the score of ideological bias. There is some semiphilosophical foliage of

[5] Even there, so I have been reminded by Professor E. Hamilton, there is perhaps more to praise than there is to blame.

an ideological nature but it can be removed without injury to his scientific argument. The analysis that supports his qualified free-trade conclusions is not—as it was with some contemporaneous philosophers, such as Morellet—based upon the proposition that by nature a man is free to buy or to sell where he pleases. The statement that the (whole) produce is the natural compensation of labor occurs, but no analytic use is made of it—everywhere the ideology spends itself in phraseology and for the rest recedes before scientific research. In part at least, this was the merit of the man: he was nothing if not responsible; and his sober and perhaps somewhat dry common sense gave him respect for facts and logic. In part it was good fortune: it matters little if his analysis has to be given up as the *psychology* it was meant to be if at the same time it must be retained as a *logical* schema of economic behavior—on closer acquaintance, the *homo economicus* (so far as Adam Smith, the author of the *Moral Sentiments*, can in fact be credited or debited with this conception at all) turns out to be a very harmless man of straw.

Marx was the economist who discovered ideology for us and who understood its nature. Fifty years before Freud, this was a performance of the first order. But, strange to relate, he was entirely blind to its dangers so far as he himself was concerned. Only other people, the bourgeois economists and the utopian socialists, were victims of ideology. At the same time, the ideological character of his premises and the ideological bias of his argument are everywhere obvious. Even some of his followers (Mehring, for instance) recognized this. And it is not difficult to describe his ideology. He was a bourgeois radical who had broken away from bourgeois radicalism. He was formed by German philosophy and did not feel himself to be a professional economist until the end of the 1840's. But by that time, that is to say, *before* his serious analytic work had begun, his vision of the capitalist process had become set and his scientific work was to implement, not to correct it. It was not original with him. It pervaded the radical circles of Paris and may be traced back to a number of 18th century writers, such as Linguet.[6] History conceived as the struggle between classes that are defined as *haves* and *havenots,* with exploitation of the one by the other, ever increasing wealth among ever fewer *haves* and ever increasing misery and degradation among the *havenots,* moving with inexorable necessity toward spectacular explosion, this was the vision then conceived with passionate energy and to be worked up, like a raw material is being worked up, by means of the scientific tools of his time. This vision implies a number of statements that will

[6] See especially S. N. H. Linguet, *La théorie des Lois Civiles* (1767), and Marx's comments on him in Volume I, pp. 77 *et seq.* of the *Theorien über den Mehrwert.*

not stand the test of analytic controls. And, in fact, as his analytic work matured, Marx not only elaborated many pieces of scientific analysis that were neutral to that vision but also some that did not agree with it well—for instance, he got over the kind of underconsumption and the kind of overproduction theories of crises which he seems to have accepted at first and traces of which—to puzzle interpreters—remained in his writings throughout. Other results of his analysis he introduced by means of the device of retaining the original—ideological—statement as an "absolute" (*i.e.*, abstract) law while admitting the existence of counteracting forces which accounted for deviating phenomena in real life. Some parts of the vision, finally, took refuge in vituperative phraseology that does not affect the scientific elements in an argument. For instance, whether right or wrong, his exploitation theory of "surplus" value was a genuine piece of theoretical analysis. But all the glowing phrases about exploitation could have been attached just as well to other theories, Böhm-Bawerk's among them: imagine Böhm-Bawerk in Marx's skin, what could have been easier for him than to pour out the vials of his wrath on the infernal practice of robbing labor by means of deducting from its product a time discount?

But some elements of his original vision—in particular the increasing misery of the masses which was what was to goad them into the final revolution—that were untenable were at the same time indispensable for him. They were too closely linked to the innermost meaning of his message, too deeply rooted in the very meaning of his life, to be ever discarded. Moreover, they were what appealed to followers and what called forth their fervent allegiance. It was they which explain the organizing effect—the party-creating effect—of what without them would have been stale and lifeless. And so we behold in this case the victory of ideology over analysis: all the consequences of a vision that turns into a social creed and thereby renders analysis sterile.

Keynes' vision—the source of all that has been and is more or less definitely identified as Keynesianism—appeared first in a few thoughtful paragraphs in the introduction to the *Consequences of the Peace* (1920). These paragraphs created *modern* stagnationism—stagnationist moods had been voiced, at intervals, by many economists before, from *Britannia Languens* on (1680)—and indicate its essential features, the features of mature and arteriosclerotic capitalist society that tries to save more than its declining opportunities for investment can absorb. This vision never vanished again—we get another glimpse of it in the tract on *Monetary Reform* and elsewhere but, other problems absorbing Keynes' attention during the 1920's, it was not implemented analytically until much later. D. H. Robertson in his *Banking Policy and the Price Level* presented some work that amounted to partial implementation of the idea of abortive saving. But with Keynes this idea remained a side issue even in the *Treatise on Money*. Perhaps it was the shock imparted by the world crisis which definitely broke the bonds that prevented him from fully verbalizing himself. Certainly it was the shock imparted by the world crisis which created the public for a message of this kind.

Again it was the ideology—the vision of decaying capitalism that located (*saw*) the cause of the decay in one out of a large number of features of latter-day society—which appealed and won the day, and not the analytic implementation by the book of 1936 which, by itself and without the protection it found in the wide appeal of the ideology, would have suffered much more from the criticisms that were directed against it almost at once. Still, the conceptual apparatus was the work not only of a brilliant but also of a mature mind—of a Marshallian who was one of the three men who had shared the sage's mantle between them. Throughout the 1920's Keynes was and felt himself to be a Marshallian and even though he later on renounced his allegiance dramatically, he never deviated from the Marshallian line more than was strictly necessary in order to make his point. He continued to be what he had become by 1914, a master of the theorist's craft, and he was thus able to provide his vision with an armour that prevented many of his followers from seeing the ideological element at all. Of course this now expedites the absorption of Keynes' contribution into the current stream of analytic work. There are no really new principles to absorb. The ideology of underemployment equilibrium and of non-spending—which is a better term to use than saving—is readily seen to be embodied in a few restrictive assumptions that emphasize certain (real or supposed) facts. With these everyone can deal as he thinks fit and for the rest he can continue his way. This reduces Keynesian controversies to the level of technical science. Lacking institutional support, the "creed" has petered out with the situation that had made it convincing. Even the most stalwart McCullochs of our day are bound to drift into one of those positions of which it is hard to say whether they involve renunciation, reinterpretation, or misunderstanding of the original message.

V

Our examples might suggest that analytically uncontrolled ideas play their role exclusively in the realm of those broad conceptions of the economic process as a whole that constitute the background from which analytic effort sets out and of which we never succeed in fully mastering more than segments. This is of course true to some extent—

the bulk of our research work deals with particulars that give less scope to mere vision and are more strictly controlled by objective tests—but not wholly so. Take, for instance, the theory of saving which does appear in a wider context in the Keynesian system but might also, factually and theoretically, be treated by itself. From the time of Turgot and Smith—in fact from still earlier times—to the time of Keynes all the major propositions about its nature and effects have, by slow accretion, been assembled so that, in the light of the richer supply of facts we command today, there should be little room left for difference of opinion. It should be easy to draw up a summarizing (though perhaps not very exciting) analysis that the large majority of professional economists might accept as a matter of course. But there is, and always has been, eulogistic or vituperative preaching on the subject that, assisted by terminological tricks such as the confusion between saving and nonspending, has succeeded in producing a sham antagonism between the writers on the subject. Much emphasized differences in doctrine for which there is no factual or analytical basis always indicate, though in themselves they do not prove, the presence of ideological bias on one side or on both—which in this case hails from two different attitudes to the bourgeois scheme of life.

Another instance of sectional ideology of this kind is afforded by the attitude of many, if not most economists, toward anything in any way connected with monopoly (oligopoly) and cooperative price setting (collusion). This attitude has not changed since Aristotle and Molina although it has acquired a partially new meaning under the conditions of modern industry. Now as then, a majority of economists would subscribe to Molina's dictum: *monopolium est injustum et rei publicae injuriosum*. But it is not this value judgment which is relevant to my argument—one may dislike modern largest-scale business exactly as one may dislike many other features of modern civilization—but the analysis that leads up to it and the ideological influence that this analysis displays. Anyone who has read Marshall's *Principles*, still more anyone who has also read his *Industry and Trade*, should know that among the innumerable patterns that are covered by those terms there are many of which benefit and not injury to economic efficiency and the consumers' interest ought to be predicated. More modern analysis permits to show still more clearly that no sweeping or unqualified statement can be true for all of them; and that the mere facts of size, single-sellership, discrimination, and cooperative price setting are in themselves inadequate for asserting that the resulting performance is, in any relevant sense of the word, inferior to the one which could be expected under pure competition in conditions attainable under pure competition—in other words, that economic analysis offers no material in support of *indiscriminate* "trust busting" and that such material must be looked for in the particular circumstances of each individual case. Nevertheless, many economists support such *indiscriminate* "trust busting" and the interesting point is that enthusiastic sponsors of the private-enterprise system are particularly prominent among them. Theirs is the ideology of a capitalist economy that would fill its social functions admirably by virtue of the magic wand of pure competition were it not for the monster of monopoly or oligopoly that casts a shadow on an otherwise bright scene. No argument avails about the performance of largest-scale business, about the inevitability of its emergence, about the social costs involved in destroying existing structures, about the futility of the hallowed ideal of pure competition— or in fact ever elicits any response other than most obviously sincere indignation.

Even as thus extended, our examples, while illustrating well enough what ideology is, are quite inadequate to give us an idea of the range of its influence. The influence shows nowhere more strongly than in economic history which displays the traces of ideological premises so clearly, precisely because they are rarely formulated in so many words, hence rarely challenged—the subject of the role that is to be attributed in economic development to the initiative of governments, policies, and politics affords an excellent instance: groupwise, economic historians have systematically over- or understated the importance of this initiative in a manner that points unequivocally to prescientific convictions. Even statistical inference loses the objectivity that should in good logic characterize it whenever ideologically relevant issues are at stake.[7] And some of the sociological, psychological, anthropological, biological waters that wash our shores are so vitiated by ideological bias that, beholding the state of things in parts of those fields, the economist might sometimes derive solace from comparison. Had we time, we could everywhere observe the same phenomenon: that ideologies crystallize, that they become creeds which for the time being are impervious to argument; that they find defenders whose very souls go into the fight for them.

There is little comfort in postulating, as has been done sometimes, the existence of detached minds that are immune to ideological bias and *ex hypothesi* able to overcome it. Such minds may actually exist

[7] I am not aware of any instances in which the rules of inference themselves have been ideologically distorted. All the more frequent are instances in which the rigor of tests is relaxed or tightened according to the ideological appeal of the proposition under discussion. Since acceptance or rejection of a given statistical result always involves some risk of being wrong, mere variation in willingness to incur such a risk will suffice, even apart from other reasons, to produce that well-known situation in which two statistical economists draw opposite inferences from the same figures.

and it is in fact easy to see that certain social groups are further removed than are others from those ranges of social life in which ideologies acquire additional vigor in economic or political conflict. But though they may be relatively free from the ideologies of the practitioners, they develop not less distorting ideologies of their own. There is more comfort in the observation that no economic ideology lasts forever and that, with a likelihood that approximates certainty, we eventually grow out of each. This follows not only from the fact that social patterns change and that hence every economic ideology is bound to wither but also from the relation that ideology bears to that prescientific cognitive act which we have called vision. Since this act induces fact finding and analysis and since these tend to destroy whatever will not stand their tests, no economic ideology could survive indefinitely even in a stationary social world. As time wears on and these tests are being perfected, they do their work more quickly and more effectively. But this still leaves us with the result that some ideology will always be with us and so, I feel convinced, it will.

But this is no misfortune. It is pertinent to remember another aspect of the relation between ideology and vision. That prescientific cognitive act which is the source of our ideologies is also the prerequisite of our scientific work. No new departure in any science is possible without it. Through it we acquire new material for our scientific endeavors and something to formulate, to defend, to attack. Our stock of facts and tools grows and rejuvenates itself in the process. And so—though we proceed slowly because of our ideologies, we might not proceed at all without them.

THE COMMUNIST MANIFESTO IN SOCIOLOGY AND ECONOMICS

Reprinted from *Journal of Political Economy,* June 1949, 199-212.

THIS paper is to appraise the position of the *Communist Manifesto* in the history of scientific sociology and economics and incidentally in Marx's own scientific work (Secs. III and IV). Some of the necessary framework will be provided and some extra-scientific aspects will be noticed first (Secs. I and II). But I wish to emphasize at the outset that this is in no sense an essay in Marxology, that is, in what has by now become a special discipline of Marx the man and the thinker; and also that, but for an inevitable minimum, I shall neglect many of those things that readers might expect to find in a centenary appraisal. Very obviously, the *Manifesto* was more than a piece of analysis. But it is as a piece of analysis that I am going to discuss it, without any intention, if this need be added, of either debunking or glorifying it.

I

Friedrich Engels' Preface to S. Moore's English translation of the *Manifesto*, dated London, January 30, 1888, tells us all we need to know about the nature of the publication, the conditions under which it appeared, and its fortunes. Later research, including the work of the Marx-Engels Institute, has added a number of details and corrected others, none of which, however, is of importance to our purpose.[1] But Engels' Preface itself *is* important for us in several respects.

First, Engels made it quite clear that the pamphlet should not be called the manifesto of a communist *party*, for the communist group that "commissioned" Marx and Engels to write its "platform" did not amount to anything like what is usually meant by a "party." The Communist League, successor of the League of the Just, was a small group founded for purposes of education and propaganda that should not have been called a "workingmen's association" either, for both its original German membership and the allies that it found later in various Western capitals of Europe consisted mainly of isolated individuals who were intellectuals rather than manual workers. The group, dissolved in 1852 (after the "Communist trials" of Cologne), was numerically insignificant and is not known to have exerted any influence on the contents of the *Manifesto*. Viewed from the standpoint of the latter, it was hardly more than a "letterhead."

Second, Engels' Preface explains why the classic document of modern socialism should have been called the *communist* manifesto. In 1847, so he told his readers,

[1] We merely note, from Engels' Preface, that the *Communist Manifesto* was written, in German, in January, 1847, and "sent to the printer" (a small firm in London) in February; that the first French translation became available before June of the same year and the first English one (in G. J. Harney's *Red Republican* [London]) in 1850; that the first American translation was published in the periodical of a brokerage firm—*Woodhall and Claflin's Weekly;* that a Russian translation (Bakunin's) appeared in 1870, another (Plekhanov's) in 1882. There were several translations into other languages before the end of the 1880's, i.e., before the German Social Democratic party placed itself on Marxist ground. The authentic German edition of 1872 is of particular interest because of Marx's and Engels' joint Preface to it.

socialism had become a respectable middle-class movement, i.e., it had ceased to be a working-class movement and revolutionary. Using a later expression, we may say that socialists—or, more correctly, some of them—had become "reformist." Still more important was it for Marx and Engels to distance themselves from the various groups of "utopian" socialists that were then no longer being taken seriously. Rather than risk being mixed up with these groups, they resolutely ranged themselves with the "crude, roughhewn, purely instinctive communism" which they attributed to at least a portion of the working class. This resolve accounts for, and in part excuses, Marx's and Engels' failure to recognize doctrinal priorities of utopian writers in several important points.

Third, with admirable tact and feeling, Engels "considered himself bound to state that the fundamental proposition which forms its [the *Manifesto*'s] nucleus,[2] belongs to Marx," while reserving his own claims to the extent that both he and Marx had been moving independently of each other toward that proposition for "some years before 1845"—perhaps since 1843. For this he offered his *Condition of the Working Class in England in 1844* as evidence which there is no reason to refuse, on the understanding that the undeniable difference between the two men in depth of comprehension and analytic power be appropriately balanced against the fact that in those years Engels was certainly farther along, as an economist, than was Marx.

Fourth, Engels was far from wishing to claim for the *Manifesto* any causal importance in the course of social history; in fact, he could not have done so without contradicting the Marxist interpretation of history. But he claimed much too much for the First International (p. 4), which, "on its breaking up in 1874, left the workers quite different men from what it had found them in 1864."[3] And, on the lower level on which a Marxist is bound to keep when speaking of a mere document, Engels was the victim of a similar optical delusion as regards the *Manifesto*. For him, the *Manifesto* not only "reflects, to some extent, the history of the modern working-class movement" but also is "the common platform acknowledged by millions of workingmen from Siberia to California" (p. 5). This must mean, if anything, that the history of the modern working-class movement is correctly interpreted by the fragmentary theory of the *Manifesto*—whereas it is quite clear that it is not, because, not to mention other reasons, the increasing social and political weight of the working class has been a result of increasing real wages per head, hence the consequence of a development the very possibility of which Marxism (especially in 1848) explicitly denied. It must also mean that the ideology of the proletariat, or of a large part of it, was (in 1888) correctly rendered by the class-struggle ideology of the *Manifesto*—whereas it is equally clear that this was not the case for the

[2] We shall deal with this "nucleus" at length (Secs. III and IV below), since it contains all that is of scientific interest in the *Manifesto*. But Engels' brief rendering of it (on p. 6 of the International Publishers ed.; page references throughout text are to this edition) is strongly recommended to the reader's attention. Were it not for considerations of space I should quote it in full.

[3] The question of the achievements of the First International has been merged in mist, owing to the joint efforts of its adherents and its enemies, both of whom vied with each other, for opposite reasons, in exaggerating its influence. But it should be clear that it did not amount to a great deal, since the trade-union element that was represented lent but qualified support and since the rest of the membership consisted of persons whose own opinion about their importance was shared by nobody except a few police officers.

large majority of workers and that, at best, only small minorities then followed the Marxist flag. However, so imbued are many of us with the idea that the argument of the *Communist Manifesto* reflects *either* social reality *or* the modal workman's genuine attitude toward his class position in capitalist society that it seems worth while, before we proceed, to scrutinize this part of the Marxist saga.

The reader will presently be able to satisfy himself that I have no intention of minimizing the intellectual performance embodied in the *Communist Manifesto*. But no amount of respect for it can alter the fact that its position in the history of socialist thought is closely wound up with the acceptance of Marxism, first, by small but efficient groups in France and Russia and, second and more important, by the great Social Democratic party of Germany (Erfurt Program, 1891). But this acceptance which raised the *Manifesto* to the place it occupies now was not a conversion to the one and only possible truth, not a victory of light over darkness, not the socialist day of Damascus, but a tactical move that was very possibly a tactical mistake—as the comparison of German and English developments suggests. Some doubters—not less stalwart socialists than the Marxists—arose practically at once, and the revisionist controversy was in full swing before long. If the party was unable to make short work of these doubters and had to be content with a formal recantation that did not mean much, this was because the masses, especially the trade-unions, responded to them and failed to take kindly to the class-struggle philosophy of the *Manifesto*. True, extensive pedagogical efforts in the party schools eventually did convert an increasing number of them; but substantially that situation—the unavowed rift between the party, which was dominated by Marxist intellectuals, and the trade-unions, which were much more directly under the control of the workmen—persisted and created difficulties throughout because the masses felt that the Marxist ideology was not their own but *that it was imposed upon them by intellectuals who had adopted another intellectual's idea of what their ideology ought to be.*

II

All that matters for us, within the limited purpose of this paper, is to be found in the first of the four sections of the *Manifesto*. Not that the other three are uninteresting: here and there, we are impressed by a sparkle or an arrestingly bitter phrase or a clever squib. But they belong to the historian of political thought rather than to the historian of economic analysis. We may therefore deal summarily with them.

Let us glance at the last section first, the one that issues in the resounding call—"workingmen of all countries, unite!"—and, immediately before that, in the treacherous phrase which sounds so wrong in the light of more recent developments, namely, that in a revolution "the proletarians have nothing to lose but their chains." For the rest, this section discusses the principle of temporary tactical alliances with nonsocialist parties and in its two pages contains a number of statements that Marx and Engels themselves felt to be obsolete in 1872. We also notice, with a wry smile, the admonitory statement that "communists disdain to conceal their views."

The third section on socialist and communist literature is devoted to the inevitable task of discrediting all the groups that sponsored competitive (and highly substitutable) currents of thought. Everything considered, the job is well done, and our quarrel should not be with what Marx and Engels wrote but with those who take this sort of thing seriously. There is, however, a point about this series of vituperations that is of interest to the man primarily concerned with analysis. Each indictment—especially that of the "reactionary" socialism of the feudal and official classes and that of the pseudo-socialism of the bourgeois class, not so much that of the utopians—is drawn up according to a definite schema. Marx and Engels realized that every group or "movement" needs some ideas with which to verbalize itself, some interest from which to derive support, and some organization through which to act. Within their general frame of thought (see below, Sec. III) this conception took a particular form: the interest was defined as economic class interest; the organization as well as the ideas were purely derivative and determined by the circumstances of the class and the means that its position in the economic and social structure put within its reach. And they proceeded to analyze the various types of socialism and quasi-socialism at which they aimed in terms of this method. They refrained, of course, from applying the principle involved to communism of their own brand, but, however distorted by the bias inseparable from their polemical purpose, it worked fairly successfully with "feudal" and "bourgeois" socialisms or reformisms: there is, e.g., a considerable amount of truth, even though not the whole truth, in their analysis of the manner in which sectors of the aristocracies and gentries of Europe were driven back upon prolabor policies by the rise of the bourgeois power.[4]

In the second section Marx and Engels attended to two very necessary tasks. The one was to protect the communism which they meant to stand for against popular aspersions. Following a hallowed practice of all ages, they selected these aspersions wisely and stated them at the lowest possible level—just as radicals do today. Aided by this device, they again did a good job—a masterpiece, in fact, in eluding the opponents' strong points and replacing fact and reasoning by emphatic assertion—"the workingmen have no country"—whenever convenient. The necessity of the other task arose from the fact that no group can do without an "immediate program" unless it is prepared to put itself (politically) out of the running. It was all very well to proclaim the principles of organizing the proletariat so as to enable "it"[5] to step into the position of a ruling class, to conquer political power, and to wrest—but, mind, "by degrees"—all capital from the bourgeoisie, "to centralize all instruments of production in the hands of the state . . . and to increase the total of productive forces as rapidly as possible" (p. 30).[6]

[4] The spiteful subsection on German or "true" socialism (subsumed in the category of "reactionary socialism") should not go unmentioned. It is disfigured by personal resentments that are natural in a man who once had been a would-be *Privatdozent;* but it contains some things that are not only amusing but also have the kind of truth that is in every malevolent caricature. I could however not hope to earn the gratitude of my readers by going into this matter.

[5] Lenin was the first regular socialist to admit clearly that the proletariat never could or would emancipate "itself," i.e., without being officered by intellectuals.

[6] This is as near as Marx ever went in drawing the contours of the socialist economy. As everybody knows, his scientific work was entirely devoted to explaining the capitalist process with a view to proving that it would, by virture of its logic, turn into socialism. He thereby created a difficulty for his followers which they never overcame—this was done for them by economists of bourgeois complexion, especially by Barone. By implication, however, that passage in the *Communist Manifesto* covers more ground than it seems to do at first sight, as the reader will easily perceive. Observe in particular

But followers, if there were to be any, were bound to ask: Yes; but what *now?* And Marx faced the question.

In presenting his answer, he was very obviously aware of a difficulty: the decalogue of measures that he felt able to draw up was sure to sound insipid after all the glowing rhetoric that had gone before. So he proffered comfort to the faithful, first, by *calling* these measures "despotic inroads on the rights of property and on the conditions of bourgeois production"[7] and, second, by pointing out—very truly—that these measures, "though economically insufficient *and untenable* [my italics]," tend to "outstrip themselves" and will necessitate further inroads upon the old social order.

After this, no further comment is needed on the decalogue (p. 30), from the abolition of property in land and the heavily progressive income tax, through the government national bank and the "extension of factories . . . owned by the state," to the free education of all children in public schools, except this. Section 8 reads: "Equal obligation of all to work. Establishment of *industrial armies* [my italics], especially for agriculture." But for this Hitlerian item and the extension of public enterprise, the program might have secured J. S. Mill's blessing, had it been submitted to him. Anything really incompatible with the bourgeois economics of the time—so far as represented by J. S. Mill—was conspicuous by absence, e.g., any tampering with profits or with free trade.

III

For the purpose of analyzing the scientific contents of the *Manifesto*[8] (Sec. I) we shall introduce a distinction that is not to everyone's taste and in particular entirely non-Marxist[9] but presents decisive expository advantages—the distinction between economic sociology and economics. By "economic sociology" (the German *Wirtschaftssoziologie*) we denote the description and interpretation—or "interpretative description"—of economically relevant institutions, including

that Marx—who thereby proved how deeply rooted he was in eighteenth-century rationalism—took it for granted that the "proletariat," freed both from bourgeois inhibitions and from the capitalist whip, would have no more pressing business than to expand society's "productive forces."

[7] Thus conservative Republicans of our day have the authority of Marx himself for calling "a heavy progressive income tax . . . a despotic inroad on the rights of property"—respectfully submitted.

[8] By anticipation, I thus recognize that the argument of the first section of the *Manifesto* does come within the range of empirical science. Nevertheless, I shall admit and even emphasize that it also formulates an ideology: in fact, I have done so already in the preceding part of this paper. There is, however, no contradiction in this: an ideological conception may be developed or implemented by scientific tools of analysis, and a scientific piece of work may contain any amount of ideology, i.e., of extra-scientific preconceptions. I hope that this will become clear as we go along (I have tried to explain this point also in my Presidential Address at the American Economic Association's annual meeting of 1948; see *American Economic Review*, March, 1949). For the time being, it is sufficient to state that ideologies are not necessarily "wrong," that is, not necessarily incapable of scientific verification and that, even if they are, they do not necessarily destroy the scientific nature and value of the analysis with which they are amalgamated.

[9] It is an essential feature of the Marxist system that it treats the social process as an (analytically) indivisible whole and uses only one conceptual schema in all its parts. Example: most of us use the concept "social class" for the purposes of sociology only; in the "pure" economics of today there are no classes in this sense but only classes in the sense of economic categories, i.e., of sets of individuals that have some economic characteristic in common. But with Marx the social class that is a living, feeling, acting sociological entity is also the class of his economic theory. One can fully recognize and even admire the Marxist conception—from the standpoint of which the economic classes of "pure" economy look like bloodless specters whose relations to one another are stripped of their "social content," as Marxists say—and yet consider it an impediment to effective analysis.

habits and all forms of behavior in general, such as government, property, private enterprise, customary or "rational" behavior. By "economics"—or, if you prefer, "economics proper"—we denote the interpretative description of the economic mechanisms that play within any given state of those institutions, such as market mechanisms. Or, to use a felicitous, if not completely synonymous, turn of phrase of Professor G. Colm, economic sociology deals with the problem of how people came to behave as they do at any time and place; and economics with the problem of how they do behave and what economic results they produce by behaving as they do. No question of principle is involved in this distinction. It is simply an expository device that, in itself, is incapable of being "right" or "wrong" and is to be judged merely from the standpoint of the categories "convenient" or "inconvenient." This economic sociology of the *Manifesto*, imbedded in a historical sketch that has been rightly called, by Professor S. Hook, a "miracle of compression," is far more important than its economics proper and will be dealt with first. It contains, more or less definitely, at least three contributions that are all warped by ideological bias but are all of the first order of importance.

1. THE ECONOMIC INTERPRETATION OF HISTORY[10]

So far as I can see, the historical sketch referred to describes changes in social structures and in their cultural complements in terms of economic change alone, both as regards the manner in which "feudal society" had disintegrated and as regards the manner in which "bourgeois society" was disintegrating. Such events as the colonization of overseas countries that widened markets and, later on, steam and machinery that revolutionized industrial production and passed sentence of economic death on the artisan's crafts, and hence on the artisan's world, are clearly visualized as steps in a purely economic process that is conceived of as going on autonomously, according to its own law, carrying its own motive power within itself. And all the rest of social life —the social, political, legal structure, all the beliefs, arts, habits, and schemes of values—is not less clearly conceived of as deriving from that one prime mover— it is but steam that rises from the galloping horse. These two propositions define Marx's economic interpretation of history.[11] Marx may not, when he wrote

[10] I take this opportunity to call attention to the new edition of Professor M. M. Bober's *Karl Marx's Interpretation of History* (1948).

[11] For Marx and most of his followers the "materialistic" aspect of this theory was, of course, very important. It should be observed, however, that no materialism—in the philosophical sense—is implied in its acceptance. All that is needed is assent to the proposition that the economic structure and an individual's or group's location in it exert a very strong influence on his or its thought and behavior. This is quite compatible, e.g., with a belief in the freedom of will or any other religious or metaphysical conviction, for it is possible to admit that, statistically and historically, people yield to that influence and to hold, nevertheless, that, on metaphysical and moral principle, they are not absolutely compelled to do so. To this extent, the term "materialistic interpretation of history" or "historical materialism" is a misnomer. Furthermore—as has been admitted by several staunch Marxists, e.g., by Plekhanov—the economic interpretation of history *per se* does not condemn ideas, e.g., moral ones, to insignificance or, e.g., artistic creations to dependence upon the prevailing mode of production so completely as my own analogy with the steam that rises from the galloping horse might suggest; this analogy was intended to render Marx's own version of his theory, but now it is important to note that this theory retains meaning and, as a working hypothesis, usefulness if that version be modified. In fact, it is clear, on the one hand, that Marx's own account of the historical process implies the recognition of psychological links—forms of reaction—that are not reducible to "objective" conditions of production; and, on the other hand, that noneconomic factors must enter the picture in order to explain why and how a given social situation, dominated by conditions of production, "produces" a phenomenon so completely incommensurable with them as is a given work of art.

the *Manifesto*, have been so fully in possession of these two propositions as he was when he wrote the Preface of *The Critique of Political Economy* (1859; English trans., 1911)—the almost desperate brevity of the *Manifesto* leaves room also for a somewhat different interpretation. Presumably Engels was right, however; and, if he was, then the birth of the economic interpretation of history dates from 1844. Marx's claims to originality and priority have often been called into question. But they are at least as good as Darwin's. Only Saint-Simon seems to me to have any right to figure as a genuine forerunner; the cases for other candidates rest, I believe, largely on their sponsors' inadequate comprehension of what the economic interpretation of history really is—no mere emphasis upon the historical importance of economic conditions or, still worse, interests[12] comes near it.

Assuming, then, that Marx intended to present, by way of application, the economic interpretation in the *Communist Manifesto*, we must, with a brevity that rivals that of the *Manifesto* itself, try to formulate an appraisal of the importance of this contribution to economic sociology. Of course, we shall do so in the light of the further information that Marx supplied in the *Critique* and in the first volume of *Capital*.

In the first place, it is a working hypothesis. Marx himself, as he tells us in the Preface to the *Critique*, considered it as "the leading thread in my studies." As such, it works sometimes extremely well, e.g., in the explanation of the political and cultural changes that came upon bourgeois society in the course of the nineteenth century; sometimes not at all, e.g., in the explanation of the emergence of feudal domains in western Europe in the seventh century—where the "relations of production" between the various classes of people were imposed by the *political* (military) organization of the conquering Teutonic tribes. We may indeed qualify the hypothesis in various ways, e.g., by allowing for the effect of past conditions of production, or else define the concept of relations or conditions of production so widely as to include almost all the relations and conditions observable in human groups. But the reader will readily perceive that on this road we rapidly lose not only the glamour but also the explanatory value of the hypothesis. Still, if we do not pursue it some of both the glamour and the value may be salvaged.

In the second place, it must not be forgotten that Marx (deeply rooted as he was in eighteenth-century ideas and in the German philosophy that continued eighteenth-century traditions) had an enemy to fight and an obstacle to overcome that barred the way toward an acceptable theory of history—the doctrine of the "general progress of the human mind" that made a purely intellectual process the causally important independent variable in social history, the doctrine that prospered so well from Condorcet to Comte and J. S. Mill. If the economic interpretation had done nothing else except to beat back *this* kind of thing by compensatory overemphasis of "objective" economic conditions, it would, because of this merit alone, have to stand high in the history of economic as well as of general sociology. On this

[12] It is relevant to note that even Engels, in his address at Marx's grave, defended historical materialism on the ground that, obviously, economic interests must loom large in any attempt at explaining the historical process. Unless we attribute this slip to an occasion that was not propitious to careful formulation, this would mean that the loyal ally failed, in this point, to fathom Marx's thought. In some respects, his book on historic materialism rather strengthens this suspicion.

score, historiography, especially German historiography, owes much to it.

In the third place, finally, the Marxist proposition that it is not men's conscious thought which determines their modes of existence but their modes of social existence which determine their conscious thought (Preface to the *Critique*)—which anticipates so much of later psychology—is readily recognized as a major contribution toward the theory of economic and political behavior and as a big step away from uncritical individualism, even though we may not be prepared to accept it as it stands.

2. THE MARXIST THEORY OF SOCIAL CLASSES

The text of the *Manifesto* begins with the following sentence: "The history of all society that has existed hitherto is the history of class struggles."[13] Neither for historians nor for sociologists or economists were social classes a discovery—for the economists the less so because most of them, and especially the English classics, had at that time not yet fully adopted the distinction between social classes and economic categories but were still in the habit of using the sociological entities, manual laborers, capitalists, and landlords, in their economic reasoning:[14] for Ricardo the attorney-general was not yet a laborer like the street sweeper. Nor was it necessary to discover that every type of class structure, whether legally recognized or not, spells superordination and subordination—every schoolboy knew this. Finally, nobody can ever have failed to see that class structure is the source of many groupwise antagonisms—the most unhistorical economist must have heard of peasant wars and *hoc genus omne*. Nevertheless, Marxists are right in claiming that the sentence quoted contains the principle of a theory of the social process that was novel and specifically Marxist in the same sense as was the economic interpretation.[15] This theory may be conveyed in three steps.

First, Marx's classes are defined exclusively in economic terms: the social process of production determines the classwise relations of the participants and is the "real foundation" of the legal, political, or simply factual class positions attached to each. Thus the logic of any given structure of production is *ipso facto* the logic of the social superstructure.[16] This is so obviously untrue that it

[13] To the edition of 1888 Engels added a qualifying footnote (in which he refers to his own *Origin of the Family, Private Property, and the State*) which limits the proposition to societies other and later than "primaeval village communities," which he seems to have regarded as classless and communistic. At that time, this was prevalent doctrine.

[14] Throughout, Marx saw a decisive merit in this and was correspondingly severe on those who, like J. B. Say, had begun to divorce economic categories from the social classes of sociology. Needless to say, he knew why: the divorce might spell an advance in analysis, but it tended to obliterate the all-important class antagonisms.

[15] That is to say, there was a number of forerunners, of whom, once more, Saint-Simon was the most important; but we may still attribute to Marx—in the sense that may again be illustrated by the, in this respect, analogous case of Darwin's theory of natural selection—a theory which he stated and developed with unsurpassable force. In view of the connection which will presently be indicated between the Marxist theory of social classes and his formulation of the economic interpretation of history, it is important to observe that the two are not logically inseparable, i.e., that they do not imply each other. A little reflection will satisfy the reader that it is *possible* to hold each of them without holding the other.

[16] In expounding Marx's doctrine on classes, I continue to borrow from his later works, particularly the *Critique* and the first volume of *Capital*. But I do not think that I thereby read anything into the *Manifesto* that is not there. I have not even the slight doubt that, as the reader will have observed, made me hesitate in the case of the economic interpretation of history. Even the significant term "class culture" occurs in the *Manifesto:* this part of Marx's ideology or analysis, then, was, so I believe, fully developed (never to be altered) by 1847.

seems more important, than to show this, to warn the reader against jettisoning *a limine* a proposition that, though untenable, does contain an important element of truth: no class can keep a position above the proletariat—not at least anywhere outside utopias—without some, even though possibly a modest,[17] economic complement, for which, accordingly, it is in most cases ready to fight and the increase or decrease of which is also, in most if not all cases, correlated with the increase or decrease of its social weight. The objection to Marx's theory is not that he saw and emphasized this element but that he related the class phenomenon causally to it: in many cases the causal nexus is the other way round; in all the others the nexus between the structure of production and the class structure embodies, at best, an immediate cause through which analysis must cut in order to reach more fundamental ones.

But Marx weakened his economic theory of the class structure still further in order to fulfil his *ideological* desire to come out with the great battle array between bourgeoisie and proletariat. For prebourgeois society he was ready enough to recognize a complicated interplay of a multiplicity of classes that keeps more closely in touch with observed reality. He also recognized that these prebourgeois classes are hardy plants that take a long time in dying. But as a tendency that was bound to prevail in time, he held that society was more and more splitting up into those two "hostile camps." The difficulty with this is *not* that the persistence of the "old" middle class—the farmers or peasants and the artisans—might defer socialist possibilities to an indefinite future or even that this "old" middle class might altogether fail to disappear. The difficulty is that the capitalist process creates a "new" middle class that fills continuously the whole range between the *grande bourgeoisie*, of which Marx was thinking, and half-starved laboring masses. Bordering on the very rich and the very poor, and sometimes hostile to both, it constitutes a "class" of its own. Observe: such a pattern does not necessarily preclude advance toward socialism; but it might preclude advance toward socialism on Marxist lines and for Marxist reasons.

Second, it is characteristic of Marx's theory of classes that the classwise relations determined by the structure of production are exclusively viewed as antagonistic. From first to last, Marx seems to see nothing but opposition of interests between them: essentially and inevitably, their relation to each other is struggle ("class war"). And from first to last they are relations between oppressors and oppressed, exploiters and exploited. If these and similar terms meant nothing but value-judgments, there would be nothing more to be said—everybody, if he so pleases, is free to consider himself exploited by the $(n - 1)$ other inhabitants of the globe. But the analyst who means more than this is not free to give in to what is clearly an ideological postulate.[18] The complex texture of individual and group relations con-

[17] "Modest" refers to the share of the individual member only.

[18] Of course, by "class antagonism" Marx meant (and so do I) only the "objectively" determined opposition of classes. He did not mean (and neither do I) conscious hostility or will to hurt and fight, although these things do enter into the class consciousness which he was trying to *teach* the proletariat. He even went so far as to say that the immediate aim of the communists is "formation of the proletariat into a class" for the conquest of political power (p. 22). This looks like a slip at first sight, and in a sense it was. But we may correct it into "to awake the proletariat to its class position."

tains at least as many strands of co-operative as strands of antagonistic color and, in addition, others that change their color according to circumstances.[19] Still the antagonisms exist, though they are frequently sectional ("vertical") rather than classwise ("horizontal"). And there is some excuse for "compensatory over-emphasis" on them, though Marx's attempt to substantiate them in his economic theory, namely, by his exploitation theory of interest, was a complete failure.[20]

Third, it was *this* conception of the nature of social classes and *this* conception of the nature of their relation to one another which Marx chose for pivots of his theory of history: it is they which, in his system, implement the economic interpretation of history. Now let us carefully distinguish two different and separable aspects of this.

We have already observed that the economic interpretation of history—no matter whether or not we accept Marx's formulation of it—can also be implemented, i.e., be made to work as an instrument of explanation, in other ways; there is no need to graft a theory of classes upon it and to make such a theory of classes, whatever it be, the only link between the economic interpretation of history and everything else, especially the explanation of the economic process.[21] But, if this is done, it can be done also by means of other conceptions of the nature of social classes and their relations to one another. And if in this case a quite different picture of society should result, the man who paints it would still have to acknowledge indebtedness to, or at least the priority of, Marx's picture. In other words, the idea of making social classes and relations between them the pivots of the historical process and the conception of class culture, and so on, *might* prove analytically valuable, even if we refuse to accept Marx's particular theory of social classes.

3. THE MARXIST THEORY OF THE STATE

Policy is politics; and politics is a very realistic matter. There is no scientific sense whatever in creating for one's self some metaphysical entity to be called "The Common Good" and a not less metaphysical "State," that, sailing high in the clouds and exempt from and above human struggles and group interests, worships at the shrine of that Common Good. But the economists of all times have done precisely this. While perfectly aware, of course, of the fact that the business process must be understood from the businessman's interest, most of them have been blind to the no less obvious fact that the political process and hence political measures that affect economic life must be understood from the politician's interest. Political science should have been from the first what it is slowly beginning to be now, namely, an investigation into the realities of political life, in the widest sense of the term, in which it includes also the social psychology of electorates and of parties, the behavior of bureaucratic organisms, of political bosses and pressure groups, and

[19] "Objectively" speaking, see preceding footnotes. The psychological reflexes of the objective state of things are not without importance, but they are another matter.

[20] I shall say at once that no such attempt was made in the *Manifesto:* several passages point toward, but do not amount to, a *theory* of this type.

[21] This statement is not intended to convey a criticism. Every Marxist can accept it because acceptance would still leave him free to hold that implementation of the economic interpretation by means of a theory of social classes is the "best" or even the "only true" manner of implementing it. I am only trying to emphasize once more that to do so means the introduction of a new idea not already contained (logically implied) in the economic interpretation.

the like. The English classics, and particularly Adam Smith, understood these things instinctively, even though they failed to see the necessity of going into them explicitly. For instance, nobody can read the Fourth Book of the *Wealth of Nations* carefully without observing that there Adam Smith argues for laissez faire as much because of his clear perception of what politics and politicians are as on purely economic grounds. Though other examples could be adduced, it still remains true that a large majority of economists, when discussing issues of public policy, automatically treated political authority and especially government in the modern representative state as a kind of deity that strives to realize the will of the people and the common good. And political science itself was in general as little concerned about the facts of its subject matter and as prone to philosophize on this very same common good and popular will. It was, therefore, a major scientific merit of Marx that he hauled down this state from the clouds and into the sphere of realistic analysis.

Unfortunately, recognition of this merit must be qualified in the same manner in which we had to qualify the merits of his theory of social classes. On the one hand, he would have accepted my slogan—policy is politics—only for the vicious bourgeois world. When the proletariat has destroyed capitalist property relations and capitalist class culture, there will be, at least after a transitional stage, no classes, hence no class politics, and "the free development of each" will be "the condition for the free development of all" (p. 31). The state will wither away, and, as Lenin of all men was to aver again, government of men will be reduced to government of things in the manner of a post office. There is no need to comment on this except in order to point out that it simply amounts to replacing one ideology by another. On the other hand, for the world as it is or was, government or the executive in the modern democracy "is but a committee for managing the common affairs of the whole bourgeoisie" (p. 11), and parties are simply identified, on principle at least, with Marxist classes. This is completely unrealistic and perfectly inadequate to account for the facts of political life and for the results that follow therefrom. Politics as it is can never be understood by anyone who does not start from the analysis of the political group and in so doing discovers that, though relation of social classes (not, however, Marxist ones) is hardly ever absent, it hardly ever tells the whole truth. But the reader will readily see that, in spite of all this, the essential point must be credited to Marx: he will always remain the founder of modern political science even though not a single one of his propositions should stand the test of further research.

IV

The first thing about the "economics proper" of the *Communist Manifesto* that must strike every reader—and a socialist reader still more than a nonsocialist one—is this: After having blocked out the historical background of capitalist development in a few strong strokes that are substantially correct,[22] Marx launched out on a panegyric upon bourgeois achievement that has no equal in economic literature. The bourgeoisie "has been the first to show what man's activity can bring about. It has accomplished wonders far surpassing Egyptian pyramids, Roman aqueducts, and Gothic cathedrals" and "by the rapid improve-

[22] I believe that most historians will agree that it would be difficult to improve Marx's statements *within the same space.*

ment of all instruments of production . . . draws all nations, even the most barbarian, into civilization . . . it has created enormous cities" and "during its rule of scarce one hundred years has erected more massive and more colossal productive forces than have all preceding generations together . . ." and so forth. No reputable "bourgeois" economist of that or any other time—certainly not A. Smith or J. S. Mill—ever said as much as this. Observe, in particular, the emphasis upon the *creative* role of the business class that the majority of the most "bourgeois" economists so persistently overlooked and of the business class *as such*, whereas most of us would, on the one hand, also insert into the picture nonbourgeois contributions to the bourgeois success—the contributions of nonbourgeois bureaucracies, for instance—and, on the other hand, commit the mistake (for such I believe it is) to list as *independent* factors science and technology, whereas Marx's sociology enabled him to see that these as well as "progress" in such fields as education and hygiene were just as much the products of the bourgeois class culture—hence, ultimately, of the business class—as was the business performance itself. Never, I repeat, and in particular by no modern defender of the bourgeois civilization has anything like this been penned, never has a brief been composed on behalf of the business class from so profound and so wide a comprehension of what its achievement is and of what it means to humanity.

Whatever the function of these passages is in a document that purported to be the manifesto of a "party," there cannot be any doubt about their significance for economic analysis. And Marx did not lose the opportunity to add a number of touches that make this significance more precise.

First of all, the creative role of the business class is, by identity, a revolutionary role. This must not be taken as a mere reflex of Marx's philosophical position according to which any creation involved "revolution." The revolution in question is a "constant revolutionizing of production," creation that spells the obsolescence and consequent destruction of any industrial structure of production that exists at any moment: capitalism is a process, stationary capitalism would be a *contradictio in adjecto*. But this process does not simply consist in increase of capital—let alone increase of capital by saving—as the classics had it. It does not consist in adding mailcoaches to the existing stock of mailcoaches, but in their elimination by railroads. Increase of physical capital is an incident in this process, but it is not its propeller.

Second, this incessant economic revolution tends to revolutionize the preceding social and political structure and class civilization. It breaks up the medieval environments that fettered but also protected the individual and the family. By destroying the feudal aristocracy, the peasants, and the artisans, it also destroys the moral world of feudal aristocrats, peasants, and artisans. It changes the *mind* of society. "It has drowned the most heavenly ecstasies of religious fervour, of chivalrous enthusiasm, of philistine sentimentalism in the icy water of egotistical calculation. It has resolved personal worth into exchange value . . . stripped of its halo every occupation hitherto honored and looked upon with reverent awe . . . has torn away from the family its sentimental veil" (p. 11)—in short, it has created the godless utilitarian attitude to life. It has replaced the "idyllic" traditionalism of the Middle Ages by haste and insecurity all round, for bourgeois and workman alike. Above all, it has replaced the highly differentiated groups of the "oppressed" of old by what Marx believed was a homogeneous, nondescript, internationalist proletariat. All this is no longer "economics proper"; it is an essential link that connects Marxist economics with Marxist sociology and social psychology. And he who denies the force and grandeur of this vision is as hopelessly wrong as is he who takes it literally.

But, third, there are three purely economic features in that picture, all of which were essential to Marx's vision of the capitalist process, all of which might be developed analytically in different directions, but none of which was formulated by Marx in such a way as to enable us to attribute to him definite "theories" of them.

To begin with, all economists know, at least by hindsight, that capitalism tends to evolve the giant concern, though some of us seem disposed to deny the necessity of this feature of capitalist evolution. Marx *saw* it and *saw* its necessity (p. 10) or thought he saw it, but no professional economist will deny that much more than his hints at explanation would be necessary to establish it in a manner that would stand, or indicate that it could stand, scientific tests. Marshall's falling average-cost curves might be invoked, along which firms, ever growing, rush on toward monopoly or oligopoly; but there is no trace of this in the *Communist Manifesto*. Again, there are the "crises" that are adduced as an illustration of the proposition that "for many decades the history of industry and commerce is but the history of the revolt of modern productive forces against . . . the property relations that are the conditions for the existence of the bourgeoisie and its rule" and in which breaks out "the epidemic of overproduction." Except for the recognition of the phenomenon (also of its "periodicity") and of its economic and political importance, this does not amount to much and is suggestive of Fourier's *crises pléthoriques*. If there be a theory implied in this passage (pp. 14–15), it is not the one that might be attributed to the full-fledged Marxist system.[23] Finally, there is the *vision* that the capitalist process not only creates the "proletariat" but also, by virtue of its inherent logic, steadily deteriorates its condition. It is *this* element which is supposed to account for capitalism's imaginary inability to do what every previous form of society had been able to do, viz., to feed its slaves or serfs; "and here it becomes evident, that the bourgeoisie is unfit any longer to be the ruling class" and that "its existence is no longer compatible with society (p. 21). This foreshadows *that* breakdown theory which Marx was to develop in the first volume of *Capital* and which, after many prevarications, was eventually abandoned by his followers. But in the *Manifesto* it lacks even so much substantiation as it was to receive later. All that is offered in support of the contention that real wages tend to decrease is that "the price of a commodity, and therefore also of labor is equal to its cost of production" and that "the cost of production of a workman is restricted, almost entirely, to the means of subsistence that he requires for his maintenance, and for the propagation of his race," which sounds like highly crudified Ricardianism (p. 16). Except for this passage, which is clearly inadequate to establish the contention, the *Manifesto* displays even less training in technical economics than we

[23] Marx never worked out any explicit theory of business cycles, although his writings are full of fragments that his followers have tried to build into one. But it is safe to say that he outgrew both overproduction and underconsumption theories, even though traces of both were retained throughout.

might be disposed to attribute to Marx in 1847. So far as these purely economic items are concerned, there is not even much that is specifically Marxist, that is, much that anticipates Marx's technical economics of the 1860's. The word "exploitation" occurs, but there is little to point toward the particular exploitation theory he was to develop. "Capital" holds pride of place, but there is nothing of the elaborate capital theory of his later days. In the matter of value, there is that indication that Marx then followed, more or less, the Ricardian version of A. Smith's theory but no sign of what eventually he was to make of it himself.

All this, I think, answers the problem of the place of the *Communist Manifesto* in Marx's own development as an economist. This answer agrees both with the available evidence and with the opinion of Marxists. The known facts of his career as well as the story he told in the Preface to the *Critique of Political Economy*[24] make it practically certain that, up to and including 1843, he had not taken any serious interest in economics. The desultory reading, mainly of the works of French "utopian" socialists, that he may have done before amounted to as much as desultory reading generally does. As would the average educated person, he doubtless believed himself to be getting along much faster than he was. In Paris, partly led on by Engels, he made more substantial progress but principally on the line of economic sociology, as was natural for a man who came from philosophy. Even by 1847 he was hardly an economist at all: it was during the 1850's that he became one, and one of the most learned ones who ever lived, working away for all he was worth in the British Museum and in the little apartment in Dean Street. But the social vision that this work has to implement was quite set when he wrote the *Communist Manifesto* not only as regards economic sociology but also as regards economics. Nothing essential was ever added to it or jettisoned from it. And the vision implied a program of research. We may, therefore, call the *Manifesto* the prelude to the whole of Marx's later work in a sense in which this cannot be averred of any other of his writings published before 1848. It foreshadowed not only the themes to be developed and the lines to be followed but also the difficulties that he was bound to encounter. Further research, factual and theoretical, was bound to yield results at variance with the hard-and-fast contour lines that had been drawn, once and for all, by the man who was no economist as yet. His inability to establish these contour lines to his own satisfaction, coupled with his unwillingness to give them up, created the intellectual situation that speaks to us from all his later works.

HARVARD UNIVERSITY

[24] The word "Critique" should not be taken in the sense that it carries in common parlance, but in the sense that it carried in the German philosophy of that or, rather, a somewhat earlier time. The analogy with *Critique of Pure Reason* will convey the point, especially if we remember that by "political economy" Marx did not mean the science or literature of political economy but the subject of it—the economic process itself.

ENGLISH ECONOMISTS AND THE STATE-MANAGED ECONOMY

Reprinted from *Journal of Political Economy*, Oct. 1949, 371-382.

I. INTRODUCTION

IN THE past, economic analysis has reaped rich harvests from English discussions of economic emergencies such as the one about monetary policy during and after the Napoleonic Wars. Hence it is natural to ask what analytic harvest England's postwar problems and the Labour government's efforts to grapple with them have produced. With insignificant deviations, this essay is entirely devoted to an attempt to answer this question. Readers will please bear in mind that this purpose places severe restrictions upon my argument. Obviously, economists' reactions to the present course of events in any given country also offer other aspects, and among them several that may be more important or interesting than the one I have singled out. Moreover, we shall not be able to cover all that is relevant even to our restricted purpose. A great part—perhaps the chief part—of the contributions that English economists have made to economic analysis during the last few years consists in researches of the type that is best exemplified by national-income accounting and cannot be dealt with here. Finally, it will not be possible to do full justice to the publications listed in note 1, considered as individual performances. In partial atonement, I shall preface what I have to say by a brief paragraph of general description.

Written by men of unquestioned standing, these books are all recommended, if recommendation be necessary at all, to the attention of the American professional and general public. Baster's little essay is an excellent discussion of the various forms of restrictionism that, among other things, should also do good

[1] A review article of the following works:

The Little Less, By A. S. J. BASTER. New York: Macmillan Co., 1947. Pp. 161. $2.00.

Central Planning and Control in War and Peace. By SIR OLIVER FRANKS, K.C.B. Cambridge, Mass: Harvard University Press, 1947. Pp. 61. $0.75.

Are These Hardships Necessary? By ROY HARROD. London: Rupert Hart-Davis, Ltd., 1947. Pp. 178. 5*s* net.

Ordeal by Planning. By JOHN JEWKES. New York: Macmillan Co., 1948. Pp. 248. $3.75.

Planning and the Price Mechanism. By JAMES EDWARD MEADE. New York: Macmillan Co., 1948. $2.50.

The Economic Problem in Peace and War. By LIONEL ROBBINS. New York: Macmillan Co., 1948. Pp. 86. $1.50.

Where no other title is mentioned, page references are to these works. A few other publications will be mentioned in the appropriate places.

service in classroom work.[2] It presents succinctly one of the most important tendencies of our epoch and also shows that this tendency is not confined to the policy of any particular party. Sir Oliver Franks's brief pamphlet consists of three lectures delivered at the London School of Economics. Mr. Harrod's brilliant diagnosis of the English situation of roughly two years ago is all that we should have expected from a scientific economist of his rank and no longer needs any introduction: no reader can fail to derive pleasure and profit from the Ricardian trenchancy of its argument, whether or not he agrees with either the diagnosis or the theoretical background from which this diagnosis is derived. Professor Jewkes's vigorous attack upon planning and planners reaches out to the fundamental questions of the capitalist order and therefore touches upon present vicissitudes within a wider frame; thus falling out of line with the rest, its weighty argument will have to be dealt with separately. Professor Meade's admirable book, barring some technical details of relatively minor importance, might have been written by J. S. Mill and is "liberal-socialist" in the same sense as are the latter's *Principles*, or as they would have been had Mill beheld the present situation. Evidently, there was plenty of reason for Meade to ask himself: "Am I a planner?"[3] Professor Robbins, in the little book that reproduces the Marshall lectures delivered at Cambridge in the spring of 1947, moves far away from what I conceive to have been his earlier moorings. English war economy receives all but unqualified commendation. Peace, as Franks points out on page 17 of his pamphlet, is indeed very different from war. But Robbins draws no very strong conclusions from this unchallengeable fact. He surveys possible courses of action during the transitional period with perfect detachment, giving his due to every conceivable devil. In the end, professing himself "not yet" persuaded of the virtues of "collectivism," he seems to envisage the "competitive order" as the eventual outcome of present vicissitudes.

There is a reason weightier than convenience of exposition for dividing our argument into three parts, which we shall respectively identify by the headings "Socialism," "Laborism," and "Readjustment," avoiding as much as possible the next to meaningless term "Planning."[4] There is, or so I believe, a long-run tendency toward a genuinely socialist organization of English society in the sense of an organization that vests the control ("ownership") of means of production—the production program—and the claim to the imputed returns from means of production other than labor with a central agency of society, an agency that may, but need not, consist of government and parliament. From this tendency we must distinguish mere laborism—much the same thing that orthodox Socialists, with a derogatory connotation, call "reformism"—which we define as a state of things in which labor is the ruling class and in which economic as well as any other policy is geared to its interests to the exclusion of all others, with the possible exception of the farming interest. This pattern does not in-

[2] In particular, it has occurred to me that the little book might be especially useful in classes on economic theory, where it is impossible to go systematically into contemporaneous fact, while it is highly desirable, at the same time, to enliven arrays of theorems by well-chosen examples of factual patterns.

[3] See R. F. Kahn, "Professor Meade and Planning," *Economic Journal*, LIX (1949), 1–16.

[4] See, however, Dr. Pigou's interesting article, "Central Planning and Professor Robbins," *Economica*, XV (February, 1948), 17 ff.

volve the transfer of economic activity from the sphere of private to the sphere of public concerns or complete abolishment of private property in means of production. Something different again is the set of problems created by the war and by the necessity of readjusting the English economy to the conditions of the postwar world. Clearly, none of these three topics can be treated without reference to the other two: readjustment problems look very different to a society controlled by trade-unions and to a society controlled by the landed gentry and the "merchants." And the given degree of the propensity to socialize—or, if you prefer, the given degree of decay of capitalist society—makes a lot of difference in the extent to which, with more or less enthusiasm, the political world espouses reformist desires, from social insurance, housing subsidies, and so on down to gratis wigs. Nevertheless, there is point in keeping these three topics distinct, if only in order to show how they interact to produce the English problem. Failure to do so is perhaps the most important cause of the confusion that prevails in a confused discussion.

II. THE ISSUE OF SOCIALISM

Many of us are in the habit of seeing nothing but tactics in the refusal of official and unofficial, Russian and non-Russian, Communists to recognize anything specifically socialist in the policy or policies adopted by the English Labour party ever since fifty-one Labour members took their seats, in 1906, on House of Commons benches. But if we define the structural idea of socialism as we did above and if we neglect the talk and the writings of intellectual henchmen and interpreters, we are bound to admit that, to this day, practically everything that has been sponsored, done, or proposed by the Labour party qualifies, in fact, much better for the title of "laborism" than it does for that of "socialism." This is obviously true for the period before 1914, but it holds true also for the interwar period, when, both in office and out of office, the labormen simply "administered" or helped in "administering capitalism," although they did so from their own standpoint and should receive credit instead of blame for it. The only question is how far this applies to the present Labour government as well. And, since we are now trying to abstract from laborite and readjustment policies, it might seem as if this question were raised only by the nationalization program. This program may, indeed, pass muster as a first step on the road to gradual or piecemeal socialization. But, so far, every item, even steel, has proved capable also of other motivations, that is, of motivations specific to the sectors nationalized; and it would hardly do to accept such measures as the nationalization of the Bank of England—the Imperial Bank of Russia was a state bank—or the nationalization of railroads or of mining or of utilities and so on as proof positive of socialist intentions. It is true that the socialist aspect has been strongly emphasized. It is also true that the nationalization policy is coupled with an attitude toward private enterprise in general that amounts to sabotage (see below, Secs. III and IV). And, finally, it is true that laborite policies, though not necessarily socialist in themselves, may pave the way—the specifically English way—toward socialism. Nevertheless, it is not on these grounds that the existence of a "tendency toward socialism" should be averred; we must go much deeper into economic and cultural processes if we are to find out whether such a tendency exists or whether, to plagiarize the *Times*,[5] the Labour government, like *all* its predecessors, is merely seeking for a "habitable halfway house."

Frequently taking issue with the reasons which I have offered elsewhere for believing that during the last half-century England has, in fact, been slowly "maturing toward socialism," Jewkes courageously raises the question of principle on a broad front.[6] He stoutly denies that the businessman is *actually* obsolete, a proposition which no serious economist and not even many governmental hewers of wood and drawers of water (and salaries) would assert, but which Jewkes demolishes with a force all his own (chap. ii). He attacks at least some of the current slogans about monopoly (chap. iii)—though he accepts others readily enough—about mass unemployment (chap. iv), and about the comparative prosperity (chap. viii) and stability (chap. ix) to be expected from planned and nonplanned societies. He even—though somewhat hesitatingly—finds it "difficult to take seriously the theory of secular stagnation in the light of these conditions," i.e., the conditions that prevailed in the United States in 1947 (p. 151). Throughout, but especially in chapter x, he puts upon the relation between private property and enterprise, on the one hand, and human dignity and independence—"freedom"—on the other, all the emphasis that, from his standpoint, it deserves.

This, then, is a thoroughly honest, as well as able, book that speaks the ethos of free-enterprise civilization with no uncertain voice and should be studied, page by page, by every intelligent reader on this side of the Atlantic—by "radicals" and "fellow-travelers" even more than by those who already embrace the free-enterprise creed. I am sorry that I cannot leave it at this. Full allowance must, of course, be made for the popular purpose of the book, which in part explains that, in several points, Jewkes fails to do full justice to the possibilities of his own argument.[7] But he seems to accept Keynesianism wholesale—more, at all events, than is justifiable at this hour of the day (see, e.g., p. 59)—without observing that the popularity of Keynes with his (Jewkes's) opponents is not without good reason.[8] And he says very little about the pivotal question of taxation (see below, Sec. IV), which need only be left as it is in order to make full and genuine socialism practically inevitable before long. If one weighs carefully this point and all the implications of a number of concessions which Jewkes makes or implies, one is left wondering whether the free-enterprise system that he visualizes is worth troubling about, while, on the other hand, the formidable task of reconstructing one that will work *successfully* emerges in its true dimensions.

[5] As quoted by Jewkes, p. 12 n.

[6] This being a review article, if not a review, I do not feel free to reply to his courteous and interesting criticisms, though I fail to recognize my argument in the statements attacked.

[7] For instance, nothing more than correct theory is needed in order to make a much stronger case on the subject of "monopoly" than Jewkes presents. In a spirit of Gladstonian liberalism he fails to stress that "big business" is responsible for the standard of life which American labor has attained. Instead, he pays an unmerited compliment to the thoroughly irrational attitude toward largest-scale business of the American economists, public, legislation, judicature, and administration.

[8] Similarly, Professor Robbins gives thanks to the late Lord Keynes—also, it is true, to Professor Robertson!—for having "awakened me from dogmatic slumber" (p. 68). Of course, nobody except Robbins himself can tell us whether he was dogmatically slumbering or not. However, I submit that such statements, if they are not to be misunderstood by future historians, should be more carefully phrased, or these historians will set down the current decade of English economics as an analogue to the period of post-Ricardian sterility, though they may be unjust in both cases.

Most English economists touch upon the socialist issue (in our sense) lightly or not at all. Robbins' statement that was quoted earlier seems to express something like a common opinion: there are very few straight socialists of scientific standing—I do not count Meade as a socialist—still fewer thoroughgoing adherents of the free-enterprise system, and the majority is "not yet" convinced. But this is the hall mark of a transitional state.[9] Of course, socialism may be defined in many ways other than ours. In popular parlance there are almost as many definitions as there are writers. Sir Stafford Cripps, for instance, so Jewkes reminds us (p. 210), has actually declared that "the prime principle of the socialism for which we stand lies not in the methods of organization of our society that we adopt but in the high purpose at which we aim." If, however, we define as we did, then we arrive at a conclusion that looks paradoxical at first sight: there is (if I am right) a long-run tendency toward socialism in our sense; laborism, as will be presently explained, is the method by which this tendency works itself out; but, so far as practical politics is concerned, *there is for the moment no socialist issue at all*, or, if readers prefer, the specifically socialist issue per se is for the moment not on the political docket. Weaker, however, than the momentary drive toward socialism is the resistance to it.

III. LABORISM

In Europe, the English labor movement was the first to abandon socialism as a practical goal and to settle down to a consistent policy of improving labor's position within the given framework of capitalist society. The present government and, except for readjustment, its policy are the logical outcome of a development that, asserting itself through trade-unionism, began with collective bargaining and with efforts to provide the funds for rudimentary social security and eventually established labor in the arena of politics, the decisive victory being won by the passing of the Trade Disputes Act of 1906.[10] Office and now not only office but also power have followed in due course. The interest of labor *as a class* rules supreme, and, of all that this implies, two things are particularly relevant to the economist's professional concerns. First, the wage contract and all that hangs thereby have become a political affair and are no longer left to the forces of the market. The wage rate is a political datum and is to be protected and, so far as possible, augmented as a matter of course; other interests count mainly, if not wholly, only so far as their neglect can be shown to affect the labor interest injuriously, at least *pro futuro*. Second, taxation is again, as in the times of Louis XV, to produce a maximum of revenue for the benefit of the ruling class which, in this case, implies not only the possible maximum of public expenditure for the benefit of labor but also the reduction to a minimum of incomes other than wages: laborism and not, as ortho-

[9] Of course, there are "individualist" diehards, like Sir Ernest Benn. But his *Government to Death* has not, so far as I know, evoked much response. See also the more business-like article by Lord Brand, "Private Enterprise and Socialism," *Economic Journal*, LVIII (September, 1948), 315 ff.

[10] The Trade Dispute bill was the result of the report of a royal commission that was appointed in 1903 when the Balfour government was in power. The attitude of the conservative party and of Balfour himself is most interesting (see Mrs. Blanche E. C. Dugdale's biography of her uncle [1937], e.g., II, 21). The act is a landmark because, relaxing the law of conspiracy as regards "peaceful picketing" and exempting trade-unions from liability in action for damages for torts, it was the first to recognize labor as a *privileged* class to which the law of the land was not to apply.

dox Marxists would have it, imperialism is the policy of the latest stage of capitalism; labor has replaced Mme DuBarry.

Of course, nobody can be blind to these facts. Economists have perhaps been slow in inserting them into their "general economics," but they are recognizing some of them, indirectly at least, in one way or another, e.g., by reasoning on the assumption of the "downward rigidity of wages." Moreover, in the case of the large contingent of laborite economists—and of all the Marxo-Keynesians—it is not surprising to find that those facts are tacitly accepted and that the economic problems that arise from them are dealt with according to the principle of letting sleeping dogs lie—the old slogans concerning the tyranny of the capitalist still doing duty whenever convenient. But our little sample does not contain any professed laborites or any Marxo-Keynesians. All the more interesting is it to notice that they, too, accept the premises of laborism tacitly or all but tacitly. This is true even of Jewkes. But it is also true of Robbins, who does not seem to think it worth while to emphasize that the "competitive order," which he prefers "as yet" to collectivism, means not one thing but two: it undoubtedly means the proportionality of marginal rates of substitution and prices which pure competition (if it ever could exist) might be supposed to realize (in perfect equilibrium, which never exists); but it also means a motive force which is bound to be ground into dust between the millstones of present wage and tax policies. Mead, whom it is a pleasure to congratulate on his success in presenting the mechanism of competitive pricing in an elementary form, does refer cautiously to "incentives"—consideration of which even prevents him from giving unqualified support to Lady Rhys Williams' scheme of universal personal allowances, for which he displays much sympathy (pp. 42 ff.)—and even to various possibilities of improving the present situation by tax reductions in the higher brackets,[11] which is perhaps all that we are entitled to expect from a "socialist," however "liberal." But such ideas, though they do honor to his economist's conscience, are all but completely snowed under by the articles of a fundamentally equalitarian creed and in practice spell acceptance of laborism, though not of genuine socialism.[12] Harrod displays no interest at all in the economic and cultural problems that laborism raises. I understand, however, that he holds the laborite creed with a vengeance—to the point, that is, of advocating complete elimination of income from interest. Again, this—minus the last-mentioned point—seems to express a well-nigh general opinion, and a fascinating sociological phenomenon to boot. Had we space, it would be interesting to trace back this preference of economists for a laborite civilization to Marshall, Cairnes, and so on, and to show how it acquired a sharper edge in the works of Pigou—to reveal the old and unbroken tradition that slowly gathered the force to overcome economic scruples, the only ones that Marshall and Cairnes ever had. But, preferences apart, one would think that there are purely professional problems incident to this

[11] On inheritance (pp. 47 ff.) he proves himself a particularly faithful pupil of J. S. Mill.

[12] It is curious to note how impressions from past conditions survive. Throughout, Meade is seriously concerned about the objectionable existence of "the rich." But there are probably less than a hundred people in England who after taxes receive an income of £6,000 (equal to less than half in 1914 purchasing power if an upper-bracket index of cost of living be applied) or more a year. This means that laborism has done full work—there are no rich people left except that owners of capital assets may still consume their capital, as Meade does not fail to notice with disapproval (p. 49).

laborite civilization—problems concerning England's future, for instance—that should interest economists, at least with reference to a situation of suppressed inflation. Pigou's works might have provided starting points. But there is little to observe of all this.[13] So, if critics find fault with the Labour government's policy of readjustment, they should not forget that they accept its premises themselves.

IV. POSTWAR READJUSTMENT

Thus the work of almost all English economists centers in the problems of postwar readjustment under the conditions set by the long-run tendency toward socialism (in our sense) and by the pattern of laborism rather than in the problems of that tendency and of that pattern themselves. Both in its monetary and in its "real" aspects, postwar readjustment is a process that is well known to every economist. Modern analysis has a number of improvements to offer upon earlier views on the subject—most of them anticipated by the Atwoods and other writers of the nineteenth century—the practical upshot of which consists mainly in suggestions about how to mitigate the jolt that inevitably accompanies the vanishing of the mirage of war inflation. But, substantially, those earlier views are as valid as they have ever been. We are not saying anything new when we state that England, unless she is able and willing to live indefinitely upon foreign aid, must, within the probable span of the Marshall plan, so adjust her economic process as to make it produce the goods and services that she is going to consume plus the goods and services that will procure her imports,[14] including in both items the appropriate allowances for maintenace, renewal, and restocking. If there is to be any "progress" at all, something must be added for net investment and capital export: the latter is even necessary in order to safeguard any status quo that might be decided on; or else this status quo, in an economy so largely dependent on international exchanges, would be at the mercy of every untoward event that might occur. The "target practice" of the English government may or may not be wise or necessary; but, fundamentally, it does nothing but express these necessities. With intact capitalism all round, this process of readjustment along with the downward revision of consumption and the upward revision of production schedules would be largely "automatic" except in the spheres of money, credit, and public finance, which bring to the fore the familiar conflict inherent in any treatment of inflationary situations: measures that are likely to bridle inflation are, at the same time, likely to bridle production.[15] In the conditions set by the pattern of laborite society[16] a policy that runs exclusively in

[13] As an example, I may, however, mention Pigou's own article on "The Food Subsidies," *Economic Journal*, LVIII (June, 1948), 202 ff.

[14] As Professor Jewkes has justly emphasized, the importance of the loss of British overseas investments has been much exaggerated. Income from these investments was £205 million in 1938. In 1946 it was £150 million. The difference is, in fact, "insignificant in relation to the real difficulties of the nation" (p. 215).

[15] I have been much impressed by the superficiality with which, both in England and in the United States, the problems of inflation are being dealt with. Everyone realizes, of course, that the old quantity-theory treatment is of little value. But few seem to realize that the modern treatment by means of income analysis is very little better. That is, few writers posit the true problem: How to adjust the economic process in such a manner as to make it cease to produce further inflation. This is illustrated by the sweeping condemnation by economists in both countries of all tax reductions whenever there is inflationary pressure.

[16] This aspect has been well treated by W.A. Lewis, "The Prospect before Us," *Manchester School*, May, 1948.

terms of money, credit, and taxation carries implications that may put it out of court.[17] Hence, suppressing inflation by "direct controls," that is, measures to enforce restriction of consumption and expansion of production in the hope that this would do something toward the gradual improvement of the situation, was all that it was possible to do immediately—the rest must be achieved by careful and circuitous steering, if at all. And, allowing for the troubles, subterfuges, and phrases of the harassed politician, we may say, I conceive, that this is precisely what has been done, at least since the balance-of-payments crisis of August, 1947.[18]

English economists have certainly not failed in their first duty to their country, which was to teach the ABC lesson, so sorely needed in an age of economic illiteracy,[19] viz., that the basic problem is one of *domestic* adjustment: the government, like all governments in such situations, has displayed an understandable proclivity to claim that everything, including their domestic economic policy, was for the best and ideally successful except for the evidently unconnected difficulties about the balance of payment, particularly the vexing "shortage of dollars." With practical unanimity, economists explained the error involved in this,[20] and Harrod in particular must be singled out for admiring compliment for having bravely testified to the simple truth that "this allegation of a 'world dollar shortage' is surely one of the most brazen pieces of collective effrontery that has ever been uttered" (p. 43). A necessary qualification of this salutary lesson will, however, have to be mentioned below.

But I have been surprised to find English economists *almost* equally unanimous in their disapproval of the government's attitude toward investment. Harrod actually went so far as to make retrenchments in the government's investment program the pivot of his recommendations;[21] I get the impression that, according to him, excessive investment is the main internal maladjustment and that

[17] Therefore, I find it difficult to understand Jewkes's arguments on pp. 234 and 240 of his book. To eliminate inflation by withdrawing purchasing power by taxation (and also, we might add, credit restriction that means either rationing of credit or, temporarily, a very high interest rate) is feasible if there is something left to tax in industry or in the higher-income brackets. As it is, English industry does not look as if it could stand much more fiscal punishment (as will presently be emphasized again), and an increase of taxation of this kind is likely to have an inflationary effect (I am not sure that this does not also hold true of the credit restriction recommended by Von Haberler in his brilliant review of Harrod's book in *Review of Economics and Statistics*, XXX [May, 1948], 141–43). So we are left with an increased taxation of wages and farmers' incomes or an equivalent reduction of welfare expenditure. But this would upset the comparative quiet in the labor market (even so, money wages keep on rising) and eventually lead to troubles, including open inflation, which I cannot imagine Jewkes is prepared to face. I take, however, the opportunity to point out that, under conditions of suppressed inflation, i.e., when existing masses of purchasing power have not as yet taken full effect, there is an argument for (the right kind of) a capital levy that does not exist in open inflation. This has been partially recognized by J. R. Hicks ("The Empty Economy," *Lloyd's Bank Review*, n.s., No. 5 [July, 1947], pp. 10–11).

[18] For a presentation of the case (more or less) for the government, see T. Balogh, "Britain's Economic Problem," *Quarterly Journal of Economics*, Vol. LXIII (February, 1949). As everyone knows, the hope that inflationary pressure would decrease has not been proved entirely futile; and restrictions are accordingly being relaxed gradually.

[19] The term is F. Graham's (see *American Economic Review*, XXXIX [March, 1949], 553).

[20] This has been done by all our authors. But see, in addition, D. H. Robertson's address on "The Economic Outlook," *Economic Journal*, Vol. LVII (December, 1947), and Sir Hubert Henderson, "Cheap Money and the Budget," *Economic Journal*, Vol. LVII (September, 1947). The refreshingly original articles by Meade on "National Income, National Expenditure, and the Balance of Payments," *Economic Journal*, Vols. LVIII (December, 1948), and LIX (March, 1949), move on a level of analytic refinement higher than the literature under survey but must also be mentioned in this connection.

[21] His advice has, in fact, been taken.

retrenchment on this item will remove balance-of-payments difficulties. Others go nearly as far, if not quite. Of course we must not overlook the fact that they all include in investment subsidized housing and other long-range provisions for consumer's services and that, to this extent, their criticisms of the Labour government amount to no more than partial recognition of the fact that England's economy suffers from excess consumption and undersaving.[22] Also the charge against the government's policy may simply reduce to malinvestment, but then it should be based upon the merits or demerits of each individual case and not be proffered in general. This includes cases in which the government undertakes or instigates capital outlays the rates of return on which do not cover at least the rate of interest that a free capital market would evolve. Perhaps this is all that is really meant. But then it should be made clear that the government is being criticized on these grounds only and not because it undertakes or encourages genuine investments in the sense alluded to, which, though they may be inflationary in the short run, have the opposite effect eventually—even if they involve major reconstruction.[23] A labor government that is still more than are any other governments under the temptation to neglect its nation's future deserves credit and not blame for its efforts to foster industrial investment within the breathing space afforded by the Marshall windfall. In fact, we might expect criticism to run in the opposite direction; for the government, though it professes to foster industrial investment and in individual lines actually does so, at the same time compensates, perhaps overcompensates, this by depleting industrial capital through its policy of expenditure—mainly on the social services and on food subsidies—and of taxation. The former will presently create an untenable situation,[24] especially if rearmament is to be taken seriously. The latter, quite apart from any question of incentive, dries up the only source—since there is no longer private saving to speak of—of noninflationary finance even for purposes of restocking and maintenance.[25] A volume would be

[22] I fail to understand why English—and, still more, American—economists touch upon this subject so gingerly, as if there were something improper in it. A man has tuberculosis or he has not. No wish to be tactful excuses the physician from recognizing the fact, if it is a fact.

[23] See, e.g., Hicks, in his otherwise excellent article already referred to (*op. cit.*, p. 9): "One of our difficulties is that we have got into a state of mind which looks upon a major reconstruction of British industry as one of our major obligations. But, as things are, major reconstruction is not a thing which we can possibly afford." As a result of my speculations on the question of how it was possible for one of England's foremost economists to pen those lines—while he has nothing to say about outlay on beer—I have but one explanation to offer: an attack of Keynesian paralysis that prevented him from seeing anything except short-run expenditure effects. It is interesting to note that this particular distemper is, if anything, still more endemic in the United States, where Keynesians complained around 1946 about the capital outlays or programs of capital outlays of American corporations—though they also complained about steel shortage in due course.

[24] It has done so already (note added July 15).

[25] This is a simple consequence of applying high rates of taxation, without taking account of replacement costs, in and after an inflation. The profits tax and the taxation of undistributed profits, higher in any case than is compatible with keeping up venture capital in a world of rapid technological change, are in such situations increased much above their nominal rates. Shortage of capital is therefore one, though not the only, reason why comparisons between the "productivities" of the industries of England and the United States, however much "corrected," yield the familiar result. Of course, the tax situation per se is not much worse in England than it is here; and the radical outcry against the apparently high profits after taxes of American corporations may eliminate all the difference there is. But it needs no emphasis that similar policies may produce different results in countries so differently circumstanced. For a brief presentation of the English situation see, e.g., S. P. Chambers, "Taxation and the Supply of Capital for Industry," *Lloyd's Bank Review,* n.s. No. 11 (January, 1949), pp. 1–20.

necessary in order to establish these statements satisfactorily. The reader is requested to bear in mind that this is no part of the purpose of this essay. I have no wish to criticize, let alone to "proffer advice" to, anyone or any country. I merely wish to mention problems which there is sufficient prima facie evidence for believing to be interesting and to express astonishment at the relatively slight attention which they receive in the literature under survey.[26]

To return to the lesson in the economic alphabet. Economists who take it upon themselves to teach such unpromising pupils are naturally tempted to extol the powers of competitive pricing, Harrod and Meade being shining examples. Up to a point they are quite right, of course: everyone should know by now—or have Lange, Lerner, and a host of others really written to no purpose?—that there is nothing specifically capitalistic but only general economic logic about the price system that pure competition tends to establish in a near-equalitarian society and under approximately normal conditions (which include absence of rapid technological development). But not only the socialists of the old tradition and people who are more conspicuous for their enthusiasm about "welfare" and "justice" than for their economic competence but also professional economists have felt that *this* lesson has gone too far.[27] And these are also right; for some of the exponents of free pricing fail to make clear to their readers—in one or two cases one has an impression that it is not quite clear to themselves—that the rosy propositions about competitive pricing do not apply even in the rarefied air of pure theory without exceptions and qualifications; that, if they are to apply to actual patterns and especially to the highly irregular pattern of modern England, this would have to be carefully established; and that, in particular, it will not do to accept "consumers' sovereignty" as a *noli me tangere*. I think that both sides are missing a great opportunity for original contributions by dealing so cavalierly—and, in fact, with nothing but very old phrases—with these problems.[28] We

[26] But, as already pointed out, the question of incentive fares better, though Hicks (*op. cit.*, p. 8), after recognizing that English taxes on profits are "one of the factors making for low productivity," arrives at the conclusion that, unless the total tax burden be reduced, any reduction "must be judged to be a wrong course." I think that this judgment neglects the necessity for a proper division of labor between politicians and economists. Moreover, in the 1920's, when a German Socialist (and Marxist) minister of finance, who was nevertheless a good economist, wished to give relief to the upper-income brackets, I remember having read in the (Marxist) organ of his party an article in which it was explained that the income tax may become "the most terrible scourge" of the proletariat: it is not always so impossible, as we uncritically assume, to talk sense to organized labor. On the question of incentive, see, *inter alia*, S. P. Chambers, in *Lloyd's Bank Review*, n.s., No. 8 (April, 1948), pp. 1–12.

[27] All "planners" felt like this, of course, but also others; see, e.g. Sir Hubert Henderson, "The Price System," *Economic Journal*, LVII (December, 1948), 467 ff.

[28] Let me exemplify, by the last of our three points, the uncritical belief that so many seem to harbor in the virtues of consumers' choice (and a similar argument goes for free choice of employment). First of all, whether we like it or not, we are witnessing a most momentous experiment in malleability of tastes—is not this worth analyzing? Second, ever since the physiocrats (and before), economists have professed unbounded respect for the consumers' choice—is it not time to investigate what the bases of this respect are and how far the traditional and, in part, advertisement-shaped tastes of people are subject to the qualification that they might prefer other things than those which they want at present as soon as they have acquired familiarity with these other things? In matters of education, health, and housing there is already practical unanimity about this—but might the principle not be carried much further? Third, economic theory accepts existing tastes as data, no matter whether it postulates utility functions or indifference varieties or simply preference directions, and these data are made the starting point of price theory. Hence they must be considered as independent of prices. But

do not stand to learn novelties from either. We get plenty of sense, on both sides. But it is all old stuff, defended by analytic tools that were available a hundred years ago.

This amounts to saying that the discussion of England's problems in general and of the state-managed economy in particular is unduly influenced, *on both sides*, by convictions that have become traditional. Also, it is unduly influenced by naïve delight in planning—"which is such fun"—and downright bureausadism, on the one hand, and resentment of vexations and inefficient types of control, on the other. Jewkes devotes to a well-chosen selection of examples of this bureausadism some of the most effective pages of his admirable book[29] that have been conveniently overlooked by hostile reviewers. But, in spite of his protest against any distinction between planning and inept planning,[30] we must recognize that, considered from the relevant standpoint—namely, the standpoint of the vested interests of the trade-unions—the Labour government's planning, which is not more specifically socialist than the logic of free pricing is specifically capitalist, cannot be pronounced a failure and that in the given conditions the necessity for planning or regulation cannot and should not be denied. As regards the first point, the fact is that labor has been carried through the national emergency without unemployment, with rising real wages,[31] and with decreasing hours—and, if this is all that matters, it is no doubt possible to speak of success.[32]

The second point is best illustrated by the import and export policy. It was, of course, a merit in the analysis of the early classics to have pointed out that, generally speaking and as a first approximation, import restrictions and export bounties do not accomplish what they are intended to accomplish. But this first approximation neglected—in part, perhaps, for pedagogical reasons—all the advantages that a nation may reap, in a disturbed and developing world, from a great many mercantilist tricks. In England's present situation I, for one, find it difficult to accept, e.g., Harrod's brief argument for all but unrestricted multilateralism, nondiscrimination, and freely interchangeable currencies. Such ideas have their place, as have the high-sounding phrases of the Declaration of Policy in our own Foreign Assistance Act of 1948.[33] But there seems to be little point

considerable and persistent changes in prices obviously do react upon tastes. *What, then, is to become of our theory and the whole of micro-economics?* It is investigations of this kind, that might break new ground, which I miss.

[29] See esp. pp. 217 ff., which should be made required reading in *any* economics course.

[30] The methodological question of how far it is permissible to distinguish between any system and the miscarriages to which it is exposed is one that merits further study. Abuse of this distinction is an obvious danger. But its necessity is not less obvious.

[31] This is very often denied on the formally correct ground that, under rationing, indices lose their usual meaning. If, however, we analyze the main items that compose the workman's standard of life—food and drink, shelter, wearing apparel, amusements, health and educational services—the denial turns out to be entirely unjustified. The *Economist*'s statements on the subject (see, e.g., the one of November 15, 1947) go rather far; but the facts presented by so unchallengeable an authority as Dr. Bowley (*London and Cambridge Economic Service* [Special Memo. No. 50], May, 1947, and article, "Wages," in the *Service's Bulletin* of November 18, 1948, pp. 133–34) tell no very different tale. Our own statement, however, also includes some items other than those that he considered.

[32] Much of the planning, of course, antedates the taking-of-office by the labor men. An example is the Special Areas (Amendment) Act of 1937. On this policy see Jewkes's article in the *Economic Journal*, XLVIII (March, 1938), 142 ff.

[33] World-plan ideas, on the other hand, perhaps have no place at all in the practical sense. But they have at least the merit of having produced something new and original, namely, Frisch's proposals.

in losing contact with reality for their sake. As we have seen, England, her economic situation and social structure being what they are, cannot take the course that would have appealed to Ricardo. Instead, she has to maneuver back to a normal position by *all* the means at her command—credit policy, taxation, rationing, exchange and trade controls of all kinds, with devaluation, perhaps, as a final measure to help over the last few steps toward abandoning the discrimination against the dollar: her case is not one for specious simple measures à la Keynes. And among these means is mercantilist exploitation, with all the regulating or planning that this implies, of the strong or least weak points in her position. Governmental "bulk purchases" mean oligopsonistic gains; and, though the English oligopsonist may occasionally be worsted by the Argentinian oligopolist, he can in general rely on the weakness of some countries and on the forbearance of others. Gains of this kind may not be great individually, but they help somewhat. Nor is it necessary to consider such policies as mere temporary expedients. Some shaky "equilibrium"—if internal maladjustments are not too great—may be permanently secured by them. And, much though I regret to have to say so regarding the work of fellow-economists whom I respect so highly, there seems to be hardly any writer who has built the analytic complement of all this or has made any comprehensive attempt to add to our analytic engine the new parts which it requires.[34]

HARVARD UNIVERSITY

[34] This shows that analytic work is not, as some historians of economics would have us believe, exclusively conditioned by the analyst's environment. For instance, Leontief's work has been done in and for the United States, although, so far as practical application is concerned, there is more need and scope for it in England.

THE HISTORICAL APPROACH TO THE ANALYSIS OF BUSINESS CYCLES

Reprinted from *Universities-National Bureau Conference on Business Cycle Research,* Nov. 25-27, 1949.

I

In order to protect the following comments from a not unnatural misunderstanding, I want to make it quite clear right away that I have no wish to advocate the historical approach to the phenomenon of business cycles at the expense, still less to the exclusion, of theoretical or statistical work upon it. As my own attempts in the field amply prove, I am as much as anyone can be convinced of the necessity of bringing to bear upon the study of business cycles the whole of our theoretical apparatus and not only aggregative dynamic schemata but also our equilibrium analysis. It goes without saying as should be evident from the last sentence that by theory I do not only mean explanatory hypothesis — as our lamented Mitchell did — but also and even principally the tools that theory puts at our disposal. Not less am I convinced that statistical investigations and statistical methods (including all the methods that cluster around the handling of time series) are essential means for making headway. Further on I shall indicate how theory and statistics fit in with the historical approach as visualized in this paper. For the moment I only wish to emphasize that nothing is farther from my mind than any wish to start the kind of methodological discussion which the logic of the modern scientific situation has definitely made a thing of the past.

II

Economic life is a unique process that goes on in historical time and in a disturbed environment. For this and other reasons there is an argument for historical or institutional study in almost any department of economics. But I mean something more specific than that. We talk about business cycles as a scourge (some of us call them the main scourge of capitalist life) and discuss possibilities of eliminating them altogether as if this were an unchallengeable end in itself, whereas it does not seem to me open to doubt

(a) that the darkest hues of cyclical depressions and most of the facts that make of business cycles a bogey for all classes are not essential to the phenomenon of business cycles per se but are due to adventitious circumstances and

(b) that these adventitious circumstances might be eliminated and those darkest hues might be banished without interfering with the cyclical mechanism itself. It is submitted that it is possible to devise a program of policy which though not foolproof would be effective in reducing the remaining discomforts incident to business cycles to the range within which the ordinary welfare provisions of the modern state are adequate. This fact, if it be a fact, is important both scientifically and practically. From both standpoints it at least merits to be looked at more closely. But this calls for historical analysis into every cycle on record: in the first instance and before everything else cycles must be treated as historical individuals.

III

The fact envisaged may be illustrated by every major crisis in history, but it will suffice to illustrate my meaning by the depression that broke in 1929. It is my opinion that a depression of unusual intensity and duration was in fact due. But, speaking from the standpoint of the United States alone and neglecting, therefore, the relatively minor repercussions of foreign troubles, I challenge anybody to deny that the whole course of events would have been entirely different and that all the phenomena of crisis-neurosis that were such potent factors in shaping subsequent history would have been avoided if there had been no banking epidemics, if the mortgage situation had been normal and if the speculative mania had been kept in bounds (including in the phenomena that make up the speculative mania also the practice of living on unrealized speculative gains). The statistical evidence of the quantitative importance of these three factors is as overwhelming as their demoralizing effects are obvious. Nor do I think that it can be reasonably contested that in their absence there would indeed have been "business as usual" though on a reduced scale. Now the point is that those three factors were logically separable from the underlying process from which they arose and that they were practically avoidable. To establish this fully would take all the time at my disposal and more. It is only in order to give some measure of precision to my meaning that I venture to submit the following remarks:

First, by saying that the factors mentioned were practically avoidable I mean no more than that a sufficiently powerful and intelligent government assisted by a properly organized banking system could have avoided them. I do not wish to be understood to hold that the American government as it then was and to some extent still is and the American banking system could have avoided them. Now since the power and the constitution of a government and of a banking system are of course not products of chance, it would be very easy to reply that these factors were inevitable after all, but it is perhaps unnecessary to show explicitly why this objection fails.

Second, this objection apart, it is easy to see that the virulence of the banking epidemics was due to the existence of a host of inefficient Lilliput banks and to mismanagement in some of the big banks. As regards the Lilliput banks, there is of course no reason why the process of concentration so effective in other fields should not have produced a dozen or so of huge banks (each with a system of branch offices) that would have been as impregnable to the impact of the depression as were the English Big Five, except that politics and public opinion in what I believe to be unreasonable fear of big business ("money trusts" and the like) offered resistance that proved invincible. As regards the cases of mismanagement, they link up with the mortgage situation and with the speculative mania and, through these with partly inadequate quality of leading personnel. But if so we should immediately have to add that inadequate leading personnel is not an essential feature of modern financial processes.

Third, it cannot be repeated too often that the catastrophic as distinguished from merely depressed conditions in the agrarian sector were *only* due to the farmers' debt situation and that a nation that will not permit farmers' financial transactions to be controlled has only itself to blame for the consequences. The reform that would have prevented this situation from emerging is too obvious to detain us. Nor was it an essential feature of the cyclical process, that is, a feature without which this process could not do its work, that urban real estate credit was in still worse case.

Fourth, speculative manias are quite obviously one of the reasons why in any historical or statistical description, American business fluctuations are so much more marked than they are in European countries. I think most people will agree that it is not possible to control speculative excesses by interest-rate and credit-rationing policies; but there are other means of controlling them.

This analysis could be made very complete but so could the analysis of any other crisis on which we have sufficient material, that is to say, from at least the 18th century on. Intellectually speaking it is evidently no very deep problem to explain why John Law's ventures went wrong and why their failure had the consequences it did have. All this may be very trite. I believe it is. But — I have taken care before that this should not be misunderstood — as guide to depression policy historical analysis of cyclical vicissitudes is all the same worth a ton of dynamic schemata. As I have said, the policies to which they point are not foolproof. There is no tablet, the swallowing of which will immunize the system against events such as those which we have glanced at. But neither are such policies difficult to devise. They need sound sense, moral courage and, of course, an environment that does not fall from one hysteria into another.

IV

It seems to me important. scientifically and practically, to bring out that all these phenomena are accidental in the sense defined and yet play a role that may very well decide the fate of capitalism. Since this can only be done by detailed historical case studies, the argument for the historical approach to business-cycle research seems established. In reality, however, we have established only half of it and, so far as the scientific aspect is concerned, the less important half. For historical research is not only required in order to elucidate the nature and importance of the non-essentials dealt with so far, but also in order to elucidate the underlying cyclical process itself. This underlying process as depicted in the more important time series suggests indeed dynamical schemata that may be framed in such a way as to fit practically any contour. In particular, it is obvious that the ups and downs of aggregate investment will by themselves account for most of the surface phenomena that we usually associate with business cycles.[1] And these ups and downs

[1]Including the behavior of aggregate expenditure on consumption. Mere precedence or lagging of absolute quantities is of course not necessarily significant. See e.g., R. Frisch, *Propagation and Impulse Problems* in Essays in Honour of Gustav Cassel, 1933. The distinction between propagation and

lend themselves beautifully to description by means of dynamic models, especially if we introduce the now well-established distinction between induced and autonomous investment. Familiar properties of differential, difference, mixed difference and differential and integro-differential equations then give us all, or almost all, we seem to need in order to "rationalize" our material. They give us oscillations the possibility of which the untutored mind would never suspect and historical description would never suggest — the most striking instance being afforded by the theory of "oscillators".[2] But not only is it necessary to look to the historical material for verification of the postulates involved and to give it an opportunity for suggesting others to us; but it is also necessary to bear in mind that those ups and downs of (corrected or uncorrected) investment expenditure are themselves only a surface phenomenon and that we must try to see what there is behind it — which means that we must investigate historically the actual industrial processes that produce it *and in doing so revolutionize existing economic structures.* Unless we do this, investment, especially autonomous investment,[3] is a mere label for a blank space and if we fill this blank space by some such thing as "expectations" we are filling a blank with another blank.

impulse problems will presently be used below. Meanwhile we note the methodologically interesting fact that it may be — I think it is — true that it is in the sphere of production rather than in the sphere of consumption that we ought to look for explanation of the cyclical movement and at the same time wrong to infer this from the observation that the maximum in the production of capital goods usually precedes the maximum in the production of consumers' goods. (Not everyone will approve of this formulation; it is chosen for the sake of brevity.)

[2]An oscillator is a quantity that does not oscillate or act intermittently itself, yet produces oscillations in some other quantity or set of quantities on which it acts — I take this opportunity in order to point out two errors into which the builders of exact models are prone to fall in the excitement of the chase: First, if they are proof against the layman's error that some factor, if it is to qualify for a "causal" role in the cycle, must itself be of an oscillatory nature, they often imply that such a factor must be aggregative in nature because cyclical situations are defined in terms of conditions obtaining in the whole economy; second, they often take pride in the fact that theories embodied in an exact model will "explain" *all* the phases of cycles, including turning points, by a single argument and make it possible to dispense with separate theories for the individual phases — this *may* be an advantage but it also may result in misconstructing the whole phenomenon.

[3]But induced investment also because it is decisively influenced by autonomous investment.

It is tempting to define the resulting relation between the two "indispensables," the historical analysis and the dynamic model, by means of the concepts, Impulse and Propagation Problems. But it would not be quite correct to say that historical analysis gives information as regards impulses and dynamic models as regards the mechanisms by which these impulses are propagated through the system or, to put it differently, as regards the manner in which the economic resonator reacts when "irritated" by the impulse. Very roughly this is so and I should be quite content if my audience accept the thesis that the role of the econometric model (which includes the statistical element) is to implement the results of historical analysis of the phenomenon and to render the indispensable service of describing the mechanics of aggregates. But the econometric models do more than this — they "explain" situations which in turn "explain" or help to "explain" impulses. And the reverse is also true. For instance, it may be possible to show — personally I believe it is — that *at least* the major prosperities and depressions from the last decades of the 18th century on can all be "explained" without appeal to endogenous oscillations of the elastic type though the existence of the latter is of course not denied. But whether this is so or not can be established only by finding out what actually happened in each instance in the economic organism. It is even likely that there are a great many "waves" running along simultaneously that are of entirely different nature, some being of an oscillatory character and others not.

V

Nothing has been said so far as regards the nature of the historical information required. In a sense, the compilation of long time series (and it is extremely important to note that for fundamental problems of analysis, only long time series are of any use and that time series that start in 1919 are almost completely valueless) is in itself work in economic history. This work is indispensable of course, but it is not what I wish to draw attention to. Apart from the measurements it yields, a set of time series per se does not so much solve any problem as state in quantitative terms what problem there is to solve. In another sense, it might be thought (and this is the idea of the National Bureau of Economic Research) that annalistic description of business situations and other events that might conceivably have any relevance (the annals of the National Bureau of Economic Research even include the marriage of Queen

Victoria) is all that is required. Such annals have their value. They facilitate the interpretation of the time series and are useful as a check upon theoretical analysis. But they tell us very little about industrial processes of change and their effects upon the structure of the economy. To let the murder out and to start my final thesis, what is really required is a large collection of industrial and locational monographs all drawn up according to the same plan and giving proper attention on the one hand to the incessant historical change in production and consumption functions and on the other hand to the quality and behavior of the leading personnel.[4] The rationale of this requirement can be very briefly stated at the expense of my being more dogmatic than I have any intention to be. First of all it can be established, but it may be taken as intuitively clear, that no society would display *that kind of fluctuations* which we usually identify as business cycles, if consumption and production functions remained unchanged over time. To this proposition, it is, however, necessary to add two qualifications: (a) such a society would be still exposed to wars and other political disturbances and to the occurrence of good and bad harvests. Any investigator who is prepared to base his explanation of the business cycle on either or both of these two sets of factors would of course not agree with my proposition and I in turn, placing myself on his standpoint, would agree with him; (b) among short-run fluctuations there is the one that used to be called the 40-month cycle (I usually refer to it as the Kitchin cycle): These fluctuations and perhaps still shorter ones may possibly be explained by some such schema as Metzler's inventory cycle. Hog cycles, sheep cycles, coffee cycles and other such phenomena may be included in the same category. To all this my thesis does not apply either, or rather I cannot aver that it does, because it would lead too far to discuss my doubts on this point.

But all those cycles that do not belong in either of the two categories just mentioned can be reasonably assumed to be absent from a society of the kind envisaged. It has often been said that there may not be much left of cycles if we do exclude these. But whether this is so or not is again a question which can be answered only by detailed historical inquiry that yields generalizations through making us understand individual situations. In any case, if there are

[4]The term, consumption function, is used here in a sense too obvious to require explanation which has nothing whatever to do with the Keynesian consumption function.

factors inducing cycles of a different sort at all then these factors must be connected with changes in the consumption and production functions or if we do not think much of the autonomous change in taste, of the production functions alone. Now in order to construct a schema that will describe the modus operandi of these changes, it is necessary to refer to industrial history which, when the analytical work is done, will again provide verifications, checks, amplifications, qualifications, and also tell us where we might expect oscillatory movements to play a role. Theoretical and statistical analysis is in this task as necessary as is the historical work. In fact they are inseparable because there is an incessant give and take between them. But I am not contradicting this if I say that the most serious shortcoming of modern business-cycle studies is that nobody seems to understand or even to care precisely how industries and individual firms rise and fall and how their rise and fall affects the aggregates and what we call loosely "general business conditions."

Also, it should not be forgotten, that there are many individual problems about business cycles which can only be solved on the basis of such understanding. An instance is the question of the effects of given degrees of monopoly in an economy upon the processes of prosperity and depression. Without the kind of experience that industrial history supplies, all we have to say about this question reduces to reckless assertions or trivial speculations.

BIBLIOGRAPHY OF THE WRITINGS OF JOSEPH A. SCHUMPETER[1]

Reprinted from *Quarterly Journal of Economics,* Aug. 1950, 373-384.

SUMMARY

I. Books and pamphlets, 373. — II. Articles, 375. — III. Book reviews and review articles, 381.

I. BOOKS AND PAMPHLETS

Das Wesen und der Hauptinhalt der theoretischen Nationalökonomie. München und Leipzig: Duncker & Humblot, 1908. Pp. xxxii+626.

Japanese translation by Professors Kimura and Yasui, published by Nihon-Hyoronsha, 1936. Pp. 706. Second edition, 1950.

Wie studiert man Sozialwissenschaft? (Schriften des sozialwissenschaftlichen akademischen Vereins in Czernowitz, Heft 2), 1910. Pp. 28. Second edition, München und Leipzig: Duncker & Humblot, 1915. Pp. 54.

Theorie der wirtschaftlichen Entwicklung. Leipzig: Duncker & Humblot, 1912. Pp. viii+548. [Preface dated Vienna, July 1911.]

Second revised edition (subtitle first appears with this edition, *Eine Untersuchung über Unternehmergewinn, Kapital, Kredit, Zins und den Konjunkturzyklus*). München und Leipzig: Duncker & Humblot, 1926. Pp. xiv+369. [Preface dated Bonn am Rhein, October 1926.]

Third edition, 1931. [Mere reprint of second edition.]

Fourth edition (unchanged except for a new foreword), 1935. Pp. xxi+369. [Foreword dated Cambridge, Mass., end of 1934.]

Italian translation (abridged), *La teoria dello sviluppo economico,* translated by G. Demaria and K. Mayer (Nuova collana di economisti stranieri e italiani, Vol. V: Dinamica economica). Turin, 1932, pp. 17–182.

English translation, *The Theory of Economic Development: An Inquiry into Profits, Capital, Credit, Interest, and the Business Cycle* (translated by Redvers Opie, with a special preface by the author). Cambridge, Mass.: Harvard University press, 1934. Pp. xii+255. Second printing, 1936; third printing, 1949.

French translation, *Théorie de l'Evolution Économique; Recherches sur le Profit, le Crèdit, l'Intérêt et le Cycle de la Conjuncture* (published as Vol. II in la Collection scientifique d'Économie politique à la Librairie Dalloz). Paris, 1935. Pp. xi+589. [Translated by M. Jean-Jacques Anstett with a long introduction by M. François Perroux. This introduction has also been published as a separate volume under the title *La Pensée Économique de Joseph Schumpeter.* Paris: Librairie Dalloz, 1935. Pp. 216.]

Japanese translation by I. Nakayama and S. Tobata (with a special preface written for the Japanese edition). Tokyo: Iwanami-Shoten, 1937. Second edition in preparation, 1950.

Spanish translation, *Teoria del Desenvolimiento Economico: una investigación sobre ganancias, capital, crédito, interés y ciclo económico.* (Translated by J. Prados Arrarte.) Mexico: Fondo de Cultura Economica, 1944. Pp. 363.

Epochen der Dogmen- und Methodengeschichte (Grundriss der Sozialökonomik, I. Abteilung, Wirtschaft und Wirtschaftswissenschaft). Tübingen: J. C. B. Mohr (Paul Siebeck), 1914, pp. 19–124. Second edition, 1924.

Japanese translation by I. Nakayama and S. Tobata, to be published by Iwanami-Shoten of Tyoky in 1950.

[1] The compiler of this bibliography will be grateful for any additions or corrections. Because Joseph Schumpeter possessed no copies of many of his earlier writings and because many of the German articles (even books) are not to be found in American university libraries, it has not been possible to produce a complete and accurate bibliography. — E. B. S.

Vergangenheit und Zukunft der Sozialwissenschaft (Schriften des sozialwissenschaftlichen akademischen Vereins in Czernowitz, Heft 7). München und Leipzig: Duncker & Humblot, 1915. Pp. 140.

Die Krise des Steurstaats. Graz und Leipzig: Leuschner & Lubensky, 1918. Pp. 74.

Zur Soziologie der Imperialismen (first published as two articles in the Archiv für Sozialwissenschaft; later in book form). Tübingen, 1919. Pp. 76.

Grundlinien der Finanzpolitik für jetzt und die nächsten drei Jahre. Printed by the Austrian Government (D. ö. Staatsdruckerei 8140219), Vienna, October 17, 1919.

Das deutsche Finanzproblem. First published as four articles in *Der deutsche Volkswirt;* later as a pamphlet (No. 2 in Der Schriftenreihe des deutschen Volkswirt), Berlin, 1928.

Business Cycles: A Theoretical, Historical and Statistical Analysis of the Capitalist Process. New York and London: McGraw-Hill Book Co., Inc., 1939. 1st ed., 2 vols. Pp. xvi+ix+1095.

In preparation, 1950:

German translation to be published by Vandenhoeck & Ruprecht, Göttingen.
Spanish translation to be published by Revista de Occidente, Madrid.

Capitalism, Socialism and Democracy. New York: Harper & Brothers, 1942. Pp. x+381.

Revised second edition, 1947. Pp. xiv+411.

Enlarged third edition, 1950. Pp. xiv+425.

English edition, *Capitalism, Socialism and Democracy.* London: Allen & Unwin Ltd., 1943. Pp. x+381.

Revised second edition, 1947. Pp. xii+412.

Third edition with new preface, 1950.

Spanish translation, *Capitalismo, Socialismo y Democracia.* Buenos Aires: Editorial Claridad, 1946. Pp. 431.

German translation, *Kapitalismus, Sozialismus und Demokratie.* Bern, Switzerland: A. Francke, 1946. Pp. 488. (Introduction by Edgar Salin, Part V omitted.)

In preparation, 1950:

French translation to be published by Editions Payot of Paris.

Italian translation to be published by Arnaldo Mondadori Editore, Milan.

Japanese translation to be published by Toyo Keizai Shimpo (The Oriental Economist Publishing Co.), Tokyo.

Rudimentary Mathematics for Economists and Statisticians (with W. L. Crum). New York: McGraw-Hill Book Co., Inc., 1946. Pp. ix+183.

Spanish translation *Elementos de Matematicas para Economistas y Estadigrafos* (with W. L. Crum). Mexico and Buenos Aires: Fondo de Cultura Economica, 1948. Pp. 183.

To be published in 1950 or 1951:

Ten Great Economists: from Marx to Keynes. (Essays on Marx, Walras, Menger, Marshall, Pareto, Böhm-Bawerk, Taussig, Fisher, Mitchell, and Keynes, with an appendix containing three short essays on Knapp, von Wieser, and Bortkiewicz; three of these essays — those on Walras, Menger, and Böhm-Bawerk — have been translated from the German.) To be published by the Oxford University Press in the United States and by Allen & Unwin in England.

Imperialism and Social Classes. (The two long essays, originally published in German in 1919 and 1927, have been translated into English for the first time.) To be published by Augustus Kelley in New York, Allen & Unwin in England; Japanese edition by Iwanami-Shoten.

History of Economic Analysis. (A long two-volume work on which Schumpeter had been working for eight or nine years and which was nearly completed at the time of his death.) To be published by the Oxford University Press in the United States, by Allen & Unwin in England, and by Vandenhoeck & Ruprecht in Germany.

II. Articles

1905

"Die Methode der standard population," *Statistische Monatsschrift*, Vol. XXXI (New Series, Vol. X), Vienna, 1905, pp. 188–91.

"Die Methode der Index-Zahlen," *Statistische Monatsschrift*, Vol. XXXI (New Series, Vol. X), Vienna, 1905, pp. 191–97.

"Die Internationale Preisbildung," *Statistische Monatsschrift*, Vol. XXXI (New Series, Vol. X), Vienna, 1905, pp. 923–28.

[These three articles were reports to the statistical seminar conducted by Inama-Sternegg and Juraschek at the University of Vienna — the first two were given in the winter term 1903/4 and the last in the winter term 1904/5. The *Statistische Monatsschrift* was the Monthly Statistical Bulletin of Austria.

1906

"Über die mathematische Methode der theoretischen Ökonomie," *Zeitschrift für Volkswirtschaft, Sozialpolitik und Verwaltung*,[2] Vol. XV, pp. 30–49.

"Professor Clark's Verteilungstheorie," *Zeitschrift für Volkswirtschaft*, Vol. XV, pp. 325–33.

"Rudolph Auspitz," *Economic Journal*, Vol. XVI (June 1906), pp. 309–11.

1907

"Das Rentenprinzip in der Verteilungslehre," *Schmollers Jahrbuch für Gesetzgebung, Verwaltung und Volkswirtschaft*, Vol. XXXI, pp. 31–65, 591–634.

1909

"Bemerkungen über das Zurechnungsproblem," *Zeitschrift für Volkswirtschaft*, Vol. XVIII, pp. 79–132.

"On the Concept of Social Value," *Quarterly Journal of Economics*, Vol. XXIII (February 1909), pp. 213–32.

1910

"Über das Wesen der Wirtschaftskrisen," *Zeitschrift für Volkswirtschaft*, Vol. XIX, pp. 271–325.

"Marie Esprit Léon Walras," *Zeitschrift für Volkswirtschaft*, Vol. XIX, pp. 397–402.

"Die neuere Wirtschaftstheorie in den Vereinigten Staaten," *Schmollers Jahrbuch*, Vol. XXXIV, pp. 913–63.

1911

"Gründungsgewinn in Recht und Wirtschaft," *Zeitschrift für Notariat Österreich*, Vol. IV, p. 31.

1913

"Zinsfuss und Geldverfassung," *Jahrbuch der Gesellschaft österreichischer Volkswirte, Vienna*, 1913.

"Eine 'dynamische' Theorie des Kapitalzinses: Eine Entgegnung," *Zeitschrift für Volkswirtschaft*, Vol. XXII, pp. 599–639.

"Ausserungen zur Werturteilsdiskussion im Ausschuss des *Vereins für Sozialpolitik*," paper presented at seminar in Düsseldorf, privately printed for distribution to seminar members.

[2] Titles of German periodicals given in full the first time mentioned and abbreviated thereafter.

1914

"Die 'positive' Methode in der Nationalökonomie," *Deutsche Literaturzeitung*, Vol. XXXV.

"Das wissenschaftliche Lebenswerk Eugen von Böhm-Bawerks," *Zeitschrift für Volkswirtschaft*, Vol. XXIII, pp. 454–528.

"Die Wellenbewegung des Wirtschaftslebens," *Archiv für Sozialwissenschaft und Sozialpolitik*, Vol. XXXIX, pp. 1–32.

1916

"Das Grundprinzip der Verteilungstheorie," *Archiv für Sozialwissenschaft*, Vol. XLII, pp. 1–88.

1917

"Das Bodenmonopol: Eine Entgegnung auf Dr. Oppenheimers Artikel," *Archiv für Sozialwissenschaft*, Vol. XLIV, pp. 495–502.

"Das Sozialprodukt und die Rechenpfennige: Glossen und Beiträge zur Geldtheorie von heute," *Archiv für Sozialwissenschaft*, Vol. XLIV, pp. 627–715.

"Volkswirtschaftliche Seminare" (Bericht an Universität Graz).

1919

"Zur Soziologie der Imperialismen," *Archiv für Sozialwissenschaft*, Vol. XLVI, pp. 1–39, 275–310. (Also in book form, 76 pp.)

"Finanzpolitische und wirtschaftliche Ausblicke," *Die Woche*, 21/26, pp. 679–80.

1920

"Sozialistische Möglichkeiten von heute," *Archiv für Sozialwissenschaft*, Vol. XLVIII, pp. 305–60.

"Max Webers Werk," *Der österreichische Volkswirt*, No. 45 (August 7, 1920), p. 831.

1921

"Carl Menger," *Zeitschrift für Volkswirtschaft*, Vol. I (New Series), pp. 197–206.

1923

"Angebot," *Handwörterbuch der Staatswissenschaften* (fourth edition), Vol. 1, pp. 299–303.

"Kapital," *Handwörterbuch der Staatswissenschaften* (fourth edition), Vol. 5, pp. 582–84.

1924

"Der Sozialismus in England und bei uns," *Der österreichische Volkswirt*, Nos. 11 and 12/13 (December 13 and 20, 1924), pp. 295–297, 327–30.

1925

"Eugen v. Böhm-Bawerk," (*Neue österreichische Biographie*), Vol. II, Vienna, 1925, pp. 63–80.

"Kreditpolitik und Wirtschaftslage," *Berliner Börsencourier*, No. 603.

"Edgeworth und die neuere Wirtschaftstheorie," *Weltwirtschaftliches Archiv*, Vol. XXII, pp. 183–202.

"Kreditkontrolle," *Archiv für Sozialwissenschaft*, Vol. LIV, pp. 289–328.

"Oude en nieuwe bankpolitiek," *Economisch-Statistische Berichten*, Rotterdam, 1925.

1926

"Konjunkturforschung," *Berliner Börsencourier*, Nos. 157 and 159.

"Gustav v. Schmoller und die Probleme von heute," *Schmollers Jahrbuch*, Vol. L[3], pp. 337–388.

"G. F. Knapp," *Economic Journal*, Vol. XXXVI (September 1926), pp. 512–14.

"Steuerkraft und nationale Zukunft," *Der deutsche Volkswirt*, Vol. I (October 1, 1926), pp. 13–16.

"Subventionspolitik," *Berliner Börsencourier*, No. 87.

1927

"Cassels Theoretische Sozialökonomik," *Schmollers Jahrbuch*, Vol. LI[2], pp. 241–60.

"Sombarts dritter Band," *Schmollers Jahrbuch*, Vol. LI[3], pp. 349–69.

"Zur Frage der Grenzproduktivität: Eine Entgegnung auf den vorstehenden Aufsatz von Willem Valk," *Schmollers Jahrbuch*, Vol. LI,[5] pp. 671–80.

"Unternehmerfunktion und Arbeiterinteresse," *Der Arbeitgeber*, Vol. XVII, No. 8.

"Die sozialen Klassen im ethnisch homogenen Milieu," *Archiv für Sozialwissenschaft*, Vol. LVII, pp. 1–67.

"Zur Einführung der folgenden Arbeit Knut Wicksells [Mathematische Nationalökonomie]," *Archiv für Sozialwissenschaft*, Vol. LVIII, pp. 238–51.

"Die Arbeitslosigkeit," *Der deutsche Volkswirt*, Vol. I (March 11, 1927), pp. 729–32.

"Finanzpolitik," *Der deutsche Volkswirt*, Vol. I (April 1, 1927), pp. 827–30.

"Finanzpolitik und Kabinettssystem," *Der deutsche Volkswirt*, Vol. I (April 8, 1927), pp. 865–69.

"Geist und Technik der Finanzverwaltung," *Der deutsche Volkswirt*, Vol. I (May 13, 1927), pp. 1028–31.

"Finanzausgleich (Das deutsche Finanzproblem; Reich, Länder und Gemeinden)," *Der deutsche Volkswirt*, Vol. I (June 3 and June 10, 1927), pp. 1123–26, 1156–59.

The four articles listed above on Finanzpolitik were reprinted as a pamphlet under the title *Das deutsche Finanzproblem*, No. 2 in Der Schriftenreihe des deutschen Volkswirt, Berlin, 1928.

"Friedrich v. Wieser," *Economic Journal*, Vol. XXXVII (June 1927), pp. 328–30.

"Die goldener Bremse an der Kreditmaschine," *Die Kreditwirtschaft*, Vol. I, pp. 80–106.

"Deutschland," (in: *Die Wirtschaftstheorie der Gegenwart*,) published by Mayer-Fetter-Reisch, Vienna, 1927, pp. 1–30.

"The Explanation of the Business Cycle," *Economica*, Vol. VII (December 1927), pp. 286–311.

Preface to Enrico Barone, *Grundzüge der theoretischen Nationalökonomie*, translation and appendix by Hans Staehle. First edition, Bonn, 1927; second edition, Bonn, 1935.

1928

"Unternehmer," *Handwörterbuch der Staatswissenschaften*, fourth edition, Vol. VIII, pp. 476–87.

"Staatsreferendar und Staatsassessor," *Schmollers Jahrbuch*, Vol. LII[2], pp. 703–20.

"Erbschaftssteuer," Der deutsche Volkswirt, Vol. III (October 26, 1928), pp. 110–14.

"Wen trifft die Umsatzsteuer?" *Der deutsche Volkswirt*, Vol. III (November 16, 1928), pp. 206–08.

"The Instability of Capitalism," *Economic Journal*, Vol. XXXVIII (September 1928), pp. 361–68.

"Die Tendenzen unserer sozialen Struktur (Vortrag vor dem Verein zur Wahrung der Interessen der chemischen Industrie Deutschlands, December 8, 1928)," *Die Chemische Industrie*, Vol. LI, pp. 1381–87.

"Der Unternehmer in der Volkswirtschaft von heute," in *Strukturwandlungen der Deutschen Volkswirtschaft*, Berlin, 1928, pp. 295–312.

A revised enlarged version in a later year, pp. 303–326.

"Lohngestaltung und Wirtschaftsentwicklung," *Der Arbeitgeber*, Vol. XIX, pp. 479–82.

"International Cartels and Their Relation to World Trade," in *America as a Creditor Nation*, edited by Parker T. Moon, New York, 1928.

1929

"Die Wirtschaftslehre und die reformierte Referendarprüfung," *Schmollers Jahrbuch*, Vol. LIII^2, pp. 637–50.

"Das soziale Antlitz des deutschen Reiches," *Bonner Mitteilungen*, No. 1, pp. 1–12.

"Lohnpolitik und Wissenschaft," *Der deutsche Volkswirt*, Vol. III (March 22, 1929), pp. 807–10.

"Grenzen der Lohnpolitik," *Der deutsche Volkswirt*, Vol. III (March 28, 1929), p. 847. Dazu Nachbemerkung, Vol. III (May 3, 1929), p. 1022.

"Was vermag eine Finanzreform?" *Der deutsche Volkswirt*, Vol. IV (October 18, 1929), pp. 75–80.

"Ökonomie und Soziologie der Einkommensteuer," *Der deutsche Volkswirt*, Vol. IV (December 20, 1929), pp. 380–85.

"Ökonomie und Psychologie des Unternehmers" (Vortrag in der 10. ordentlichen Mitgliederversammlung des Zentralverbandes der deutschen Metallwalzwerks- und Hütten-Industrie E. V. in München). Leipzig, Haberland, 15 pp.

"Le rôle économique et psychologique de l'employeur," *Informations sociales*, International Labor Office, Geneva, Vol. XXXI (1929).

1930

"Wenn die Finanzreform misslingt . . . ," *Der deutsche Volkwirt*, Vol. IV (February 28, 1930), pp. 695–699.

"Wandlungen der Weltwirtschaft," *Der deutsche Volkswirt*, Vol. IV (September 19, 1930), pp. 1729–33.

"Mitchell's Business Cycles," *Quarterly Journal of Economics*, Vol. XLV (November 1930), pp. 150–72.

"Rudolf Auspitz," and "Eugen v. Böhm-Bawerk," *Encyclopaedia of the Social Sciences*, Vol. II, p. 317 and p. 618.

Preface to F. Zeuthen, *Problems of Monopoly and Economic Warfare*, London, 1930.

1931

"The Present World Depression," *American Economic Review*, Vol. XXI (Supplement, March 1931), pp. 179–83.

"Dauerkrise?" *Der deutsche Volkswirt*, Vol. VI (December 25, 1931), p. 418 ff.

"Das Kapital im wirtschaftlichen Kreislauf und in der wirtschaftlichen Entwicklung," *Kapital und Kapitalismus, Veröffentlichungen der deutschen Vereinigung für Staatswissenschaftliche Fortbildung*, Bernhard Harms, Berlin, 1931, pp. 187–208.

"Les Possibilités Actuelles du Socialisme," *Année Politique Française et Étrangère.*

"The World Depression with Special Reference to the United States of America."

"The Theory of the Business Cycle."

"The Present State of Economics. Or on Systems, Schools and Methods."

"The Present State of International Commercial Policy." Four articles in Japanese, published in Japanese periodicals during 1931.

1932

"Ladislaus von Bortkiewicz," *Economic Journal*, Vol. XLII (June 1932), pp. 338–40.

"A German View: World Depression and Franco-German Economic Relations," *Lloyds Bank Limited Monthly Review*, March 1932, pp. 14–35.

"Weltkrise und Finanzpolitik," *Der deutsche Volkswirt*, Vol. VI (March 4, 1932), p. 739 ff.

"Kreditpolitische Krisentherapie in Amerika," *Der deutsche Volkswirt*, Vol. VI (July 22, 1932), p. 1415 ff.

1933

"The Common Sense of Econometrics," *Econometrica*, Vol. I (January 1933), pp. 5–12.

Der Stand und die nächste Zukunft der Konjunkturforschung. Festschrift für Arthur Spiethoff. Foreword and contribution by Joseph Schumpeter, München 1933, pp. 263–67.

1934

"Depressions," in *The Economics of the Recovery Program*, New York and London: Whittlesey House, McGraw-Hill Book Co., pp. 3–21.

Italian translation, Turin: Einaudi, 1935.

Spanish translation, Madrid, 1935.

"The Nature and Necessity of a Price System," *Economic Reconstruction*, Report of the Columbia University Commission. New York: Columbia University Press, pp. 170–176.

1935

"The Analysis of Economic Change," *Review of Economic Statistics*, Vol. XVII (May 1935), pp. 2–10. Reprinted as Chapter 1 of Part I of *Readings in Business Cycle Theory*, Philadelphia, 1944.

"Allyn Abbott Young," *Encyclopaedia of the Social Sciences*, Vol. XV, pp. 514–15.

"A Theorist's Comment on the Current Business Cycle," *Journal of the American Statistical Association*, Vol. XXX (Supplement, March 1935), pp. 167–68.

Preface to D. H. Robertson, *Das Geld*, tr. by K. Bode, Vienna.

1936

"Professor Taussig on Wages and Capital," in *Explorations in Economics:* Notes and Essays Contributed in Honor of F. W. Taussig, New York, pp. 213–222.

1937

Author's Preface to Japanese Edition of "Theorie der wirtschaftlichen Entwicklung" by Professor Joseph Schumpeter (6 pages) with a list of Schumpeter's writings by S. Tobata (12 pages). Separately reprinted from the Japanese edition, tr. by I. Nakayama and S. Tobata, published by Iwanami-Shoten, Tokyo, 1937.

1940

"The Influence of Protective Tariffs on the Industrial Development of the United States," *Proceedings of Academy of Political Science*, Vol. XIX (May 1940), pp. 2–7.

1941

"Alfred Marshall's *Principles:* A Semi-Centennial Appraisal," *American Economic Review*, Vol. XXXI (June 1941), pp. 236–48.

"Frank William Taussig," *Quarterly Journal of Economics*, Vol. LV (May 1941), pp. 337–63. (With A. H. Cole and E. S. Mason.)

1943

"Capitalism in the Postwar World," in *Postwar Economic Problems*, Seymour E. Harris, ed., New York: McGraw-Hill, 1943, pp. 113–126.

Preface to Bernard W. Dempsey, *Interest and Usury*, Washington, D. C.: American Council on Public Affairs, 233 pp.

1946

"Capitalism," in *Encyclopaedia Britannica*, 1946, Vol. IV, pp. 801–07.

"Keynes and Statistics," in "Keynes' Contributions to Economics — Four Views," *Review of Economic Statistics*, Vol. XXVIII (November 1946), pp. 194–96.

"The Decade of the Twenties," in "The American Economy in the Interwar Period," *American Economic Review, Proceedings*, Vol. XXXVI (May 1946), pp. 1–10.

"John Maynard Keynes: 1883–1946," *American Economic Review*, Vol. XXXVI (September 1946), pp. 495–518.

"L'Avenir de l'Entreprise Privée devant les Tendances Socialistes Modernes," in *Comment Sauvegarder l'Entreprise Privée*, Montreal, 1946.

1947

"Keynes, the Economist," in *The New Economics: Keynes' Influence on Theory and Public Policy*, Seymour E. Harris, ed., New York: A. A. Knopf, 1947, pp. 73–101.

"Comments on a Plan for the Study of Entrepreneurship," Widener Library, HUH 775, January 13, 1947.

"The Creative Response in Economic History," *Journal of Economic History*, Vol. VII (November 1947), pp. 149–59.

"Theoretical Problems of Economic Growth," *Journal of Economic History*, Vol. VII (Supplement 1947), pp. 1–9.

1948

"There is Still Time to Stop Inflation," *Nation's Business*, Vol. XXXVI (June 1948), pp. 33–35, 88–91.

"Irving Fisher's Econometrics," *Econometrica*, Vol. XVI (July 1948), pp. 219–31.

1949

"Economic Theory and Entrepreneurial History," in *Change and the Entrepreneur*. Prepared by the Research Center in Entrepreneurial History, Harvard University, Cambridge, Mass.: Harvard University Press, pp. 63–84.

"English Economists and the State-Managed Economy," *Journal of Political Economy*, Vol. LVII (October 1949), pp. 371–382.

"Science and Ideology," *American Economic Review*, Vol. XXXIX (March 1949), pp. 345–59.

"Vilfredo Pareto (1848–1920)," *Quarterly Journal of Economics*, Vol. LXIII (May 1949), pp. 147–73.

"The Communist Manifesto in Sociology and Economics," *Journal of Political Economy*, Vol. LVII (June 1949), pp. 199–212.

"The Historical Approach to the Analysis of Business Cycles," Universities-National Bureau Conference on Business Cycle Research, New York, November 25–27, 1949.

1950

"Wesley Clair Mitchell (1874–1948)," *Quarterly Journal of Economics*, Vol. LXIV (February 1950), pp. 139–55.

"March into Socialism," *American Economic Review*, Vol. XL (May 1950), pp. 446–56.

III. Book Reviews and Review Articles

1906

"Otto Karmin: *Zur Lehre von den Wirtschaftskrisen.*" *Zeitschrift für Volkswirtschaft, Sozialpolitik und Verwaltung,* Vol. XV, pp. 95–97.

"H. Deutsch: *Qualifizierte Arbeit und Kapitalismus.*" *Zeitschrift für Volkswirtschaft,* Vol. XV, pp. 98–99.

"Johannes Leonhard: *Neue Feststellung des Wertbegriffes und ihre Bedeutung für die Volkswirtschaft.*" *Schmollers Jahrbuch für Gesetzgebung, Verwaltung und Volkswirtschaft,* Vol. XXX², p. 1271.

1907

"J. W. Schiele: *Über den natürlichen Urspring der Kategorien Rente, Zins und Arbeitslohn.*" *Schmollers Jahrbuch,* Vol. XXXI¹, pp. 395–98.

"M. E. Waxweiler: *Esquisse d'une sociologie.*" *Economic Journal,* Vol. XVII (March 1907), pp. 109–11.

1908

"J. B. Clark: *Essentials of Economic Theory as Applied to Modern Problems of Industry and Public Policy.*" *Zeitschrift für Volkswirtschaft,* Vol. XVII, pp. 653–59.

"Einige neuere Erscheinungen auf dem Gebiete der theoretischen Nationalökonomie.

1. E. R. A. Seligman: *Principles of Economics.*
2. W. Stanley Jevons: *The Principles of Economics.*
3. Leon Polier: *L'idée du juste salaire.*
4. L. Querton: *L'augmentation du rendement de la machine humaine.*
5. W. Hasbach: *Güterverzehrung und Güterhervorbringung.*
6. H. v. Leesen: *Frédéric Bastiat.*
7. A. Rudiger-Miltenberg: *Der gerechte Lohn.*
8. Thomas Nixon Carver: *The Distribution of Wealth.*
9. Frank A. Fetter: *The Principles of Economics, with Applications to Practical Problems.*"

Zeitschrift für Volkswirtschaft, Vol. XVII, pp. 402–20.

1909

"Rudolf Kaulla: *Die geschichtliche Entwicklung der modernen Werttheorien.*" *Schmollers Jahrbuch,* Vol. XXXIII², pp. 1261–62.

The following six book reviews follow one another in the *Zeitschrift:*

"Irving Fisher: *The Nature of Capital and Income.*"

"Heinrich Mannstaedt: *Die kapitalistische Anwendung der Maschinerie.*"

"G. de Molinari: *Questions Économiques à l'ordre du jour.*"

"Ira Ryner: *On the Crises of 1837, 1847, and 1857 in England, France and the United States.*"

"Minnie Throop England: *On Speculation in Relation to the World's Prosperity, 1897–1902.*"

"W. G. Longworthy Tailor: *The Kinetic Theory of Economic Crises.*"

Zeitschrift für Volkswirtschaft, Vol. XVIII, pp. 679–85.

1910

"Alfred Weber: *Über den Standort der Industrien.*" *Schmollers Jahrbuch,* Vol. XXXIV,³ pp. 1356–59.

"Otto Conrad: *Lohn und Rente.*" *Jahrbucher für Nationalökonomie und Statistik,* Vol. XCIV, pp. 827–31.

"E. v. Böhm-Bawerk: *Kapital und Kapitalzins: Positive Theorie des Kapitals.*" *Archiv für Sozialwissenschaft und Sozialpolitik*, Vol. XXXI, p. 271.

"J. Conrad: *Grundriss zum Studium der politischen Ökonomie, 4. Teil: Statistik.*" *Archiv für Sozialwissenschaft*, Vol. XXXI,p. 256.

"Otto Neurath und Anna Schapire-Neurath: *Lesebuch der Volkswirtschaftslehre.*" *Archiv für Sozialwissenschaft*, Vol. XXXI, p. 256–57.

"Eugenie Fabian-Sagal: *Albert Schäffle und seine theoretisch-nationalökonomischen Lehren.*" *Archiv für Sozialwissenschaft*, Vol. XXXI, p. 271.

"Hermann Levy: *Monopole, Kartelle und Trusts in ihren Beziehungen zur Organisation der kapitalistischen Industrie.*" *Archiv für Sozialwissenschaft*, Vol. XXXI, pp. 285–86.

"Alfred Lansburgh: *Depositen und Spargelder.*" *Archiv für Sozialwissenschaft*, Vol. XXXI, p. 297.

"Vilfredo Pareto: *Manuel d'économie politique.*" *Archiv für Sozialwissenschaft*, Vol. XXXI, p. 257.

"Gustav Schmoller: *Grundriss der allgemeinen Volkswirtschaftslehre*, Part 1." *Archiv für Sozialwissenschaft*, Vol. XXXI, pp. 257–58.

"Adolf v. Wenckstern: *Staatswissenschaftliche Probleme der Gegenwart*, Vol. I." *Archiv für Sozialwissenschaft*, Vol. XXXI, p. 258.

1911

"Wilhelm Lexis: *Allgemeine Volkswirtschaftslehre.*" *Archiv für Sozialwissenschaft*, Vol. XXXII, pp. 865–67.

"Heinrich Niehuus: *Geschichte der englischen Bodenreformtheorien.*" *Archiv für Sozialwissenschaft*, Vol. XXXII, pp. 873–74.

"Albion W. Small: *The Meaning of Social Science.*" *Archiv für Sozialwissenschaft*, Vol. XXXII, pp. 868–70.

"Neuere Erscheinungen auf dem Gebiete der Nationalökonomie.

1. F. Lifschitz: *Untersuchungen uber die Methodologie der Wirtschaftswissenschaft.*
2. Josef Grunzel: *Allgemeine Volkswirtschaftslehre.*
3. W. Hohoff: *Die Bedeutung der Marxschen Kapitalkritik.*
4. Charles Gide: *Cours d'économie politique.*
5. G. Ruhland: *System der politischen Ökonomie.*
6. Walther Jacoby: *Der Streit um den Kapitalsbegriff.*
7. Heinrich Pesch, S. J.: *Lehrbuch der Nationalökonomie.*
8. F. Lifschitz: *Zur Kritik der Böhm-Bawerkschen Werttheorie.*
9. Adolf Weber: *Die Aufgaben der Volkswirtschaftslehre als Wissenschaft.*
10. Soda Kiichiro: *Geld und Wert. Eine logische Studie.*
11. Irving Fisher: *The Rate of Interest, its Nature, Determination and Relation to Economic Phenomena.*
12. Joseph Herbert Davenport: *Value and Distribution, a Critical and Constructive Study.*
13. Robert Schachner: *Australien in Politik, Wirtschaft und Kultur.*
14. Charles A. Conant: *A History of Modern Banks of Issue.*"

Zeitschrift für Volkswirtschaft, Vol. XX, pp. 240–52.

1912

"Neue nationalökonomische Lehrbucher und Lehrbehelfe.

1. W. Lexis: *Allgemeine Volkswirtschaftslehre.*
2. H. R. v. Schullern zu Schrattenhofen: *Grundzüge der Volkswirtschaftslehre.*
3. E. Schwiedland: *Einführung in die Volkswirtschaftslehre.*

4. F. W. Taussig: *Principles of Economics.*
5. L. H. Haney: *History of Economic Thought.*
6. O. Spann: *Haupttheorien der Volkswirtschaftslehre.*
7. O. and A. Neurath: *Lesebuch der Volkswirtschaftslehre.*
8. K. Diehl and P. Mombert: *Ausgewählte Lesestücke zum Studium der politischen Ökonomie.*"

Zeitschrift für Volkswirtschaft, Vol. XXI, p. 281 ff.

"R. Stolzmann: *Die soziale Kategorie in der Volkswirtschaftslehre,* und *Der Zweck in der Volkswirtschaft.*" *Schmollers Jahrbuch,* Vol. XXXVI[1], pp. 928–34.

1913

"Franz Oppenheimer: *Theorie der reinen und politischen Ökonomie.*" *Zeitschrift für Volkswirtschaft,* Vol. XXII, p. 797.

The following twelve reviews follow one another in the *Archiv:*

"A. Adler: *Leitfaden der Volkswirtschaftslehre.*"

"Quaritsch: *Kompendium der Nationalökonomie.*"

"Georg Mollat: *Volkswirtschaftliches Quellenbuch.*"

"Sp.-C. Haret: *Mécanique sociale.*"

"James Bonar: *Disturbing Elements in the Study and Teaching of Political Economy.*"

"Ernst Bundsmann: *Das Kapital, wirtschaftstheoretische Skizzen.*" *Archiv für Sozialwissenschaft,* Vol. XXXVI, pp. 244–6. [Erwiderung Bundsmann, *ibid.*, pp. 677–79.] [Entgegnung auf Bundsmanns Erwiderung, *ibid.*, p. 679.]

"Irving Fisher: *De la nature du capital et du revenu.*"

"Lavergne: *Théorie des Marchés Économiques.*"

"T. Lloyd: *The Theory of Distribution and Consumption.*"

"Achille Loria: *La synthèse économique, étude sur les lois du revenu.*"

"René Maunier: *L'origine et la fonction économique des villes.*"

"Henry L. Moore: *Laws of Wages.*"

Archiv für Sozialwissenschaft, Vol. XXXVI, pp. 238–258.

1915

"Karl Schlesinger: *Theorie der Geld- und Kreditwirtschaft.*" *Archiv für Sozialwissenschaft,* Vol. XLI, pp. 239–42.

1927

"R. G. Hawtrey: *The Economic Problem.*" *Weltwirtschaftliches Archiv,* Vol. XXVI, pp. 131–33.

"Heinrich Dietzel: *Die Bedeutung des 'Nationalen Systems' für die Vergangenheit und die Gegenwart.*" *Archiv für Sozialwissenschaft,* Vol. LVIII, pp. 415–16.

"Friedrich B. W. Hermann: *Staatswirtschaftliche Untersuchungen.*" *Archiv für Sozialwissenschaft,* Vol. LVIII, pp. 416–17.

"Edwin R. A. Seligman: *Essays in Economics.*" *Archiv für Sozialwissenschaft,* Vol. LVIII, pp. 417–18.

"C. A. Macartney: *The Social Revolution in Austria.*" *Economic Journal,* Vol. XXXVII (June 1927), pp. 290–92.

1928

"Carl Landauer: *Grundprobleme der funktionellen Verteilung des wirtschaftlichen Wertes.*" *Weltwirtschaftsliches Archiv,* Vol. XXVII, pp. 24–27.

"L. V. Birck: *The Theory of Marginal Value.*" *Weltwirtschaftsliches Archiv,* Vol XXVIII, pp. 24–26.

"Bonn und Palyi: *Festgabe für Lujo Brentano.*" *Zeitschrift für Volkerpsychologie,* Vol. IV, pp. 101–02.

"Carl Rodbertus: *Neuere Briefe über Grundrente.*" *Zeitschrift für Volkerpsychologie,* Vol. IV, pp. 102–03.

1932

"G. H. Bousquet: *Institutes de science économique.*" *Economic Journal,* Vol. XLII (September 1932), pp. 449–51.

1933

"J. M. Keynes: *Essays in Biography.*" *Economic Journal,* Vol. XLIII (December 1933), pp. 652–57.

"Wilhelm von Winkler: *Grundzüge der Statistik.*" *Schmollers Jahrbuch,* Vol. LVII, pp. 136–39.

1934

"Joan Robinson: *The Economics of Imperfect Competition.*" *Journal of Political Economy,* Vol. XLII (April 1934), pp. 249–257.

1936

"J. M. Keynes: *General Theory of Employment, Interest and Money.*" *Journal of the American Statistical Association,* December 1936, pp. 791–95.

1942

"George J. Stigler: *The Theory of Competitive Price.*" *American Economic Review,* Vol. XXXII (December 1942), pp. 844–47.

1944

"Harold J. Laski: *Reflections on the Revolution of Our Time,*" *American Economic Review,* Vol. XXXIV (March 1944), pp. 161–64.

1946

"F. A. Hayek: *Road to Serfdom.*" *Journal of Political Economy,* Vol. LIV (June 1946), pp. 269–70.

1950

"Elmer Clark Bratt: *Business Cycles and Forecasting*" (third edition). *Journal of the American Statistical Association,* Vol. XLV (March 1950), pp. 140–42.

ELIZABETH B. SCHUMPETER.

TACONIC, CONNECTICUT.